Women and the Law of Property
in Early America

LANGDON G. WRIGHT

Studies in Legal History

Published by The University of North Carolina Press
in association with the American Society for Legal History

Editor: G. Edward White

W O M E N

and the Law of Property
in Early America

Marylynn Salmon

The University of North Carolina Press

Chapel Hill and London

Manufactured in the United States of America

92 91 90 89 88 5 4 3 2

Library of Congress Cataloging in Publication Data
Salmon, Marylynn, 1951–
Women and the law of property in early America.
(Studies in legal history)
Based on the author's thesis (Ph.D.)
Bibliography: p.
Includes index.
1. Married women—United States—History.
2. Women—Legal status, laws, etc.—United States—
History. 3. Separate property—United States—History.
I. Title. II. Series.
KF524.S24 1986   346.7304   85-20865
ISBN 0-8078-1687-6   347.3064
ISBN 0-8078-4244-3 (pbk.)

To Mary Beth Norton

Contents

Acknowledgments

Many colleagues and friends have been generous with their time in helping me understand the intricacies of women's legal history. It is a pleasure to thank them at last, in a public way. Mary Maples Dunn directed my Ph.D. dissertation, which forms the core of this work. She had the wisdom to know that students need to find their own way, with a maximum of encouragement and a minimum of interference. My years at Bryn Mawr College under her tutelage were extremely happy ones. Norma Basch, Mary Beth Norton, Lisa Pollak, and Carole Shammas also read and criticized the entire manuscript. Their different perspectives allowed me to understand my own much better. Their comments saved me from errors, oversights, and unclear writing.

Others read individual chapters or sections of the manuscript. The comments of Lloyd Bonfield, Toby Ditz, Clive Holmes, Stanley N. Katz, Kathy Peiss, and Linda Shopes were very helpful. I have benefited over the years from conversations with a number of historians, including Carol R. Berkin, Lois Green Carr, Suzanne Lebsock, and Lorena S. Walsh. Elizabeth Read Foster taught me that scholarship in legal history requires patience and attention to detail. I am grateful for her lessons and example.

Joseph O'Rourke assisted me with the technical problems of collecting and organizing research materials, and producing a polished manuscript on a word processor. He saved me untold hours of tedious labor and lightened the burden of the hours that could not be avoided. His patience and understanding attest to his unusual good nature.

Having the opportunity to present portions of the manuscript at seminars proved valuable. I wish to thank the participants in the Philadelphia Center for Early American Studies seminar (1979–80); the Columbia Seminar on Early American History (1982–83), especially John M. Murrin; and the seminar of The Johns Hopkins University Program in Atlantic History, Culture, and Society (1984–85), especially Jack P. Greene. At the Conference on Women in Early America sponsored by the Colonial Williamsburg Foundation and the Institute of Early American History and Culture in 1981, James Henretta provided much-needed encouragement in addition to criticism.

Parts of the book appeared elsewhere in different form. I am grateful for permission to include excerpts from "Equality or Submersion? Feme Covert

Status in Early Pennsylvania," originally published in *Women of America: A History*, edited by Carol R. Berkin and Mary Beth Norton (Houghton Mifflin Company, 1979); "The Legal Status of Women in Early America: A Reappraisal," *Law and History Review*, Volume I (1983); and "Women and Property in South Carolina: The Evidence from Marriage Settlements, 1730–1830," *William and Mary Quarterly*, 3rd ser., 39 (1982).

Financial support came from Bryn Mawr College, the Mrs. Giles Whiting Foundation, the Philadelphia Center for Early American Studies, and the University of Maryland Baltimore County. Without it, I could not have continued my studies.

Librarians and staff members at the Bucks County Historical Society, the Historical Society of Pennsylvania, the Library Company of the Baltimore Bar, the Maryland Hall of Records, the South Carolina Department of History and Archives, and the University of Pennsylvania Biddle Law Library offered assistance and service with good grace. I am indebted in particular to Kai-Yun Chiu, Paul Gay, and Linda Stanley.

Finally, I want to acknowledge a large personal and professional debt to Mary Beth Norton. Many years ago she recognized the need to help a quiet young woman who lacked the confidence to pursue a career in history on her own. Mary Beth's faith in me, and her efforts in my behalf, speak to her support of all women historians. I dedicate this book to her.

Preface

The vitalization of social history as a field in the 1960s and early 1970s had a profound effect on the study of American legal history. A new legal history emerged that emphasized the relationship between law and society. Increasingly, legal historians focused on the interplay between social and legal change. Studies of the law in isolation gave way to investigations that focused on interactions—the effect of economic policy on legal developments, the relationship between slavery and the law, and the effect of colonial settlement on English legal forms.[1]

My work in women's history has profited from the varied approaches of the new legal historians. Although most legal history, like a great deal of social history, continues to ignore gender, the emphasis on studying law and society together has created a receptive atmosphere for studies in women's legal history. I have benefited as well from the increasing vitality of women's history as a field of inquiry. It is no accident that the great majority of work in women's legal history is a product of the last decade, years in which the pursuit of a history of American women has intensified and grown to encompass virtually all disciplines.

Women's legal history focuses on three primary concerns that indicate the influence of the new legal history as well as women's history.[2] First, we want to understand how the law functioned in practice, as well as in theory, because we want to know how legal rules affected women's day-to-day lives. To that end, we read cases as well as commentaries. Such a goal generally entails a double burden, because current knowledge does not cover adequately even the rudiments of legal theory. We must first learn the law and then search for materials revealing its application.

Second, historians of women's legal status are centrally concerned with understanding the meaning of change over time. We want to know if a development marked progress or decline. Was it good, or bad; was it part of a trend? At this point we often come into conflict with other historians (and, occasionally, with each other), for it is difficult to say conclusively that a change was or was not for the best. Protective legislation, for example, can be seen in many lights, and early Americanists are still plagued by the knotty problem of how to define the legacy of the American Revolution.[3] Sometimes historians studying women and the law become tired of this debate over progress and decline, and we ask ourselves if other questions might prove more profitable. It is problematical to categorize legal change, and we often end up arguing unnecessarily among ourselves. Ultimately, however, we come back to it. Understanding the nature of legal change over time is one of our most pressing concerns because, to return to the first point, such changes shaped women's lives, in practice, on a day-to-day basis.

The third concern is perhaps the most important of all to the field; it encompasses the working of the law in practice as well as the meaning of change over time. Historians of women's legal status perceive the law as a powerful form of social control, and therefore we seek to uncover the relationship between law and social policy. Law is coercive as well as representative of community values. Throughout history, male-defined rules have controlled women's behavior. We need to know what the rules were, what goals they served for men, why women accepted them, and how they shifted as the role of women in society changed.

In the pages that follow I address the three concerns of women's legal history in a study of property law between 1750 and 1830. Several areas of the law are important for developing a comprehensive definition of the property rights of American women. Conveyancing and contract law demonstrate the comparative legal powers of wives and husbands over family property. Divorce, separate maintenances, and alimony reveal contemporary perceptions of the marital bond and what reasons jurists thought were valid for dissolving it. Divorce cases also hold information about the standard of living deemed acceptable for women residing apart from their husbands. The law of separate estates indicates the degree of independence lawmakers were willing to allow propertied women. Provisions for widows, like alimony, serve to define the status of women within the family by specifying what part of joint property was rightfully theirs. Inheritance law also allowed me to study the property rights of women at all social and economic levels. These topics became the focus of my research.

In focusing on property law I hoped to learn something about the status of women in colonial and early national society.[4] Although a woman's legal rights constitute only one of several strands necessary for defining her status, control over property is an important baseline for learning how men and women share power in the family. Unraveling the rules on women's ownership and control of property seemed essential, then, for arriving at a general understanding of women's changing role in the family and society at large. Yet the law remains suspect as a category to some feminist scholars.

The emphasis among women's historians is on understanding the realities of women's lives. To that end, legal sources often are overlooked or employed casually, for they are perceived as prescriptive rather than as a reflection of women's activities and position in society. In studies of widows, for example, historians of early America have been more intent on analyzing the content of wills and counting the number of administratrices than on understanding the intricacies of dower rights. Colonial women of business have been heralded without a comprehension of the rules of contract governing their activities. And for decades the mere existence of a vehicle for granting women separate estates, the marriage settlement, was interpreted as a sign of women's relative equality in the realm of family property, despite the fact that no one knew how settlements worked, or even why they usually were made.[5]

It is a mistake, I believe, to emphasize custom over formal rules of law when discussing the status of women in times past. What women could or could not do within their own communities often was determined by a wider social context that included formal rules of law. Exceptions, moreover, cannot be explained until we first understand norms. If a rule of law states that after marriage a woman cannot be sued without joining her husband, and yet we see suits involving married businesswomen and their customers in county court records, we may be led to conclude that the formal rule was not enforced at the local level and that therefore women could own property separately from their husbands. Yet upon closer examination of the formal rules of law we will discover that courts recognized married women's capacity to act independently in the marketplace provided they had their husbands' written, or even tacit, consent. Without that consent, however, women could do nothing on their own under the law. What might be perceived as a customary exception, then, actually represented an established legal precedent. We cannot understand custom, in short, unless we understand law.

In addition, the significance of attempts to avoid formal law and establish an alternative local custom will not be recognized unless we know what the rules of law were that communities wanted to avoid. In Pennsylvania, for example, couples so rarely obtained the required private examination of the wife before selling their land that the courts were compelled to enforce the technically illegal sales in order to uphold secure land titles. In this instance, women lost a valuable legal protection as a result of the prevalence of custom. Similarly, so few couples in Connecticut made marriage settlements giving wives separate property that courts there developed no precedents for enforcing them. As a result, settlements became effectively illegal in the colony and state. Examples such as these prove that formal law can provide valuable insights into customary behavior in the management of marital property.

Given this study's emphasis on developing a general definition of the property rights of women, many important questions have been left aside. In particular, I have made no effort to distinguish between the treatment of women in different socioeconomic groups, or between blacks and whites. Obviously, the property rights of all women were not the same, because access to the law marked the first right necessary to exercise all others. In early America, many women enjoyed a right to property only when their communities believed that supporting it would help keep the women off relief rolls. Free blacks, slaves, servants, and poor women all suffered under handicaps that significantly altered the portrait of women's rights presented here.

Students of American law face the unenviable task of dealing with a multitude of legal systems. For the purposes of this study, it is important to realize that each colony and state developed its own set of rules for governing women's property rights. Although each jurisdiction originally based its legal system on England's, no two evolved in precisely the same way. It has been necessary, therefore, to concentrate on a number of jurisdictions that offer a useful comparative perspective. The colonies and states chosen for this study were Massachusetts, Connecticut, New York, Pennsylvania, Maryland, Virginia, and South Carolina. They represent a range of settlement patterns, religious views, landholding and labor systems, and demographic experience. Although a study of all jurisdictions is ideal, the use of several that can provide such useful comparative information is certainly productive.

I chose an intercolonial comparative perspective because it seemed impossible to compare English and American legal practice. Little work on the history of Englishwomen has appeared in the literature. In addition, recent work in the legal history of early modern England depicts a highly complex system of local land law that operated alongside the law enforced by the courts of the Crown. Although American comparisons with English common law and equity law principles are important, and have been made in the pages that follow, they cannot provide us with a complete picture. They distort, because we know so little about the application of standard rules in the mother country. Intercolonial comparisons do not present similar interpretive problems. They also allow us to mark the appearance of particular developments and standards in different parts of the country at different times. In the process of comparing colonial and early national rules, we can trace the beginnings of regional distinctiveness in American law.

It also seemed wrong to focus on comparisons of English and American law without emphasizing seventeenth-century evidence. The answers to many of our questions about Anglo-American comparative law lie in the earliest years of settlement. My own work, however, focuses on the years 1750 to 1830, the decades surrounding the Revolution and leading up to

passage of the first married women's property acts. Where it seemed necessary to follow particular statutory provisions back into the seventeenth and
early eighteenth centuries, I did so, and the task revealed interesting regional
differences in the early application of English law. I made no systematic
attempt, however, to analyze the rights of women before the middle of the
eighteenth century. As a result, most questions of comparative Anglo-American law are best left aside, rich soil for future work in women's legal history.

My inquiry into the property rights of American women revealed above all
else a picture of their enforced dependence, both before and after the Revolution. Single women functioned on a legal par with men in property rights
(although they did not enjoy the political rights associated with property
ownership in early American society), but wives exercised only a truncated
proprietary capacity. No colony or state allowed married women, or femes
coverts, as lawmakers termed them, the legal ability to act independently with
regard to property. Only under certain circumstances, at particular times, in
precise ways, could a wife exercise even limited control over the family estate,
including what she contributed to it. Under property law, the male head of
household held the power to manage his own property as well as his wife's.

The one outstanding exception to this generalization concerned wives with
separate estates. Under equitable rules enforced in some of the colonies and
states, married women could own and control property separately from their
husbands. If their marriage settlements gave them the power to do so, femes
coverts could act as though they were femes soles, or unmarried women, in
managing settlement property. Yet even this exception did not spell meaningful independence for American women, for they could make marriage settlements only if their husbands consented. Without such consent, no feme
covert could create a binding separate estate of her own property. A relative
or friend could give a woman separate property over the objections of her
husband, but even that right made her dependent on the goodwill of others.
Even more significant for demonstrating the ineffectiveness of trusts is the
fact that few women had them. The law of separate estates was important, not
because many women actually succeeded at utilizing the vehicle of the trust,
but because it continually pushed outward the boundaries of what women
might do under the law.

Despite the promise of republicanism, American independence had little
direct effect on the legal status of women. My research has revealed only
three changes that occurred as a direct result of independence, one involving
divorce law and two, the law of inheritance. After the Revolution all of the
states studied, with the exception of South Carolina, broke from English
tradition and allowed absolute divorce. In the colonial period Connecticut

and Massachusetts had enforced divorce statutes, but the other colonies either had not tried to enact statutes or had seen their attempts disallowed by the English Privy Council. Independence from Great Britain permitted American lawmakers to follow their inclinations on the subject of divorce. Rules varied considerably from place to place, but the availability of divorce in several states for the first time gave abused or deserted wives important new legal rights. Even in South Carolina, chancellors defended their right to order legal separations and alimony against the rising protests of husbands, as more unhappy wives sought financial help and protection from the Court of Chancery. In inheritance law, reforms benefited women in two ways. Most important, jurists everywhere in the new United States abandoned the English law of primogeniture and the colonial rules on double shares for eldest sons in cases of intestacy. Daughters gained increased rights to family property as a result of the republican emphasis on equality. In addition, post-revolutionary South Carolina lawmakers went even further in reforming the laws of intestacy, by making the rights of widows and widowers more nearly equal.

Other changes in women's property rights cannot be traced directly to the influence of independence from England. In fact, most developments demonstrate a continuing reliance on English precedents, as American courts followed rules designed by the jurists of the mother country in the post-revolutionary decades. For the most part, these late eighteenth- and early nineteenth-century shifts in property law gave women increased rights to family property. The regressive rules that appeared from time to time serve to remind us of the inconsistencies of legal change, but on the whole the period saw an increase in women's autonomy with regard to property. The greater availability of divorce and legal separations; the enforcement of direct contracts between wives and husbands; the acceptance of the law of separate estates in New England; stricter observation of private examination procedures in Pennsylvania and New York; and the appearance of statutes such as Connecticut's giving married women the right to devise (1809), South Carolina's emphasizing equality between the inheritance rights of widows and widowers (1792), and Massachusetts's granting formal recognition to feme sole traders (1787)—all point toward increasing solicitude for women's property rights.

No sudden revolution in the legal status of married women occurred during the period studied. Wives remained femes coverts in 1830, just as in 1750. But steady improvements in the ability of wives to own and control property, especially in the rules on separate estates, indicate that the married women's property acts represented the end of an evolutionary process, not a radical break from postrevolutionary trends, as historians once thought. The forces of change—increasing economic diversification and instability, legal professionalism, improvement in women's education, shifting attitudes toward marriage that arose with liberal divorce laws, and the enhanced social roles of women that came with republican motherhood—were not revolutionary, but they could not be stopped, and over time they brought about dramatic changes in women's lives.[6] Most important, although the ideal of equality espoused in the Declaration of Independence did not work immediately to allow women greater autonomy, it represented a powerful weapon for future use, a weapon that nineteenth-century advocates of women's rights would not ignore for a second. In this sense, the influence of the American Revolution is still being felt today.

Women and the Law of
Property in Early America

Diversity in American Law

The most pervasive problem I encountered in studying the property rights of early American women had little to do with either women or the law of property. It was how to explain the remarkable diversity in colonial laws. No two colonies (and later, states) came to precisely the same conclusions about how to manage property under the law. Often rules varied only slightly, but sometimes the differences were major ones. Before we look closely at the specific legal areas covered in this study, it should prove useful to consider in a general way the forces behind legal diversity in the colonies. Although it is often impossible to pinpoint precisely why one unusual rule developed in a particular place, we can learn about the wider forces behind legal diversity by considering several developments together. What follows, then, are some introductory comments about the nature of legal diversity in the colonies.

First, it is important to remember that there was great variation in English law, perhaps particularly property law.[1] Colonial jurists were accustomed to regional diversity. Rules on widows' dower rights, conveyancing practices, and feme sole trader actions shifted between counties and boroughs in seventeenth- and eighteenth-century England. London had many standards all its own. When we recall in addition the tremendous variation in the reasons for settlement of the colonies, the differing English backgrounds of the settlers, dates of settlement, and the varied legal experience of early colonial lawmakers, standardization of the law in America can scarcely be expected.

Moreover, no one ever envisioned a single colonial code of laws. From the earliest days of settlement, legislative bodies in the colonies held the power to create laws suited to New World conditions. Contemporaries accepted the fact that life in America required the institution of rules unknown at home, and life everywhere in America was not the same. Chattel slavery, the need to promote clearing of wilderness lands, and the creation of a new religious leadership in New England and Pennsylvania all demanded innovation among American lawmakers. Change became not only acceptable but desirable in many areas of the law. Once a system supporting deviation from English law was in place, the colonists held a great deal of freedom to develop their own solutions to the legal problems of the day. Given the failure of the mother country to supervise colonial development to any meaningful degree throughout most of the seventeenth century, lawmakers developed systems based on their own values and needs with relative ease.[2] Colonial law therefore often differed from the common law considerably. Because so little is known about English local law, it is impossible to say whether colonial rules imitated certain county or borough standards, but that possibility must be acknowledged for some developments. Others clearly arose from the specific New World needs of the settlers.

Legal historians have recognized for some time that colonial lawmakers deviated from English standards, adapting both local customs and the common law to their own circumstances. In *Law and Authority in Early Massachusetts* (1960), George L. Haskins debunked an older theory favoring uniformity in colonial law. His conclusion soon came to represent a new consensus: "The conditions of settlement and of development within each colony meant that each evolved its own individual legal system, just as each evolved its individual social and political system. Geographical isolation, the date and character of the several settlements, the degree of absence of outside supervision or control—all had their effect in ultimately developing thirteen separate legal systems."[3] By the early 1960s, then, historians agreed that the common law was not transported wholesale to America and that colonial legal systems diverged sharply from one another. Since that time, however, little detailed work on colonial law has appeared to demonstrate regional distinctiveness, and Haskins's work on the evolution of the law in Massachusetts has not been imitated elsewhere.

In the following chapters, instances of regional variation in the rules governing women's property rights appear again and again. It was the norm for each jurisdiction to develop its own standard. Diversity stemmed from several general causes and many specific ones. First and perhaps most important, in many instances there was simply no obvious solution to the problem of how to handle women's property after marriage. When English law proved unsuitable or undesirable to colonial lawmakers, multiple solutions to any given question presented themselves. Therefore, even in colonies with similar backgrounds, different rules sometimes evolved. In Virginia, for example, slaves became defined as realty for the purpose of apportioning widows' dower, while Maryland retained the common law rule defining all movable estate as personalty. Virginia widows therefore inherited a share of their husbands' slaves only for life, whereas widows in Maryland gained absolute rights to some slave property. Because dower in Maryland included a share of personalty as well as the standard widow's thirds in realty, women there had a considerable advantage. Virginia's modification of the common law rule in this instance was not necessary, but to some lawmakers it seemed logical to attach valuable slave property to lands, since neither could be utilized fully without the other. The new rule restricted widows to a life estate in slaves as well as lands, and therefore remained consistent with the general purpose of dower. Women still received the property they needed to support themselves, but they did not gain enough for meaningful independence. Maryland lawmakers apparently were more concerned with making a clear distinction between personalty and realty, and with promoting the ready sale of slaves. Their system also worked to keep land and slaves together to a certain extent, since widows always received both as dower. If widows gained greater shares of family estates as a result of this policy, that outcome seemed relatively unimportant to Maryland officials. Both systems solved some of the problems associated with the high value of personal property in slaves and a widow's need for laborers in a plantation economy. Neither system was ideal.

Examples like this one are common. Depending on the talents, inclinations, and prejudices of influential men in any given colony, laws developed in one direction or another. Thus Massachusetts required wives' signatures in sales or mortgages of family lands, whereas Connecticut (until 1723) did not. Connecticut gave widows dower only in lands their husbands owned at death; widows in Massachusetts held a claim on any realty owned during the marriage. Maryland allowed widows a full dower share in personalty, while Virginia restricted the widow to a child's share of personalty as dower. Pennsylvania had a feme sole trader statute making special provisions for deserted wives, and New York left women to cope under the few available English common law precedents designed to give relief to the families of deserters. In each of these cases, similar social conditions produced diverging rules of law, for no obvious social or economic reason.

Some variations in the rules on women's property rights occurred as a result of the timing of settlement of different colonies. English law on issues such as dower changed in the seventeenth century, so that in following English law Maryland and South Carolina, for example, adopted different standards. Whereas Maryland followed the early seventeenth-century English rules of allowing dower in personalty, South Carolina adopted the rule established by the end of the century, that men had the right to bequeath all of their personalty to whomever they pleased.

The most startling distinctions in colonial laws appeared not within regions but between regions, and here the forces for change are more readily apparent. Connecticut and Massachusetts developed a system of laws for dealing with women's property that differed significantly from the standards of Maryland, Virginia, and South Carolina. Although the gap between New England and the South was widest, Pennsylvania and New York also differed in several respects from both North and South.

The settlers of New England came to America determined to create a society shaped by the teachings of their faith. The law played an important role in assisting them to build their New World utopia, as demonstrated by Haskins and others.[4] It is not surprising, then, to find Puritan lawmakers in Connecticut and Massachusetts developing rules on family property that agreed with their ideological concerns. When necessary, the Puritans readily revised the common law of England. Unlike settlers in royal or even proprietary colonies, they had charters that gave them considerable freedom to do so, and their radical bent demanded rather than discouraged reform.

New Englanders gave male heads of household more control over family property, including what wives inherited or earned, than was common elsewhere. In Connecticut, until 1723, all real property a woman brought to her husband in marriage became his absolutely, to sell or mortgage as he saw fit. Normally a husband acquired absolute rights only to his wife's personalty. Similarly, throughout the period studied, a wife in Massachusetts had no right to a private examination at the time of a sale or mortgage of family property. The examination served to guarantee court officials that a woman entered into a conveyance voluntarily, and not because her husband was forcing her. Obviously, in Massachusetts the possibility of male coercion was not a serious concern. Widows in Connecticut fared badly compared to widows elsewhere. Normally a woman received dower in whatever lands her husband possessed during the marriage, but in this New England colony she could claim only a share in the lands her husband owned at death. Such a limit meant that she had no power to influence the sale or mortgage of her husband's realty. These and other examples are discussed fully in the text that follows. What is important to note here is the fact that Connecticut and Massachusetts changed standard English common law rules adopted in the other colonies. Puritan lawmakers worked under a set of assumptions that differed from those of other Englishmen, and they did not offer married women the usual protections for their estates.

On one level New Englanders sought not to deny women property rights but to simplify some of the complications of English land law. They changed many aspects of property law, not just those affecting wives and widows.[5] The establishment of recording practices, abolition of primogeniture, and tightening of judicial controls over the administration of estates all pointed to a desire for more clear and efficient management of land than was known in England. Reform in the rules on conveyancing, dower, and wives' separate estates conformed to this general desire for simplification. English law on marital property was confusing because the rules required a balancing of conflicting interests within the family. What the Puritans attempted to achieve in their revision of the law was the elimination or at least minimization of conflicting interests, a goal that went beyond mere simplification.

Like their contemporaries, the Puritans emphasized a hierarchy of relationships among all members of society.[6] Within seventeenth-century English families the father and husband wielded absolute authority. A wife, like her children, owed the family head obedience in religious and secular matters. Unlike their contemporaries, however, Puritans possessed the conviction to act according to their beliefs. Rather than offering only mouth service to the patriarchal ideal, the Puritans created a social and legal system in America that personified it. They changed a number of standard English rules and procedures that openly acknowledged conflicting interests between spouses and therefore worked against the patriarchal ideal.

Consider for a moment the problem of land conveyances. Under English law a husband could not sell land his wife brought to the marriage without her consent, indicated by her signature on the deed and her declaration in a private examination that she acted of her own free will and not under the coercion of her husband. Husband and wife both had to appear before the local authorities to acknowledge the deed. Procedures of this kind gave a wife equal status with her husband before the law. They admitted that she possessed rights in the land he could not abrogate. They also acknowledged the possibility of conflicting interests: he might want to sell her land against her wishes; she might need protection from his coercion.

Other rules carried similar implications of separate interests within the family. To protect their dower rights, widows held the power to oppose land sales or mortgages by their husbands. During widowhood, the women could sue for their thirds in the lands transferred without their consent, and find favor in courts of law. Men therefore did not have absolute powers of control over their own estates. Marriage settlements creating separate estates for wives represented probably the sharpest division of interests within the family. Beginning in the late sixteenth century in England a woman or her relatives and friends could arrange a contract under which she or her trustee would retain full managerial rights over her separate property. Either personal or real property placed in such a trust could not be touched by the woman's husband or his creditors. Women with separate estates gained protection under the rules of equity, and their husbands lost traditional common law marital rights under which they had access to all their wives' property.

In Connecticut and Massachusetts lawmakers changed English law on conveyancing, dower, and marriage settlements to reduce the possibility of separate marital interests. As previously noted, they increased men's power to control their wives' estates, eliminating or changing procedures designed to protect women from coercion. They also improved the ability of husbands to control their own property and discouraged the use of separate estates. The rejection of English rules created to grant women independent rights within the family was a logical step to seventeenth-century Puritans. Not only did requiring a wife's signature on a land deed and a private examination complicate the law and make conveyancing more expensive and time-consuming, it also contradicted a central tenet of Puritanism: the wife's submission to her husband's will. An obedient and dutiful wife did not need to express her public approval of a conveyance arranged by her spouse. His decision represented her will. As William Gouge explained in *Of Domestical Duties*, a couple "are yoak-fellows in mutuall familiaritie, not in equall authoritie. . . . If therefore he will one thing, and she another, she may not thinke to have an equall right and power. She must give place and yeeld."[7] Similarly, to the Puritans, separate estates created by contract represented the worst element of English family law, designed to facilitate not only separate interests but in many instances separate residences as well. Often separate estates in England served as the basis for informal divorces, a practice the Puritans frowned upon. In the eyes of conservative New Englanders, the procedure had been developed to support a decadent system of marital relations based on an exchange of property rather than love and companionship. Proper families needed laws to bind them together, not draw them apart. Finally, widows did not need to protect their own interests. Puritans assumed that in the event a man's estate could not provide adequate support for his surviving spouse, the children of the marriage would care for their mother out of feelings of love and duty.

In short, the rules of law adopted in Connecticut and Massachusetts assumed that families would be loving, considerate, and interdependent. Protective strategies for wives and widows could be reduced because they were viewed as unnecessary, restrictive, and perhaps even destructive of family harmony. Connecticut, even more than Massachusetts, tended to restrict the independent property rights of wives. It is interesting to note the more extreme position of Connecticut, because the founders of that colony long have been regarded as Puritans with a vengeance. As Perry Miller observed, "New Haven was the essence of Puritanism, distilled and undefiled; the Bible Commonwealth and nothing else." He also believed that "the Colony of New Haven is the ideal laboratory in which to study the germ of Puritanism."[8] The historic opposition of Connecticut law to wifely autonomy in the management of property speaks well, then, to Puritan ideals about the family. Faithful Puritans believed that "our Ribs were not ordained to be our Rulers: They are not made of the head to claim Superiority. . . . They desert the Author of nature that invert the order of nature. The Woman was made for the man's comfort, but the man was not made for the woman's command. Those shoulders aspire too high, that content not themselves with a room below the head."[9] Good Puritan women trusted their husbands, and later their sons, to take care of them.

Support for the contention that New England legal reforms resulted from ideological influences comes from the colony of Pennsylvania, where similar forces were at work. Although settled considerably later than either Connecticut or Massachusetts, the Quaker colony followed some of the same rules of law. Pennsylvania did not require private examinations until the end of the colonial period, and dower included a share only in what a husband owned at his death. To support creditors' rights the Pennsylvania General Assembly also took the unusual step of making all of a deceased man's estate liable for his debts. Under the common law the widow received her dower share before creditors could make their claims on the estate, but in William Penn's colony, from the earliest days of settlement, lands were made liable for a man's debts. Indigent widows became dependent on children, other relatives, or the local community. In Pennsylvania, as in New England, a reform tradition coupled with an emphasis on family unity allowed lawmakers to ignore or change rules of English law.[10]

Southern law was not based on such high ideals. Maryland, Virginia, and South Carolina tended to follow English rules closely on matters of land conveyancing, private examinations, dower, and separate estates. Traditional safeguards against male coercion found strong support in the South. Women exercised the legal right to veto land conveyances arranged by their husbands (at least so far as their inheritance or dower rights were concerned). Widows in Maryland and Virginia even gained over Englishwomen in their dower rights, because they retained the right to shares of personalty. Southern women also enjoyed greater protection for their separate estates, since courts there enforced marriage settlements strictly and followed the most current English practices.

Southerners imitated English law more closely than their New England counterparts because they lacked an ideological commitment to change.[11] Instead, their backgrounds necessitated adherence to English forms, particularly in property law. Most southern elites—those men who influenced the development of law and politics—came to America unwillingly. They gave up a life they loved at "home" for the primitive colonial environment solely for financial reasons. Southerners sought and gained large tracts of land, exploited the labor of both white indentured servants and African slaves, and produced for export such crops as tobacco (considered base and nasty by their countrymen), all with the end of making themselves richer than they would have become in England. Many succeeded at the price, they thought, of their dignity. Americans in the southern colonies felt themselves to be inferior to the English in culture, lifestyle, politics, and law.[12] Their sense of inferiority caused them to adhere as closely as possible to English forms. As Carole Shammas observed about seventeenth-century Virginians, "The low opinion of Virginia at 'home' [England] and the motives behind most planters' migration seemed to militate against the majority of the immigrant elite taking the colony's institutions, honors, or anything besides their own estates, seriously."[13] Southerners therefore looked to England for solutions to their problems, not only because they often were too busy (making money) to institute innovations themselves, but also because they believed in the superiority of English culture, government, and law.

Shammas's comment speaks to another point. Southern planters gained their greatest satisfaction from managing, enlarging, and improving upon their estates. Their self-esteem was very much tied up with the land, and they hoped to make their family seats as luxurious as those of the English upper ranks. They wanted to be respected for their financial accomplishments. One observer noted that Virginians possessed an "extraordinary *Ambition* to be *thought well of*" in England.[14] Imitation of English cultural forms, particularly in the management of large estates, made them careful to duplicate established rules on property. Primogeniture and the use of jointures and marriage settlements therefore found favor in the South, though not in the North. Perhaps, to the less secure planters of Maryland, Virginia, and later, South Carolina, such forms represented desirable cultural norms as well as established rules of law. They could be overturned only at the risk of losing continuity with English society.

Finally, the harsh demographic realities of life in the early South necessitated reliance on protective strategies for wives.[15] Few couples reached old age together, and in many families the death of one spouse occurred within a decade of the marriage. Remarriage was the norm for survivors, with children experiencing one, two, or several changes in parental authority before reaching adulthood. As Mary Beth Norton has observed, although the English patriarchal ideal certainly existed in southern families, high mortality rates undermined it at several points. Demographic disruption made it difficult—and sometimes unwise—for men to exert full patriarchal control over family members.[16] Women needed the power to safeguard their own interests, since they could not depend on either husbands or children to outlive them. Protection of wives' dower and inheritance rights in land conveyancing stemmed, then, from a commitment to English procedures, and also from the necessities of southern colonial life.

Perhaps the most radical legal change instituted by some of the American colonies was the elimination of chancery courts. Connecticut, Massachusetts, and Pennsylvania refused to establish separate courts of equity, though New York, Maryland, Virginia, and South Carolina had them. Because chancery administered trust estates, the vehicle under which wives owned property separately from their husbands, the presence or absence of an equity court virtually determined a colony's position on female separate estates.

Opposition to chancery as a separate court was the crux of the matter. According to Stanley N. Katz, "No colonial legal institution was the object of such sustained and intense political opposition as the courts dispensing equity law."[17] Puritans and Quakers, and other reform-minded Englishmen as well, disliked the court for its time-consuming and expensive procedures (everything had to be submitted to the court in written form), its reliance on the independent judgment of a chancellor rather than a jury, and in particular, its association with the prerogative powers of king or governor. Pennsylvania's single attempt to establish a chancery court failed, for example, out of widespread distrust of the governor who had set himself up as chancellor.

Puritan legal reformers in England did not succeed in abolishing the High Court of Chancery as they had hoped, but in America the Puritans got what they wanted. Because opposition centered mainly on the structure and procedures of the court rather than on the substance of equity law, certain essential areas of equity—mortgages, for example—were placed under the jurisdiction of the courts of common law. Wives' separate estates were never mentioned in the statutes designating jurisdiction, however. Apparently, this was not an area of equity deemed essential by lawmakers, even though historians have found several examples of prenuptial contracts executed by New England couples. Pennsylvania courts of common law did administer separate estates when they sat periodically as dispensers of "equity," but they never developed the detailed set of rules and precedents enforced in colonies with independent courts of chancery.

Settled by entrepreneurs and adventurers rather than social reformers, New York, Maryland, Virginia, and South Carolina felt no qualms about duplicating the court structure of the mother country. In fact, as noted, they wanted to recreate English forms as much as possible. In time, courts of chancery in these jurisdictions developed into sophisticated bodies capable of handling the most intricate of equity suits. They supported female separate estates fully, adopting English precedents as they appeared and gradually expanding the right of wives to own property in their own names. With regard to separate estates, then, the colonies enforced different rules at least in part because of Puritan and Quaker hostility to chancery courts, which New York and the South did not share.

New Englanders entertained unusual opinions about another controversial area of the law—divorce. Here again, the Puritans once had hoped to reform English law on the question, but had to content themselves with establishing a new standard in New England.[18] As early as 1552 Puritan divines had advocated a liberalization of divorce law. According to Nancy F. Cott, a document released in that year, the *Reformatio Legum Ecclesiasticarum*, "regarded marriage as a civil contract rather than an indissoluble sacred bond."[19] The treatise suggested allowing absolute divorce with the right to remarry for adultery, desertion, continued absence without word, and uncontrollable enmity or cruelty. England never accepted the radical proposal, but Connecticut and Massachusetts permitted absolute divorce for virtually identical causes. No other colony followed suit. Although legal separations could be obtained from both common law and equity courts, absolute divorce was not available outside New England until after the Revolution—at least in part because England refused to countenance further deviation from its law on this point.

Diversity in colonial law cannot be explained easily. Obviously there were a number of forces at work in creating the divergent legal codes, some more rational than others. Many stemmed from the concerns of the Puritans and Quakers, who came to America intent on creating more perfect societies than they had known in England. They revised the law as part of their general effort at reform. Other settlers wanted to recreate what was familiar to them, and changed English law only in response to new legal problems, not out of a dissatisfaction with established solutions to the old. Often lawmakers in different colonies faced similar needs to devise new legal forms appropriate to life in America. Occasionally, as in loosening old common law restrictions on waste, they arrived at the same conclusion. More often, however, varying solutions to similar problems surfaced because no obvious answer existed. Precise causes for individual differences—one man's brainstorm, another's prejudice, the effect of a particular legal decision—can only be surmised without detailed work in seventeenth-century legislative records. At this point, we can only conclude that the overall aim of jurists was similar, despite varying modes of attacking the problems. In colonial America, lawmakers sought social stability above all else. In arriving at statutes and precedents, they hoped to enforce standards of behavior appropriate to their values. Puritan and Quaker emphasis on the family as a loving, interdependent unit resulted in a reduction of protective strategies for wives: the family could be depended upon to care for all its members according to their needs. By making women more dependent on husbands and children, lawmakers hoped, in fact, to strengthen the family. Too often, as cases demonstrate, their ideals were not matched by reality.

English law, and the law of the jurisdictions that attempted to duplicate it, achieved a more modern stance by offering women extended protection for their property rights. Recognizing that men held the balance of power in the family, jurists sought to improve the position of women by enforcing private examinations, demanding women's signatures on land deeds, supporting separate estates, and guaranteeing common law dower to all widows. By thus increasing women's ability to act autonomously in managing property, lawmakers reduced men's power slightly. Under this framework, a more equal balance of power stabilized family relationships by giving women some leverage over their husbands' actions. As will be shown, women often chose not to utilize the safeguards designed for their benefit, especially separate estates. Autonomy frightened most women in the colonial and early national periods. In many instances, it was only when husbands proved abusive or wasteful that women sought to control their own financial affairs. It would take an improvement in the social position of women generally before they could begin to appreciate the importance of independent action, and that would not come until well into the nineteenth century.

Conveyances

Unity of person, the principle advertised so well by William Blackstone in his commentaries on English law (1765–69), represented little more than an ideal in Anglo-American law. As a legal concept, it underwent almost continual change in the seventeenth and eighteenth centuries. But although unity of person suffered revision, jurists never abandoned it completely. As an ideal, lawyers, judges, and lawmakers all upheld the principle. For early Americans, as for the English, spousal unity represented a goal of the law, hoped for but never realized, worshiped and ridiculed at the same time. In this study, unity of person is employed just as colonial and early national jurists employed it, as a benchmark. The first goal, therefore, is to understand exactly what Blackstone and his Anglo-American contemporaries meant by the concept.[1]

UNITY OF PERSON

Under the common law, women and men gained certain rights and responsibilities after marriage. No longer acting simply as individuals, together they constituted a special kind of legal partnership, one in which the woman's role was secondary to the man's. Restrictions limited a married woman's ability to act at law.[2] At marriage, her husband gained the right and responsibility for prosecuting suits in her name as well as his own. She could not institute a suit without him. In suits involving only the rights of the husband, the wife did not join.[3] Such was the uneven nature of unity of person, which limited the activities of the wife while broadening those of the husband.

After marriage, women acting alone could not execute valid contracts. Nor could they convey the property they brought to their marriages or earned with their husbands. They also lost the power to act as executors or administrators of estates and as legal guardians. With their husbands, however, femes coverts could do all of these things. Coverture notwithstanding, women who contracted, conveyed, and administered jointly rather than alone did so with the sanction of the law. Men, in contrast, did not need the consent of their wives in executing most contracts and conveyances, and never needed to join in actions as executors, administrators, and guardians. Men also possessed the legal right to devise their estates, whereas women could do so only with the express consent of their husbands. Even then, their right extended only to personal property.

Restrictions on feme covert activities were a necessity, given the nature of property law. The inability of wives to act as individuals at law arose as a corollary to their inability to own property. After marriage, all of the personal property owned by a wife came under the exclusive control of her husband. He could spend her money, including wages, sell her slaves or stocks, and appropriate her clothing and jewelry. With regard to real property his rights were almost as extensive. He made all managerial decisions concerning her lands and tenements and controlled the rents and profits. A conveyance of a woman's real estate was another matter, however. No husband could sell or mortgage real property without the consent of his wife. The common law sanctioned conveyances only when wives freely agreed to them, although "free" consent sometimes was difficult to determine in court.[4]

Unity of person meant that once they married, a man and woman had to cohabit for the rest of their lives. Legal separations or divorces remained rare and were frowned upon for all social classes. The law required men to support their wives and children. If they refused, they could be prosecuted. At death, men had to devise at least two-thirds of their estates to their immediate families. If men died intestate, their families received all of their property.

The law of husband and wife thus bound the interests of spouses closely together. Ideally the system should have worked. If men always acted wisely and fairly, the common law rules on marital relations might have served everyone well enough. To say that they did not is only to state the obvious. Unity of person was based on the perfect marriage, and therefore it inevitably created hardships in marriages that were less than ideal.

Reform in the common law concept of unity of person thus arose out of necessity. Jurists had to provide remedies for the cases when men, either purposefully or out of ignorance, abused their extensive powers. In particular, the courts acted to protect women from damaging bargains, mortgages, and sales of real estate by their husbands. Despite the principle of unity of person, they gave women significant rights to property—rights that men had to respect.

The most significant property right of women was dower, a share of the real property owned by husbands during marriage that was designated for the support of widows. Acting alone, men could not alienate property to deny their wives dower. Unless a wife consented to a sale or mortgage of family real estate, the title of the purchaser was never secure. Years after the execution of any conveyances to which she was not a party, a woman could sue for her dower right in the lands and find support from courts of law. Dower was a necessity in a legal system that denied women the ability to provide for their own financial security during widowhood.[5]

Women who purchased or inherited land, or received it in a deed of gift, exercised the same powers they held over dower lands. Husbands could not alienate their wives' realty unless the women agreed. This rule evolved because of the differing provisions governing property owned by childless women and mothers. Under the common law, a woman without children held absolute rights to her own estate. Although her husband managed it during the marriage, at his death it did not become a part of his general estate. Instead, it remained in the possession of the widow, who in addition received a one-third share of her husband's real property as dower. Similarly, if the woman died first her husband did not inherit her estate. It returned to her own family. These provisions changed once a couple had a child. Then the husband became "tenant by the curtesy," the lifetime manager of his wife's estates. His new position resulted from the guardianship rights he exercised over their children. Only when he died would they inherit their mother's lands. Heiresses, then, had special rights and responsibilities over property. The law recognized their need to protect their own estates, safeguarding them in the only way it recognized as valid, by demanding evidence of their consent to all conveyances.

As a remedy for women's legal incapacities during marriage, dower and inheritance rights were ineffective. They assisted women only insofar as purchasers feared future rather than present claims. Until the death of the family patriarch, women held no legal means to oppose purchasers, and death, of course, could lie many years in the future. Despite the fact that dower or inheritance rights represented only a potential risk, however, few purchasers relished agreements made without the consent of sellers' wives. Their hesitancy to buy land or extend mortgages without the consent of women was wise, for in most of the American colonies widows' claims against purchasers found support in the courts. To ensure honest conveyances, courts in England had developed procedures for ensuring women's property rights, procedures that the colonies adopted with varying degrees of commitment. Heiresses of realty thus had special rights to control the disposition of property that never, in an absolute sense, became their husbands'. The law recognized women's need to protect their own property by demanding evidence that they had consented freely to any conveyance instigated by men. Under the common law, lands could not be sold or mortgaged in an attempt to circumvent women's property rights.[6]

The ancient procedure by which Englishwomen conveyed property was the fine, a legal action in which seller and buyer engaged in a fictitious lawsuit before a court of record. The title passed when the court found judgment for the purchaser, as it always did in collusive suits of this nature.[7] Part of the procedure involved a conference with the seller's wife, held apart from her husband and called a private examination, during which a judge attempted to determine her true wishes regarding the sale. If her husband were forcing her to execute the deed, she could reveal his coercion during the meeting.[8]

Fines developed in medieval England. As William Searle Holdsworth wrote, "It was an old rule, and one common to many Germanic nations, that possession by order of a court gave to the possessor an undisputed title as against all the world after the lapse of a short period—generally a year and a day."[9] The strength of the fine made it the favored conveyance of married women from roughly the thirteenth century. By the seventeenth century some manorial and borough courts no longer required the fine and recovery procedure for feme covert conveyances. Instead, they replaced it with the simpler bargain and sale. The anonymous author of an eighteenth-century legal treatise, *The Laws Respecting Women*, wrote that in London, for example, local courts developed a less expensive and more streamlined procedure. "By the custom of *London*, and that of several other cities, a married woman may bar herself by a deed enrolled on which she is privately examined; and this custom was confirmed in 34 & 35 *Hen.* 8. by a positive statute."[10] Holdsworth thought that Sir Francis Moore (1558–1621) invented the bargain and sale. In any case, it was 1621 when an English court first recognized the procedure as valid, and by the second half of the seventeenth century, it was commonplace.[11] In some areas of England, then, jurists employed a simpler method than fines for releasing the dower right of women. In early America, the courts followed the newer procedure almost exclusively.

There were many reasons for the colonists to reject the common law on fines. In the first years of settlement, court officers may have been unsure of the proper way to execute a fine, or they may have opposed the more complicated and expensive procedure on principle. Because deeds of bargain and sale also were recognized by English courts, it was easy for the colonists to adopt that procedure for transferring estates. In most colonies, therefore, after an initial period of confusion when husbands often conveyed family property alone and women's rights to join in conveyances were ignored, jurists adopted deeds of bargain and sale that included private examinations.[12]

The examination procedure required by most colonial courts was fairly standard. When a woman wanted to execute a conveyance of real property, she and an officer of the court, who was usually a judge of common pleas, went alone into a separate room where he read the contents of the deed to her, ensuring himself that she understood its meaning. He then asked if she freely agreed to a conveyance of her ownership or dower rights in the property, and if she answered affirmatively he noted that she had done so on the face of the deed or on an attached certificate. This acknowledgment by a woman barred her forever from establishing claims to the property.

Jurists designed private examinations to protect wives from the coercive powers of their husbands. Coercion, the ability of men to force women into executing deeds, was a recognized legal principle in seventeenth- and eighteenth-century Anglo-American society.[13] Official acknowledgment of coercion forced courts to seek procedures that could mitigate its impact, and the most important of these was the private examination. It was not a foolproof method of control, for a woman's fear of her husband might cause her to lie during the inquiry, but it was the only means the courts developed for protecting women. In theory, private examinations gave women who opposed conveyances the opportunity to seek help from local officials. Even more important, the procedure stood as a formal statement attesting to the property rights of women.

SOUTHERN RULES ON CONVEYANCING

In at least two colonies, Maryland and Virginia, the settlers followed English bargain and sale procedures on feme covert conveyances from the middle of the seventeenth century. In 1674, when Virginia lawmakers enacted a statute on feme covert conveyances, they pointed out that colonial custom already adhered to the simpler procedure rather than the fine and recovery. The preamble to "An Act empowring ffeame coverts to make good acknowledgment of sales of lands" duly noted that "the legall way in England of passing estates where the inheritance is in a ffeame covert, is by way of ffine and recovery." But in Virginia, "for many yeares, wee haveing noe ffines and recoveries," the usual form of conveyance was a joint deed executed and acknowledged by husband and wife, "the wife being first privately examined by the court whether she acknowledge the same ffreely." The statute con-

firmed this long-standing practice of Virginians and made it a legal requirement for all future conveyances involving married women.[14]

Maryland lawmakers acted in an identical fashion. Shortly after the General Assembly developed specific regulations for establishing titles to land in
1671, it recognized the need for rules governing feme covert acknowledgments and private examinations. In 1674, just as in neighboring Virginia,
Maryland lawmakers wrote a statute outlining the required procedures. To
convey the estate of a married woman, a judge of a court of common pleas
had to question her "privately and secretly," that is, apart from her husband,
and ask "whether she do make such Acknowledgment willingly and freely,
and without being induced by any Force or Threats used by her Husband, or
through Fear of his Displeasure?"[15]

Shortly after South Carolina became an independent royal colony in 1729,
the General Assembly enacted a conveyancing statute similar to those of
Maryland and Virginia. The statute probably continued a practice known to
earlier settlers. North Carolina's first statute requiring private examinations
appeared in 1715, and it seems likely that the procedure spread to the
southern section of the colony as well, although at that time the two sections
constituted independent jurisdictions. In any case, South Carolinians believed that they needed a precise description of women's conveyancing rights
in their new code of laws. The conveyancing statute of 1731 explained that
"no office or offices have hitherto been established whereby any fine might
be passed for barring any feme covert of her right and inheritance, or of her
dower or thirds, in any lands or tenements."[16] Instead, South Carolina
matrons conveyed real property by joint deeds executed with their husbands.
Moreover, "by the practice of late years," women had been examined privately by the chief justice of the province to determine whether they acted
freely, "without any compulsion, dread or fear of their said husbands."[17] The
colonial assembly approved this practice and made it a legal requirement for
all future conveyances. South Carolina jurists, accustomed already to administering private examinations, probably saw the law as a confirmation of old
procedures rather than as a creator of new policy.

All three southern colonies strictly enforced their statutes on feme covert
conveyances. Unless a woman signed and acknowledged a deed of sale or
mortgage with her husband, and signified her free consent apart from him,
she could not convey a legal title to real estate. Jurists in the South regarded
the procedure as necessary for women's financial security. Southern decisions throughout the colonial and early national periods indicate the serious
manner in which courts of law supported this female prerogative.

One of the earliest surviving cases focusing on the enforcement of a private examination is *Carroll* v. *Warren*, tried in Maryland before the Court of Chancery in 1736.[18] From the trial record it appears that Sarah Curtis owned considerable property under the will of a former husband. In 1711 her then husband, Michael Curtis, prevailed upon her to convey her lands, but he did not fully explain to her the nature of the conveyance he had in mind. Sarah believed that the deed she executed was a long-term lease, whereas in reality Michael agreed to sell the property to Charles Carroll outright. John Warren, Sarah's heir at law and the defendant in the case, reported in his deposition that when Sarah learned of the sale "she was much troubled in mind, declared that she never had that it was false, that there never was any such thing mentioned to her that she had only been askt to join with her Husband in a lease or leases of some Tenements on part of the Lands and Mannors aforesaid but never to give away her Right and Title to any part thereof." After she learned of her husband's deceit in obtaining her signature, "the grief thereof broke her Heart," and she remained estranged from him until her death several years later.[19] Moreover, she constantly refused to correct several imperfections in her deed of acknowledgment, leaving the title unclear and liable to a dispute at law.

The chancellor ruled in favor of John Warren's claim to the property on the grounds that the deed was obtained and acknowledged improperly. He noted that at the time of executing the deed there were clear requirements for conveying feme covert estates in Maryland. The procedures were not followed even though Charles Carroll was an able practitioner of the law and fully cognizant of the need for obtaining correct statements. That the proper forms were not followed, he observed, must have been due to the deceit practiced on Sarah Curtis to gain her signature, for "it plainly appeared even from the mouth of Samuel Williamson the Justice of the Peace who certified her acknowledgment that her Willingness and Consent was not so Voluntary as it ought to have been but that on the contrary some importunate perswasions were made use of to prevail with her to sign such deed."[20] These circumstances, added to the fact that Carroll still owed part of the purchase price, resulted in a verdict favoring the heir at law.

In *Carroll* v. *Warren*, a Maryland court recognized the right of married women to exercise at least some control over conveyancing. The stand is echoed by a Virginia decision from the same period. In *Jones* v. *Porters* (1740), the court threw out a conveyance executed by William and Jane Porter in 1703 because the feme covert's private examination had not been recorded.[21] According to a statute enacted in 1734, if a deed had no notation concerning the examination, the assumption had to be that it had been omitted.[22]

Another Virginia case, *Harvey and Wife* v. *Pecks* (1810), concerned the same issues.[23] In their attempt to overturn a sale of property made in 1745, the heirs of Lydia Peck claimed that she had been a victim of fraud and coercion. They noted that Lydia never signed the deed of conveyance executed by her husband, nor did any public record attest to her private examination. As their attorney argued, such evidence constituted adequate proof of coercion, for Lydia "must be presumed to have been under the coercion of her husband, without direct evidence to the contrary." The court agreed, noting that Lydia Peck "never relinquished her right" to the land in question.[24]

Support for women's property rights in conveyancing continued in the South throughout the late eighteenth and early nineteenth centuries. As Chief Justice Pendleton of the Virginia Supreme Court noted in 1797, "A feme covert can't pass her legal title without a deed, accompanied by a privy examination, to evince that she does not do it under her husband's influence." Otherwise, he continued, "she might be dragged before the justices, and the oath administered in the husband's presence, under the influence of some signal terror before communicated and kept up."[25]

Despite Pendleton's opinion to the contrary, even strict rules on private examinations could not always protect women, a fact demonstrated by a Maryland case heard by the Court of Chancery in 1761. In *Bissett v. Bissett*, a married woman revealed the manner in which her husband forced her to surrender all her real estate.[26] Ann Atkinson was a widow with considerable property when she married David Bissett, "who had not any Real and but a very inconsiderable Personal Estate." Soon after the marriage he asked her to convey all of her property to him in fee simple. Ann refused initially, but his continued ill treatment finally forced her to consent. She reported in her deposition to the chancellor that her husband "did often and at Sundry Times cruelly beat and with Approbrious Language abuse your Oratrix menacing and threatening her at the same time with a repetition of such Ill-Usage unless she consented to such Conveyance."[27] By these methods David forced Ann to sign away her lands. They executed a deed of bargain and sale, and Ann acknowledged it according to law, submitting to a private examination.

The conveyance took place in 1755. After David's death in 1761, Ann attempted to regain title to her own lands by bringing a suit in chancery against David's son, who was acting as his father's administrator. She claimed that her acknowledgment was void because it had been gained through her husband's force. David's son based his defense on the correct form of the deed and acknowledgment, which was executed according to the legal requirements. He told the court that the law must support proper acknowledgments, "as otherwise property would be rendered altogether Vague and incertain If no Rights that could be Devised nor no Act of the Legislature that could be formed could Assure the same or Effectually Barr."[28] He denied the claims of physical abuse made by his stepmother, pointing to her acknowledgment in court that she signed the deed voluntarily.

The Maryland Court of Chancery dismissed Ann Bissett's petition for relief, ruling that it could not admit evidence to invalidate a deed executed according to law. The decision on *Bissett* v. *Bissett* shows the potential ineffectiveness of the examination procedure in cases of wife abuse. A woman who wanted protection from the courts had to ask for it before executing a deed of conveyance, and yet such a move would surely expose her to increased beating, ill-treatment, and as Ann Bissett put it, "Moroseness and Sourness of Temper" from her husband.[29]

NORTHERN RULES ON CONVEYANCING

In contrast to southern practice, the legislatures of colonial Connecticut, Massachusetts, Pennsylvania, and New York exhibited a more casual attitude toward feme covert acknowledgments. Connecticut wives possessed no property rights at all until 1723. During the seventeenth century and the first two decades of the eighteenth century, women had no private examinations because they had no right to sign joint deeds with their husbands. The situation in Massachusetts was much the same. There wives did sign joint deeds, but no procedure existed for taking their private examinations. Pennsylvania and New York law echoed that of Massachusetts. Although both jurisdictions eventually enacted statutes requiring private examinations, they did so late in the colonial period, 1770 for Pennsylvania and 1771 for New York.

In seventeenth- and early eighteenth-century Connecticut, women lost even the minimal proprietary capacity granted to them under the common law. They possessed no right to control property after marriage, including what they acquired themselves by purchase, gift, or inheritance. According to Connecticut practice, all family property belonged to the husband as head of his household. He exercised absolute power over everything and could buy, sell, mortgage, and lease lands alone. Wives did not join in real estate transactions, and they possessed no right to oppose them. Private examinations were unheard of.[30]

The situation in Connecticut demonstrates a strong, self-conscious commitment to the principle of unity of person. Lawmakers in the colony, determined to view husband and wife as one legal being, refused to grant women the power to influence their husbands in any decisions regarding the management of family property. Connecticut courts failed to recognize feme covert property rights until 1723, when the legislature finally passed an act significantly reforming the law on conveyancing. The statute, "An Act for preventing the Sales of the Real Estates of Heiresses, without their Consent," required the concurrence of a wife to any property sale by her husband.[31] After 1723 she had to acknowledge the deed before a justice of the peace in a manner similar to that employed in the South. Enforcement of the new procedure was strict, as Justice Ingersoll of the Supreme Court of Errors noted almost a century later. In a discussion of Connecticut history on the law of conveyancing he wrote, "The statute of this state put the matter beyond all dispute, as it made every contract of a *feme-covert*, with respect to her real estate, void, except a deed executed by her with her husband, and acknowledged before proper authority."[32]

Significantly, the Connecticut conveyancing statute included two new requirements designed to protect the property rights of married women. First, women had to join their husbands in signing deeds, and second, they had to demonstrate their free consent. Both provisions indicated a new acceptance of the right of married women to own property. In addition, the second provision marked the recognition of male coercion as a legal principle in Connecticut.

Unlike their neighbors in Connecticut, Massachusetts lawmakers never gave formal recognition to the principle of coercion. Women did not have private examinations, nor were they required to acknowledge deeds of conveyance in court. All the law demanded to validate a conveyance of real property by a feme covert was her signature, which could be taken at home. If the husband alone acknowledged the deed in public, that was sufficient.[33] In *Fowler* v. *Shearer* (1810), Chief Justice Parsons observed, "Estates have never in this state been conveyed by fine, in which the wife might be examined, and by her consent be barred by the fine."[34] Instead, he pointed out, the wife could convey her estate by simply signing the deed with her husband.

In *Catlin* v. *Ware* (1812), the Supreme Court of Massachusetts considered the validity of a deed of conveyance signed by a feme covert but acknowledged only by her husband.[35] The court accepted the deed, despite Mrs. Catlin's contention that she never signed it. Her signature, she said, was forged, and she never acknowledged the conveyance in court. In ruling against her claim, the court noted the irrelevance of a woman's failure to acknowledge any deed of conveyance. The written opinion stated unequivocally, "We think an acknowledgment unnecessary. One party to a deed acknowledging it gives notoriety to it, and that is the whole that is necessary. . . .

Neither was an acknowledgment by the wife necessary in order to make the deed binding on her. She must know her own acts, and is bound by such, as the law authorizes her to execute."[36] With these words, the court indicated its refusal to recognize the possibility of fraud or coercion; it continued to support deeds signed by women at home rather than in public, and never acknowledged.

Justice Sewall criticized Massachusetts policy on feme covert conveyances in his opinion on the case of *Dudley* v. *Sumner* (1809).[37] Here a woman signed the deed, but only her husband acknowledged it. Sewall believed that the court should overthrow the deed because such a procedure afforded so little protection to the wife. He favored adopting the English practice of requiring a private examination of the wife at the time of recording:

> This, on principle well and long established, I have thought of consid-
> erable importance; and more so in this country than in England, be-
> cause here there are few marriage settlements, and consequently the
> wife is generally under the absolute control of her husband. It is
> necessary, therefore, to protect her property against arbitrary coercion,
> that the only means of defending it, which the law has provided as a
> shield to her incapacity, should be kept sacredly for her protection and
> security. This can never be the case, if a deed, signed jointly by her and
> her husband, without any other ceremony whatever, shall be effectual
> to deprive her of her freehold and inheritance.[38]

Justice Sewall and his supporters never effected a change in Massachusetts law on conveyancing. Throughout the eighteenth and early nineteenth centuries, a woman simply signed her name to a deed to convey her estate. It could be done at home rather than in court. No one attempted to discover if her husband forced her into the transaction, or even if she understood the meaning of her signature. By choosing to ignore the principle of coercion, Massachusetts lawmakers afforded men essentially full control over the conveyancing of family lands.

Pennsylvania lawmakers refused to admit the need for private examinations until 1770.[39] Before that time some couples did request the procedure when entering into a sale or mortgage, but it was not a legal necessity. Pennsylvanians transferred land as did the other colonists, by deeds of bargain and sale that included the signature of the wife, but not necessarily her private examination. Thus, although the Quaker colony did not follow the early Connecticut pattern of denying femes coverts all rights to property, legal protections for those rights were negligible. Fines were unknown and courts did not enforce feme covert acknowledgments. The leniency of the law on conveyancing adversely affected the financial security of married women by denying them the opportunity to influence business decisions made by their husbands. Purchasers and creditors safely ignored the opinions of women, secure in the knowledge that widows could not attach conveyed property for their inheritance or dower rights.

Simple conveyancing procedures without feme covert examinations existed unchallenged in Pennsylvania until 1764. Then, in the case of *Davey* v. *Turner*, counsel for the plaintiff made an attempt to introduce the English practice of conveying by fines.[40] The dispute arose because a couple conveyed the lands of the wife to trustees for their joint use during the marriage, and then to the survivor absolutely. The wife died first, childless, and so the lands descended to her husband under the terms of the postnuptial trust. The woman's legal heir (probably her nephew) contested this disposition of the property, arguing that the deed of conveyance to trustees was void. He noted that according to the common law tradition, a feme covert could transfer her estate only by executing a fine, with examination by writ. Here there was a simple contract rather than a fine, and an incomplete examination, "for though it is set forth, that she declared she executed the deed freely, yet it does not appear the deed was read, or the contents made known to her, without which she could not be said to become a party."[41] Peter Turner, the husband and defendant in the case, argued in support of the deed that he had executed with his wife on the basis of Pennsylvania custom. His counselor noted that "from the first settlement of the province" land was conveyed by simple deeds, and that fines, never employed, were unnecessary in Pennsylvania. If a deed were overthrown for want of a fine and acknowledgment, it would create great confusion in land titles, he told the court. Most titles in the colony stood without fines, supported under the legal maxim *communis error facit jus*. As for the argument that Sarah Turner did not enjoy the protection of a proper examination, the facts did not prove it. The plaintiff argued that the acknowledgment was incorrect because certain information was missing, but according to Pennsylvania usage, "it must be taken, the magistrate did his duty," rather than that he did not.[42] In all likelihood, the counselor argued, Mrs. Turner had a full and private examination. The court agreed.

Thus in *Davey* v. *Turner* the Supreme Court supported an informal deed of conveyance, rejecting a plea for more careful procedures in conveying the estates of married women. Too many deeds depended on the validity of such arrangements, and the court believed that to overthrow them after a long history of support would be "very mischievous."[43] After cautious consideration, the justices voted unanimously in favor of Peter Turner's claim to the property of his wife.

The precedent established by *Davey* v. *Turner* remained the law for several years as Pennsylvania authorities continued to support deeds executed with or without private examinations. Then, in 1768, the practice was challenged once more in the courts, this time with positive results for women. The case was *Lloyd* v. *Taylor*, a land dispute involving a feme covert's informal transfer of property.[44] In *Davey* v. *Turner* the question revolved around an improper examination, but in *Lloyd* v. *Taylor* there was no examination at all. Furthermore, parol evidence indicated that Mercy Lloyd was forced into the sale against her will and subsequently had been dissatisfied with the transaction. Lloyd's son Thomas hoped to overturn her conveyance on this point and claim the property as his own.

The attorney for Thomas Lloyd argued that private examinations were a necessity to protect the interests of women. If Pennsylvanians wanted to persist in rejecting the formal fine and recovery procedure, they should at least recognize the need for private examinations. As in *Davey* v. *Turner*, however, the court decided against strengthening the conveyancing procedure. Concern for the security of land titles is evident in the opinion on the case, which notes "that it had been the constant usage of the province, formerly, for femes coverts to convey their estates in this manner, without an acknowledgment or separate examination; and that there were a great number of valuable estates held under such titles, which it would be dangerous to impeach, at this time of day."[45] Here it appears that the justices saw the danger of coercion by husbands as secondary to the need for secure land titles. The court refused to accept testimony aimed at proving Mercy Lloyd's unhappiness with the deed because the danger of recognizing it was potentially so great.

The conservative decision of the Pennsylvania Supreme Court on *Lloyd* v. *Taylor* must have disturbed the colonial legislature. Two years later, in 1770, the assembly enacted a statute that reformed conveyancing practices. "An Act for the better confirmation of the estates of persons holding or claiming under feme-coverts, and for establishing a mode by which husband and wife may hereafter convey their estates" confirmed land titles held under previous conveyancing methods and stated that in the future all femes coverts would have to acknowledge deeds privately when transferring their rights to real property.[46] In this way the assembly hoped to provide greater protection for the property rights of married women. As Justice Tilghman observed, "Although it was reasonable to confirm the estates of innocent purchasers, acquired under a mistaken principle pardonable in the infancy of the province, yet it was high time to put a stop to a practice under which the rights of married women were left too much unprotected."[47]

Tilghman's words speak to a trend in eighteenth-century American law that has been traced by John M. Murrin: anglicization.[48] By 1770 jurists often felt embarrassment at the "mistaken principles" of their local legal systems. Increased communication between the colonies and with England allowed courts and legislatures to see where their own rules deviated from the norm. At the same time the early colonial desire for simplification of the law was giving way to an appreciation of the advantages of more sophisticated forms. Women's private examinations did complicate the law of conveyancing, but as Tilghman realized, they also offered women a significant protection for their property rights. As a result of the increasing professionalization of the law in the late eighteenth century, procedures such as the private examination were finally adopted in Pennsylvania (and New York, as will be discussed below).

Some women in Pennsylvania did take advantage of their expanded property rights after 1770, employing their new legal power to influence business decisions made by their husbands. Thus in 1794 a Pennsylvanian, John Dickinson, arranged to buy a piece of property from Matthew Crips. The two men agreed to a purchase price of seventy-five pounds, but apparently Crips's wife did not think much of her husband's bargain. In a letter to Dickinson, Crips noted that the sale could be made only "on condition of paying £100 instead of £75 . . . for my wife Elizabeth thinks it is too low at £100 and says she will never sign or confirm the lots for any less."[49] Demonstrably, women in Pennsylvania such as Elizabeth Crips exercised a new control over their own financial well-being after 1770.

Wherever a woman lived, her wishes concerning a sale or mortgage could be overruled in spite of protective legislation. As seen in *Bissett v. Bissett*, some men coerced their wives into saying that they acted freely in executing conveyances. At other times men simply went ahead and sold property without informing their wives. Later the women did not exert the legal right to sue for their inheritance or dower rights because they did not want to disagree publicly with their spouses. This was what happened in the case of a Pennsylvania judge, Thomas McKean, and his wife, Sally. In 1779, when Sally was away from Philadelphia visiting friends, the judge decided to sell all of his real property so that he could buy a country estate "whereon I may live cheap, and spend the remainder of my days in comfort." A few days later he wrote to his wife, enclosing the news that he had sold a piece of her property, but nothing yet of his own. Her response to that information must have been furious, judging by the next letter McKean wrote to her: "I am to get the full value of the lott at the Bridge, and more than I believe any other person will ever offer for it—An unwillingness to sell it as it was your's made me ask a price I did not expect to get, but it turned out otherways and I am contented, only you appear to be otherwise. . . . I thought you loved a Country life, but now you seem to prefer the Town—agreed; we will continue in one. The general character of the Lad[ies] is, that they are fickle, ever changing, & never satisfied, but I flattered myself you were an exception."[50] It appears that Sally McKean never contested this sale of her property in a court of law. She preferred to suffer the consequences of her husband's action in silence. So, undoubtedly, did many other women whose rights were not given adequate protection under the law.

Jurists in Pennsylvania hoped that the new rules on conveyancing would help women like Sally McKean by making both husbands and purchasers more wary of transacting business alone. But the legislative goal for reform in conveyancing was never realized fully. Although Pennsylvania law in the eighteenth century moved closer to the practices of the southern colonies, it still did not match their efforts in guaranteeing protection for the property rights of married women. Local officials and county courts remained negligent. They enforced the new provisions poorly or neglected them altogether, and by their actions opened the way for numerous disputes at law. Enacting a statute was not enough to change the customary behavior of Pennsylvanians.

In the years leading up to the Revolution, New York law on conveyancing mirrored that of Pennsylvania. According to the custom of the colony, women entered into land transactions with their husbands and often enjoyed the protection of private examinations. There were no statutes requiring these procedures, however, and therefore lands could change hands without the knowledge and consent of female owners.[51] Moreover, just as in Pennsylvania, recording practices remained informal. Local justices sometimes neglected to note the participation of a feme covert even when she did join in a conveyance, or recorded only sketchy information about her examination. By the second half of the eighteenth century, purchasers no longer willingly tolerated such informality, and the New York legislature moved toward strengthening procedures on feme covert acknowledgments.

In "An Act to confirm certain ancient Conveyances and directing the Manner of proving Deeds to be recorded," enacted in 1771, New York lawmakers duplicated Pennsylvania policy.[52] They recognized all conveyances already executed without feme covert acknowledgments, but ordered different procedures for the future. Under the new law, not only did femes coverts have to sign and acknowledge conveyances, they also had to signify their consent in meetings with court officials held apart from their husbands. Two nineteenth-century cases, *Jackson* v. *Gilchrist* (1818) and *Garlick* v. *Strong* (1832), demonstrate the change in New York law after 1771, and also reveal something about earlier practices.

Jackson v. *Gilchrist* focused on the validity of a colonial land sale.[53] In 1711 Joshua and Ann Hunloke sold land held in Ann's right. Ann appeared in court to acknowledge the deed, but no record survived to attest to her separate examination. Her fifth-generation descendants attempted to over-throw her conveyance on the basis of this omission from the record. Their effort proved unsuccessful for two reasons. First and most important, the statute of 1771 specifically supported all colonial conveyances made without feme covert acknowledgments. Although counsel for the Hunloke descendants argued that such a statute went against a long-standing common law tradition demanding precision in conveyances, the Supreme Court justices remained firm in their commitment to the legislature's intent. Second, the court believed that even without the statute of 1771, the conveyance was valid according to colonial law. As Chief Justice Thompson pointed out in the majority opinion of the court, New York never had accepted the common law rules on conveyancing. The colony never enforced fines, nor, in his opinion, was it likely that any of the other colonies had done so. He cited *Davey* v. *Turner* and *Watson* v. *Bailey* from Pennsylvania and *Fowler* v. *Shearer* from Massachusetts to support his point.[54] Obviously the chief justice was un-aware of southern practices on conveyancing. Because feme covert acknowl-edgments with private examinations never had formed a part of the law of New York, Thompson concluded, Ann Hunloke's descendants could not claim that improper procedures nullified her deed.

Garlick v. *Strong* indicates that women in the nineteenth century, including the complainant in this case, used the statute of 1771 as leverage in opposing the transactions of their husbands.[55] The bill in *Garlick* v. *Strong* was filed by Mrs. Garlick against her husband. She complained that he was trying to overturn an agreement they made concerning the sale of a piece of family property worth two thousand dollars. In exchange for releasing her dower right, Mrs. Garlick had insisted that half the purchase price be reserved for her separate use. She feared that her husband would leave her penniless when he died because he had already sold a great deal of their property. This thousand dollars she needed as security for herself and her children.

Mr. Garlick argued that husbands and wives could not make bargains concerning property, and that therefore his agreement to place half of the purchase price into a trust for the use of his wife could not be enforced. But the Chancery Court ruled against his argument. Women had the right to withhold their consent from conveyances of family property. Mrs. Garlick's agreement to sign a release in exchange for a payment to herself was valid and enforceable according to equitable principles. More than that, the court actively approved her attempt to protect some portion of the family estate, "her husband having wasted most of his property by intemperance."[56]

Additional cases demonstrate the new commitment in New York to women's property rights. In *Humphrey* v. *Phinney* (1807), Chief Justice Kent supported a widow's right to dower in land alienated by her husband without her consent.[57] In *Jackson* v. *Cairns* (1822), the court voided a conveyance despite the fact that the woman had joined in the deed, because she did not acknowledge it "according to the statute."[58]

As in Pennsylvania, women in New York after 1771 theoretically had the power to prevent sales and mortgages of family lands. But women lost much of their ability to influence their husbands in both these states when courts adopted loose standards for determining compliance with the rules. In the early national period the two jurisdictions followed virtually the same path in interpreting their statutes on conveyancing. Judges accepted informal acknowledgments and incomplete certificates. In the South, meanwhile, strict standards were applied. This contrast is worth studying, for it exemplifies the varying attitudes of the early states on women's property rights.

ENFORCEMENT OF PROCEDURES

In the majority of Maryland cases from both the colonial and early national periods, courts dismissed defective acknowledgments automatically.[59] Judges enforced the precise form of the acknowledgment by voiding all of those that did not fulfill the stated requirements. Thus, in *Hawkins's Lessee* v. *Gould* (1804), the court voided a transfer of property made in 1683 because it had not been executed properly.[60] The seller's wife was not listed as a grantor on the deed, and the officer of the court had taken her acknowledgment improperly. Although counsel in favor of the conveyance argued that an "ancient" deed should not be construed as strictly as a modern one, the court dismissed his point at once. Statutes existed in 1683 for regulating feme covert deeds, and they should have been followed in this case.

A similar decision is found in *The Corporation of the Roman Catholic Clergymen's Lessee* v. *Hammond* (1805).[61] Here the Maryland Court of Appeals ruled against a conveyance executed in 1706 because authorities did not conduct the examination of the feme covert according to the statute. Justice Chase wrote, "The certificate of the acknowledgment should be in the manner the law directs, and unless so done, the acknowledgment is defective, and the deed cannot operate so as to bar the female covert."[62]

Jurists in Maryland demanded precise adherence to the statutory formula.[63] From the cases of *Hawkins* v. *Burress* (1804) and *Heath* v. *Eden* (1805), it appears that even minor omissions were enough to invalidate conveyances. In both of the acknowledgments under dispute, only one part of the statement was missing, the phrase stating that the woman conveyed her rights without fear of ill-usage by her husband.[64] Other words in the recorded acknowledgments could have been interpreted to include such a meaning, but the courts were adamant in requiring inclusion of all phrases. They maintained that the technical words required by the conveyancing statute could not be modified without harmful effects for the women whose rights needed protection.[65]

In a late eighteenth-century case, *Flanagan's Lessee* v. *Young* (1782), the court ruled against a conveyance because the form of the acknowledgment was recorded incompletely.[66] It stated only that the deed had been acknowledged according to the provisions of the act of assembly, without reciting the required words. Because two justices of the peace witnessed the deed, the court had to decide on the very point that appeared in the Pennsylvania case of *Davey* v. *Turner*. Could they assume that an officer had done his full duty in taking a woman's statement of consent simply because he said that he had done so? Counsel for the plaintiff argued that the court should make such an assumption, but the justices decided otherwise. They insisted that feme covert acknowledgments were too important to pass on insufficient evidence. It must appear on the face of the deed that the prescribed conveyancing procedure was observed. "If a particular form of notice be prescribed, it must be fully set out and precisely pursued, and an allegation that due notice was given not being sufficient, all inferior jurisdictions ought to show they have proceeded according to that power which they have by law."[67]

Virginia law followed the same principles. In fact, in Virginia the General Assembly had moved early and decisively to head off problems concerning incomplete recording by local officials. In 1734 lawmakers enacted a statute that specifically made all feme covert conveyances void unless the court clerks recorded their private examinations.[68] In the preamble to the section on private examinations, they noted that despite several judicial decisions voiding deeds due to inadequate recordings, "the point is still constantly disputed." To establish a strict standard, therefore, the assembly ordered "that the law shall always be held, and it is hereby declared to be therein,

according to the said judgments, and shall never hereafter be questioned."
And in the future, the clerk of the court "shall always . . . record her private
examination" after taking the acknowledgment of any feme covert.[69]

The reforming statute did not entirely end disputes about private examinations. Only a few years later, in 1740, a test case made its way into court. In
Jones v. *Porters*, it appeared from the record that no one had recorded the
private examination of a feme covert who conveyed land with her husband.[70]
This omission was sufficient to void the conveyance, under both the statute
of 1734 and the weight of earlier judicial decisions. The court did so in this
case without hesitation.

The tough Virginia stand on recording continued into the nineteenth
century. As discussed above, the decision on the case of *Harvey and Wife* v.
Pecks turned on the failure of a clerk to record, or perhaps even to take, the
private examination of Lydia Peck.[71] As her attorneys argued, the deed was
"a mere nullity. . . her privy examination and relinquishment not having been
taken." They continued, "Indeed, it may be denied that she ever signed it at
all; for the probate of a deed said to have been executed by a married woman,
without privy examination, is entirely extrajudicial."[72] Without evidence attesting to a woman's free will, the court had to assume the use of coercion.
Here, apparently, force had been used, although it had come from the
purchasers rather than Lydia's husband.

Nineteenth-century South Carolina jurists enforced a similar standard, as
evidenced by the opinion of the Court of Appeals in Chancery in *Ewing* v.
Smith (1811).[73] Here a feme covert conveyed her separate estate, held under
a marriage settlement, without undergoing a private examination. In its majority opinion, the court strongly criticized such a mode of proceeding despite
the fact that English chancery decisions supported it. In England, married
women with separate estates could act just as though they were femes soles
who did not need private examinations. South Carolina, however, refused to
follow English precedent on this point of law. Chancellor Waties explained
his position by noting, "It is indeed true as a general rule, that an absolute
right of property, gives an absolute right of disposition; but this rule is only
applicable to persons of full legal capacity; and it is strange that any English
judge should have ever lost sight of the common law so far as to apply it to a
married woman."[74] In conveying her estate, he explained, a married woman
must always be examined privately to protect her against coercion. The court
therefore disallowed Ann Smith's mortgage, designed to satisfy the creditors
of her husband.

In contrast to those of South Carolina, Virginia, and Maryland, courts in
postrevolutionary Pennsylvania remained lax in enforcing feme covert ac-

knowledgments. Under the provisions of the statute enacted in 1770, justices of the peace in Pennsylvania counties had to question women to discover if they acted "voluntarily" and "without any *coercion or compulsion*" in selling lands with their husbands.[75] But the formal phraseology, although theoretically required by the legislature, rarely was used in practice. Justices of the peace, unaccustomed to taking feme covert acknowledgments in one form, continued to administer and record them haphazardly. Perhaps as a result, courts remained flexible in determining cases on forms of acknowledgments. Judges became resigned to the fact that after almost a century of informal conveyancing, precision could not be obtained. Thus Justice Yeates observed that the acknowledgments of "more than nineteen deeds out of twenty" were "miserably" defective,[76] and Justice Gibson wrote that in Pennsylvania the right of a woman was considered to be of such little consequence that her acknowledgment was "entrusted to a justice of the peace, by whom it is sometimes entirely dispensed with in fact, but often slubbered over, even in the presence of the husband himself."[77]

Under these circumstances, which differed so radically from the situation in Maryland and Virginia, Pennsylvania jurists contented themselves with asking that the intent of the legislative formula be followed, rather than its exact words. In *Watson* v. *Bailey* (1808), the Supreme Court first grappled with the problem of informal acknowledgments.[78] The disputed statement, witnessed and signed by a judge of common pleas, stated simply that the couple "acknowledged the above written indenture to be their act and deed, and desired that the same might be recorded. *She the said Margaret being of full age and by me examined apart.*"[79] The bench questioned the validity of this acknowledgment because it contained no evidence of even minimal compliance with the act of 1770. The presiding officer of the local court neglected to state that the woman conveyed of her own free will and with a full understanding of her actions. For these reasons the court refused to sanction the deed, in spite of the witnessing signature by a judge.

The opinion on *Watson* v. *Bailey* was explicit, however, in stating that it did not expect an exact compliance with the form of acknowledgment prescribed by the statute. The court demanded that feme covert statements display certain characteristics, including the occurrence of a private inquiry, the woman's knowledge of the contents of the deed and an understanding of their meaning, and evidence attesting to free consent. It did not require the use of one set of words. As Justice Yeates took care to explain, no particular form was necessary to convey a woman's estate as long as the deed demonstrated compliance with the general legislative prescription.[80]

Watson v. *Bailey* became the ruling guide for subsequent cases on feme covert acknowledgments in Pennsylvania. Following its reasoning, courts never demanded duplication of the statutory form; they asked only for substantial agreement. Of course, "substantial agreement" could be interpreted in many ways, and evidence indicates that it was. The result was almost total confusion.

In 1812, for example, the Pennsylvania courts supported a patently defective deed. In the case of *Lessee of McIntire* v. *Ward*, the certificate did not state that an officiating justice read the deed to the feme covert.[81] The court could not discover, therefore, if the woman understood the meaning of the deed or the significance of her action in transferring it. The acknowledgment fulfilled all of the other requirements, but this was an important one and according to the decision on *Watson* v. *Bailey* it was essential for establishing the validity of the deed. The justices of the Supreme Court recognized the importance of the precedent established in 1808, but they voted in favor of the acknowledgment because to them it demonstrated "substantial" compliance. Although the certificate did not state that the woman understood the contents of the deed, it did state that the title conveyed was in fee simple and that the lands involved were those mentioned in the deed of sale. This information apprised her of the key points, Chief Justice Tilghman reasoned, so that a more detailed description was unnecessary.[82] The other justices supported his opinion, with the exception of Brackenridge, who thought the court should not deviate from the standards it had established in *Watson* v. *Bailey*. According to the decision in that case, he claimed, this deed did not follow the minimal standards and should be voided.[83]

Owing partly, then, to the precedent established in *Watson* v. *Bailey*, Pennsylvania courts continued to be plagued by poorly worded deeds, at times ruling in their favor and at times deciding that the words chosen did not encompass the meaning of the legislative act. In *Evans* v. *The Commonwealth* (1818), the court disallowed an acknowledgment because no mention was made of the woman's free consent.[84] It stated that Anne Coe was of full age and separately examined, but did not state that she conveyed her property rights willingly. Justice Gibson, who wrote the opinion on the case, believed that evidence of free consent was the most important part of the acknowledgment procedure. Dispensing with this particular provision was the equivalent of neglecting the separate examination altogether. Because protection of the property rights of the wife was the primary purpose of the conveyancing statute, Gibson would not permit such an action.

These cases show an unsuccessful attempt by the courts to follow the precedent established in *Watson* v. *Bailey*. Jurists analyzed each individual acknowledgment on its merits, trying to determine if it met the necessary standards and generally making decisions on an arbitrary basis. Clearly, something had to be done to change the confusing pattern of the law on feme covert deeds. The key question remained one of wording. What form of acknowledgment should the courts demand? Under the current law, it was impossible to determine whether an acknowledgment was incomplete and obscure as a result of the opposition of the wife or the incompetence of the subscribing officer. Justice Brackenridge repeatedly advanced one solution to the problem. He advocated eliminating the recorded statement altogether, replacing it with an official assurance that the private examination had been conducted according to law.[85] His system placed ultimate responsibility on the presiding officer of the county court, whose word would stand alone as evidence of free consent by the feme covert. In Maryland and Virginia lawmakers had rejected similar proposals, believing that they invested local officials with undue authority. But in the opinion of Brackenridge, it was the most logical procedure for Pennsylvania jurists to adopt. Courts in the state found it impossible to enforce a single form of conveyance, and the interpretive distinctions they constantly were being asked to make left too much room for litigation.

In contrast to Brackenridge, Justice Gibson wanted a more careful reliance on the formula created in the conveyancing statute. His stand mirrored that taken by the Maryland and Virginia courts and was similarly designed to provide women with adequate safeguards. He advocated asking all women to recite a precisely worded statement that would express their free consent and understanding of a conveyance. Gibson felt ashamed of the cursory manner in which Pennsylvania courts handled feme covert acknowledgments. In a revealing commentary on Pennsylvania legal attitudes toward women, he wrote,

In no country, where the blessings of the common law are felt and acknowledged, are the interests and estates of married women so entirely at the mercy of their husbands as in *Pennsylvania*. This exposure of those, who, from the defenceless state in which even the common law has placed them, are least able to protect themselves, is extenuated by no motive of policy, and is by no means creditable to our jurisprudence. The subordinate and dependent condition of the wife, opens to the husband such an unbounded field to practise on her natural timidity, or to abuse a confidence, never sparingly reposed in return for even occasional and insidious kindness, that there is nothing, however unreasonable and unjust, to which he can not procure her consent. The policy of the law should be, as far as possible, to narrow, rather than to widen, the field of this controlling influence.[86]

Despite the opposition of men like Gibson, Pennsylvania did adopt a less regimented method for taking feme covert acknowledgments. In 1826 the legislature passed an act validating all deeds from husbands and wives to *bona fide* purchasers, regardless of form. All conveyances executed before a judge or other authorized officer of the court were guaranteed "as if all the requisites and particulars of such acknowledgment mentioned in the act to which this is supplementary [that of 1770], were particularly set forth in the certificate thereof."[87]

The new provision was tested immediately in the courts. In *Tate and Wife* v. *Stooltzfoos* (1827), Samuel and Jane Mary Tate sued for recovery of lands she had conveyed during a previous marriage.[88] They made no attempt to claim that Jane Mary executed the deed under coercion. Instead she and Samuel based their case on the inadequacy of the acknowledgment, which read, "Before me, the subscriber, one of the associate judges of the court of common pleas in and for the county of Lancaster, came James Cochran and Jane Mary, his wife, and acknowledged the within instrument of writing to be their act and deed, and desired that the same might be recorded as such. Witness my hand, etc., 28th May 1796."[89] This certificate, far from omitting a part of the statutory phraseology, neglected to mention that any examination of the woman occurred at all. On this basis the Tate case was a strong one. No post-1770 precedent existed in Pennsylvania for dispensing entirely with the examination of a feme covert. According to the presiding justices, however, the acknowledgment sufficed under the reforming statute of 1826. They supported the deed.

Pennsylvania courts thus recognized a principle that the courts of Maryland and Virginia rejected. In Pennsylvania, an official signature to a deed obviated all inconsistencies or omissions in the form of the acknowledgment, whereas in the southern states the law required a local official to prove his observance of each separate regulation in writing, on the face of the deed. New York law, as demonstrated by the decision on *Jackson* v. *Gilchrist*, imitated Pennsylvania law on this question. In New York, as in neighboring Pennsylvania, courts assumed that local officials followed the procedures set out in the conveyancing statutes. If an omission occurred in the record, the courts overlooked it on the assumption that it was an error in recording rather than in practice. In *Jackson* v. *Gilchrist*, Chief Justice Thompson explained the reasoning of the court when he noted that a justice of the peace "could hardly have been guilty of so absurd and nugatory an act, as to give a formal certificate, that the parties came before him *to* acknowledge the deed, if they did not actually acknowledge it." With regard to a feme covert's examination, he explained further, "Nor are we to conclude, that because the certificate does not state a private examination of the wife, that no such examination took place."[90]

Despite the shortcomings of private examinations, the procedure did offer women some protection and leverage. Without them, women in northern jurisdictions suffered in comparison to southern women. The matrons themselves sometimes realized the differences in their situations with regard to property control, as evidenced by an exchange between a Philadelphian, Mary Biddle, and a granddaughter who was a resident of Maryland. Mrs. Biddle advised the younger woman to use Maryland law for protection against her husband's creditors. The granddaughter was encountering difficulties with her gambling husband, and Mrs. Biddle suggested that she refuse to help him in paying his debts. She wrote, "I am informed that he cannot dispose of his property without your consent. If so, and I hope it is, never give your consent. It is only making him a prey to gamesters, the worst of villains." She noted astutely that under Maryland law, "if he gives them his bond, and they should sue him, they cannot recover." In an effort to bolster the morale of her granddaughter, Mary Biddle concluded, "When you married the estate was equally yours, and dearly have you earned it. I allow that it seems hard that a wife should refuse to pay her husband's debts, but they are not just debts."[91] The precise meaning of Mary Biddle's letter becomes clear when it is learned that her husband lost most of their family property through his own poor management. The older woman must have envied the right of her granddaughter to influence the activities of her husband, a right that she, as a Pennsylvania wife, had not enjoyed.

Although all of the colonies experienced difficulty in enforcing their laws on property in the early decades of settlement, some tried harder than others to follow standard common law rules. Statutes in Maryland and Virginia included guidelines for protecting the property rights of women from the beginning of the colonial period. The same rules applied in the Carolinas, and South Carolina moved soon after its establishment as a separate colony to confirm the procedures. Courts in all three colonies enforced the statutory requirements to the letter. Northerners, however, even after establishing rules for the recording of deeds, did not have the same degree of commitment to following common law rules on women's participation. Connecticut completely ignored the property rights of women for almost a hundred years. Massachusetts, New York, and Pennsylvania omitted any mention of private examinations from their colonial conveyancing statutes. Eighteenth-century cases indicate that custom did not make up for the absence of statutory requirements. In the New England and middle colonies, men sometimes sold lands on the authority of their signatures alone. Courts and assemblies accepted the practice.

Everywhere in the colonies early courts evinced great concern with protecting legal titles to real property. The first colonial laws on property focused on the urgent need for recording. In order to protect the rights of purchasers and creditors, lawmakers demanded precise deeds, signed, acknowledged in court by the seller(s), and recorded. They wanted to head off litigation on fraudulent deeds, secret mortgages, and unfair exchanges. All would serve to upset delicate colonial credit arrangements and to discourage potential settlers and investors. To avoid such complications, colonial authorities sought to protect legitimate titles to property by requiring recording. At first they did not entirely succeed. Every colony had at least one or two statutes confirming titles held without the benefit of properly executed and recorded deeds, and demanding more care for the future. Undoubtedly, in the earliest days of settlement in all the colonies, women's rights were overlooked, sacrificed to the need for secure land titles even though some of the titles resulted from unfair dealings. Eventually, however, the laws on acknowledgments and recording were established and followed closely. Then women gained an advantage because their rights could not be ignored safely by purchasers.

In the eighteenth century, as their legal systems became increasingly sophisticated, all of the northern colonies were forced to confront the problem of what to do about women's property rights. Connecticut, one of the oldest colonies and well along in its development by 1723, moved first to correct long-standing errors in its rules on feme covert conveyances. It adopted the southern practice of requiring women's signatures on deeds of conveyance and evidence of their free will in signing. Pennsylvania reluctantly followed suit shortly before the Revolution, perhaps prodding neighboring New York into similar action by the force of example. Although neither Pennsylvania nor New York ever enforced its statute according to the standards followed in the South, the new laws did indicate a growing conformity in American law. By the middle of the eighteenth century high courts in many colonies were beginning to keep and even to publish their decisions. Communication increased, and more and more jurists became aware of the shortcomings and strengths of their own systems. They started to express their ideas for change in their written opinions, and occasionally succeeded in instituting legal reforms. Lawyers may have helped to change the law as well, by citing cases from other colonies and the mother country in their arguments before the bench. As demonstrated by cases like *Lloyd* v. *Taylor* and *McIntire's Lessee* v. *Ward*, judges and legislatures in northern jurisdictions found it increasingly difficult to defend systems that ignored old common law customs concerning the property rights of women. Only Massachusetts completely refused to accept the new standards.

Although American laws on feme covert deeds grew more and more alike in the eighteenth century, some important differences remained. Customary procedures from the early colonial period had a tremendous staying power, as seen in the nineteenth-century debates over the wording of female acknowledgments. Southern judges diligently demanded precision in female acknowledgments and private examinations because they believed that less-strict rules would endanger land titles, making property rights in general uncertain. Once a formula evolved for conveying estates, they would not overturn it. But jurists elsewhere also feared uncertainty in property law. Unlike southerners, however, they claimed that keeping land titles secure required allowance for clerical errors, official oversights, and greater control by husbands. Their rules demanded flexibility in taking feme covert acknowledgments. In Maryland, Virginia, and South Carolina, courts found it possible to secure estates while guarding the property rights of women. In one way or another, no northern jurisdiction offered the same degree of protection. Although southern judges and legislators repeatedly voiced concern for the rights of married women, their colleagues spoke mainly about the need for secure land titles. The contrast is a striking one.

The differences in American rules on conveyancing suggest two interpretations. We may regard the customs of New England and the middle colonies as progressive because jurists there believed that women were capable of safeguarding their own interests. As one judge in Massachusetts observed, a woman "must know her own acts and is bound by such as the law authorizes her to execute." His statement sounds modern, reflective of twentieth-century legal policy in the United States. In comparison to northerners, southerners behaved in an overprotective, patriarchal fashion because they placed so much emphasis on female helplessness. By preventing women from acting for themselves, they effectively kept women in a subservient position.

A second interpretation places southern practice in a more favorable light. Because courts in Maryland, Virginia, and South Carolina accepted the existence of coercion, they acted consistently in demanding both female acknowledgments and private examinations. Northern jurists, who also admitted the possibility of coercion, essentially acted against their principles in failing to enforce private examinations. They did not, for example, extend other safeguards to women to make up for irregular conveyancing practices. Nor did they expand the property rights of women to give them the greater control and independence their conveyancing theories posited. As an ideal, unity of person found greater favor in the North, where courts gave men more control over family property.

Although Anglo-American culture as a whole taught the importance of wifely submission, only the colonies of Connecticut, Massachusetts, and Pennsylvania created laws on the assumption that women would indeed be submissive. If a husband believed that the family could prosper from a sale of his wife's lands, then according to contemporary standards she should agree. Private examinations and the necessity of obtaining women's signatures on deeds acknowledged the possibility that some women would disagree with their husbands. Lawsuits involving women's participation in conveyances also advertised specific instances when wives failed to achieve submission. A policy supporting the standard common law rules might serve, then, to undermine the family by recognizing the legitimacy of women's autonomous decisions regarding property. Realizing this possibility, the Puritans and Quakers acted in one way or another to reduce women's autonomy. Their goal was to strengthen the family.

Colonists elsewhere, and their English contemporaries, were not so ready to assume that a woman's submission always served the best interests of her family. Women might have legitimate interests apart from those of men, interests that they needed to protect. By recognizing the possibility of separate interests within a marriage, jurists in the South accepted reality over an ideal. This is not to say that southern wives necessarily occupied a more enviable position within the family than the wives of New Englanders or Pennsylvanians. The law offered southerners greater protection, but we do not yet know what group in early America created the most beneficial climate for women. It is possible that northerners accepted the limitations of their laws on conveyancing precisely because families in New England and Pennsylvania were stable and basically harmonious. But if strong families could be achieved only by reducing or eliminating the autonomy of wives, then we must question whether the ends justified the means. This is an issue that historians of the family have yet to address.

Contracts

In one way or another, everything women owned before marriage became their husbands' afterwards. A significant result of this social policy was the inability of femes coverts to contract. No agreement a woman made could be enforced against her because she owned nothing the court could seize to meet a judgment. Even a woman's contract to provide services was unenforceable. According to common law rules, a woman's services belonged to her husband. They could not be given to another unless he consented.[1]

Although the most important rationale for denying women the right to contract was their lack of control over property, judges and authors of legal treatises discussed other reasons as well. Blackstone claimed that unity of person prevented the law from recognizing a contractual ability in women, particularly for agreements they might make with their husbands. He wrote, "A man cannot grant any thing to his wife, or enter into covenant with her: for the grant would be to suppose her separate existence; and to covenant with her, would be only to covenant with himself."[2]

Tapping Reeve, Connecticut Supreme Court justice and author of the first treatise on domestic relations published in the United States, disagreed with Blackstone's analysis. He argued that Blackstone, to whom he referred as "the elementary writer," was wrong in his claim that husband and wife were one under the law.[3] The matter was more complicated. According to Reeve, several doctrines assumed the independent legal existence of femes coverts, including the right to inherit real property and the ability to commit crimes. Therefore, "To say they are one person, is a figurative expression only and not a legal one."[4]

Reeve believed that it was fear of male coercion that prevented courts from recognizing women's contracts. As he put it, "The law considers the wife to be in the power of the husband; it would not, therefore, be reasonable that she should be bound by any contract which she makes during the coverture, as it might be the effect of coercion."[5] Judicial acceptance of coercion as a factor in the relations of husbands and wives made all financial transactions by women suspect, particularly those that directly affected their husbands. According to this reasoning, the law acted for the good of women by removing their contractual capacity.

In addition to coercion, Reeve discussed a second factor responsible for the restrictive rules on women's contracts. These rules resulted in part from the great respect of the law for male marital privileges. Women could not enter into any agreements that might result in court actions against them, for if women could be imprisoned their husbands would be denied sexual and household services. The right of a husband to the person of his wife "is a right guarded by the law with the utmost solicitude; if she could bind herself by her contracts, she would be liable to be arrested, taken in execution, and confined in a prison; and then the husband would be deprived of the company of his wife." This circumstance, Reeve concluded, "the law will not suffer."[6]

Although married women could not contract alone, women who contracted jointly with their husbands acted according to law. Women also could contract as the agents of men.[7] As Blackstone observed, "A woman indeed may be attorney for her husband; for that implies no separation from, but is rather a representation of, her lord."[8] To enable a wife to buy or sell real estate or commodities, a husband generally had to provide her with a letter of attorney.[9] Under such a power a woman essentially lost her common law status as a feme covert and became, with regard to her contractual abilities, a feme sole. Men could not avoid the agreements their wives made under letters of attorney, just as they could not under letters of attorney issued to other persons.

The law sometimes allowed a married woman, as the agent of her husband, to contract without a letter of attorney. When a couple operated a business together, there were times when it became necessary for the woman to act for her husband. One Pennsylvania jurist explained, almost apologetically, "She would be considered in such instance as his *agent*, or, in the more uncourtly though legal phrase, as his *servant* acting by his command."[10] Under the concept of agency, courts supported normal agreements made by a wife in the course of running the family business, if she entered into them on a regular basis with the knowledge and consent of her husband. Without his permission, however, a woman's action could bind neither of them into a contract of any kind. Permission could be given either before or after an agreement, but it was dangerous for a husband to wait too long before expressing his disapprobation. The law interpreted a lengthy silence as consent.

In the Pennsylvania case of *Webster* v. *McGinnis* (1812), for example, a husband was able to overthrow a bargain made by his wife because he acted quickly to show his disapproval.[11] Here the wife, who ordinarily ran her husband's tavern in his absence, contracted to provide a stage line with regular provisions, including hay and oats for the horses and board for the drivers, over an extended period of time. But the bargain was a poor one according to the husband, and he refused to honor it. The Supreme Court of Pennsylvania supported his decision. Chief Justice Tilghman reasoned that while the law did enforce contracts made by wives under some circumstances, it was not obliged to do so in this case. He wrote, "It is a well settled principle, that the husband is not bound by the contract of the wife, unless by some act or declaration prior or subsequent to the contract, his consent may be fairly inferred." In this instance the husband did not consent to his wife's contract, Tilghman noted. In addition, it was not the type of contract the wife of an innkeeper normally made; it was not part of the "ordinary business" of a tavern.[12] Tilghman's colleagues on the bench agreed with him. Justice Yeates reasoned, "Furnishing a line of stages with hay and oats, and the driver with refreshment for months to come, exhibits a case very distinct from the common accommodations of an inn. . . . I do not consider the articles furnished to the plaintiff in error, to be within the usual routine of the business of an inn, but am of opinion, that we cannot deem the wife the agent or servant of the husband."[13]

In addition to executing contracts, a wife could act as the agent of her husband in receiving payments from lessors or purchasers of goods.[14] Although payment to a wife was not strictly legal under the common law, long practice had sufficed to make it legitimate in many instances. As one judge noted in deciding a Pennsylvania case, "A husband is often from home. Nothing is more common than to pay the wife, in his absence, a debt due to her husband."[15] In cases of this nature, the husband legitimized his wife's receipt by expressing tacit consent to her action.

A South Carolina case, *Willingham* v. *Simons* (1792), demonstrates judicial reasoning on the principle of tacit consent.[16] Here the chancellor ruled that a wife could accept payment for slaves sold by her husband, even though the acceptance was "to all intents illegal."[17] He supported the payment because subsequent actions of the husband attested to his consent, which was the key to decisions on feme covert contracts. When a man appeared to agree with his wife's bargains or receipts, he was bound to support them. When he showed immediate and unquestionable disapproval, as the husband did in *Webster* v. *McGinnis*, they could be overturned by legal process. In *Willingham* v. *Simons*, the husband testified that although he initially agreed to sell several of his slaves, he later reconsidered, deciding not to accept payment but ask for their return instead. Before he had the opportunity to inform either his wife or the purchaser of his plans, however, they concluded the bargain without him. Had Mr. Simons immediately rejected the payment, he could have voided the agreement, but he hesitated for some time. That hesitation ruined his case. Because he could not prove that he had renounced his wife's bargain, he could not convince the court to return the slaves.

Similar decisions demonstrate acceptance of this policy elsewhere in America. Agreements that technically could be construed as improper found support when consent by spouses softened the issues.[18] Thus some courts allowed femes coverts to purchase lands or sign leases with the permission of their husbands.[19] These rights were based strongly on the concept of agency, for without a separate estate a woman who made a purchase or paid rent necessarily employed family funds. The courts believed that men who did not want their wives to execute deeds could easily prevent them from doing so. Moreover, the acquisition of land generally represented a benefit to any man's estate, and therefore the law assumed that a husband would not object to any such purchase by his wife.

FEME SOLE TRADERS

In one area of property law, the principle of tacit consent became particularly important to women. Some jurisdictions allowed femes coverts to own and operate businesses in their own names, if their husbands expressed their approval either through written documents similar in purpose to powers of attorney or through tacit consent.[20] If married women lived in areas that recognized the law of feme sole traders, as they were called, they could execute binding contracts, sue, and be sued just as though they were single. Such rights were essential if women wanted to operate their own businesses, but unfortunately for many women, feme sole trader rights were ill defined.

The Laws Respecting Women contains an outline of English rules on feme sole traders. We learn that under the laws of English markets, "a Feme-covert is warranted by law to sell goods in open market, and her husband cannot reclaim any goods so sold, provided such woman is usually accustomed to trade for herself." According to Blackstone, the notoriety of a feme sole trader was the key to determining her legal right to sell goods. If a buyer realized that a woman was a feme covert "not usually trading for herself," he would not be able to press a claim against her husband for the delivery of goods.[21] In rural areas, women often sold the surplus of farm products grown or made by the family. What this statement does not tell us, however, is whether the husband or the wife had the legal right to the money made at the market.

In London, married women who carried on businesses separately from their husbands became feme sole traders. Several cases reported in *The Laws Respecting Women* demonstrate the desire of London courts to make married women liable for their own business debts.[22] Courts issued commissions of bankruptcy against feme sole traders, and held them liable for their own executions in cases of debt. Under the custom of London, "If a feme-covert trades by herself, in any trade with which her husband doth not intermeddle, and buys and sells in that trade, there the feme shall be sued, and the husband named for conformity only." Most important, "If judgment be given against him, execution shall be only against the feme."[23] The most significant factor in determining whether a woman acted as the agent of her husband or as a feme sole trader was her independence. If a husband had nothing whatsoever to do with her trade, the wife alone became responsible for her contracts. Her property could be seized and sold on execution. It is not clear if she could also be imprisoned, but presumably her status as a feme sole dealer made that a possibility. A husband who allowed his wife to act independently ran the risk of losing her "services."

Evidence on American law concerning feme sole traders varies considerably among the colonies and states. Pennsylvania and South Carolina enacted statutes on the subject in the colonial period, but among the other jurisdictions studied, the only one to follow suit was Massachusetts, which did so considerably later, in 1787. It is surprising to find colonial assemblies silent on feme sole dealerships, for towns such as Boston, New Haven, and New York must have had many women occupied in trade.[24] The absence of statutory provisions demonstrates a common theme in early American law. Custom and precedent dominated statutory law in many areas, particularly those concerning women and the family. Specific laws to govern the activities of feme sole traders do not always appear in the record because courts and legislatures developed other methods of dealing with women who worked outside the home. The doctrine of necessities, rules allowing deserted women to own separate property, private empowering acts, and divorces or legal separations obviated the need for feme sole trader statutes in many instances. Thus, even in jurisdictions without specific statutes on women in business, some femes coverts did act independently in operating shops and taverns. Their legal rights were susceptible to challenge, however, which made the statutory provisions of colonial South Carolina and Pennsylvania particularly valuable.[25]

South Carolina demonstrated a strong commitment in the colonial and early national periods to the right of married women to act as feme sole traders. Two colonial statutes enacted in 1712 and 1744 governed the activities of independent businesswomen. The first, "An Act for the better securing the payment of debts," made feme sole traders liable for the debts they contracted on their own accounts. Apparently several women had pleaded coverture as a means of avoiding their creditors' demands. To prevent such fraud, the statute made any feme sole trader liable at law for the payment of her own debts "as if such woman was sole and not under coverture."[26] The law must have benefited the traders as much as their customers, because it made dealing with them less risky. The traders' ability to gain credit undoubtedly improved under such a regulation.

The act of 1712, obviously designed to protect the populace from scheming businesswomen, was followed thirty-two years later by a similar law protecting feme sole traders from dishonest customers. In 1744 the assembly wrote, "Sole traders are often under difficulties in recovering payment of debts contracted with them, by reason of the absence of their husbands, in whose names they are obliged to sue for all debts due to them, sometimes not being able to produce any power or authority from their husbands." To correct the problem, created in part as these words suggest by the assembly's own failure to establish a legitimate mode for determining who could be a feme sole trader, the act provided a way for women to sue without their husbands. Thereafter they conducted lawsuits in their own names and named their husbands in the suits only "for conformity."[27]

This statute strengthened the legitimacy of women dealing as sole traders but still did not define the position or require formal registration. That step was not taken until 1823, when "An Act to regulate the mode in which married women shall become Sole Traders or Dealers" passed the legislature.[28] For the first time the law required married women to announce their intentions of dealing as feme sole traders, and register as such. It is important to note that the statute of 1823 gave women freedom to declare themselves sole traders, perhaps against the wishes of their husbands, although that point is not clear. The act declared "that no woman having a husband living, shall be entitled, either at law or in equity, to the rights of a free dealer, unless she shall give notice by publication in a public newspaper, of her intention to trade as a sole trader, which notice shall be published at least one month, and in case there is no newspaper published in the district, then the notice shall be published in the same way as sheriff's sales."[29] Such a notice did have to state the name of the trader's spouse, his address, and his occupation,[30] but there was no requirement of his public declaration of consent to her business activities. Perhaps the law assumed that any husband who allowed his wife to advertise her intentions to become a feme sole trader was thereby expressing his tacit consent. It is possible, however, that a woman could claim feme sole trader status even without his consent. The supposition is an intriguing one, but unfortunately there are no cases to prove the point.

Although the law did not require formal registration of feme sole traders until 1823, some women took the precaution of registering before that date. Throughout the public records of early South Carolina are sprinkled copies of agreements between husbands and wives attesting to women's rights as feme sole dealers.[31] Women and their husbands rightly assumed that written documents most safely established their respective rights and responsibilities, and from one court case tried in the late eighteenth century it is clear that reliance on the doctrine of "tacit consent," although correct under the law, could cause problems.

The case of *Magrath v. Robinson* (1795) focused on a dispute over the administration of a deceased woman's estate.[32] The deceased, Ann Robinson, had acted during her life as a feme sole trader, but there were no documents attesting to her husband's consent. Under the law of South Carolina, it was not clear if Robinson's mother could inherit her estate. The administrators, who also were managing the estate of Ann's husband, John, were unsure how to distribute the properties. They had no proof that Ann had any right to hold property independently of her husband. At her death, they reasoned, her property should have been combined with his, including the real estate she held under titles in her own name. The task of Ann Robinson's mother (her heir at law) became one of proving her daughter's status as a feme sole trader under the doctrine of tacit consent.

When this case appeared, South Carolina had no statute for determining feme sole trader status. The acts of 1712 and 1744 recognized the existence of independent businesswomen in the colony and state and authorized them to carry on suits in their own names, but did not explain how the law should define feme sole traders. In Ann Robinson's case, her status remained unclear because she never signed an agreement with her husband, although witnesses' testimonies established the fact that John Robinson knew and approved of his wife's business ventures. It was clear to the couple's acquaintances that Ann Robinson was successful in business, even more so than her husband, who was portrayed as an indolent man. As one witness testified, she was an "active industrious woman. . . . all the money that was made, was made almost solely by her means." He believed that she could at times command as much as twelve or fifteen hundred pounds, because "she used to buy the refuse Negroes of a Cargo; nurse them up, and sell them out again, by which means she made a great deal of money."[33] Another witness testified that her own husband sometimes borrowed money from Mrs. Robinson, and a third that when one of the woman's customers offered to pay Mr. Robinson, he was told to "go and settle with her, as she acted for herself, and had the note."[34]

In passing judgment on the case, the South Carolina judges in Chancery emphasized the testimony of witnesses, who demonstrated John Robinson's knowledge of his wife's activities. He clearly consented to her conducting a business separate from his own, and acknowledged before various people her economic independence. Had he wished to exert his common law rights over her property, he could have done so on numerous occasions, but instead he left her to control her own business as she pleased. By South Carolina law his acquiescence implied consent, and that consent was adequate to give Ann Robinson all the rights of a feme sole trader. As the opinion noted, "We think that unless a woman could shew a regular deed under the hand and seal of her husband constituting her a Sole Trader; no stronger Case than the present can be produced which ought to empower a Feme Covert to be a Sole Trader; especially as there is no particular Law which defines the mode by which she is to be made so."[35] The court ruled that her estate should not be combined with her husband's, but administered instead as her own separate property. Ann Robinson's mother therefore was able to inherit.

The evidence available to legal historians on the tradition of feme covert businesswomen in South Carolina indicates a liberal standard, especially when compared to the situation in other colonies and states. Pennsylvania, for example, imitated South Carolina in outlining rules for the protection of feme sole traders and their customers early in the eighteenth century, but the Pennsylvania model differed significantly. Whereas South Carolina legislation allowed any woman to become a feme sole trader, the Pennsylvania statute limited the role to women whose husbands did not support them.

"An Act concerning feme-sole traders," enacted by the General Assembly of Pennsylvania in 1718, provided that the wives of "mariners and others, whose circumstances as well as vocations oblige them to go to sea" could act as feme sole traders "during their husbands' natural lives."[36] Under the terms of the act, women who regularly lived with their husbands did not qualify. The reasoning behind this distinction appears in the preamble to the statute. Pennsylvania lawmakers realized that women needed help in maintaining themselves and their families during the absences of their husbands.

How much better than public assistance was a law allowing them to support themselves. As the statute declared, some of these women were "industrious and take due care to pay the merchants they gain so much credit with, as to be well supplied with shop-goods from time to time, whereby they get a competent maintenance for themselves and children." Undoubtedly the lawmakers thought it even more important that many of the women were able "to discharge considerable debts, left unpaid by their husbands at their going away."[37] The assembly took action, therefore, to support hardworking matrons by giving them the legal status of feme sole traders. In addition, the assembly provided that the estates of absent husbands should be held for the use of the wives and children, unless there was evidence to show that other provision had been made for their maintenance.

Pennsylvania lawmakers acted defensively in establishing these guidelines for feme sole traders. As a last resort, women could take on the breadwinner role usually held by men. In cases of long absence or desertion by husbands, women would be allowed to carry on trades, contract, sue, and be sued under the protection of the colonial government. Women whose husbands lived at home could act similarly, however, only if their husbands consented. The distinction centers not so much on a wife's proclivity to work, which one assumes few men below the highest social ranks would oppose. Rather, the statute addresses the issue of control over the profits and assets earned by a woman's labor. The statute of 1718 on feme sole traders guaranteed deserted women the right to keep their property separate from their husbands'. It did not offer the same protection to feme sole traders who lived with their husbands or whose husbands lived separately but continued to provide some support. Those women had to have evidence of their husbands' consent in order to keep separate property. The issue of consent implies that even in Pennsylvania and South Carolina, feme sole trader rules and customs did not give many women meaningful financial independence. Unless a man agreed to the feme sole trader activities of his wife, either openly through a written agreement or tacitly, they became technically illegal.[38]

Massachusetts waited until the end of the eighteenth century to enact rules on women in business and in doing so duplicated Pennsylvania policy. Only abandoned wives came under the terms of the act, which allowed them to apply for the right to contract, convey real estate, sell personal property, sue, and be sued. The law stated clearly that a woman could act as a feme sole trader "during the absence of her husband from this Commonwealth, and no longer." If her wayward spouse returned while she had unfulfilled contracts, he became responsible for them, but her suits at law did not abate at his return. She could continue them in her own name.[39]

Massachusetts case law on feme sole traders indicates judicial reticence to grant all women the possibility of financial independence. Unless a woman applied in a formal manner for feme sole trader status, she might well find herself outside the law in contracting to provide goods or services, or selling a piece of property. When she did apply and demonstrate need, her rights under the act were supported. For example, in 1804 Lydia Bachelor found help from the courts when her husband opposed a conveyance of land she had made during his extended absence. She had complied with the terms of the statute of 1787, by asking permission from the county court to sell the property and giving notice of her intent in a local newspaper for three weeks. Therefore, the court found her conveyance valid despite the objections of her wandering spouse.[40]

Other judicial decisions concerning feme sole traders were less supportive. In *Commonwealth* v. *Cullins* (1804), the Supreme Judicial Court of the state refused to accept an indictment for theft made in the name of a feme sole trader.[41] The court required the indictment to be made in the name of the husband, even though he had been living for six or seven years in the "East Indies" while she carried on a business in Massachusetts in her own name. In the eyes of the law, she owned no separate property, perhaps because she had never applied for feme sole trader status under the statute.

In *Russell* v. *Brooks* (1828), the Supreme Court found that a woman was not a feme sole trader in spite of the fact that she had supported herself for six years, simply because her husband occasionally visited her.[42] To qualify as an independent dealer under the terms of the act, a woman could have no contact at all with her husband. In this case it was proved to the court that Joshua Swan abandoned his wife and that from 1815 to 1818 he lived in Boston with another woman, "but passed Sunday with his wife at Lexington as often as twice a month."[43] In 1818 Joshua moved to Georgia; he returned to Massachusetts for a short while in 1819 but then traveled south once more, this time to Alabama, where he died in 1821. During his wanderings he became insolvent. Meanwhile, Eleanor Swan continued to operate the family business of "manufacturing articles of fur" and prospered, leaving a small estate at her death. Controversy arose over the distribution of Eleanor's property—did it belong to her heirs or the creditors of her husband? The court decided to favor the husband's estate in this case, ruling "that the husband was entitled to the earnings of the wife before his death."[44] Joshua Swan's desertion did not make his wife a feme sole trader, because he had continued to see her and had not renounced his marital rights.

In the case of Joshua and Eleanor Swan, one issue seemed of particular importance to the court. It took special notice of Joshua's residences, noting where he lived during what periods. Under Massachusetts law, the status of a feme sole trader depended heavily on whether her husband resided within the state. The statute of 1787 applied only to women whose husbands were not living in Massachusetts. As soon as a husband returned to the state, he regained his marital rights. Under Massachusetts case law as defined in two suits heard before *Russell* v. *Brooks*, the wives of men who lived in different countries or states held special rights to act as feme sole traders. They did not need to apply for feme sole trader status under the statute.

Gregory v. *Paul* (1818) and *Abbot* v. *Bayley* (1827) indicate greater willingness on the part of the Massachusetts Supreme Court to recognize women's independent property rights than was demonstrated in *Russell* v. *Brooks*.[45] Both Deborah Gregory and Phebe Abbot were deserted by their husbands. After abandonment in her native England, Gregory traveled to the United States. Phebe Abbot was deserted in New Hampshire and subsequently moved to Massachusetts. According to English precedent, adopted by the Massachusetts court in both cases, women whose husbands lived permanently in another country, or by extension, state, could act as femes soles with regard to property.[46] The law recognized that women living alone had to have separate property in order to support themselves, and allowing them to carry on suits at law to protect that property could not affect male marital privileges. As the courts reasoned, a man living elsewhere "could not complain if his wife should be taken and imprisoned for debt; for he had renounced her society."[47] Both women, therefore, found support for their property rights. Gregory was permitted to receive an inheritance of personal property, and Abbot allowed to sue in her own name.

Significantly, neither the recorded arguments of the counselors nor the judicial opinions on these cases mentioned the provisions of the statute of 1787. It was not, apparently, a factor in establishing the separate property rights of the women. First, there is no record that either woman applied for protection under the terms of the act. Their failure to do so may indicate that the law was unknown to women in the state. Such a conclusion is strengthened when we recall that the feme sole trader in *Commonwealth* v. *Cullins* also failed to comply with the terms of the statute. In fact, the 1818 decision of the court supporting Deborah Gregory may have been a judicial attempt to obviate the need for formal compliance with the Massachusetts law on feme sole traders. It was not serving its purpose, for women continued to act unofficially as independent traders, neglecting to obtain judicial consent to their activities and to publish notices in local newspapers. The court discovered that existing English precedents on marital rights served their interests better than the statute in protecting women's property rights. By extending specialized English common law rules to the cases of Deborah Gregory and Phebe Abbot, the Massachusetts Supreme Court successfully improved the property rights of married women.

English precedent gave particular support to the property rights of women in only two instances, however. The wives of men who were banished from England or "abjured the realm" to escape prosecution for crimes automatically became feme sole traders.[48] English jurists reasoned that in both instances, the rationales for denying women the right to contract were removed. The marital rights of a man who lived outside of England could not be affected by his wife's imprisonment for debt, for he had lost them already. Neither could coercion be an issue, for he could not gain access to his wife. Because these were the legal arguments for denying women's contractual abilities, once both fears were eliminated there was no logical reason for restricting women.

The desire of the justices of the Massachusetts Supreme Court to use English precedents in novel ways indicates a progressive tendency. In neither *Gregory v. Paul* nor *Abbot v. Bayley* had a husband abjured the realm or been banished from it. These were simple cases of desertion and nonsupport. Yet the justices chose to see the cases as falling within one of the few English precedents supporting independent property rights for women. According to Justice Putnam, who wrote the opinion on *Gregory v. Paul*, "The fact and circumstances which should be considered as proof of having abjured the realm, have been liberally regarded." Following his own inclinations, he concluded that Deborah Gregory's case "comes within the spirit of the rule of the common law, founded on reason and necessity, in cases of exile." Although Putnam admitted with regard to Gregory's husband that "he has not, it is true, abjured *his* country," yet his abandonment of his wife and her subsequent removal to the United States amounted to the same thing. She had been forced to abjure, and therefore the law could regard her as a feme sole trader. As Putnam saw the issue, "Miserable, indeed, would be the situation of those unfortunate women whose husbands have renounced their society and country, if the disabilities of coverture should be applied to them during the continuance of such desertion. If that were the case, they could obtain no credit on account of their husbands, for no process could reach him; and they could not recover for a trespass upon their persons or their property, or for the labor of their hands. They would be left the wretched dependents upon charity, or driven to the commission of crimes, to obtain a precarious support."[49] Putnam and his peers on the Massachusetts bench believed that it was their duty to provide a remedy in cases of abandonment.

Consequently, they ruled that deserted women could own separate property when they lived in a different country or state from their husbands.

The Massachusetts decisions on *Gregory* v. *Paul* and *Abbot* v. *Bayley* demonstrate why all the colonies did not enact specific statutes to govern feme sole trader status. Common law rules already offered some women assistance when their husbands abandoned them, and jurisdictions could enforce and enlarge them if they chose. The rule cited by the court in *Gregory* v. *Paul* was an important one. Another, even more commonly applied provision was termed the doctrine of necessities. Under it, any woman whose husband left her temporarily—or, by extension, permanently—could charge his estate for the family's necessary support. Local shopkeepers who provided her with food, clothing, medicine, and other essential items could sue the husband's estate if he refused to pay the bills, and seize his property on execution.[50]

AGENTS OF NECESSITY

Under the doctrine of necessities, the purchases made by a wife had to be such as she usually made for the provision of the family. In this sense, the rule was the same as that in cases of agency. She acted as the agent of her husband for all normal transactions, and he was obliged to honor her contracts. As Tapping Reeve put it, "If a wife should purchase at a merchant's store, such articles as wives in her rank in life usually purchase, the husband ought to be bound; for it is a fair presumption that she was authorized to do so by her husband. If, however, she were to purchase a ship or yoke of oxen, no such presumption would arise, for wives do not usually purchase ships or oxen."[51]

When husbands remained absent for extended periods of time on business, the power of their wives to make binding contracts increased. The law reasoned that over the course of months or years women needed more than common powers to contract for necessities.[52] There were also occasions when the courts supported women whose husbands adamantly refused to pay for essential support. Under the law, husbands had to provide wives with suitable maintenances and when they refused, they became liable to prosecution. Thus men who advertised in newspapers that they would not pay for the purchases of their wives could not, technically, enforce their prohibitions in courts of law. Unless a woman deserted her husband or committed adultery, he was responsible for her support. According to Zephaniah Swift, "A general warning in the gazette, or newspaper, not to trust her, will not be a sufficient prohibition."[53] A husband could, however, prohibit a particular shopkeeper from selling to his wife, or ask him to refuse her certain items. As long as the prohibitions were precise and reasonable, they would hold up in a court of law.[54]

That colonial shopkeepers as well as wives understood the law on necessities is demonstrated well by a Maryland divorce case, *Pattison* v. *Pattison*, tried in 1736 and 1737.[55] Jeremiah Pattison beat and abused his wife repeatedly during their first year of marriage. Finally, he forced her out of their home (actually, *her* home by a former marriage), refusing to allow her to take her clothes and other personal items. Such treatment shocked the women of the community, who advised Jane Pattison to buy some clothes on credit at the shop of a local merchant. As Eleanor Dorrumple reported to the chancellor during the trial, "About 8 years ago she this deponent met the Complainant together with several other Women of the Neighborhood at the Home of Doctor James Somerveill that the Complainant was then very bare of Cloaths and was perswaded by the other Women to go along with this deponent to the Store of one Isaac Johns to take up necessaries for herself."[56] Jane allowed herself to be convinced of the justice of her action, and went to the merchant. He thereupon "offered to Credit her with Goods to the Value of £50 on the defendants Acco[un]t."[57] Jane refused to purchase that much, but did run up a bill for eight or nine pounds, for which her husband became liable. He reacted by posting just the sort of notices Swift believed were ineffective under the law—bills placed in public places warning all persons to refuse his wife credit.

The doctrine of necessities most often covered the needs of women like Jane Pattison, who needed credit to purchase essential food and clothing. But the doctrine could be applied to support other, more businesslike activities of femes coverts. The Pennsylvania feme sole trader statute, for example, contained clauses reserving the estates of absconding men for the support of their families. Such a statutory provision duplicated in purpose the judicially defined doctrine of necessities.[58] It was entirely appropriate for the provisions to appear in a law outlining the feme sole property rights of deserted women, for the aim of all sections of the law was the same, financial support for women. Similarly, in a nineteenth-century Connecticut case, *Rotch* v. *Miles* (1818), the Supreme Court of Errors relied on the doctrine of necessities to support the property rights of a woman who operated a boardinghouse after the desertion of her husband.[59] When he returned to the state several years later, the court even ordered him to pay the debts that she had contracted for rental of the property.

Throughout the eighteenth and early nineteenth centuries, courts relied on the doctrine of necessities to support the property rights of women with unusual needs. Another kind of support came not from the courts but from legislatures. Lawmaking bodies occasionally used private empowering acts to help women who needed release from their common law disabilities. To prevent women from becoming public charges, assemblies allowed them feme sole trader privileges in specific instances—the right to sell family property in the absence of their husbands or the ability to accept and spend an inheritance, for example.[60] Private empowering acts also benefited creditors, of course, by enabling women to employ family property to pay debts. Jurisdictions with feme sole trader statutes simply saved their assemblies the burden of passing private bills.

In 1744 a Virginia woman, Susannah Cooper, requested a private empowering act.[61] Her husband, Isles, had abandoned her in 1720, after only three years of marriage. Creditors took all the family property, leaving Susannah and her young son in "utmost misery and distress." Susannah Cooper's situation exemplifies the contradictions in colonial attitudes toward the property rights of married women. In her community, she lived out her life as a married woman under the law. Through her diligence and hard work, she accumulated a small estate consisting primarily of several slaves. But while Susannah could accumulate property, paying only with cash or limited credit, one assumes, she could not dispose of it. Her husband owned everything she had and she could not sell or devise it without his permission. As explained in the private act passed to remedy her awkward legal status, "No purchaser will treat with her on account of her coverture." Moreover, persons with whom she did business over the years took advantage of her helplessness at law. "In her present unhappy situation, she is exposed to many injuries, some persons committing trespasses on her tenements, and others refusing to perform their contracts and agreements with her; for which wrongs and injuries, she is advised she can maintain no action in her own name, unless her husband be actually dead."[62] Susannah wanted the right to prosecute suits at law and make binding contracts. Even more important, she wanted the power to write a will, under which she could devise her estate to her son. The General Assembly of Virginia granted her these rights, and in exchange she gave up all dower claims she had in Isles Cooper's estate. Unfortunately, it is not clear whether Susannah reaped any benefits from her private act. The English Privy Council may never have approved it.

A Maryland woman, Susannah Tracy, approached both the Court of Chancery and the colonial assembly for help in managing her estate early in the eighteenth century. After her husband, Thomas, abandoned her, she discovered that she could not convey lands she had inherited from a former husband. To remedy the situation the Court of Chancery confirmed a deed of conveyance executed by Susannah without her husband, and the assembly passed a private act allowing her to lease lands and keep the proceeds for her own use.[63] The Massachusetts assembly acted similarly when it enacted laws allowing Mary Evans, "Wife of Jonathan Evans," to mortgage property she inherited from her father and permitting Abigail Conqueret, "Wife of Lewis Conqueret, Mariner," to prosecute a suit for assault "as though she was sole and unmarried."[64] Both women were abandoned by their husbands and unable to act alone under traditional common law forms.

Despite examples such as these demonstrating their usefulness, private empowering acts remained rare throughout the period studied. Women turned to local officials and the courts more often than to legislative bodies for help in overcoming their legal disabilities; or they suffered in silence rather than attempt to fight the established rules of the common law. One important exception to this pattern concerns private acts of divorce and separation, which some colonies and states employed as an alternative to judicial divorce. Of necessity, acts granting women the right to separate from their husbands had to grant either feme sole trader rights or alimony. Private divorce acts thus often served as empowering acts as well. Although historians have not investigated the implications of divorce or separation on the property rights of women in early America, that perspective is valuable for understanding both the willingness of courts to grant divorces and the effect of an increasing divorce rate on the legal rights and disabilities of married women. Private divorce acts, judicial decrees of divorce in common law courts, and chancery support of separate maintenances all provided some women with independent property rights.

Few formal guidelines existed in eighteenth- and early nineteenth-century law for governing women's contractual rights. Most of the jurisdictions studied had no statutes for defining the legal status of feme sole traders, and no jurisdiction enacted a law to cover women who contracted as the agents of their husbands. In this area of the law, precedent and custom rather than statute usually established the rules that determined when a woman's contract was enforceable and when it was not. Only investigations of local court records will reveal how women actually fared under such a system, but evidence concerning the decisions of higher courts and the private bills enacted to assist individual women indicate that informality in the law could be dangerous.

On one question concerning women's business activities the rules did not bend. When a woman lived with her husband she could not sign a contract or prosecute a suit at law unless he consented. Male marital privileges included the right to control a wife's activities as a feme sole trader. Even when a husband absented himself for long periods of time without cause or explanation, upon returning home he regained the right to control his wife's business dealings. Perhaps most important, unless a man allowed his wife to keep her earnings as separate property, even if she were a feme sole trader, they became his. He could change his mind at any time and refuse to allow her control over future earnings. Such rules reveal the legal dependency of businesswomen who had no formal marriage settlements delineating their right to control separate property.

If, as some historians have argued, married women in the eighteenth century owned and operated businesses more often than their nineteenth-century descendants, the law gave them scant protection for their property rights. Hemmed in by male prerogatives, women ventured into the business world of men with handicaps. Only in South Carolina did married women enjoy formal recognition of their personal right to act as feme sole traders. Elsewhere, jurists provided for the needs of deserted women only, or handled cases on an individual basis through the courts. Until women gained the right to own property in their own names under the married women's property acts, they encountered sharp restrictions on their business activities. The law assumed that women would not act independently of their husbands.

Divorce and Separation

Some couples in colonial and early national America executed contracts of a very private and special nature. They contracted to live apart and divide their assets so that each spouse could support a separate household. In instances of conflict, or when a mutual desire to live apart could not translate itself into action without court intervention, individuals requested divorces from judicial or legislative authorities. Such divorces necessitated a division of family property or a decree of alimony for support of an innocent wife. Thus the law of divorce and separation can reveal a great deal about attitudes toward women's rights to family property.

In the colonial period, most divorce provisions mirrored those of English law. Divorces *a vinculo matrimonii*, or absolute divorces with the right to remarry, were rare. Divorces *a mensa et thoro*, or separations from bed and board, were more readily available but still uncommon. Some colonial assemblies refused to allow any divorces at all, although equity courts provided a remedy in cases of abuse and abandonment by ordering separate maintenances out of the husband's property. Such separations were the equivalent in effect, if not in terminology, of divorces *a mensa et thoro*. Other colonies developed more liberal divorce policies than were known in the mother country. Even in these jurisdictions, however, divorces remained uncommon and were considered disgraceful.[1]

In addition to divorces *a vinculo matrimonii* and *a mensa et thoro*, couples in many jurisdictions had a third option. Under the rules of contract law as enforced by courts of equity, husbands and wives could execute binding separation agreements between themselves. Couples generally made private contracts to live apart and divide property in the form of postnuptial trusts. Until late in the eighteenth century, most equity courts refused to enforce direct contracts between husbands and wives, but they would support agreements made through third parties. Hence the prevalence of postnuptial trusts as private separation agreements.[2] Common law courts refused to recognize the validity of any contracts made between husbands and wives, whether directly or through third parties.[3] The law of private separation agreements, therefore, was based exclusively on equitable principles and enforced only in jurisdictions that recognized them. Of the colonies and states studied here, Connecticut alone falls outside this category.[4]

Outside the law, couples exercised yet other options. Although technically illegal and therefore unenforceable, agreements to separate made without formal contracts or the intervention of third parties must have occurred on a regular basis. In numerous instances men resorted to simple desertion, generally abandoning their property along with their families. Often no legal action was taken against them, and women lived out their lives in the awkward legal position of femes coverts without husbands. If men left without a trace and were unheard of for seven years, the law assumed death, giving their "widows" the freedom to remarry.

The most bizarre divorce option to modern ears was the wife sale, a folk custom of early modern England that made its way to the colonies.[5] Wife sales occurred after couples had agreed between themselves to separate. Symbolic "sale" of the wife, usually to a prearranged buyer who might be the woman's paramour or a relative, represented an acceptable form of divorce in some communities. Both church and court officials generally ignored the ritual and its effects, presumably in an effort to promote local harmony. The procedure followed in a wife sale demonstrates with graphic precision the inferior status of women in early modern Anglo-American society, for in the most primitive instances the woman was led to market in a halter and auctioned off to the highest bidder.

Other local customs surface in the record now and again, revealing popular dissatisfaction with the limited divorce options recognized by law. In Pennsylvania, for example, one community relied on arbitrators to settle accounts between a woman and man who wanted to live apart. After dividing their property, a permissible step in Pennsylvania, the arbitrators went beyond the law in ordering "that Fry and his wife should separate, and either should be at liberty to marry who they pleased."[6] Apparently the option of applying to the state Supreme Court for a formal divorce, a possibility by 1787 when the arbitration occurred, did not seem viable to the Frys and their neighbors. As such a case of community initiative demonstrates, popular attitudes favored easier divorce laws long before lawmakers acted to create them.

ENGLISH PRECEDENT AND AMERICAN POLICY

In England, the ecclesiastical courts heard all cases of marital discord. They granted absolute divorces to couples whose marriages were adjudged void ab initio, for such reasons as bigamy, sexual incapacity, and consanguinity (blood relationship). All children of the unions became illegitimate. Ecclesiastical courts granted divorces from bed and board for adultery of either spouse, desertion, and cruelty. Innocent women received financial support in the form of alimony—usually biannual or annual payments in cash. Divorces from bed and board did not bestow the right to remarry, as did divorces *a vinculo*, and the children remained legitimate if conceived before the separation. The English courts of chancery heard all disputes arising from private separation agreements created by postnuptial trusts.[7]

Late in the seventeenth century the House of Lords introduced a new kind of divorce, designed to benefit noblemen whose wives proved adulterous. If a man first obtained a divorce *a mensa et thoro* from the ecclesiastical courts, and successfully prosecuted a civil suit for damages against his wife's paramour, he could obtain a private bill of divorce from Parliament giving him the right to remarry. His wife could also remarry, with one significant restriction. She could not marry the man who was her proved lover and the cause of the divorce.[8] Ostensibly English lawmakers designed this form of divorce to protect the property of noble families. Adulterous wives were dangerous: they could deceive their husbands into making heirs of other men's sons. To protect legitimate heirs, such women had to be put aside. Because adulterous husbands could not introduce spurious offspring as legitimate, there was no point in allowing women parliamentary divorces. No woman received one until 1801.[9] The rules on remarriage indicate, however, that more was at stake than the protection of hereditary estates. Men also sought to punish and control unfaithful women.

Work on divorce by Nancy F. Cott for Massachusetts and by Henry Cohn for Connecticut demonstrates that the Puritans believed in the value of liberal divorce laws. Both Massachusetts and Connecticut granted divorces *a vinculo matrimonii* for causes unrecognized in the mother country. Although the Massachusetts General Court did not formalize grounds for divorce, decrees indicate that men received absolute divorces for their wives' adultery and women received absolute divorces if their husbands neglected or abused them in addition to committing adultery. According to Cott, there is no evidence that separations from bed and board were granted in seventeenth-century Massachusetts, but in the eighteenth century women received them for cruelty and men and women for desertion. Two men won absolute divorces for desertion.[10] Connecticut refused to grant separations from bed and board for any cause.[11] All divorces in Connecticut were absolute and gave the right to remarry. They were available from both the courts and the legislature for adultery, desertion, fraudulent contract, and seven years' absence without word. Legislative divorces also could be obtained for cruelty.[12]

In the colonial period only Massachusetts and Connecticut enacted statutes providing for absolute divorce and enforced them on a regular basis. Historians believe that this radical departure from English law indicates the degree to which Puritan theories influenced Massachusetts and Connecticut lawmakers. As early as 1552 Puritan divines had advocated specific reforms in the ecclesiastical court rules on divorce. In a treatise authorized by Parliament, *Reformatio Legum Ecclesiasticarum*, reformers suggested allowing absolute divorces for adultery, desertion, continued absence without news, and cruelty or hatred. The Puritans did not view marriage as a sacrament, sacred in the eyes of God and the churches, but simply as a civil contract, and therefore dissolvable. Although such reforms never found support in early modern England, New England Puritans attempted to enforce them. Perhaps their belief in the family as an arm of government required policies designed to strengthen the family unit. In their eyes, absolute divorces benefited society by dissolving dysfunctional unions.[13]

New England willingness to change English law has long been noted by historians.[14] The Puritans felt no need to adjust their principles to the demands of a government and legal system they believed corrupt and long overdue for reform. But New England fervor did not extend elsewhere. The radical divorce tradition of Connecticut and Massachusetts lawmakers stands in marked contrast to the laws of the other colonies studied. Nowhere else did colonial lawmakers break with English tradition and change the rules for granting absolute divorces. In 1705 the colonial assembly of Pennsylvania authorized annulments for consanguinity and affinity and divorces *a mensa et thoro* in cases of adultery, bigamy, sodomy, and buggery, but the law contained no provision for divorces *a vinculo matrimonii*.[15] Later in the colonial period, the Pennsylvania assembly attempted to imitate the English parliamentary practice of granting divorces *a vinculo matrimonii* by private bill. The Privy Council opposed such an intrusion on Parliament's prerogatives, however, and in 1773 disallowed a divorce bill enacted in Pennsylvania. At that time the Crown issued instructions to all colonial governors demanding that they void any divorce bills enacted in the future.[16]

Colonial New York, Maryland, Virginia, and South Carolina were even less innovative on the question of divorce than Pennsylvania. New York changed an early policy favoring absolute divorce, and refused to allow remarriage after 1675.[17] There is no evidence that the southern colonies ever granted absolute divorces. Legal separations were another matter, however. All the southern colonies and New York administered them through their courts of chancery. Although no jurisdiction formalized the grounds by statute, separations generally could be obtained for desertion and cruelty, and occasionally for sexual offenses such as adultery, homosexuality, or bigamy. While their more radical northern neighbors were granting absolute divorces, then, the colonies with equity courts adopted a policy of support for separate residences and alimony in the tradition of English divorces *a mensa et thoro*.[18]

Requests for separations usually came from abused or abandoned wives who sought both protection in living alone and alimony. Colonial policy on separations demonstrates a powerful tradition of paternalism. Jurists reasoned that because the law gave men so much power over women, it had an obligation to protect women when husbands abused that power. This sense of obligation, although present in many areas of the law, is particularly evident in the cases on separate maintenances, for here the courts came face to face with the most dangerous shortcomings of the laws on women's property rights. Again and again chancellors noted the helpless condition of abused or deserted wives, their need for financial support, and the duty of the judicial system to provide assistance.

Thus in *Taveroon v. Taveroon*, tried in South Carolina in 1726, the chancellors acted the role of intermediary between husband and wife.[19] They ordered Stephen Taveroon to pay his wife forty shillings a week as a separate maintenance, because she could not live in their home in safety. Despite the straitened financial circumstances of the couple, which the court acknowledged, and the desire of Stephen to have his wife return home, the chancellors thought it "Equitable" for the woman to receive a separate maintenance. In 1736 the South Carolina Chancery acted similarly to protect Ruth Lowndes by requiring her husband Charles to "give Security for his good Behaviour towards her." The court awarded Ruth a separate maintenance consisting of various household utensils and furnishings, a sidesaddle, a slave woman and two children, and fifty pounds in current money.[20]

The history of divorce in colonial New York, Maryland, and Virginia imitates that of South Carolina. Chancellors ordered separations and payment of alimony in cases of abuse. In colonial Maryland, however, a challenge arose to the jurisdiction of the Court of Chancery early in the eighteenth century. To Thomas Macnamara, an abusive husband, it was not clear that the Chancery had a legal right to provide a remedy for his wife.[21] When he was ordered to give her clothing and personal items and pay fifteen pounds a year for support, he claimed that under Anglo-American law only an ecclesiastical court could divorce *a mensa et thoro*. Chancellor Seymour dismissed his argument, however, answering that "the Infancy, Low Circumstances and present Constitution of this province prevent us from being Able to pursue [an ecclesiastical suit] here for want of the said Courts or Maintenance for the proper Oficers of them."[22] Seymour allowed Macnamara the right to appeal the decree to England, but ordered him to follow it in the meantime. After being imprisoned three separate times for failure to comply, Macnamara finally acknowledged his obligation to meet the court's demand and began paying alimony. No record of an appeal to England has survived, if any was ever made.

Margaret Macnamara received her separation on the grounds of cruelty and sexual misconduct.[23] It appears, however, that charges of cruelty and desertion or nonsupport, rather than sexual misconduct, most readily convinced judges to grant women support. In Maryland, no woman used a sexual offense alone as a reason for requesting the help of the court, although women expected the charge to bolster the legitimacy of their requests. The testimony of neighbors and relatives attests to the serious nature of sexual offenses, but although adultery or homosexuality were disturbing to the morals of most settlers, charges of nonsupport and abuse formed the basis of every complaint. The sexual double standard worked to deny women separations for the infidelity of their husbands. In a suit for alimony in Maryland, a woman's main obligation was to prove her inability to provide for herself when living separately from a dangerous or negligent man.[24]

After winning independence, many of the new states moved quickly to reform their laws on divorce. Pennsylvania imitated the New England model by providing for judicial divorces on several grounds. In 1785 the Pennsylvania legislature enacted a statute granting jurisdiction over cases of divorce to the state Supreme Court. Appeals were allowed to the High Court of Errors and Appeals. Men and women subsequently obtained divorces *a vinculo matrimonii* for adultery, willful desertion of four years' duration, bigamy, and knowledge of sexual incapacity before marriage. Divorces *a mensa et thoro* became available for the same causes and, in addition, for cruelty.[25]

Massachusetts and New York followed suit in enacting postrevolutionary divorce statutes. In 1786 Massachusetts lawmakers formalized grounds for the first time. Absolute divorces were obtainable for adultery, impotence, and criminal conviction carrying a prison sentence of seven years. Husbands and wives could obtain separations for desertion, and wives could obtain them for nonsupport.[26] New York enacted its first divorce statute in 1787. Absolute divorces became available from the Court of Chancery for the single cause of adultery. Legal separations still were available for cruelty and desertion, as they had been in the colonial period. In 1813 the state assembly authorized the granting of divorces *a mensa et thoro*, thereby adding legitimacy to Chancery practices.[27]

Connecticut maintained its liberal prerevolutionary statutes on divorce, although the appearance of a three-year residency requirement in 1796 indicated the state's unwillingness to become the divorce capital of the new nation. Connecticut's fears had validity, as demonstrated by the actions of one Pennsylvania woman, Beulah Torbert. According to Supreme Court Justice Jasper Yeates, "It appeared to us that Mrs. Torbert left her husband without cause, refused to return to him on overtures made her, and prosecuted him for adultery without cause, merely to found certain proceedings against him for a divorce, in the state of Connecticut." Yeates made his remark in the case of *Torbert v. Twining*, tried in 1795.[28]

Virginia and Maryland did not enact statutes creating new divorce policies, but their assemblies did begin to enact private bills of absolute divorce.[29] Petitioners applied directly to the legislatures for divorces, and the grounds were not formalized. In 1827 Virginia lawmakers changed their procedure somewhat, granting jurisdiction to circuit superior courts of chancery over annulments and separations from bed and board for adultery and cruelty. The legislature retained the sole authority to grant absolute divorces until 1848. Then that power also was delegated to the chancery courts, which granted them only on a charge of adultery, as in New York.[30] In Maryland, divorces remained a sole legislative function even later than in Virginia. It was 1842 before the Maryland legislators relinquished jurisdiction to the courts.[31] At that time, county courts of equity gained the power to decree divorces both *a vinculo* and *a mensa et thoro*.

Of the jurisdictions studied, then, only South Carolina neglected to develop a legislative policy on divorce. In the colonial period, South Carolina lawmakers had reasoned that only ecclesiastical courts had jurisdiction over divorces *a vinculo*. Because there were no ecclesiastical courts in South Carolina, there could be no absolute divorces. After the Revolution, the assembly continued its policy of opposition. Although South Carolina lawmakers now had the authority to legislate for divorce, they chose not to do so. Absolute divorces and annulments could not be obtained for any cause whatsoever. As Chancellor Desaussure explained in *Vaigneur v. Kirk* (1808), "The legislature has uniformly refused to grant divorces, on the ground that it was improper for the legislative body to exercise judicial powers. And it has as steadily refused to enact any law to authorize the courts of justice to grant divorces *a vinculo matrimonii*, on the broad principle that it was a wise policy to shut that door to domestic discord, and to gross immorality in the community."[32] Despite the continued absence of statutory rules to govern divorces, courts of chancery in South Carolina ordered separations from bed and board for cruelty and desertion, as they had in the colonial period.[33] In most cases they did not use the term "divorce," but their orders were identical to those creating divorces *a mensa et thoro* in other jurisdictions.

Given the unique characteristics of South Carolina as a slave society, it could not recognize the legitimacy of absolute divorce. Divorces most often were granted for adultery, but divorce for husbands' extramarital affairs was impossible in a social climate condoning masters' sexual exploitation of slaves. To allow white women the freedom to divorce for male adultery would have meant placing severe restrictions on men's sexual behavior. That South Carolina more than Maryland or Virginia accepted the inevitability of male sexual license and refused to control it through the possibility of legislative (if not judicial) divorce is consistent with what historians know about the diverse cultures of southern slave societies. In *White over Black*, Winthrop D. Jordan pointed to the unusual prevalence of miscegenation in South Carolina during the eighteenth and early nineteenth centuries.[34]

According to Jordan, South Carolinians were less careful to conceal interracial liaisons than were other eighteenth-century slaveowners in the colonies. In this respect, they resembled the residents of the West Indies more than those of the mainland settlements. White women in South Carolina tolerated miscegenation by attempting to ignore it. Their own sexuality suffered as a result of the inevitable tensions in their marital lives. Jordan describes the plantation mistresses as "aloof from the world of lust and passion, a world which reeked of infidelity and Negro slaves"; in social situations they appeared formal and stiff.[35]

Bertram Wyatt-Brown stresses the difference between northern and southern attitudes toward male sexual continence in *Southern Honor*. Whereas middle-class northerners were beginning to extol the male virgin in terms similar to those traditionally reserved for females, southerners continued to approve of men's sexual freedom. Young white men were expected to have intercourse with blacks in order to gain sexual experience. Married men who remained discreet and followed the rules in pursuing their sexual liaisons with slaves encountered no criticism. The problem was ignored in polite mixed society, and not perceived as a problem at all among men.[36]

According to Wyatt-Brown, divorce remained rare in the South as a whole and absent in South Carolina because it threatened male honor. As he explained, "The problem was not just protection of women, but of male self-image and reputation before the world: honor. . . . Descriptions of misbehavior inevitably forced men to consider the consequences of patriarchal authority should they take the wife's part in such disputes."[37] Although men undoubtedly did seek to protect their honor by restricting access to divorce for themselves as well as their wives, they also were safeguarding their sexual privileges. Wives were forced to ignore their husbands' illicit behavior because they possessed no legal power to prevent or control it. They could not divorce, or in most cases even obtain legal separations. It is unsurprising that the most successful complaint in southern divorce law was a wife's adultery. In both Maryland and Virginia, the first private divorce acts (1790 and 1803, respectively) went to men whose wives gave birth to mulatto infants.[38] Men's honor, and their sexual rights, could not condone a woman's unfaithfulness, particularly with a black man.

THE QUESTION OF SUPPORT:
SEPARATE MAINTENANCES

Whether in North or South, when a marriage broke up, so did family property. Divorces *a vinculo matrimonii* often required a final disposition of all property owned by the husband and wife, although at times courts ordered awards of yearly alimony for women. When all the family property had to be divided by the courts, they proceeded according to the rules on inheritance. Women usually received one-third to one-half of the estate owned during the marriage.[39] The award could consist of either real or personal property or both, depending on the circumstances of each case. Divorces *a mensa et thoro* generally included provisions for monetary payments to the wife, while the husband maintained his marital right to control family property. That variations on these patterns are common in the records, however, indicates legislative and judicial willingness to meet the needs of individuals. In determining alimony, moreover, chancellors could be affected by the behavior of the parties, granting more or less according to their impressions of the conduct involved. Women guilty of adultery received no alimony at all, and even the conduct of innocent women was subjected to close scrutiny. Thus in *Peckford* v. *Peckford* (1828), a suit for divorce on the basis of the husband's adultery, the New York chancellor noted, "If the wife had been perfectly discreet, prudent, and submissive to her husband, I should have allowed her half of this property." Because she had traveled to England against the wishes of her husband and "exposed him to temptation," he awarded her only a life annuity equal to the value of one-third of their property.[40]

In states with separate courts of equity, lawmakers gave jurisdiction over questions of property to the chancellors. The tradition grew out of chancery's control of cases concerning women's property rights, as well as the special ability of the masters in chancery to settle matters of account. Thus, even when legislative bodies enacted private bills of divorce, as in the Chesapeake states after the Revolution, chancery courts continued to exercise authority over separate maintenances.

Chancery courts in Maryland enforced both divorces *a mensa et thoro* and private agreements to live apart and divide property. The chancellors also heard all suits for alimony by women who received legislative divorces. In Maryland, then, all decisions concerning the division of property, even those arising from absolute divorces ordered by the assembly, came from the chancellors. This practice began early in the colonial period, with the case of *Galwith* v. *Galwith* (1689), and continued into the nineteenth century, despite an attempt by the legislature to assume jurisdiction in *Crane* v. *Meginnis* (1829).[41] In this case the Court of Appeals overturned a legislative decree of alimony because it represented a usurpation of judicial powers. As Justice Earle observed, a suit for alimony was distinct from a suit for divorce in Maryland, and recoverable only from the Chancery Court or the Court of Appeals. Because suits for alimony had always been heard by chancellors, the legislature could not now take over jurisdiction.

Before the Revolution, Pennsylvania rules on separate maintenances followed the usual guidelines, but with passage of the divorce statute of 1785, the law on alimony developed an unusual twist. Under the laws of the state, only divorces from bed and board gave a woman the right to alimony. Absolute divorces did not carry alimony, for they ended all marital obligations, including the wife's right to financial support. Couples in Pennsylvania did divide family property at the time of divorce, but in poor or even middling families, the right to a share of collective assets meant less to women than the right to a portion of their husbands' earnings.[42] Significantly, the other jurisdictions studied did not adopt similar policies. They granted innocent women alimony, even in cases of absolute divorce.

In Pennsylvania, men and women could choose which kind of divorce they wanted, whether absolute or from bed and board, for most grounds. Under the act of 1785, both kinds of divorce were available for adultery, bigamy, desertion of four years' duration, and knowledge of sexual incapacity before marriage. But until 1815, divorces for cruelty, or forcing a woman to leave her home, brought only separations from bed and board. After 1815, a woman could make an election in a case of cruelty.[43] It is interesting to note that when a choice was available, some women preferred separations with alimony to absolute divorces. Their decision may indicate that they preferred the financial security of a decree of alimony to the right to remarry.[44] Given the poor preparation for earning their own livings that most women received in early America, their behavior is hardly surprising.

Barbara Klingenberger was one Pennsylvania wife who preferred alimony to the right to remarry. In her original petition to the Court of Common Pleas of Westmoreland County, she asked for a divorce *a vinculo matrimonii* with alimony. It was not possible to grant such a request under the laws of the state, and therefore the court decreed a divorce from bed and board with alimony. Barbara apparently was satisfied with the decree, but her husband appealed to the Supreme Court, arguing that because Barbara had asked for an absolute divorce, she should have been granted one. In his opinion on the case, Chief Justice Tilghman noted the inconsistencies of Barbara's petition, but decided that she wanted alimony. He wrote, "The petition was informal, and prayed for things which were inconsistent, viz.: a divorce from the bond of marriage and alimony; and perhaps, alimony was to the petitioner, the most important of the two."[45] He pointed out that Barbara had not appealed the decree or reapplied for a divorce *a vinculo*.

In Massachusetts, a provincial statute of 1695 had given the Superior Court of Judicature jurisdiction over alimony. According to Cott, however, in the colonial period the governor and council usually determined the kind and amount of support. Alimony usually consisted of cash payments to women, proportionate in amount to the family's wealth and status in the community. Cott discovered that men frequently refused to pay alimony. She concluded aptly, "Petitioners who won separate bed and board thus had an ambiguous success, not being allowed to remarry, nor released from the economic constraints of the marriage contract, nor guaranteed current support."[46]

Cott's statement indicates that under Massachusetts law women divorced *a mensa et thoro* did not enjoy the legal status of femes soles. In the eyes of the law they remained married, and therefore they could not contract, sue, or be sued in their own names. Women must have suffered considerable economic hardship under such divorce decrees. Divorces *a vinculo matrimonii* did not similarly handicap women. They became femes soles again, earning independence in the marketplace as well as in the household.

Given the lack of financial autonomy awarded to women divorced from bed and board, it is interesting to note that this was the only form of divorce granted to women in Massachusetts on the grounds of desertion and cruelty, although women who charged their husbands with adultery in addition to desertion or cruelty could receive absolute divorces.[47] Obviously Massachusetts jurists believed sexual misconduct to be the worst offense against the sanctity of the family. Cases of nonsupport, desertion, or cruelty did not excite the full compassion of the courts. That these charges were also the ones made almost exclusively by women indicates a sexual bias in the handling of divorce decrees. Women in eighteenth-century Massachusetts noted the distinction and apparently took it into account in bringing suits for divorce and separation. Cott observed that whereas men always sued for absolute divorces, women did not. "They requested divorce or, if that were not possible, whatever the governor and Council were willing to grant."[48]

The Massachusetts policy on divorces *a mensa et thoro* was in agreement with the policy on feme sole traders generally. No colonial statute outlined a procedure for granting married women independence in commercial affairs. Such a statute did not appear until after the Revolution. The creation of a formal policy at that time probably also affected the granting of divorces. Separations from bed and board for the cause of desertion were no longer technically necessary after 1787. Women could apply for feme sole trader status instead. In fact, their rights under the statute were stronger than their rights under Massachusetts divorce law, if Cott is correct in her assessment that separated women did not automatically earn feme sole trader status. Passage of the statute of 1787 may have served, then, as an alternative to divorce in Massachusetts.

Connecticut policy on separate maintenances differed significantly from that of Massachusetts. No divorces *a mensa et thoro* were granted in the colony or state. Until 1811, the courts also refused to recognize or enforce private agreements between husbands and wives to separate and divide property. In Connecticut, couples either were married or were not. There was no in-between status by which some marital privileges were recognized, such as a wife's right to support, and others were not. Connecticut law followed the suggestions outlined in the Puritan reform treatise of 1552. The reformers did not advocate divorce *a mensa et thoro*, and neither did Connecticut lawmakers. In this New England colony and state, therefore, couples received absolute divorces for desertion of three years' duration, seven years' willful absence without word, and cruelty, as well as for adultery.

Although Connecticut earned criticism from other jurisdictions for its liberal divorce policy, the policy was retained throughout the colonial and early national periods. Apparently the rules served the interests of residents well, perhaps in part because divorce substituted efficiently for rules allowing married women independent property rights. The General Assembly of Connecticut never enacted laws to govern the legal rights of independent businesswomen or women living separately from their husbands on an informal basis. Lawmakers believed that women already had a remedy in the rules on divorce, because each Connecticut divorce decree gave the husband and wife the legal status of unmarried persons. For women this included the right to own and control property and prosecute suits at law. In addition, each divorce included a division of family property. Courts made the decisions about how to divide the family estate, and there was no set policy. Under the terms of the statute, however, the woman could receive no more than the equivalent of her inheritance right in cases of intestacy—one-third to one-half the real and personal property owned at the time of the divorce.[49]

According to one contemporary observer, Zephaniah Swift, Connecticut divorce policy was responsible for the jurisdiction's failure to recognize both separate maintenances under postnuptial trusts and feme sole trader rights. Because deserted women could sue for divorce and be granted feme sole status if they proved their suits, other provisions for their protection and support were unnecessary. His reasoning is worth quoting at length:

> By a particular custom of the city of London, if a married woman carry on a trade, in which her husband does not intermeddle, she may be sued as a single woman. In Equity the separate estate of a married woman, living as a single woman on a separate maintenance allowed by the husband, on a separation after marriage, has been subjected to the payment of her contracts. . . . It may be said, that when the law recognized the idea of a separate estate of the wife, and a separate living from the husband, it necessarily involved the idea of a power of contracting, and being sued as a single woman. But in this state our courts have had no occasion to take these principles into consideration, for we have not introduced the practice of separate maintenance, and living of the husband and wife. Nor is it very probable that we ever shall, as the granting of divorces, renders such separations unnecessary; and this may be considered as a strong argument in favour of the policy of our law, for these separations necessarily arise from the indissoluble nature of the marriage contract, by the English law.[50]

Swift's opinion is supported by the findings of Linda K. Kerber on Connecticut divorces in the eighteenth century. In *Women of the Republic*, Kerber reports that the typical petitioner for divorce was "a woman whose husband had deserted her, usually leaving her economically troubled, if not desperate."[51] Because divorce freed a woman to control her own earnings and estate as well as to remarry, she had a great deal to gain from a favorable decree. Moreover, the lack of any other clear economic option may have prompted more women to sue for divorce in Connecticut than otherwise would have.

Swift erred in his belief that Connecticut would never recognize separate maintenances. After the Revolution the state did not long resist the policy of support demonstrated elsewhere for separate maintenances administered through trustees. All the other states studied, including neighboring Massachusetts, gave legal recognition to such postnuptial trusts.[52] Particularly in jurisdictions that opposed absolute divorces, or granted them only on narrow grounds, private separation agreements served a vital social function.

EQUITY LAW AND PRIVATE SEPARATION AGREEMENTS

The colonies and states with conservative policies on absolute divorce, New York, Maryland, Virginia, and South Carolina, lent particularly strong support to private separation agreements. Their policy grew partly out of a strong commitment to marriage settlements. Under equitable rules and principles, postnuptial settlements could be agreements to separate, and if they were made through trustees, courts of chancery felt the same obligation to enforce them as other marriage settlements. Despite their greater reluctance to grant absolute divorces, particularly in the colonial period, the jurisdictions with courts of chancery allowed the equivalent of divorce *a mensa et thoro* at the will of the parties. Such a policy denotes in some sense a liberal attitude toward divorce, for even in Connecticut a petitioner had to demonstrate cause to win a court-ordered separation.

Although jurists supported postnuptial contracts to separate, conservative attitudes surfaced in postrevolutionary judicial decrees. For example, although equity courts increasingly supported direct contracts between husbands and wives, that is, contracts executed without trustees, they did not extend the new principle to separation agreements.[53] Unless executed as trusts, private agreements to live apart and divide property were liable to be overthrown. A dislike of separations, which were increasing rapidly in number in the postrevolutionary era, prompted courts to enforce private separation agreements only when forced to do so by the weight of judicial precedent. If executed as postnuptial trusts designating a division of property between husband and wife, the courts had to enforce them, not because they were socially acceptable agreements to live apart but because they were legal agreements to divide property. Given a choice, some jurists would have preferred to stop the practice.

Just like the other colonies and states with equity courts, New York supported private separation agreements made through the medium of trustees. New York imitated English practice in this area of the law beginning in the colonial period, and did not change its policy after the Revolution despite the growing opinion among jurists that separation agreements went against good public policy.[54] New York chancellors refused, however, to support private separation agreements when the law behind them was not absolutely clear. In *Carson* v. *Murray* (1832), for example, the Chancery Court supported a separation agreement because it was made through trustees, whereas in *Rogers* v. *Rogers* (1834) it refused to validate an agreement made directly between a husband and wife, without the intervention of a third party.[55] In *Rogers* v. *Rogers*, the chancellor expressed his disapproval of private agreements by men and women to live apart. He claimed to support them only as standard postnuptial trusts, and not as contracts beneficial in themselves to society. Like Swift, the New York chancellor opposed giving couples the right to separate at will. He wrote, "It is impossible for a *feme covert* to make any valid agreement with her husband to live separate from him, in violation of the marriage contract and of the duties which she owes to society, except under the sanction of the court; and in a case where the conduct of the husband has been such as to entitle her to a decree for a separation. The law of the land does not authorize or sanction a voluntary agreement between husband and wife. It merely tolerates such agreements when made in such a manner that they can be enforced by or against a third person acting in behalf of the wife."[56] Without that intervening third party, he felt no compunction about voiding the contract.

The chancellor from New York thus echoed sentiments expressed by southern jurists who opposed divorces but supported private agreements to separate. At times the contradiction in policy was acknowledged openly, both by attorneys and by judges. As one New York jurist observed, "However strange it may seem . . . that the agreement for a separate maintenance, which is merely auxiliary, should be enforced, whilst the principal agreement, viz. for a separation, is held to be contrary to the spirit and policy of the law, yet the decisions on the subject seem too numerous and uniform to be easily shaken."[57] Even though some early United States chancellors were unwilling to admit it, separation agreements served an important social function in a country that considered divorce a disgrace, and yet gave women few property rights unless they were separated legally from their husbands. Agreements to divide property also acted as a vital force behind the nineteenth-century movement to allow divorce at the will of the parties.

Connecticut jurists, although long opposed to contracts of any kind between husbands and wives, eventually bowed to the public will and accepted private separation agreements. In *Nichols* v. *Palmer* (1811), the Connecticut Supreme Court decided five to four to support a postnuptial trust dividing property and establishing separate residences.[58] Swift dissented from the majority opinion. He staunchly criticized the willingness of equity courts to support private separation agreements and argued for upholding the long-standing Connecticut policy against them. As he reasoned, "Although the marriage contract, is, in our law, considered to be of a civil nature only, yet there is a certain sanctity attached to it, which forbids us to degrade it to a level with ordinary contracts, and to permit the parties to dissolve it *ad libitum*."[59] Swift believed that if couples could agree to separate on their own, without submitting their grievances to a court of justice, they would do so hastily. A proceeding at law, moreover, prevented one party from taking advantage of another. He warned in dire tones, "This decision proclaims to all who are married, that they have the right to separate by mutual consent, as whim, fancy, or passions may dictate. This is to foster that unfortunate propensity to change, which is productive of misery in society, beyond the power of description."[60]

A majority of Swift's peers on the bench were not so pessimistic. They foresaw no great danger in supporting separate maintenances; they believed, in fact, that some couples would benefit from the option. Not all women and men wanted to sue for absolute divorces, with their accompanying publicity. Perhaps, Justice Smith observed, they were embarrassed to prosecute a suit at law, or concerned with upsetting their families. "Perhaps, they have children who are to be disgraced and whose feelings are to be wounded, by a public disclosure of a crime in one of their parents."[61]

There were additional legitimate reasons for women to desire separate residences, reasons that were not recognized by the state statutes on divorce, despite their relatively liberal nature. At the time of *Nichols* v. *Palmer*, cruelty could not be claimed as a ground for judicial divorce in Connecticut. To obtain a divorce for cruelty a woman had to apply to the state legislature by private bill. Such a step brought even more public notice than a proceeding at law. As Justice Baldwin argued, "What harm, then, is done to morality, or what sound principle of policy is impugned, by permitting the parties, on good cause, to separate by agreement, and thus save the parties the painful task of exposing the follies or the vices of partners, to obtain a compulsory separation, or the disgrace and misery of themselves and families, by fruitless attempts to live together in harmony[?]"[62] Although Baldwin agreed with Swift that Connecticut law should not support separations at the will of the parties, he believed that, on the whole, agreements to separate served a good purpose. Separations without cause, he maintained, could be overturned by judicial process when they were discovered.

Postrevolutionary fears concerning the increase in divorce suits appeared in southern jurisdictions as well as in the North. Chancellors regretted the necessity for the rising number of divorces *a mensa et thoro* issuing from their courts. They believed, however, that their awards of separate maintenance were morally expedient. Male defendants did not always agree. In South Carolina, Virginia, and Maryland after the Revolution, husbands challenged the right of chancery courts to order divisions of property and awards of alimony. Perhaps requests by wives for separate maintenances were increasing in these jurisdictions as well as in the North, and men therefore had a pressing reason for questioning the chancellors' decisions. In addition, the absence of statutory guidelines on divorces *a mensa et thoro* gave husbands the necessary opening to oppose established judicial precedents.

In *Purcell* v. *Purcell* (1810), Virginia chancellors faced a challenge to their jurisdiction over divorces *a mensa et thoro*.[63] Counsel for the defendant, Charles Purcell, argued that the court did not have the right to issue a decree for separate maintenance. The chancellor dismissed his argument on the grounds that when there was no remedy at law, a court of equity had to provide one. Such was the rule of "every well regulated government."[64] When Ann Purcell won her suit, her husband immediately demanded the right to appeal. The chancellor refused to allow it unless the man agreed to support his wife while his suit was pending. This he refused to do, claiming that the court had no right to order such a payment. In making this claim, however, Charles Purcell was arguing against established precedent in Virginia, as the chancellor pointed out. He noted that the Chancery "had the highest authority in support of the principles which he had laid down, to wit, the universal sense of the country, as declared every day, with great propriety, in such cases in the County Courts, and in no instance had an appeal from their decisions ever been taken, which proved that where they acted, they had done right, and with which the people were perfectly satisfied." When the husband went directly to the Virginia Court of Appeals with his case, the justices unanimously refused to hear it. They were satisfied with the decree of the chancellor and determined that "the doctrine of alimony may now be considered as settled."[65]

In Maryland, the division of authority between the assembly and the Court of Chancery in cases of divorce and alimony indicates a deeply entrenched belief in the propriety of Chancery's jurisdiction over cases concerning married women's property. Maryland jurists believed that the Chancery, not the legislature, could best discover the intricacies of family finances and make a proper disposition. Their attitude demonstrates well why chancery courts so often handled suits for divorce in early America, and also indicates why husbands were not successful in challenging that jurisdiction after the Revolution.

Before the Revolution, suits for separate maintenances in South Carolina revealed no dispute over the jurisdiction of the Chancery, despite the failure of the legislature to provide statutory guidelines on divorce. After the Revolution, however, chancellors found it necessary to defend their practice of ordering separations and payment of alimony. Thus, in the case of *Jellineau* v. *Jellineau*, counsel for Francis Jellineau disputed the right of the court to order a separate maintenance.[66] The chancellor refused to recognize his argument, noting with Revolutionary flair,

> It has been contended by defendant's counsel that this Court has not the power to decree a separate maintenance for a wife, however harshly treated by her husband, unless a divorce has been previously obtained, or unless there be an express or implied agreement, on their separation, for that purpose. The cases cited from the English books to establish this doctrine, may be good law in England, where ecclesiastical Courts have competent jurisdiction to grant divorces *a mensa et thoro*. But in this State there is no such Court, and hard would be the lot of females if they alone should be obliged to submit to any degree of cruelty from their husbands, without any redress.[67]

He refused to shape South Carolina law around the laws of England, and ordered an immediate separation. In 1809 the Chancery met a similar challenge. Counsel for the male defendant in *Prather* v. *Prather* contended that "this Court has no jurisdiction in such case, and cannot interpose its authority to give any relief."[68] The argument was dismissed as simply incorrect.

As a result of such challenges, South Carolina chancellors took special care in the years after the Revolution to explain their reasons for granting separate maintenances. Despite the continuing opposition of the legislature to any form of divorce, the Court of Chancery would not condone abandonment or violence. In cases of abuse, for which the common law gave no remedy, equity law had a duty to provide one. As Chancellor Desaussure explained in *Prather* v. *Prather*, "It is shocking to think that such conduct, so inhuman in itself, so injurious to innocent and helpless women, and so mischievous to society, should pass unheeded and unchecked in a civilized country. It is the boast of our jurisprudence, that for every wrong there is a remedy, and for every injustice an adequate and salutary redress. But this would be a vain and empty boast, if for such a case as this there was no remedy."[69]

At other times the chancellors seemed to forget that they had no authority to use the word "divorce." In *Taylor* v. *Taylor*, tried in 1811, Chancellor James pondered, "Will this Court proceed to pronounce a divorce between the parties and separate them forever?"[70] Despite his finding that the husband had committed "outrages" amounting to "the highest degree of the *saevitia* of the civil law, or of the intolerable cruelty mentioned by Judge Blackstone," he decided in the negative. His wording, however, implies that he believed he was denying a divorce: "This Court will pronounce no divorce; but after such repeated outrageous conduct on the part of the defendant, it will endeavour to provide for the security and maintenance of the wife, until both parties may be somewhat cooled, and she may return with some kind of safety to her husband."[71]

Perhaps Chancellor James's unwillingness to decree a permanent rather than a temporary maintenance equated with a denial of divorce in his eyes. He and his fellows certainly realized the similarities between their separation decrees and divorces *a mensa et thoro*. As Justice Nott noted in his opinion on *Rhame v. Rhame* (1826), "Although our Courts of Equity have not the power to grant divorces, yet as the two subjects, 'divorce and alimony,' are insepara-ble companions in *England*, we must look to the causes of divorce, to ascer-tain the grounds on which alimony will be allowed."[72] In South Carolina, chancellors such as James and Nott supported the right of abused wives to live apart from their husbands, and they gave such women sufficient property to enable them to do so, commensurate with the estates of their husbands. Separations exclusively for adultery were not given in the colony and state, as they were in the other jurisdictions studied, but adultery sometimes was acknowledged as an abuse by the court, aggravating to complaints of aban-donment and personal violence.[73] Moreover, deserted women in South Carolina received property settlements, even when no acts of personal vio-lence occurred.[74] It appears, then, that when the chancellors ordered separa-tions they were most concerned with ensuring the proper support of wives. Men who failed in their duties with regard to property found little favor in the Court of Chancery. The law of South Carolina reveals an overriding concern with safeguarding the estates of women. Support of private agreements to live apart at the will of the parties, combined with the feme sole trader statutes of 1712, 1744, and 1823, amounted to a public policy allowing women to leave neglectful, abusive, and unfaithful husbands. When we consider in addition the liberal attitude of the chancellors toward separate maintenances for wives, the "divorce" policy of South Carolina was not markedly different from the policies of the New Englanders.

According to the rules of early American law, husbands had an obligation to support their wives. Under a legal system that gave male heads of household control over wives' real property and ownership of their personal property, the guarantee of support served as compensation to women for their losses. The inability of married women to contract or to prosecute and defend suits at law further increased their need for financial support. Under standard common law rules, women did not possess the means to take care of themselves; men had to care for them. In a statement explicitly outlining the judicial reasoning behind women's limited property rights, Justice Putnam of the Massachusetts Supreme Court first listed the ways in which married women found themselves restricted under the law, and then observed, "For these disabilities she is liberally recompensed by the obligations which the marriage imposes upon the husband to provide for her support during coverture, and by a claim for dower after its dissolution."[75]

Inevitably, some men chose not to protect and provide for their wives, and the law developed rules for the exceptional cases. Divorce and legal separation served as a way of correcting and compensating for dysfunctional family relations. When abusive husbands forced wives out of their homes, courts moved aggressively to remind them of their obligations. If a man was not willing to treat his wife in a way that permitted her to remain at home in safety, then he became liable to support her in living elsewhere. This premise helps to explain the attitude of American jurists toward cruelty as a cause for legal separations. Under the laws of the colonies and states, cruelty had to be severe enough so that a woman feared bodily harm or death in order to win her a separate maintenance. Occasional, slight acts of physical violence were not enough to gain judicial support for a separation, nor was what today we would call incompatibility or mental anguish.[76] Such things, although reprehensible, did not threaten life or limb. A woman could live with them. But when the degree of cruelty escalated to a level that required a wife to leave home, the courts acted uniformly in offering her help. Under American legal theory, women did not have to provide for themselves when they were forced to live separately from their husbands because of abuse or neglect.

When viewed from the perspective of divorce law, women's property rights in the early decades of the nineteenth century truly represented an ideal rather than reality. In theory, a woman did not need to own property because her husband provided for her. But in order to justify giving husbands control over what women owned at marriage as well as the profits of their labor during marriage, the law had to ensure men's financial support of their wives. During the early national period, courts and assemblies increasingly realized that their ability to guarantee women the ideal—support during marriage—was being undermined by practical considerations, including new attitudes toward marriage and divorce. In a society that was beginning to accept divorce as valid on many grounds, women living separately from their husbands became less exceptional. Society gradually realized that it could no longer deal with separated couples as deviant cases outside the ideal. They became a group representative of new views about marriage, including recognition of the individuality of husbands and wives and acceptance of conflicting interests. In response, lawmakers reluctantly adopted positions designed to reflect changing social attitudes toward marriage, separation, and property. They began to expand married women's property rights.

The spectrum of rules on divorce and alimony in the early states demonstrates that to lawmakers and jurists, there were no obvious solutions to the problem of how to define changing relationships between men and women. New York, Virginia, and Maryland, for example, did modify their strict colonial policies of opposition to absolute divorces, but their rules remained conservative in comparison to those of the New England states and Pennsylvania. All three conservative states, however, continued their prerevolutionary policies concerning divorces *a mensa et thoro* and private separation agreements, an indication of their satisfaction with those rules and their desire to preserve them.

The Pennsylvania divorce statute of 1785 gave citizens the widest range of divorce options available in early America. Lawmakers there recognized that all people did not want the same kinds of separations. In particular, all women did not want absolute divorces, especially when they included no provisions for day-to-day support. The Pennsylvania model is probably that which was most consistent with contemporary attitudes toward marital property: as long as women remained married, even though separated, they had legitimate claims on their husbands for financial support; when women obtained absolute divorces, however, all marital ties ended and husbands no longer had legal obligations to provide housing, food, and clothing.

The states with historical ties to radical Protestant religious movements developed the most liberal attitudes toward divorce. Yet Connecticut's refusal to accept divorces *a mensa et thoro* belies its liberal tradition to some extent. Why order absolute divorces but not separations from bed and board? Perhaps the middle ground of separate maintenances had no appeal to jurists in Connecticut because they believed so strongly in the husband's obligation to live with and provide for his wife. The conservative tradition of Connecticut on female separate estates points to this conclusion. Throughout the colonial and early national periods to 1811 Connecticut refused to recognize marriage settlements guaranteeing any women—even those who were happily married—separate property through third parties. Women did not need separate property in Connecticut, jurists maintained, because under the law their husbands had to provide for them. Only when attitudes toward marriage and divorce had changed significantly after the Revolution did Connecticut jurists reluctantly acknowledge the usefulness of postnuptial trusts. Ironically, acceptance of private separation agreements in Connecticut early in the nineteenth century indicates, not a retreat from the radicalism of the seventeenth and eighteenth centuries, but an expansion in juridical thinking about the purpose of divorce. Couples in Connecticut wanted the right to live apart and own separate property, even in cases where there was no basis for a court-ordered divorce *a vinculo matrimonii.*

South Carolina's policy on divorce and alimony in the postrevolutionary period was on the surface the most contradictory of any state's. Matrons there enjoyed rules allowing them significant property rights after marriage. Marriage settlements creating separate estates for women were fully recognized, as were postnuptial separation agreements created for the purpose of dividing property. In addition, South Carolina had a strong commitment to feme sole trader rights. Yet despite such general acceptance of women's financial autonomy after marriage, South Carolina refused to provide for absolute divorce. Why the contradiction?

It is important to note that although South Carolina had a liberal policy on women's separate estates, it remained the legal duty of men to provide for their wives and children. Women had no obligation to use their property for their own or their family's support. Yet jurists recognized the value in allowing women to possess property. Separate estates served as safety nets for women when men failed in meeting their family obligations. It is arguable, then, that South Carolina's unusual divorce policy served two social functions. First, it symbolized a commitment to female dependency despite a policy of support for female separate estates. Married women could control their own property and become financially independent, but they could never be fully independent of their husbands. They could never remarry. Second, the tragic sexual dynamics of slaveholding South Carolina families made it extremely difficult for lawmakers to sanction divorce and remarriage. They could not grant women absolute divorces for the sexual misconduct of their husbands. Because this was the charge that most often resulted in a divorce decree in the early United States—in New York, for example, divorces could be obtained only on a charge of adultery—South Carolinians could not grant absolute divorces at all. Women in the state may have won their high degree of economic independence within marriage partly as a result of lawmakers' inability to give them divorces when their husbands proved adulterous. In exchange for the law's acceptance of male sexual privileges, South Carolina jurists gave women the right to financial autonomy within marriage.

Although Maryland and Virginia did not duplicate South Carolina's extreme position of opposition to all absolute divorces after the Revolution, the relative conservatism of their policies probably arose from social problems similar to those that shaped South Carolina law. Absolute divorces remained rare in the southern jurisdictions, even as judges continued their traditionally strong commitment to court-ordered separations with alimony. It remained much easier, and perhaps less publicly humiliating, to win a separation in Maryland and Virginia than a divorce *a vinculo matrimonii*.

Despite the postrevolutionary increase in divorce suits, all American jurists continued to express their belief in the necessity of strong family ties. Their perspectives on how best to promote family unity varied considerably, however, and their different responses reflected the various social, religious, economic, and legal circumstances that shaped their diverse cultures. Connecticut jurists believed that the best way to protect the family as they knew it was to deny women the ability to own separate property. Absolute divorce was far better for the morals of society than opposing interests within marriage. South Carolina was forced by peculiar circumstances to argue exactly the opposite point. Married women in the state were relatively free to own and control property if they chose to do so, and their rights to court-ordered separate maintenances were also guaranteed. But they could not, under any circumstances, remarry. That rule, South Carolina lawmakers maintained, was necessary to uphold the sanctity of the family.

The other jurisdictions studied fell between the extremes represented by Connecticut and South Carolina. They recognized several kinds of divorce and determined which was most suitable in particular situations. The common theme in all jurisdictions, however, was a reluctance to grant divorces at all. Divorce represented an ultimate breakdown, not only in family relations, but also in the delicate property arrangements of husbands and wives. Only death was similarly disruptive, demonstrated by the fact that jurists frequently ordered property settlements at divorce in the same way they did at death.

Separate Estates

Separate estates, through which married women owned and controlled property independently of their husbands, evolved in England as an exception to the common law principle of unity of person. Although designed for unusual situations, separate estates clearly met the needs of many individuals and families in the propertied classes of English society. They employed and developed marriage settlements, as they were called, throughout the seventeenth and early eighteenth centuries until they became an important area of property law, theoretically accessible to all families. Administered by courts of equity rather than courts of law, marriage settlements represented both the innovative and the traditional side of the English legal system. Whereas the Chancery used them to modify and expand married women's property rights in accordance with changes in family relationships, common law courts refused to enforce them. Thus a dual system evolved for defining the legal status of women within the family.

The conflicting principles of common law and equity courts have created confusion among students of history.[1] Depending on which system is emphasized, women can be seen as holding virtually equal rights with men or few property rights at all. There can be no doubt, however, that the development of equity rules and precedents giving women the right to own, manage, convey, and devise property represented a radical breakthrough for women. It was the most significant change in the legal status of women until the advent of the married women's property acts in the nineteenth century. Because the rules fell under the supervision of courts of equity and were never defined by statute, however, they remained inaccessible to the majority of women. This explains why most historians have depicted the nineteenth-century married women's property acts as more important to women than the equitable developments of the early modern period, even though the earlier changes represented a far more radical intellectual break with accepted spousal roles and relationships.[2]

The dual system of English property law found its way to some American colonies intact. Of the colonies studied here, New York, Maryland, Virginia, and South Carolina created courts of chancery in the English fashion, thereby allowing for the easy transfer of laws and precedents on women's separate estates. Perhaps even more important than the initial transfer of a body of equity law, colonies with separate courts of chancery were able to keep abreast of English legal developments in the later seventeenth and eighteenth centuries. Their courts applied new precedents to cases as they arose in the colonies, creating a series of local decisions to assist in clarifying this changing area of the law. Colonial chancery courts did not, by and large, deviate from English precedents on women's separate estates. In particular, they did not expand on women's right to own property separately from their husbands. Occasionally, instead, they refused to recognize a case from the mother country that increased women's rights. After the Revolution, however, American chancery courts became more independent of English precedent, developing new rules of their own to deal with questions of women's property.

Colonies without separate courts of chancery often failed to adopt equitable rules on separate estates. Although common law courts frequently handled questions of equity, they did so in a piecemeal fashion, adopting rules and precedents for some areas of the law and rejecting them for others. As a result, separate estates were slighted to a greater or lesser extent in all of those colonies studied that did not have independent courts of chancery. In Connecticut, the courts refused to recognize the validity of marriage settlements giving women independent property rights. Massachusetts law shows a similar, though less extreme, reluctance to grant women independent rights to property. Separate estates under litigation after the Revolution reveal the failure of eighteenth-century Massachusetts jurists to develop a coherent body of law to govern women's property. Jurists did not know how far they could enforce equitable rules because until 1818 the colonial and state legislatures never gave them explicit jurisdiction over marriage settlements. As a result, enforcement of settlement terms became difficult, at least in the immediate postwar decades.

In Pennsylvania, common law courts enforced the terms of most settlements, but the absence of a strong tradition of equity law led to some erroneous and damaging decisions on basic issues of concern to women. Jurists there also evidenced a sharp dislike of women's separate estates, a prejudice they allowed to influence them in deciding particular cases. Unlike

Connecticut and Massachusetts, however, Pennsylvania did develop a body of local precedents supporting marriage settlements. Pennsylvania law also followed certain English developments, including support of settlements executed without trustees, that increased women's property rights. Perhaps the fact that the Pennsylvania assembly gave its common law courts full powers to hear all cases in equity, rather than delineating certain kinds of cases, can account for the distinction. In addition, it seems likely that Pennsylvanians employed marriage settlements more often than New Englanders, although that point must remain conjecture until further regional studies have been completed on the use of trust estates.

Given the unique position of the New England colonies and states on separate property for married women, discussion of that law will be reserved for the next chapter. The following analysis focuses, then, on the evolution of eighteenth- and early nineteenth-century equity law in those jurisdictions that accepted marriage settlements as valid instruments throughout the period studied. Postrevolutionary decisions on the creation and enforcement of trust estates indicate that over time, the motivation for granting women separate property focused more and more on an official acknowledgment of the right of women to protect their own property from husbands' creditors. Although such a motive for judicial support of settlements appeared early in their development, it originally had served a secondary function to preservation of landed estates for the proper support of widows and heirs. By the late eighteenth century, however, courts in the United States relied on marriage settlements as a way of granting women financial independence, particularly in cases concerning the wives of debtors. Rules on the wife's equity to a settlement, the doctrine of intentions, and the evolution of simple marriage settlements all point toward such a conclusion. When we remember that the married women's property acts of the mid-nineteenth century initially served as a way of protecting women's estates during periods of economic depression,[3] it becomes clear that property rights for women in America grew as the financial prospects of their husbands became increasingly unstable.

Marriage settlements granting women separate estates were not numerous in the period studied, although some evidence now indicates that they became more common over time.[4] Any discussion of the legal history of separate property for women must focus, then, on the theoretical importance of this alternative to the common law, rather than on the practical effects it produced. Few women had settlements, but legal discussions of the contracts that did make their way into court forced jurists to confront the contradictions in the laws on women and property. In time, lawyers, judges, and legislators came to believe that common law rules could not provide justice for women with property or women who earned wages. Under increasing pressure from the public after the 1830s, they gradually incorporated equitable remedies into the common law, making all women capable of owning property independently of their husbands. Because the law of trust estates gave women their greatest opportunity for financial autonomy before passage of the married women's property acts, it is important to study its development and use with care. An understanding of the initial appearance of separate estates in early modern England is also essential, and that is where this discussion begins.

THE EVOLUTION OF SEPARATE ESTATES IN ENGLAND

Control over trust estates constituted one of the most important branches of equitable jurisdiction in England.[5] It was the Chancery Court that first recognized the device of the married woman's trust in the sixteenth century and that encouraged its development in the seventeenth and eighteenth centuries. According to Holdsworth, *Avenant v. Kitchin* (1581–82) marked the first time an equity court supported the right of a woman to hold property separately from her husband by the force of a contract executed before marriage.[6] Maria L. Cioni claims, however, that *Mary Sankey alias Walgrave v. Arthur Goldinge* (1581) founded the concept of a married woman's separate estate. She writes, "The case established that whenever an estate was conveyed to trustees, to the separate use of a married woman, Chancery would allow her prerogative to hold or dispose of that estate unhampered by her husband's interference."[7] In any case, both authors found significant evidence in sixteenth- and seventeenth-century court reports and books on conveyancing to show a growing practice of conveying property to trustees for the use of married women. The Court of Chancery, Holdsworth wrote, "was prepared to give effect" to settlements, and at times even allowed women to exercise control over separate estates.[8]

Initially, the situation of an individual woman might affect the desire of Chancery to support or disallow her settlement. If a husband abandoned his wife or if he were wasting her estate, the court would be very likely to support her claims to property. Holdsworth discussed in particular the case of *Flecton v. Dennys* (1594), in which a wife placed one of her leases into the hands of trustees to prevent her husband from touching it. In regard to the situation of Mrs. Dennys, the chancellor wrote, "It is alleged that the said Mrs. Dennys hath been hardly forced to sell away her jointure, and to discharge the bonds and assurance for the same, and that she wanteth competent maintenance for a gentlewoman of her estate, this Court thinks it convenient, if that be true, that she should have out of the leases which were hers, and are assigned as aforesaid, some meet and convenient portion for her maintenance, answerable to the calling of Mr. Dennys, and unto her estimation and countenance, which she had before she was his wife."[9]

According to Holdsworth, then, one of the earliest motivations for the development of women's separate estates was concern for the economic well-being of wives when husbands proved either wasteful in the management of property or negligent of their family responsibilities.[10] More recent students of English law and society also have noted the connection between changes in attitudes toward women and family relationships and the appearance of marriage settlements giving wives (or widows) and younger children increased rights to property.[11] Echoing her predecessor, Cioni has observed, "Willingness to give women security moved Chancery to protect future equitable interests and to develop a new instrument, the trust, to allow married women to have separate estates."[12] Cioni found that by the end of Elizabeth's reign Chancery had developed a series of principles in support of women's separate estates.[13] It may have taken until the eighteenth century, though, before large numbers of families employed them. As Lloyd Bonfield observed in his study of English strict settlements, "In the eighteenth century there was a shift towards greater equality in the distribution of family wealth."[14] In particular, the rise in pin-money clauses in family settlements marked social acceptance of women's right to separate property.[15]

The work of Lawrence Stone offers another reason for the acceptance of women's independent rights to property in the eighteenth century. Owing in part to the rise of "affective individualism" and the "closed domesticated nuclear family," men no longer felt comfortable with laws that placed women in a helpless position with regard to property, and the women, according to Stone, were making "increasing claims . . . for sharing of power." Stone noted the connection between the decline in patriarchy and the rise of separate estates: "The hardest evidence for a decline in the near-absolute authority of the husband over the wife among the propertied classes is an admittedly limited series of changes in the power of the former to control the latter's estate and income."[16] The companionate ideal could not exist under a legal system that ignored women's needs. As fathers began to favor daughters and younger sons in their wills, they came to realize the inadequacies of the laws on women's property. Why give a daughter an estate, only to see it fall into the hands of her husband? Thus new rules on women's separate estates developed in response to the demands of propertied families for greater equity.

According to legal historians, changes in the rules of inheritance also may have prompted the new attitudes toward women's property rights. During the early modern period, there was a gradual deterioration in the dower rights of wealthy widows, owing to the increasing practice of placing family property in trusts. Although trusts were popular among the landed classes because they prevented alienation, one disadvantage was the virtual destruction of dower. As Blackstone explained the problem, "Now, though a husband had the *use* of lands in absolute fee-simple, yet the wife was not entitled to any dower therein; he not being seised thereof."[17] To correct this problem it became common to settle a certain amount of property on a couple in joint tenancy, by which the wife was entitled to the property for her life and would therefore, in the event that she outlived her husband, possess adequate means of support. Jointures also had the advantage of defining precisely what a widow's portion would be in advance, whereas dower could not be determined until after a husband's death. But in contrast to the situation with dower, widows had no common law remedy when disputes arose over jointure agreements. They had to go to Chancery, a stipulation that increased the role of that court in protecting women's property rights.[18]

It seems probable that chancellors initially were willing to support separate estates for married women because couples often made them as a part of jointure agreements. Holdsworth theorized that judges in equity were eager to expand women's rights under jointures because they had done such damage to the law of dower. Thus when pin-money clauses appeared to give women the privilege not only of owning property but of managing it as well, chancellors supported the change as a form of compensation for women's loss of other property rights, including dower.[19]

It was not until the end of the seventeenth century that legal precedents allowing married women to control separate estates were fully developed in England.[20] But once chancellors began to accept the right of a wife to act under certain qualified conditions, it did not take long for them to recognize her universal proprietary capacity. Then a proper settlement could give married women the right to act as femes soles. By the turn of the century, women who possessed trust estates could contract, sell, mortgage, or devise their property as though they had never married, providing the terms of their settlements gave them the powers to do so.[21]

The specific powers women enjoyed under their settlements were significant for determining their level of independence, for jurists interpreted the terms of marriage settlements strictly. Conservative decisions were common during the early years of English development, when landed families designed settlements more to protect their property than to give women economic independence.[22] Often settlements, written to preserve intact family estates, gave women no powers of control at all. They provided a wife simply with a guaranteed income, rather than the right to control the principal. Some settlements gave a woman one privilege while denying her others. For example, if a deed granted a feme covert the right to devise, she could not also sell or mortgage her estate. Those powers had to be granted to her in separate clauses. Similarly, a woman whose settlement gave her rights to the rents and profits of her property could exercise no control over the principal. That remained under the management of her trustees, who made all business decisions for her. Over time, these rules changed and women came to execute broad powers over their estates even when the settlements failed to delineate them.[23] But that was an eighteenth-century development.

The trend favoring women's property rights in England during the early modern period is demonstrated particularly well by the doctrine of the wife's "equity to a settlement," which first appeared in the late sixteenth century.[24] The English Chancery Court adopted separate estates so emphatically that it came to regard them as a right for every feme covert. Under certain conditions, chancellors asked men to make settlements for their wives. They ordered the creation of settlements most often when an executor or administrator refused to give a woman an inheritance, thereby forcing her and her husband to sue in Chancery for possession. Before granting them any property, the chancellor would order the husband to settle all or a part of it on his wife as a separate estate. In this way the chancellors assured themselves that they were not giving property to a husband who might take it exclusively for his own use and grant his wife no benefits from it.

American jurists' adoption of rules such as the wife's equity to a settlement demonstrates the commitment of colonial chancery courts to upholding English law. In the eighteenth century, colonial chancellors also followed English precedent in granting the beneficiaries of trusts increasing powers of control and management. Over time, American equity courts gradually developed precedents that gave women the potential for considerable independent action.

RULES ON THE CREATION OF SETTLEMENTS

At the time many of the American colonies were settled in the seventeenth century, English law dealing with separate estates still was in transition. This situation, in addition to the delays and confusion that accompanied the transfer of new legal developments to the American colonies, meant that marriage settlements remained uncommon until the eighteenth century. Most seventeenth-century colonists did not succeed in creating legally binding settlements, although extant documents indicate a few informal attempts to do so.[25] Even more important, seventeenth-century colonial society did not develop the wealth and class structure that was responsible in the mother country for the evolution of women's separate estates. Landed families in the eighteenth-century colonies, particularly in the slave-based economic systems of the South, did possess the wealth that, at least in England, had prompted the early use of marriage settlements. In South Carolina, where evidence concerning marriage settlements is most complete, documents conveying property to trustees for the use of feme coverts begin to appear in a significant number in mid-century.[26] By that time, moreover, South Carolina jurists were prepared to recognize such arrangements, owing in part to an established body of English precedents.

Despite the clear advantages of separate estates to femes coverts, few women had them. They remained uncommon throughout the eighteenth and early nineteenth centuries. Evidence from South Carolina, for example, indicates that only 1 to 2 percent of couples marrying between 1790 and 1810 wrote marriage settlements. Of this small number, most were persons of wealth, although settlements of small amounts of property also appeared. It is interesting to note that South Carolina widows created marriage settlements upon remarriage with a frequency far out of proportion to their numbers in the population. Elsewhere I have discussed these and other characteristics of the South Carolinians who employed trust estates, but investigations of settlements in other jurisdictions have not been done.[27] Therefore the discussion here must focus on the evolution of rules and precedents on female separate estates, with information on the comparative use of settlements coming from case reports rather than the documents themselves.

Proper Anglo-American marriage settlements were complicated documents, usually executed in the form of trusts. Before the English case of *Rippon v. Dawding* (1769), all valid settlements had to include trustees who nominally owned the property in the name of the feme covert (the *cestui que trust*).[28] After 1769 in England and in some American jurisdictions, simple marriage settlements—contracts made directly between a woman and a man without the intervention of trustees—also sufficed to create separate estates.[29] To create a trust estate in the normal fashion, the woman, man, and trustee(s) all joined in the execution of an "indenture tripartite," a contract stipulating the terms of the settlement. This form guaranteed the knowledge and consent of all the parties, as required by law. The indenture stated the terms of the settlement and described the property included. Recording practices varied considerably from place to place, but by the end of the eighteenth century most jurisdictions had statutes specifically requiring the registration of marriage settlements.

Settlements granting women separate estates could be created either before or after marriage, but most couples executed them before marriage. Postnuptial settlements usually resulted when a wife inherited property unexpectedly, or when her husband encountered financial difficulties that made it sensible to secure some family property from creditors.[30] For both pre- and postnuptial settlements, equitable standards demanded that in cases involving separate estates men be fully apprised of the terms of their wives' settlements. Judges refused to assist a woman who deceived her fiancé or husband into expecting a large estate, only to secure it to herself through a trustee. They viewed such an action as a fraud upon the marital rights of a husband, rights that included curtesy as well as the privilege of taking all personal property owned by his wife and enjoying the rents and profits of her real estate. A fraudulent action designed to deny a husband such important legal rights automatically negated any equitable reasons for supporting a deed of settlement. It was one of the earliest principles of the English Court of Chancery that "he that hath committed Iniquity, shall not have Equity."[31] This maxim of the law remained in force with regard to marriage settlements until the nineteenth century. Courts never supported secret trusts against the marital rights of either spouse.[32]

The law recognized variations on the standard mode of creating settlements. A woman might demand a settlement as a condition for marriage. Evidence indicates that widows frequently initiated their own settlements. No doubt they had learned from experience the value of economic independence in marriage.[33] Separate estates also could be established for women through wills. When a feme covert inherited separate property, her husband could not object to the settlement. Settlement terms were finalized by the donor and the trustee only. Jointure agreements constituted another form of marriage settlement, designed in America as in England to serve as an alternative to dower. They often were made as compensation for the loss of property a woman suffered at marriage, and generally granted her no powers of control during the life of her husband, providing only for a competent maintenance after his death.[34] Significantly, jointures found support in all the jurisdictions studied, even those that refused to enforce other types of marriage settlements. Both Connecticut and Massachusetts acknowledged the validity of jointures in their statutes outlining provisions for widows.[35]

THE WIFE'S EQUITY TO A SETTLEMENT

American courts, much like the English Chancery Court, sometimes ordered men to create trust estates for their wives. Except in Pennsylvania, equity courts closely followed English law on the wife's equity to a settlement.[36] They held that any man who sued in equity for the property of his wife had a moral obligation to settle a part or all of it on her as a separate estate. In *Helms* v. *Franciscus* (1818), Chancellor Bland of Maryland wrote regarding the wife's equity, "It is a claim founded upon natural justice; it resembles the paternal care which a Court of Chancery exercises for the benefit of orphans; and assuming the place of a parent, the court requires a settlement upon the wife, upon the presumption that it demands no more than would have been insisted on by a prudent father."[37]

Bland's demand for a settlement in *Helms* v. *Franciscus* demonstrates the commitment of some American jurists to the right of women to own separate property. Chancellors not only supported the contracts individuals made for themselves but required them for some couples. By utilizing the English concept of the wife's equity to a settlement, American courts gave separate estates increased legitimacy, and bolstered the idea that married women possessed equitable rights to own property through the intervention of trustees. Most important, it became difficult for a husband to acquire his wife's inheritance without her consent. Thus, through the intervention of equity law, women gained significant new rights to property.

In cases concerning the wife's equity to a settlement, chancellors required a specific kind of disposition. It consisted of a jointure with a provision that after the widow's death the estate descend to her children. In the South Carolina case of *Postell and Smith* v. *Skirving* (1789), the court ordered O. B. Smith "to make the usual settlement on his wife; that is to say, that the same be settled under the direction of the master, in trustees, in trust for his use during their joint lives. If she survives him, then to her heirs, executors and administrators forever: If he survives her, she leaving issue, then to him for life, and after his decease, to such issue: If he survives her, without her leaving issue, (or leaving issue, such issue should die in his life time, and without issue), then to him, and his heirs, executors, and administrators for ever."[38] Similarly, Maryland's Chancellor Bland noted that the wife's equity was "in general" a provision for herself and her children after the death of her husband.[39] This was not an absolute rule. Bland also observed that under certain conditions a woman might be given control over property during her marriage rather than after the death of her husband. In *Helms v. Franciscus* a couple quarreled furiously and parted. It appeared clear to Bland and his colleagues on the bench that Lewis Helms married Anna Wandelohr only to gain access to her fortune. In his own right he possessed no money and could do nothing to support her during their separation. Given these circumstances, the chancellors felt justified in allowing Anna to retain all of the property she recently inherited from her uncle. Bland wrote, "If the husband be insolvent, then the maintenance provided for her, is always a present one. . . . His capacity to maintain her, owing to his insolvent condition, gives her an equitable right to claim an immediate provision for her own support."[40] South Carolina courts maintained a similar position. In *Rogers v. Curloss* (ca. 1825), they ordered two men to assign all of the property their wives inherited from their father to trustees. The women earned immediate rights to the property because, as the chancellor observed, "Stephen Rogers and John Jackson are both in insolvent Circumstances."[41]

A nineteenth-century New York case, *Kenny v. Udall and Kenny* (1821), discussed how much of a woman's property should be placed in a separate estate when her husband proved unable to support her.[42] As the chancellor observed, this, rather than her right to a settlement, had become the important question by the nineteenth century. He wrote, "I consider the wife's equity, as against any assignment whatsoever and to whomsoever, to be now too well settled to be shaken. The only inquiry is, *to what extent* shall her equity be carried over her personal estate, not yet reduced to the husband's possession."[43] Noting that the law had developed no precise rules on the point, he ordered a settlement of Mrs. Kenny's entire estate. Her youth (she was still a minor), and the dishonest behavior of her husband in attempting to dispose of the property, prompted the Chancery Court to treat her liberally. Slowly, courts in the United States were accepting the idea that a woman should be given the legal ability to support herself, particularly if her husband were a debtor.

Whereas most of the states with chancery courts followed English law on the wife's equity to a settlement, Pennsylvania did not, for reasons peculiar to its judicial system. Jurists there believed that they possessed no right to impose a precedent established in an English court of equity on their common law–based system. In this instance, the absence of a separate court of chancery in Pennsylvania proved detrimental to women's interests. The case that forced a confrontation on the wife's equity in Pennsylvania was *Yohe* v. *Barnet* (1808).[44] From the facts of the case it appears that Jacob Yohe became indebted to his father-in-law, Henry Barnet, for a considerable sum. He never repaid the debt, and subsequently became insolvent. At Barnet's death intestate, his administrators distributed his estate among his children, but it proved incapable of an exact division. As a result, some of the children received land on the condition that they pay their siblings a proportionate amount of its value. Yohe received no part of the real estate, but in right of his wife he was entitled to one-fifth of its value.

Henry Barnet's heirs petitioned for a reduction of Yohe's share in proportion to the debt he owed their father. Although under common law rules women's inheritances of land could not be taken to pay their husbands' debts unless they consented, here the land had been turned into money under the Pennsylvania law for distributing intestates' estates. As personal property, Mrs. Yohe's inheritance automatically became her husband's, and therefore could be employed for the payment of his debts. Chief Justice Tilghman, who wrote the majority opinion of the court, understood the relief that an English Court of Chancery would give in such a case. He wrote, "It is to be regretted that the courts in this state are not vested with the power exercised by the Court of Chancery in England, of insisting on some provision for the wife, when the husband applies to them for the purpose of getting possession of her personal property. But we have no trace of any such exercise of power by our courts."[45] Without a Pennsylvania precedent, he felt unable to create an equitable separate estate for Mrs. Yohe.

The attitude of Tilghman and his peers is inconsistent with other aspects of the history of equity law in Pennsylvania. Although the colony and state had no separate court of chancery, its common law courts were vested with the authority to decide issues on equitable principles. Surely in a case of novel impression such as *Yohe* v. *Barnet*, they could have applied the principles of English equity law and ruled in favor of the woman's right. In 1793 then Chief Justice McKean had written, "It is a lamentable truth, there is no court clothed with chancery powers, in Pennsylvania; but equity is part of our law, and it has been frequently determined in the Supreme Court, that the judges will, to effectuate the intention of the parties, consider that as executed, which ought to have been done."[46] The decision not to follow equitable precedents in *Yohe* v. *Barnet* reflects antagonism to separate estates that adversely affected creditors' rights, especially in light of the Pennsylvania statutory requirements for distributing intestates' estates. Even more important, the decision indicates the disadvantages suffered by women who lived in jurisdictions that did not have separate courts of equity. Had Pennsylvania possessed the full armory of chancery rules and precedents, it might have followed the traditional learning on the wife's equity to a settlement. Because it did not, the justices felt free to rule according to their instincts rather than established principles. Here they decided against ordering a man to settle property on his wife.

CREDITORS' OPPOSITION TO SEPARATE ESTATES

The cautious, if not antagonistic, attitude of Pennsylvania jurists to marriage settlements developed partly in response to the arguments of creditors. The usual goals in settling property on a woman were to prevent it from being taken to pay the debts of her husband and to provide her with support. For understandable reasons, creditors disliked trust estates, particularly those made after marriage. They resented the ability of a feme covert to deny them access to her separate estate and argued that husbands as well as wives could find protection under settlements. A man who lost his own estate through business misfortunes or extravagant living, they claimed, could fall back on the income from his wife's trust property. Indebted or insolvent husbands might even attempt to preserve a portion of their own fortunes by settling property on their wives fraudulently.[47] Some men did execute fraudulent deeds, and some women, although vested with the legal power to refuse their assistance, undoubtedly supported their husbands in the event of financial crisis. Creditors believed that the existence of separate estates represented a threat to their security. Significantly, the Pennsylvania rule on the wife's equity to a settlement agreed with its dower policy favoring creditors over widows. In Pennsylvania, concern for creditors' rights overshadowed concern for the rights of femes coverts.[48]

Cases of fraudulent trusts appeared throughout the eighteenth and early nineteenth centuries. Before legislative bodies enacted recording statutes, secret trusts posed a serious problem for creditors. Even after passage of the statutes, debtors and creditors argued over the chronology of their financial dealings: were debts contracted before or after the creation of settlements? Unfortunately for both sides, statutory guidelines for the creation and recording of marriage settlements were not always either clear or strict. They varied considerably from place to place. Maryland required the registration of all trust estates beginning in 1674, with the colony's first recording statute. Virginia had done the same thing by 1710, but South Carolina lawmakers

remained negligent; they did not require registration until 1785. Pennsylvanians were similarly lax; the assembly finally enacted a recording statute in
1775, but the judicial decision upholding its application to marriage settlements did not appear until 1797. New York seems never to have required the
registration of settlements, unless they fell under the provisions of the general recording statutes. In any event, no legal dispute arose in New York to
challenge the recording of a settlement.[49]

Because trust estates were not recorded in either Pennsylvania or South
Carolina until the end of the eighteenth century, they came under frequent
attack by creditors whose interests could be affected by private agreements.
The preamble to the recording statute of South Carolina highlighted the
problem: "The practice prevailing in this State of keeping marriage contracts
and deeds in the hands of those interested therein, hath been oftentimes
injurious to creditors and others, who have been induced to credit and trust
such persons under a presumption of their being possessed of an estate
subject and liable to the payment of their just debts."[50] To avoid fraudulent
deeds in the future, the statute required all persons creating marriage settlements to record them in the office of the secretary of state in Charleston
within three months after the day of execution. All earlier settlements also fell
under the terms of the act.

Similar problems prompted the passage of a recording statute in Pennsylvania, as demonstrated by the case of *Foster* v. *Whitehall* (1797).[51] Here a
woman made a settlement with her fiancé in which she reserved the right to
devise the property she brought to the marriage. She proved the deed, but
never recorded it. When she wrote her will, she devised her estate to her
husband in fee simple, but shortly after her death her heir at law sold the
premises on the assumption that they had descended to him. In the suit to
determine ownership, the Pennsylvania Supreme Court justices supported
the heir's right. They claimed that the deed of settlement could not be
enforced against purchasers and creditors because it had not been recorded.
They noted that the legislature of the state enacted a recording statute to
avoid conflicts such as this one. "The mischief to be prevented," the court
observed, "was that secret grants or agreements should not injure the right of
bona fide purchasers, without notice."[52]

The recording of marriage settlements protected married couples as well
as creditors, and therefore careful persons often registered their settlements
even before the passage of recording statutes.[53] The courts then could
safeguard the interests of all honest parties, for almost as soon as separate
estates appeared they were abused by some persons who wished to avoid the
just claims of their creditors. An early case involving a fraudulent trust

appeared in 1726, when a heavily indebted Maryland planter attempted to protect part of his estate by settling it on his daughter for her sole and separate use.[54] Although the result of his maneuver is not known, it indicates an early need to warn creditors against the existence of fraudulent trusts. The settlement Paul Pritchard made for his wife, Lydia, in 1809 exemplifies the need for recording.[55] Pritchard contracted many debts, and some judgments had been obtained against him when he decided to convey a large portion of his real and personal estate to a trustee for the benefit of his wife. After his death several years later his creditors realized that an unjust attempt had been made to defeat their claims, and they sued Lydia Pritchard for the amounts due. The court ruled in favor of the creditors when it became clear that the majority of Paul's debts were contracted before he created the trust. The deed was set aside as fraudulent and the estate confiscated for the payment of its obligations because the date of recording revealed an intent to deceive.

Similar circumstances determined the decision of the Supreme Court of Maryland in *Kipp v. Hanna* (1820).[56] Alexander Hanna, a tradesman of ordinary means, attempted to preserve his house and furniture from creditors' demands by settling them on his family. In his defense he claimed that he executed the deed before he became indebted and in consideration of the fortune of his wife, five thousand dollars, which he had received and "agreed to settle on her."[57] But the court determined that Alexander falsely represented his activities and that the total sum of his debts, amounting to between twelve and thirteen hundred dollars, was too large in proportion to the value of his estate to permit a settlement. In their opinion on the case, the justices noted that an individual with outstanding debts could create a legal trust estate for the benefit of another person; the law required only that he possess assets to repay his debts above the value of the trust property. In this instance payment of debts clearly was not possible, and so the court ordered the sale of Alexander's home to meet the demands of his creditors.

Other cases concerning the issue of indebtedness in donors and creators of settlements demonstrate a more favorable attitude toward women's right to financial security. In all but the most obvious cases of fraud, American courts supported the creation of marriage settlements. Trust estates executed without fraudulent intent, for the valuable consideration of marriage, generally found favor in court despite a man's indebted or even insolvent condition. As Tapping Reeve observed, "A marriage settlement upon the wife and her issue, by the husband, is in a very different situation from other voluntary conveyances. The latter are always fraudulent against creditors; and it is immaterial whether the creditors are prior or subsequent to the conveyance, if the grantor were indebted at the time of the conveyance." But, he continued, "A marriage settlement, provided there is nothing unreasonable and extravagant respecting it, will be valid; although there were creditors at the time of making the settlement."[58]

Chancery's support of marriage settlements created by debtors is demonstrated well by a Virginia case, *Coutts* v. *Greenhow* (1811), for here the husband proved to be a fornicator as well as a debtor, and therefore he tested the commitment of the court on several grounds.[59] The justices discovered that Reuben Coutts lived with his wife for many years, fathering several children by her, before they married. Upon marrying, he created a settlement including a jointure for his wife and provisions for the children, despite the fact that he owed money on a mortgage. After his death, his creditors sued the estate for payment on the grounds that an indebted man could not create a valid marriage settlement and that illegitimate children could be volunteers only. Their rights could not hold up against creditors.

The court dismissed both points, apparently agreeing with the argument of the Coutts's counselor that "marriage of itself is a sufficient consideration for a settlement; not marriage and previous chastity." Reuben's debts were not large enough to destroy the settlement, because at the time he arranged for the separate estate they could be satisfied out of the remainder of his property. Although the creditors ultimately suffered owing to Reuben's failure to pay taxes on the mortgaged property, the court could not help them. To the justices, the most important factor was Reuben's desire to give property to his wife in consideration of marriage. Despite their earlier "criminal conversation," this was an honorable step. As Justice Cabell interpreted the case, "So far as relates to Mrs. Coutts, it seems difficult to imagine on what ground a doubt could have been founded. That marriage is a valuable consideration seems to be so firmly established as a general principle, as to preclude the necessity of referring to authorities."[60]

We see, therefore, strong support for settlements created in good faith even by debtors. The fact was inescapable that separate estates provided important security to all family members; supporting them was good public policy. Created openly and recorded, they gave couples an honest way to prevent creditors from seizing at least some portion of family property in the event of insolvency. Settlements therefore became more widely accepted and employed as the financial prospects of male heads of household became less secure over time. Historians of the nineteenth century, for example, have demonstrated a clear connection between the economic fluctuations and depressions associated with modern capitalism and the rise of new attitudes toward married women's independent property rights. As Norma Basch puts it in her study of the New York married women's property act, "precipitous dips in the economy" placed pressure on lawmakers to enact reform legislation. She concludes, "Much of the early support for a married women's statute focused on the economic dislocations of men; considerations of women were often secondary. Just as debtor exemption laws for household items and tools eased the lot of farmers, artisans, and some wage earners and petty traders, so might a statute separating the wife's property from that of her husband have a similar effect."[61] In the present study of separate estates before 1830, we can already see lawmakers' concern with protecting women's property from the creditors of their husbands. Even during the colonial period, courts recognized the inequity of employing wives' estates to pay husbands' personal or business debts. As the economy became increasingly unstable, these sentiments grew until by the middle of the nineteenth century Americans were ready to grant all women, not just those with separate estates, independent property rights. Thus the foundations of the radical nineteenth-century reforms are found entrenched in American law well before the Revolution.

THE DOCTRINE OF INTENTIONS

In decisions such as *Coutts* v. *Greenhow*, chancellors demonstrated their support of women's property rights. To courts of equity, settlements seemed a just compensation for the legal rights women lost at marriage. The counsel for Mrs. Coutts put the issue succinctly when he noted, "The agreement in support of a voluntary bond applies, a fortiori, to a marriage contract; first, because the woman, by entering into marriage, gives up many privileges; and secondly, because marriage alone is a valuable consideration."[62] By the middle of the eighteenth century, chancery courts had come to believe that every woman possessed a right to a separate estate. The doctrine of a wife's equity to a settlement and chancellors' willingness to recognize marriage settlements written by persons in debt demonstrate the principle. In addition, chancellors were making it easier to create separate estates by will or deed of gift. Initially they required donors to use specific, formulaic words, such as "to her sole and separate use," when giving property to a married woman, and to appoint trustees. Later, however, a donor simply had to indicate an intention that the property belong to the woman alone, independent of her husband.[63] The courts came to assume that a devise or bequest to a married woman was intended for her sole and separate use, even when words establishing a separate estate did not appear. Under the "doctrine of intentions,"

as it was called, a friend or relative simply had to express a desire for a
separate estate in order to create one; he did not have to take the necessary
legal steps, such as appointing trustees.[64]

South Carolina courts adopted the doctrine of intentions early in the
nineteenth century. *Johnson v. Thompson* (1814) exemplifies judicial use of the
guideline.[65] Here a father made a gift of personal property to his married
daughter. Her husband claimed the property and disposed of it for his own
benefit. After the woman's death her children contested his disposition. They
stated that their grandfather intended the property to go to his daughter as a
separate estate, free from the control of her husband. In deciding favorably
for the claim by the children, the Court of Appeals observed that because the
gift had been made to a feme covert, the words of the deed had to be
examined closely to determine intent. Here the words "fairly inferred" that
the estate was designed to be a separate one, and therefore the father had
possessed no right to dispose of the property.[66] The implementation of
this liberal policy in South Carolina indicates strong support for marriage
settlements.

Somewhat later, in *Lowndes v. Champneys* (1821), the chancellor explained
the position of South Carolina on the interpretation of settlements: "It is
immaterial in what form or phrase a trust of this nature creating a seperate
[*sic*] estate for the wife is described—technical language is not necessary—All
that is requisite is that the intention of the gift should appear manifestly to be
for the wife's seperate enjoyment without which the Court will not suffer the
legal rights of the husband to be superseded."[67] An inference, or the circumstances of a gift, induced the court to rule in favor of the creation either of a
separate estate or of particular powers of control over such an estate. In this
case the court supported a woman's devise of stocks purchased with the
interest of her trust property. Although she and her husband were supposed
to share the profits, he had used them consistently to purchase stock in her
name, which he then placed into the hands of her trustees. In the opinion of
the court, such activities by the husband constituted adequate proof of his
intention to give the stock to his wife for her sole and separate use. Otherwise, he could have appropriated the profits for himself. His actions vested
the woman's devise with the mark of authority, for as the chancellor wrote, "It
appears to me that a gift from a husband to Trustees implies an intention that
it should be to her [his wife's] separate use—He did not mean to do an Act
which in its operation should be a mere nullity and a mockery."[68]

Just as Pennsylvania courts refused to adopt the doctrine of the wife's
equity to a settlement, they also failed to keep abreast of developments in the
doctrine of intentions. Unlike South Carolina chancellors, the justices of the

Pennsylvania Supreme Court would not recognize the creation of a separate estate by will unless the wording was explicit. Their position is revealed in an intriguing case of family disharmony, *Torbert* v. *Twining and Story* (1795).[69]

When David Twining made his will, he devised certain lands to his married daughter, Beulah Torbert. Realizing later that the devise would place the property under the control of his son-in-law, Twining wrote a codicil in which he attempted to create a separate estate by placing the property into the hands of trustees. Under the terms of the trust, Beulah would receive the rents and profits of the land, but could exercise no control over its management. According to later testimony, "The testator declared in his last sickness, that his intention in making his codicil was, that the real estate therein devised to his daughter Beulah, should be for her sole and seperate [*sic*] use, and after he had made his codicil, he declared, that he expected he had effected his purpose, and that her husband could not intermeddle with it."[70]

Unfortunately, the will itself did not state that Beulah's inheritance was meant for her separate use. In an effort to convince the Supreme Court that such a phrase was unnecessary, counsel for the trustees argued, "No certain terms are necessary to vest a separate use of chattels in a feme covert. 3 Atky. 393. Technical words are not necessary to make a separate trust for the wife." He almost succeeded in convincing Justice Smith, who admitted to having "serious doubts on the subject." Smith admitted the relevance of the cited English precedent, and noted another one equally supportive of the trust. He also understood the effect that the doctrine of the wife's equity to a settlement would have if such a case were tried in England. Citing several authorities, Smith pointed out to his colleagues that "in England, the plaintiff's remedy against the trustees must have been in chancery, and if the husband came into equity to demand these profits, they would put terms on him and oblige him to make a proper provision for his wife."[71]

Despite such a clear presentation of English law on the doctrine of intentions and the wife's equity, a majority of the members of the Pennsylvania court decided against enforcing the separate estate. Their reason was unrelated to the issues under consideration, and reveals the danger to women of living in jurisdictions without independent courts of chancery. In *Torbert* v. *Twining and Story*, the Supreme Court exercised the ultimate power of an equity court, deciding a case on the basis of an arbitrary idea of justice rather than established precedent. As Justice Yeates reported to the court, "Even in England, I doubt greatly whether the Lord Chancellor would interpose his authority, if the same facts were disclosed to him, as came to the knowledge of the Chief Justice and myself, at the last assizes for Bucks county, judicially." He then revealed the scandalous information that Beulah Torbert had attempted to sue her husband for divorce in Connecticut, where more liberal standards on grounds for divorce prevailed than in Pennsylvania. One can almost see Chief Justice McKean shaking his head as he assented to Yeates's words by claiming, "The chancellor clearly would not interpose in such a case."[72] Both Yeates and McKean misunderstood the freedom English chancellors held at the end of the eighteenth century to judge cases against established precedent. Their lack of comprehension of equitable rules on women's separate estates led to a dangerous precedent in Pennsylvania law, as the decision on *Torbert* v. *Twining and Story* found support in subsequent cases.

Outside Pennsylvania, chancery courts maintained closer ties to their roots in English law. In addition to supporting precedents that gave women the right to employ separate estates, chancellors also became willing to interpret unclear wording of settlement terms for the benefit of women. If coercion was not an issue, courts assumed that the intent of settlements was to give the *cestui que trust*, rather than the trustee, active powers of control.[73] Although in the early years of the use of settlements, trustees played active roles and *cestui que trusts* remained passive, by the mid-eighteenth century American couples commonly gave trustees little or no control over settlement property. Many women with separate estates came to rely on trustees only for advice or protection, while directing the management of trust estates alone or with their husbands.[74]

FEME COVERT POWERS OVER SEPARATE ESTATES

Each marriage settlement contained various clauses for delineating control over settlement property. Couples could place property under the management of trustees, or they could give trustees no managerial powers at all, reducing them to figureheads. Occasionally husbands retained control over their wives' estates, and in other cases femes coverts managed their own property. The powers retained by women became significant for determining their level of independence. Some trusts gave women extensive authority over their own property, whereas others gave them none at all but instead directed trustees to pay them the rents and profits of their estates. Some settlements gave women one privilege of control while denying others. In the same vein, a woman whose settlement gave her rights to the rents and profits of her property could not regulate the principal; it remained in the hands of trustees, who made all investment decisions.

Eighteenth-century legal developments supported women's ability to control separate estates. Under passive trusts ("passive" here refers to the role of the trustee), women contracted, mortgaged, or gave away their property, often without the need to obtain consent from either husband or trustee.[75] Above all else, precise wording in a settlement became the key to its effectiveness. What powers a woman held over her separate estate and what rights her husband or trustee retained needed clear delineation.[76] Carefully constructed settlements specified each restriction or power of control separately and included sections allowing or disallowing certain basic changes in the settled property. Settlements provided the greatest degree of protection when they had precise terms, although often it was difficult for families to anticipate future situations or problems and create agreements designed to meet them.

When women exercised powers of control over separate property, courts held them liable for the debts they contracted on their own accounts, and the trust property could be taken from them and applied toward their debts.[77] Although their estates became liable, however, women theoretically could not be imprisoned for debt, even when they held property under trusts. The estate of a woman could be seized, but not her person, for the law would not interfere with the husband's right to the company and services of his wife.[78] The provision also stemmed from a fear of male coercion. As long as American courts believed that men could force women into executing damaging business agreements, they could not hold femes coverts fully responsible for their actions in executing contracts.

For many women, one of the most important reasons for creating a separate estate was protecting it from their husbands' creditors. They therefore included clauses in their settlements stating that the property could not be applied for the payment of husbands' debts. The restriction might extend only to the profits of the estate, or to both profits and principal. Yet women with powers of control over their separate estates could use the property for their husbands' benefit despite such clauses, and husbands might attempt to pressure their wives into assistance of this sort. Therefore, in creating settlements for the benefit of daughters or other female relatives, some individuals perceived a need to forbid certain kinds of future changes in the nature of the trust estates. They feared the powers of their beneficiaries to destroy the usefulness of trusts by conveying them to their husbands or wasting the principal. In 1752, for example, Ann Slann had asked the South Carolina Court of Chancery to appoint her husband as the trustee for her separate estate. Despite the obvious contradictions in allowing a husband to serve in such a capacity, the court agreed.[79] To protect women such as Ann Slann from coercion, or simply to prevent them from making damaging managerial decisions, the creators of trust estates sometimes included clauses forbidding changes or certain kinds of potentially harmful dispositions in their settlements. A deed of trust might state that it could not be altered in any way, or it might include provisions allowing a feme covert control over rents and profits, but not the principal.

Chancery courts occasionally acted to protect women from coercion even without the backing of settlement clauses restricting women's actions. Their decisions demonstrate judicial belief in the power men could and did exercise over women within the family. Coercion was not simply a legal theory in the minds of early American jurists; it was a reality they had to confront in handling cases on women's property. *Bethune v. Beresford* (1790), for example, demonstrates that South Carolina jurists feared male coercion and took seriously their responsibility to protect women from its effects.[80] Here a man, heavily in debt, entreated his wife to use her separate estate as collateral to obtain credit for their necessary living expenses. She did so, but later reconsidered and attempted to void her agreement. She claimed that a wife could not be held liable for contracts her husband asked her to make. She asked the court "whether her signing said bond binds the settled estate: And said Ann prays the court to consider that it was in a manner compulsory on her to sign said bonds; and that the natural affection a woman entertains for her husband, is so great, that at his request, and to ward off difficulties, she would join him in many transactions which might tend to injure her unless protected by the court."[81] Although there was no evidence of force or threats in the case, her arguments convinced the court. Chancellor Mathews wrote, "The situation of Mrs. B. is not that of a free agent. A wife witnessing the distress of her husband, would do any act to relieve him. This court is bound to protect her against her own misguided acts, and prevent her ruin."[82] They refused to allow the creditors access to the principal of her separate estate because they could not imagine a woman being truly independent of her husband. Men's influence was pervasive.

Almost forty years later, Maryland jurists acted on the basis of similar fears. *Lowry v. Tiernan and Williamson* (1827) determined that a feme covert entrusted with the profits of stock could not order her trustees to sell the stock and reinvest the proceeds according to the directions of her husband.[83] The court considered its decision carefully. Fear of coercion finally forced the judges to rule against Mrs. Lowry's order to change the nature of her property, on the grounds that her marriage settlement had given her no powers over the principal of the estate beyond the right to make a will if she had no children. In passing judgment, the court noted that the settlement was created to prevent Mr. Lowry from possessing the estate of his wife. How could they ignore a clear intention and give him control over the principal? The court opinion reflected their fear of coercion: "Mrs. Lowry is, besides, under the control of her husband, and the modifications proposed are for his benefit in part. . . . Are we not, in the absence of all evidence to the contrary, under these circumstances, to found the presumption, growing out of the legal relations of the parties, that this change in the trust is sought to be obtained by that influence and control which springs from their marital relations, and not from the free exercise of her own uncontrolled will and desire?"[84] With this uncertainty in mind, they would not sanction a change for the husband's benefit, even though Mrs. Lowry requested it.

When a settlement did not include any provision restricting the right of the woman to control her property, she could change or even dissolve her trust estate at any time.[85] Similarly, a woman left free to act as she pleased did not, by the end of the eighteenth century, need the permission of her trustees to exercise specific acts of control. Reeve noted that the purpose of retaining a trustee was not to restrict a woman's freedom but to protect her from the coercion of her husband.[86] Trustees were, in fact, obliged to follow the directions of a feme covert with powers of active control over her estate, and if they refused the woman could sue them in chancery. Trustees Thomas Barton and John Dickinson, for example, complied with the wishes of Elizabeth Stone when, before her death, she directed them to give her separate estate to her husband. Although the terms of her settlement arranged for descent of the estate to her children, and in lieu of children to her mother and siblings, the trustees reported that they acted at Elizabeth's "repeated instance and request."[87] The Supreme Court of Pennsylvania supported the disposition because the settlement specified that the estate was "to be at her disposal, to give to whom she should think proper in her lifetime."[88] Therefore they ruled that the trustees executed their trust properly.

Although some women wanted to dissolve their trusts or change the terms for the benefit of their husbands, more often they made adjustments to remove powers from men and invest them in themselves. At the time of marriage it might seem most appropriate for a woman to give her husband powers of active control over her property. Later, however, when he encountered financial misfortunes that threatened her estate, she might want to rescind those powers. By inserting a clause in her settlement allowing future changes in the trust, a woman who initially did not want to remove property from the control of her husband could leave it in his hands, confident that at a future date she held the power to restrict his managerial rights.[89]

As the situation of Elizabeth Stone demonstrates, the particular wording of a marriage settlement could be significant. Settlements constructed with care specified each power of control separately, to ensure a woman's various rights, and contained clauses allowing or disallowing certain basic changes in the property. It is significant, however, that when doubts arose over the meaning of settlements, as they inevitably did, courts interpreted terms to give women the widest possible control. They assumed that this was the intention, and intent rather than wording became the most important factor in judicial decisions.

CHANGING ATTITUDES TOWARD COERCION

Because women possessed powers of active control over the property they owned under settlements, jurists faced a problem in applying the traditional rules on coercion to conveyances of women's separate estates. Did women need special protection when they conveyed lands they held in their own names, supposedly free from the control of their husbands? The question proved a difficult one and prompted considerable legal debate in the early nineteenth century.

Under the laws of England as administered by courts of equity, married women did not have to undergo private examinations when they conveyed settlement property. With regard to her separate estate a woman became a feme sole.[90] She could do anything she pleased with the property as though she were unmarried, providing the settlement itself included no specific limitations. The redefinition of a married woman in this manner was a legal fiction, designed to reconcile the contradiction of permitting settlements in the first place. Although English jurists accepted separate estates for married women, they still felt compelled to administer them according to established legal rules. Thus, if a woman wanted to assume the position of a feme sole with regard to her own property, she did not, as a feme sole, require a private examination to protect her from male coercion. According to Henry Desaussure of South Carolina, this principle established itself in English chancery practice over a period of about fifty years in the mid-eighteenth century.[91]

In *Ewing* v. *Smith* (1811), the courts of South Carolina first confronted the issue of private examinations during conveyances of separate estates.[92] The case concerned the validity of a mortgage deed created by Ann Smith to satisfy the creditors of her husband, Roger. Could they allow her to convey her separate estate for the payment, not of her own debts, but of her husband's? In addition, despite the fact that men did not join with their wives in deeds executed under marriage settlements, could they allow a married woman to convey without a private examination? Ann Smith inherited considerable property from her father. Some of it he secured to her separate use by a trust deed stipulating that it could not be used to pay Roger Smith's debts. But when Roger became indebted for large sums, he asked his wife to mortgage the lands she held under the trust as security. She agreed, the couple failed to meet the repayment schedule, and at Roger's death his creditors sued for possession of the trust property.

Ann Smith's father had wanted to give her separate property to ensure her financial security in the event she outlived her husband. By her own action, however, she had destroyed that security, and her right to do so formed the basis of an extensive legal discussion in South Carolina. Following English precedent, the Court of Chancery ruled on circuit that she could make a disposition of her own property without a private examination. Chancellor Desaussure studied the English decisions with care and decided in accordance with their line of reasoning. Separate estates gave women unlimited powers, he wrote, and although it was unfortunate that wives might be subjected to the coercion of their husbands in executing conveyances, the courts could do little to protect them. When wives held separate estates, the law regarded them as femes soles in administering the property.

The case posed an interesting problem for South Carolina jurists. As the discussion by Desaussure revealed, the only reliable authorities on the question were English; few American cases had dealt with it. But in the wake of the Revolution, South Carolinians felt uncomfortable in relying exclusively on English precedents.[93] Owing in part, then, to a new feeling of independence from English precedent, the Court of Appeals overturned the decision made by Chancellor Desaussure. In his opinion on the case, Justice Waties agreed that a married woman who owned separate property ideally should be free to alienate it as she pleased, either to her husband or to any other person. But he disagreed with Desaussure's statement that the courts had no obligation to protect a feme covert from the coercion of her husband. Although he believed that an absolute right of ownership meant an absolute right of disposition, he saw the rule as "applicable only to persons of full legal capacity." Women were not such persons in early nineteenth-century society, and Waties found it strange "that English judges should have ever lost sight of the common law so far as to apply it [the rule] to a married woman."[94] In executing conveyances, he wanted all married women to have separate examinations, as a means of protecting them.

Waties felt justified in determining *Ewing* v. *Smith* against the weight of English precedents. In his mind the precedents placed women in an unfair position by removing what slight protection the law offered them. Moreover, after the Revolution South Carolina had no obligation to adhere to English law. In fact, Waties wrote, "I should feel that I was not fulfilling the purpose for which my country has been pleased to place me here, if instead of exercising my own judgment in the best manner I could in construing and applying any principle to cases as they occur, I should implicitly follow the construction given to it in similar cases by the judge of a foreign Court."[95]

In Maryland, despite judicial fears concerning coercion as demonstrated in cases such as *Lowry* v. *Tiernan and Williamson*, discussed above, the courts followed English rather than South Carolina law on the question of private examinations. They held that women with separate estates possessed full powers to sell or mortgage, just as though they were unmarried. No private examinations were necessary when settlements recognized active rights of management. Maryland reached this decision in *Tiernan* v. *Poor* (1829), a case in which a wife mortgaged her separate estate to provide security for a six-hundred-dollar debt owed by her husband, and subsequently lost it to his creditors.[96] Under her settlement Deborah Poor possessed the right to dispose of her trust property, but her lawyer maintained that as a feme covert she could mortgage it only after submitting to a private examination. No examination had been taken, he argued, and therefore the mortgage deed was void. Opposing counsel objected to the argument, citing the English precedents that South Carolina rejected. He reasoned that with regard to her separate estate Deborah was a feme sole, that as such she held all rights of management over her property, and that courts of law had no right to restrict her by requiring separate examinations.

The Maryland Court of Appeals supported English practice in *Tiernan* v. *Poor*, maintaining that women possessed active powers of control over their own property. If a wife chose to convey her estate to pay the debts of her husband or otherwise support him, that was her decision and the court would recognize its validity. They pointed out that "she was never intended to be placed in a state of pupilage with regard to her property, but left free to act as she pleased, with regard to it."[97]

Significantly, when *Tiernan* v. *Poor* was first tried before the Court of Chancery in 1826, the verdict had been different. Then Chancellor Bland dismissed the suit of Dudley Poor's creditors because he believed that the terms of Deborah's marriage settlement did not allow her to use the trust property to pay her husband's debts. Bland apparently agreed with the stand taken by the judiciary of South Carolina, but the Court of Appeals overturned his decision. The same pattern occurred in New York, where Chancellor James Kent argued against allowing women to act as femes soles with regard to their separate estates in *Trustees of the Methodist Episcopal Church* v. *Jaques* (1817).[98] Like Bland, he saw his decision overturned on appeal.[99] Kent later defended his position in his *Commentaries on American Law*. He noted that the decision of the New York Court of Errors "renders the wife more completely and absolutely a *feme sole* in respect to her separate property, than the English decisions would seem to authorize; and it, unfortunately, withdraws from the wife those checks that were intended to preserve her more entirely from that secret and insensible, but powerful marital influence, which might be exerted unduly, and yet in a manner to baffle all inquiry and detection."[100]

Kent was speaking, of course, of coercion. Under English precedent as adopted in Maryland and New York, a woman with a separate estate did not warrant the same kind of protection as a woman without one. Although the law assumed that femes coverts could be controlled by their husbands, and therefore developed a procedure for guarding against coercion, courts did not extend this protection to include the feme covert with a marriage settlement. Except in South Carolina, she could sell or mortgage without a private examination, even when she did so to help her husband. She also could act without consulting her trustee, ostensibly interposed to protect her from coercion, when her settlement did not specifically require such consultation. Finally, unless the terms of her settlement denied her certain powers, she possessed the right to take any action to manage her own property. Thus, although settlements almost always aimed at protecting women's estates from the debts of their husbands, an individual woman could use her property to help her husband, and receive no judicial protection from coercion.[101]

For Bland, Kent, and the South Carolina Supreme Court judiciary, such a policy was contradictory. They saw no reason to apply two different standards on married women's property rights. Given the acceptance of coercion as a legal principle in the early nineteenth century, they were right. If judges believed in the efficacy of male coercion, they should have taken steps to protect all women from its effects. In this regard, South Carolina's decision on *Ewing* v. *Smith* was beneficial to women despite its paternalistic qualities, and the decisions of Maryland and New York on *Tiernan* v. *Poor* and *Jaques* v. *The Methodist Episcopal Church* (the appeal) were discriminatory against women with separate property.

If we take a long historical view of female separate estates, however, a different interpretation is possible. Although the precedents on female powers over separate estates appear discriminatory, it also is clear that coercion as a legal principle was weakening by the 1820s. In part, the New York and Maryland chancellors were destroying the principle by granting married women more and more extensive rights to own and control property. They could not both support women's financial independence and claim that women were liable to pressure from their husbands. Thus the stand advocated by Kent, Bland, and others represented a commitment to earlier attitudes toward marital relations, and not necessarily the attitudes of the day. By studying in detail the evolution of one area of the law on separate estates—agreements executed without trustees—this point can be elucidated further. Once courts removed the necessity of employing intermediary parties for the establishment of trusts and allowed spouses to contract directly with each other, they further weakened the principle of coercion.

THE PROBLEM OF DEALING WITH TRUSTEES

Although courts of equity favored women in their decisions on the creation and management of trust estates, they could not always provide adequate protection. In particular, many women had to deal with incompetent, negligent, or dishonest trustees on a daily basis. Instances of abuse and ignorance demonstrate how poorly the system of separate estates worked for many women, denying them full control over their property and placing it instead in the hands of others less competent and interested than themselves.

It was not unheard of for a *cestui que trust* to be in a position in which the only way she could gain access to her own property was to sue her trustee in chancery. Some trustees simply were negligent and did not act as quickly as desired. Others were incompetent and made poor business decisions for which the trust estate became liable. At times, trustees and *cestui que trust* argued over questions of management. When trustees held powers of control, there was little or nothing that a woman could do in opposition to their wishes, short of prosecuting a lawsuit.

A Marylander, Elizabeth Wilson, found it particularly difficult to deal with her trustee, Vernon Hebb, who was her brother.[102] Elizabeth married and traveled to Europe with her husband, leaving Vernon to manage her plantation in Maryland. By 1767, when their correspondence began, she was a young widow living with her sister's family in London and trying to understand the workings of both her own property and that of her deceased husband. There were many debts to pay and the estate of Mr. Wilson was proving insufficient to cover them, a situation, Elizabeth wrote, that "prays [*sic*] on my mind and hurts my health. . . . I must submit to the hard censure of those who remain unsatisfied, this is a misery dear brother I wish not my greatest enemy to feel."[103]

The correspondence between Elizabeth and Vernon was a lengthy one, filled with her anxiety concerning her property and his nonchalance in informing her about it. She had little money and dreaded the dependence on relatives her situation made necessary. Repeatedly she wrote to Vernon, asking for information and money. She received little of either. In 1768 she wrote, "I am at a loss what to do with myself, except you make me some remittance soon. The small stock of cloaths I had when my dear Mr. Wilson left me are now near worn out, and it is not in my power to renew them, which I cant help thinking is a hardship." Vernon responded with a promise to send money as soon as he could, but reported that he had not yet collected the rent on her plantation nor sold the tobacco, because prices were so low. In 1771 Elizabeth asked for information about her property, writing "I should think my Plantation and Negroes sufficient to make me independent. I should take it kind if you will consider this, and acquaint me how my account stands with you, etc."[104] He responded by noting that her yearly profits depended so much on the market price of tobacco that they were difficult to estimate, but he believed that she could count on a yearly income of sixty pounds. It is significant that in a long letter of family news he devoted only a few lines to the management of her property.

This pattern in their correspondence continued for several years, until Elizabeth stopped receiving letters from her brother entirely during the years of the Revolution. Eventually she was forced to return to America to oversee her property herself, for, as she reported, "In the Year 1783 January 10th I wrote to E. Fenwick [a brother-in-law] to make inquiry respecting my property in Maryland, supposing that Vernon Hebb could not be living having not at that time heard from him since October 1779."[105] She learned from Fenwick that Vernon was alive and enjoyed good health. At that point Elizabeth decided to return to Maryland and turn her estate "into money," as she put it. Her suit in Chancery charged Vernon Hebb with incompetence and negligence. Deciding that a full investigation of the records was necessary to determine responsibility, the chancellor ordered the master to study the management of the Hebb plantations and settle accounts between the siblings. Before the suit ended, Vernon had paid his sister a debt of several hundred pounds.

When trustees controlled the assets of a trust fund, their poor management decisions could place female estates in financial difficulty. A significant South Carolina decision of 1809 ruled that a trust estate was liable for the debts contracted by a trustee in managing the estate, even though he acted unwisely. In *Cater* v. *Eveleigh* it was shown that a trustee purchased a saw gin to increase production on the plantation he managed, but he did not pay the full price of the machinery and eventually was sued in Chancery for the remainder of the debt.[106] In defense of the *cestui que trust*, the attorney general argued that a trust estate must not be held liable for the acts of the trustee. Granting trustees full authority to control the resources of their trusts was too dangerous. An uninformed or unsuspecting woman would be placed entirely in the power of her agent in such instances, "for the misconduct of the trustee might ruin the separate estate, if his acts were binding on it."[107] Ruling against the attorney general, the Chancery ordered payment out of the trust estate. Jurists in South Carolina believed that the danger to creditors of not enforcing payment was greater than the danger to femes coverts of subjecting their property to the actions of their trustees.

The negligence of trustees could have disastrous effects if they died unexpectedly, leaving the property they controlled in disarray. In most cases it was relatively easy for a new trustee to assume control, but at times a trustee did not differentiate clearly between his own property and that of the trust estate, or he appointed executors who were careless of the distinction. In some cases newly assigned trustees, often named not by the *cestui que trust* but by the original trustee, were simply not as solicitous of the obligation their position entailed as they should have been. Thus, in the case of *Hibben v. Scott and Brockington* (1788), we learn that Mary Hibben's trustee, James Fowler, always had conducted the management of her estate fairly and responsibly. That situation changed, however, with his death and the assumption of his duties by his son and heir.[108] A combination of negligence and ineptitude in the management of Mary Hibben's property forced her to live without income from her estate for eight years, until she won a suit in Chancery for payment.

Motives of greed often aggravated negligence or poor judgment in trustees, especially when a trustee and *cestui que trust* were related. Thus two uncles forced a young woman and her husband to accept a settlement benefiting them in case of her death. A man convinced his incompetent, alcoholic brother to grant him management of his property in an attempt to defraud the brother's wife of dower. And a brother convinced his sister to give him control over her estate in exchange for a "competent" maintenance. When this woman sued in Chancery, the court learned that for years he had enjoyed her property while providing her with only the barest essentials for survival.[109]

A startling case of family intrigue concerns the treatment Mary Philips received from her son, Edmund Jenings. Mary received three hundred pounds sterling by the will of her husband. Edmund held it in trust for her, but he never paid her the interest as directed in the will. In 1778 Mary finally initiated a suit against her own son in Chancery. At that time, to avoid a lawsuit, they reached a private agreement whereby Mary permitted Edmund to keep the principal sum of three hundred pounds if he would pay her thirty pounds a year for support. Mary withdrew her complaint, "hoping that as she had no other property, or Dependence for Support that the said Edmund Jenings would have been Punctual in paying the said annual sum."[110] He was not punctual, however, defaulting on the very first payment. She began another suit several years later for the amount of the bond Edmund had given her (one thousand pounds) pursuant to their first agreement. In an attempt to avoid paying anything to his mother for as long as possible, Edmund brought a writ of error and appealed the case to the Court of Appeals. As a result of his negligence and the delay, Mary became totally destitute and, as she reported, was "compelled to live in the Alms House of Ann Arundel County and hath wholly been supported by the public charity and the voluntary contributions of private individuals for several years past."[111]

Before a judgment could be made on the appeal, Edmund had convinced his bondsman to give up the bond, whereby Mary lost all grounds for her suit at common law. She then began a suit at Chancery to gain the original three hundred pounds left to her by her husband. She won the suit, instituted for her benefit by a trustee for the poorhouse, in 1791. At that time the court, which was sharply critical of Edmund's behavior, ordered him to support his mother according to the terms of their arbitration agreement.

This dispute between mother and son did not result solely from the callous negligence of the son. Testimony by the parties and witnesses indicates that tensions and animosities common to many families aggravated this property dispute. The major problem was the demand Mary made for cash payments—money she could use to maintain herself as she pleased. Edmund, hoping to retain his father's estate for himself, did not want to give his mother cash payments, but he did not heartlessly abandon her to the almshouse. His deposition reported that he repeatedly asked her to live with him in his own house. He perceived her refusal to do so as arrogance and wastefulness. Perhaps Edmund did not realize that for some women there was little difference between family charity and public alms.

The dangers and inconveniences of dealing with trust estates often caused women, or those acting with their best interests in mind, to restrict the degree of control granted to trustees. In the second half of the eighteenth century trustees usually were employed for form's sake only. Control over the trust property went to a woman, to her husband, or to them both together. In South Carolina, this pattern is found almost exclusively.[112] In addition, as shown above, courts of equity became more and more willing to assume that

women held powers of control when there were no settlement clauses restricting their activities. This trend may have been part of an attempt to
prevent corrupt dealings by trustees.

SETTLEMENTS WITHOUT TRUSTEES

In 1769 the English Chancery reacted to the problems of dealing with
trustees by establishing a precedent making them superfluous for the creation of separate estates. In *Rippon* v. *Dawding* the chancellors supported a
marriage settlement made directly between a woman and her fiancé, without
the intervention of trustees.[113] They ruled, ironically, that in such cases it was
appropriate to view the husband as trustee for his wife. The decision marked
a significant development in the law of women's property rights. For the first
time women with separate estates could own and administer them in their
own names. The new rule indicated a basic change in attitude toward female
contractual rights and women's rights to own property in general.

One of the earliest American cases dealing with a simple marriage settlement appeared on the docket of the Supreme Court of Pennsylvania in
1793.[114] It concerned the legality of an antenuptial agreement written in
1774 by Margaret and Matthew Henderson. Although Margaret had taken
the precaution of arranging for a separate estate before her marriage, she did
not create a trust with powers of administration. Instead, she and her fiancé
agreed between themselves that she would possess full powers to dispose of
her real and personal estate at any time during the marriage. In creating her
settlement, Margaret wanted to ensure her own and her family's continued
ownership of the land.

Margaret died childless before her husband, having executed a will in
which she gave the property to various nieces and nephews. Her heir at law
received nothing, however, and he decided to contest the will. The arguments of his attorney centered on two points: first, that the will of any married
woman was void at common law, and second, that marriage settlements
allowing devises under equity law were enforceable only when trustees administered the estate. A simple marriage settlement such as the one created
by the Hendersons had no effect on the legal heir.

Both arguments were true at the time *Barnes* v. *Hart* appeared. A feme
covert could not devise her real property unless she made formal arrangements for a separate estate, and in Pennsylvania the courts enforced marriage
settlements only when they existed in the form of trusts. Despite precedents
establishing these points in Pennsylvania, the attorney who argued in favor of

the will convinced the court to support it by emphasizing the new English rule. He quoted the following passage from the first volume of Wood's *Conveyancing*, which noted that the English Court of Chancery supported simple marriage settlements:

It was formerly doubted whether marriage was not such a suspension of the capacity of the wife to execute any effective conveyance of her property, as deprived her of the power of assenting to any alienation even of real estate, under settlement to her separate use, unless through the medium of a power, or by the interposition of a fine. But it is now settled that a wife has a capacity by her consent, of making a valid contract as to her separate estate, and that therefore a mere covenant or agreement between a woman and her intended husband, inserted in marriage articles, that she shall have a power to dispose of her real estate, without any estate being vested in trustees, out of which an appointment, by virtue of the power, may enure, will bind her heir, not only when the power attaches upon a trust, but likewise when it is applicable to a legal estate.[115]

Cases tried by the English Court of Chancery fully established the new ruling. Pennsylvania jurists therefore felt justified in following the principle. If a man wanted to consent, through a settlement, to future dispositions by his wife of real property, they would sanction that decision. Perhaps they saw the ruling as an extension of the power a husband held to allow his wife to bequeath or convey her personal estate, and his ability to recognize by tacit consent her right to contract with family property. In any case, simple agreements marked an equitable advancement in the law on separate estates and one that Justice Shippen noted was "perfectly consonant to the genius and spirit of the laws of this government." Although Shippen and his colleagues realized the purport of their decision favoring an extension of female powers, they did not seem perturbed by the possibilities. As Justice Bradford wrote, "It is easy to foresee the consequences of this decision; but it seems fully justified by the later authorities, and I am perfectly satisfied with the justice and policy of it."[116] Equitable principles forced the court to support the attempt of Margaret and Matthew Henderson to create an informal estate with powers of disposition for Margaret.

In Maryland, the first decision supporting a marriage settlement executed without trustees appeared in 1797. *Beall v. King and Woolford* also concerned the validity of a woman's will, written pursuant to an agreement made between herself and her husband before marriage.[117] The direct contract specifically allowed her to devise her own property to children by previous marriages if she died before her husband. During a serious illness Ann Woolford informed her husband, Levin, that she wanted to write her will. But Levin, believing that he already had provided well for Ann's children himself, refused to allow her to devise the property away from him and his children. Ann was so upset by their argument that she determined to broach the subject no more, but proceeded to write her will secretly, with the help of friends.

Levin contested the will after the death of his wife. He claimed that because they executed their prenuptial agreement privately, and because it did not include trustees, it was invalid. The Chancery Court of Maryland refused to accept his interpretation, however, and ruled in favor of the simple marriage settlement. As the chancellor noted, "It would be extraordinary indeed, if this Court should decide that engagement to be void . . . when it appears too, that he has had the full benefit of that consideration [marriage], for which he entered into the engagement."[118]

In 1818 the Maryland Court of Chancery indicated its continuing support for the decision on *Beall* v. *King and Woolford* when it enforced a private separation agreement made without trustees. At that time the judges noted the progress that had been made in the area of women's property rights. They observed that in earlier days simple agreements were disregarded on the grounds that a husband's right to the property of his wife could not be impeached, but in the nineteenth century such agreements were approved. The words demonstrate an acceptance of women's right to own property and point to the reforms of the mid-nineteenth century:

> It has been thought that, without putting at hazard any regulation necessary to ensure conjugal felicity, a woman might, very beneficially for herself as well as her husband, be indulged with some more latitude of free will as to contracts, and a larger extent of individuality of character in relation to the right of property. . . . [The] stern and un-gallant general rules of the common law, by which marriage so sinks the wife under the absolute sway of the husband have been made, in many respects, to yield to a better feeling, and have undergone many whole-some modifications chiefly by the direct, or indirect application of the principles of equity.[119]

Unlike the courts of Pennsylvania, Maryland, and New York, which also supported simple settlements, those of South Carolina accepted the precedent reluctantly.[120] Thus the state with the strongest tradition of support for women's separate estates had the most difficulty dealing with the concept of direct contracts between spouses. As a result of the state judiciary's attitude toward coercion, courts encouraged women to hold their property through third parties well into the nineteenth century. Courts perceived the protective function of trustees as a necessity, a characteristic providing evidence on the strength of paternalism in this preeminent slave society. It seems clear that although South Carolina courts were willing to recognize the innovation, they preferred traditional settlements in almost every case. In passing judgments that supported simple agreements they still made provisions reestablishing them into trust estates. Women could own separate property relatively easily, but they could not escape the symbolic protection of trustees.

The antipathy of South Carolina jurists to settlements made without intermediary parties does not mean that women and their families in the state favored granting active control to trustees. On the contrary, deeds of settlement gave control to the *cestui que trust* far more often than they gave it to the trustees. Jurists maintained, however, that the nominal ownership by trustees was useful as a protective shield against husbands. Thus when the court appointed a trustee to manage the separate estate of Judith Barrett, they noted that his function was "to protect the rights of the wife."[121] And when they allowed an estranged wife to dispose of her trust property without informing her trustee, they wrote that the intermediary function of the trustee was unnecessary in cases of separation. Then the coercive powers of a man were sharply reduced. The court wrote, "In general a Trustee is interposed not only to hold the legal estate for the Married Woman but to protect her from the undue influence of her husband. In this case there was no such influence to be guarded against as the husband and wife lived apart, in a state of discord and she was left to the free and uncontrolled exercise of her own discretion in the use or in the abuse of the rights of property."[122]

In at least two cases, Virginia followed the South Carolina pattern on simple marriage settlements. Although the Virginia courts supported direct contracts, they seemed to prefer trusts as a means of protecting women from coercion. The position is demonstrated well by *Tabb and Others* v. *Archer and Others* (1809) and *Randolph and Others* v. *Randolph and Others* (1809), cases involving the settlements of two sisters.[123] Here a widowed mother, Mrs. Tabb, insisted on establishing separate estates for her daughters before she allowed them to marry. Although the elder woman thought that she acted prudently in arranging for settlements, she erred in neglecting to establish trusts. Instead, she simply asked her future sons-in-law to sign direct contracts. She did not count on their duplicity. Shortly after their marriages, the two men took steps to destroy their wives' separate estates. To preserve the settlements, Mrs. Tabb found herself in court.

The justices of the Supreme Court of Appeals of Virginia criticized Mr.

Archer and Mr. Randolph for their fraudulent actions. The court supported the settlements and praised the intent of the mother in creating them. The jurists' attitude demonstrates the respectability of female separate estates in early nineteenth-century Virginia. Justice Tucker wrote, "Mrs. Tabb's conduct, from the evidence, not only seems to me to stand above every possible imputation of impropriety, but to have been highly laudable and proper, and such as every prudent and affectionate parent, whether father or mother, would have done well to have pursued in such a case." Because she acted "in the strict line of her duty," the justices decided to follow her intent and reestablish the settlements.[124] This time, however, they placed the property in trust estates and appointed trustees. Given the earlier behavior of the husbands, the court undoubtedly saw trustees as necessary intermediaries to protect the settled property from future attacks.

The Virginia decision indicates a very real belief in the efficacy of male coercion. Although courts often employed coercion as a rhetorical device, some jurists saw it as a viable force, destructive of the interests of women and potentially just as dangerous to family welfare as female independence. Virginia and South Carolina courts regarded their obligation to protect women's interests as a serious responsibility, and they balked at promoting simple settlement deeds because of it. When they could, they substituted trusts for direct contracts.

As we have seen, over the course of the second half of the eighteenth century, two developments in the law of separate estates radically changed the property rights of women. One reduced the influence of trustees; the other eliminated them altogether. First, the courts gradually expanded women's right to exercise control over settlement property without consulting trustees. Initially, settlement terms had to delineate the specific powers women could execute and courts interpreted the absence of specifications to mean that trustees held all managerial rights. Later, however, courts ruled just the opposite—that the absence of specifications gave women absolute managerial rights, and that trustees had to follow the instructions of *cestui que trusts*. Some jurisdictions even eliminated the requirement of private examinations in conveyances of real estate. Although precedents establishing these policies appeared at different times in each jurisdiction, by the turn of the century women could act independently everywhere if their settlements did not include specific restrictions.

Second, chancellors' support of simple marriage settlements represented an important advance in the law on married women's property. The law had reached a point where it recognized women's right to own and control both real and personal property separately from their husbands, and in their own names. By the end of the eighteenth century, all the courts needed to guarantee women separate property was a simple contract, executed by husband and wife, demonstrating an intent to reserve certain property for the sole use of the wife. The step from this point to passage of the married women's property acts was a relatively small one, particularly because the primary motivation for both legal developments was the same, protection of women's property from husbands' creditors.

In eliminating the requirement of trustees, the courts were following popular attitudes. Even in South Carolina, where chancellors continued to voice and act upon their fear of coercion, most couples executed marriage settlements with passive trustees. Thus, although South Carolina couples created trusts rather than simple settlements, they rarely allowed trustees to make binding decisions concerning settlement property. Either women made investment and managerial decisions themselves or in conjunction with their husbands or men held exclusive managerial rights.

Courts may have been willing to dispense with the legal requirement of trustees because so many couples already had done so in practice themselves. But changing attitudes toward coercion as a principle of law also figured in chancery's decision to support simple settlements. Remember that jurists first came to accept simple marriage settlements because they chose to see the husband as trustee for his wife. In 1827 James Kent echoed the traditional learning when he wrote, "It is not necessary that the trustee should be a stranger. The husband himself may be the trustee; and if property be settled to a married woman's separate use, and no trustee be appointed, the husband will be considered as such."[125] According to standard common law and equitable rules on coercion, however, this viewpoint was absurd. How could a man act as an intermediary to protect a woman from his own coercion? If such were the purpose of a trustee, a husband could not serve as one for his own wife. Clearly, equity courts had ceased at some point to regard trustees as primarily protectors of women. Instead, chancellors saw them as unnecessary and perhaps dangerous interlopers who could be eliminated safely.

Before reaching this conclusion, the law had to shift its interpretation of female helplessness. The shift was slow, as shown by the positions of Bland and Kent on private examinations, but as courts gave women more and more ability to control their own property, they were accepting the notion that women could take care of themselves. If women with settlements did not need the consent of trustees in executing specific powers of control, then they did not need trustees at all. Women who owned property would have to protect their own interests, particularly if they insisted on creating separate estates without trustees.

In acting to remove the requirement of trustees and support direct contracts between husbands and wives, equity courts were, in effect, throwing out the concept of coercion. By the end of the eighteenth century, legal attitudes had evolved to the point where courts believed that they could abandon coercion without endangering women. In part, the rise of the companionate ideal in marriage had made coercion anomalous as a concept.[126] Courts no longer thought that women needed special protection from their husbands. Instead, married women could rely on the remedies available to all persons in cases of coercion. Tapping Reeve explained chancery's new rationale in his treatise on domestic relations. He wrote with regard to the wife's powers of control under settlements, "A wife, as to her separate property, is a femme sole; and must so be considered, in all her actions respecting it, to act freely and without coercion.—Actual proof of duress or imposed hardship on the part of the husband, would be sufficient in chancery, to rescind her contracts respecting it, in the same manner and for the same reasons, that the contract of any other person is rescinded."[127] Chancery thereby destroyed the legal idea that husbands possessed unusual and secret means of influencing their wives. And because normal legal procedures could be assumed adequate for protecting women, there was no need for trustees in marriage settlements.

Moreover, the work of several historians in recent years has demonstrated the changing roles and status of women after the Revolution. Suzanne Lebsock and Mary Beth Norton, in particular, have pointed to a widening public sphere for women, an improved self-image, and greater independence both within marriage and without.[128] Although Linda Kerber sees the postrevolutionary position of women in more ambiguous terms, her emphasis on improved education for republican women implies that the ingredients for female independence were coalescing.[129] Now we can see that with regard to separate property, postrevolutionary women came to occupy a position of greater independence and control than was known to colonial matrons. Perhaps this explains why Lebsock found more women taking the steps to create separate estates as the nineteenth century progressed. Because English law provided the precedent for judicial support of simple marriage settlements, we cannot attribute this late eighteenth-century development to the effects of the Revolution. Instead, it reflects an increasingly egalitarian attitude toward marriage that prevailed in both England and America during the period studied. Changing attitudes toward coercion confirm this trend, but we should not forget that the strength of coercion as a concept meant that it faded only slowly from the American legal scene. Its power in a still paternalistic society helps to explain nineteenth-century lawmakers' nervousness over passage of the married women's property acts.

New ideas about contract law may have played a part in the process of change as well, although the English precedent on simple marriage settlements (1769) is early for current notions on the will theory of contract. But perhaps in the United States at the very end of the eighteenth century, the developing theories on contract did affect attitudes toward women and coercion. If the courts were backing away from the role of moral arbitrator in determining the fairness of contracts, then women with separate property, like all parties to contracts, would have to play a more aggressive role in protecting themselves. By downplaying spousal coercion, courts may have been acknowledging changes in contract law as well as changes in family relationships.[130]

Finally, it should be noted that by the turn of the nineteenth century, women who found themselves victims of coercion could do more than ask the courts for protection. They could sue for divorce. Armed with the right to separate property and to divorce, women no longer found themselves totally dependent within marriage. Their new powers gave them the ability to protect themselves, as the increase in separations after the Revolution indicates. In granting women the right to hold property in their own names, equity courts were simply acknowledging their rising independence within the family.

Separate Estates in
New England

English precedents on separate property for married women did not find support everywhere in America. Until well into the nineteenth century, the legislative assemblies of Connecticut and Massachusetts refused to give any court the power to enforce trust estates. Thus, although separate estates technically were legal, the failure of courts to enforce them amounted to a policy of opposition. As case reports demonstrate, some couples still separated their property by mutual consent; some even employed trustees as intermediaries. But if for any reason they needed the intercession of the courts to protect their property arrangements, they found themselves involved in an uncooperative legal system. As was true for women's property rights in general, informal customs—here the use of separate estates—could not provide adequate security without formal law to back them up.

OPPOSITION TO CHANCERY COURTS
AND SEPARATE ESTATES

The single most important reason for the initial failure of Connecticut and Massachusetts to enforce trust estates lies in the absence in these jurisdictions of independent courts of chancery on the English model. Without a court to administer the complicated body of equity precedents on women's property rights, New England fell behind in this area of the law. The situation in Pennsylvania, a colony that also failed to create an independent chancery, strengthens this conclusion. There, courts of common law had the power to enforce trusts, but they did not do so according to the standards followed in

New York, Maryland, Virginia, and South Carolina. If Pennsylvania courts, vested with the explicit power to support marriage settlements, encountered difficulty keeping pace with changes in this area of the law, it is consistent to find Connecticut and Massachusetts going even further afield, particularly given the Puritans' historical opposition to chancery courts.

Beginning well before migration, Puritan reformers advocated the elimination or tight control of chancery courts. With other reform-minded Englishmen, they opposed the tremendous power available to individual chancellors, who decided cases without juries on the basis of equitable principles. In the sixteenth and early seventeenth centuries, before the Chancery developed a strict tradition of following its own precedents, the decisions handed down often appeared arbitrary and high-handed. Hence the famous complaint of John Selden, "Equity is a roguish thing. For the law we have a measure . . . [but] equity is according to the conscience of him that is Chancellor, and as that is larger or narrower, so is equity. 'Tis all one as if they should make the standard for measure a Chancellor's foot."[1] That chancellors' consciences were seen as supporting the royal prerogative more often than not made the court a target of revolutionary opposition. During the Interregnum, Puritan legal reformers focused on the Chancery, and at the time of the Barebones Parliament they made a concerted effort to abolish it.[2]

Chancery survived, however. It was a necessary addition to the English legal system because common law courts remained inflexible and refused to adopt the equitable jurisdiction. As Stanley N. Katz has noted, "Most of the critics of chancery objected to the administration of the court rather than to the character of equity law."[3] They knew that the areas of law controlled by equity were essential. Because the common law could not incorporate them, chancellors would have to be tolerated.

American common law courts were not as inflexible as those of the mother country. Here, where the judicial system was built up piece by piece, often by legislative enactments, Puritan leaders could revise and reform the legal system at will. They chose to give specific areas of equity jurisdiction to their common law courts rather than to establish an independent chancery. The result was a truncated equity jurisdiction that did not cover married women's separate estates explicitly. That aspect of Puritan opposition to equity law had important ramifications for eighteenth- and early nineteenth-century matrons in Connecticut and Massachusetts.

More was at issue in New England, however, than the absence of a legal vehicle for enforcing trusts. The vehicle could have been created if the demand for one had existed. Given the early commercial emphasis of the New England colonies, it is particularly surprising that more families did not employ marriage settlements as a means of protecting at least some family property from their creditors. Perhaps a counteracting force, working against reliance on women's separate property in times of financial crisis, was the ideology of marital unity prevalent in both the common law and Puritanism. Under that ideology, women's financial autonomy represented a threat to the family rather than a safety valve. Our understanding of the status of women in early New England is still vague, but recent work does indicate that earlier, optimistic accounts of increased equality in Puritan marriages may have been overdrawn.[4] New England women served as "deputy husbands," according to Laurel Ulrich, a role that emphasized their competence in carrying on family duties normally assigned to men.[5] But Ulrich found little room for autonomy in the lives of the women she studied. As wives and mothers and servants of the Lord women defined themselves in terms of their relationships with others. They did not seek independence in their social world, and the law gave them scant opportunity for independence in the realm of family finances.

Given the general patterns in New England property law already discussed, it is not surprising to discover dislike and discouragement of female separate estates. As we have seen, married women in Connecticut had no property rights at all until the second quarter of the eighteenth century. Men had absolute rights to their wives' realty as well as personalty under rules of law that deviated sharply from the laws of England. In the next chapter it will be shown that widows of Connecticut men held fewer dower rights than widows elsewhere. They could claim only shares in what their husbands owned at death, and therefore they had no right to control the sales or mortgages of husbands' lands during marriage. Private examinations were used (after 1723) only for the conveyancing of women's own lands. Similarly, women in Massachusetts found fewer protections for their property rights than were enjoyed by many other colonial matrons. Private examinations were not required in Massachusetts, an omission of the courts that speaks to a lack of concern for spousal coercion.

Lawmakers in Connecticut and Massachusetts opposed separate property rights for women during marriage, but they supported one kind of spousal contract, the jointure. In both colonies, inheritance statutes specified the right of a couple to contract for a jointure, under which a wife was guaranteed specific property for her support during widowhood. Although in England and other American jurisdictions jointures often were made as a part of prenuptial marriage settlements, they were very different from separate estates. Jointures provided security for a woman during widowhood, not marriage. She could not exercise powers of control over jointure property, for example. New England lawmakers' support of jointures speaks to their concern for widows, and does not contradict their opposition to separate estates giving women independence as wives.

The failure of lawmakers in Connecticut and Massachusetts to develop a body of law for governing separate estates fits the pattern of opposition to women's independent control over property generally, either their own or their husbands'. According to Puritan ideas about the family, a single interest was essential. The harmony, love, and unselfishness so extolled by writers of the period left no room for the idea of separate property, particularly since women's separate estates were associated with the corrupt, aristocratic classes of English landed society, which often employed them to facilitate informal divorces. Proper Puritan matrons sought neither independence nor control in their marriages. They submitted lovingly to their husbands' authority and decisions about property, and gave up their persons and their estates to whatever fate God had in store for the family as a whole. The very idea of separate property spoke to a corruption of family life that Puritan leaders feared and sought to suppress. Although individuals still occasionally relied on marriage settlements to define the respective rights of wives and husbands, lawmakers never acknowledged the practice by assigning jurisdiction to the courts. As was true in other areas of the law, Connecticut remained more conservative on the issue of separate property than Massachusetts, and therefore the two jurisdictions will be discussed separately.

CONNECTICUT

Clear judicial opposition to separate estates surfaced in Connecticut shortly after the Revolution, in 1788, when a majority of the judges on the Superior Court ruled that trusts could not be supported by Connecticut law. The circumstances of the case under question, *Bacon* v. *Taylor*, were straightforward, so that it was an excellent test case for determining general policy.[6] Nathaniel Cornwall devised an estate of real property to his niece, placing it in the hands of a trustee, Jeremiah Bacon, for safekeeping. Cornwall directed Bacon to administer the estate for his niece and, after her death, for her children. The woman died while the children were minors, and a dispute arose between Bacon and Joseph Taylor, the children's father. Taylor seized the property after the death of his wife, claiming that as guardian to his children he was entitled to administer it in their behalf. In a decision directly opposed to all settled law on the subject, the Superior Court supported the claims made by Taylor. They ruled that because Connecticut had no doctrine of uses and trusts, the estate vested automatically in Mrs. Taylor's children at her death.

The decision of the court on *Bacon* v. *Taylor* was not unanimous. Two judges dissented from the majority opinion and wrote in favor of adopting the law on trusts, which they believed formed an important part of English equity law. They saw no reason for Connecticut to reject the principles. Zephaniah Swift echoed their position several years later. He regretted the decision of the court on *Bacon* v. *Taylor*, arguing that it had been made contrary to current legal thinking.[7] It is significant, however, that although Swift disliked the decision of his judicial peers respecting trust estates, he refused to take the issue very seriously. Trusts were simply too rare in Connecticut to cause many problems. He doubted that another case similar to *Bacon* v. *Taylor* would ever appear to prompt a reexamination of the issue. In 1795 he wrote, "Whether our courts in future, will consider this decision to be law, it is not probable will ever be determined; as there is but little prospect that another such case will ever come before them."[8]

Other jurists echoed Swift's opinion on the rarity of trusts in Connecticut.[9] The absence of a separate court of chancery and the lack of a history of enforcement of trusts undoubtedly affected popular attitudes toward using them. Certainly the application of equitable principles remained lax throughout the late eighteenth and early nineteenth centuries. But the absence of a separate court of chancery cannot alone explain the rarity of separate estates in Connecticut, for Pennsylvania had no chancery, and yet its courts enforced most English precedents on trusts and settlements. In addition, despite the absence of a chancery court, Connecticut lawmakers did manage to enforce those aspects of equity law that society deemed essential. The General Assembly granted common law courts the power to dispense equitable remedies in cases involving mortgages and jointures, for example.[10] The regular courts also received "petitions in chancery" in instances when parties believed that they could not have justice under the common law. To take one case, in 1793 Mehitable Parsons petitioned the Superior Court for relief.[11] Her husband had erred in drawing up a life insurance policy. Although he meant to provide his wife and children with the benefit of the policy, it accidentally was made payable to himself and his executors and administrators. At his death, therefore, the insurance company paid his executor, who applied the money toward the debts owed by the estate. The wife received no benefit, despite her husband's clear intent in creating the policy for her. In ordering payment to the widow, the Superior Court pointed to English chancery precedents that supported its position.

Despite a tradition of offering equitable remedies in some areas of the law,

Connecticut courts refused to enforce women's separate estates. As shown in the discussion of the Connecticut law of divorce, there is some evidence to indicate that jurists believed liberal divorce laws made separate estates unnecessary. When couples could not cohabit amicably, sharing their property under the principle of unity of person, they could divorce. And when spouses did live together in peace, they did not need separate property. That such an idea was a fallacy is demonstrated by the primary motive behind the creation and development of trusts for women, protection of their property from husbands' creditors. Yet Connecticut lawmakers discounted such a motive, as they did the premise that women might want to exercise control over their own property. Such a pattern indicates antagonism to the idea of independent property rights for women. Juridical antipathy toward separate estates is seen in several reports of cases tried in the early nineteenth century. The first was *Dibble* v. *Hutton* (1804).[12]

Dibble v. *Hutton* concerned a postnuptial contract made by Mary Hutton and her husband Samuel in 1798. She had agreed to join him in selling a piece of real estate they owned as tenants in common on the condition that she receive her share of the purchase price for her own use, as a separate estate. After selling the property, Samuel gave her some of the notes, which she kept "in her separate custody" until her husband's death. Mary had no trustee, however, nor did she and her husband ever execute a written agreement for separate property. When Nehemiah Dibble, Samuel's executor, refused to honor the contract between husband and wife and demanded the notes, Mary Hutton found herself in a precarious legal position. Unable to obtain justice in a court of common law, she turned to equity. Her petition in chancery noted that Dibble did not need the notes to pay Samuel's debts. Mary also told the court that she had received only the equivalent of dower in her husband's will. Samuel left her no share of his personal estate. She explained, "The executor has since received the money upon said notes; the estate of the said Samuel, after payment of his debts, is of the value of $20,000; but the petitioner, notwithstanding, is left dependent upon her friends for support, and has received no compensation for her land, and has no remedy at law."[13]

The county court of common pleas and the Superior Court both supported Mary Hutton's petition in chancery, but she lost her case when Dibble appealed to the Supreme Court of Errors. Antagonism to contracts between husbands and wives caused the highest state court to decide against enforcing the agreement, despite the clear equity of Mary's claim. In particular, the justices expressed their dislike of wives' separate estates. They thought English rules on such arrangements ill suited to Connecticut society. As the court explained, "The maxims of the ancient common law, on this subject, are plain and simple; our state of manners and society do not require that they should be relaxed, or qualified. The principles, therefore, which govern in the English court of chancery, ought not to be engrafted into our chancery system, but those of the common law remain unimpaired."[14] The statement indicates that the justices on the high court understood English equity principles governing separate property held without trustees. Attorneys on both sides of the case and the judiciary all acknowledged that an English court would have enforced the contract. But in such a case of novel impression in Connecticut law, the court felt free to follow its conscience rather than English precedent. It refused to sanction a wife's separate estate.

According to Nehemiah Dibble's attorney, the contract was aberrant rather than representative of attitudes toward women's property in Connecticut. Like Swift, he claimed that trusts and marriage settlements did not warrant concern because couples generally did not employ them. He eloquently voiced the conservative viewpoint on separate estates when he wrote,

Of marriage settlements, not an instance is known. We happily have never heard of forming certain exceptions to the marriage contract, when framed, that the wife need not lose her independence; nor of relations giving property to married women, to their separate use. But the idea has here been, that lines of separation were not to be drawn between husband and wife; and the generosity of our females has not allowed them to wish to keep their property from those to whom they have not refused their persons. *Our customs*, therefore, do not require the introduction of these new principles. . . . If society was here, as in England, and vast estates were depending upon the principle, there might be some reason for adopting it; but by granting this application, you destroy, at a stroke, one half of what we have ever deemed the marriage contract. That such a case was never before heard of in Connecticut, shows, that such contracts were never expected to be enforced.[15]

Arguments of counsel similar to this one appear in subsequent cases on women's property rights in Connecticut. England, with its aristocratic class structure and landholding system, might wish to encourage separate interests within marriage, but Connecticut did not. Wide use of marriage settlements in England had produced a society in which women possessed their "boasted independence." The result?—a country in which "nothing is more common, than to see my lord at one country seat, and my lady at another, pursuing, respectively, their own affairs, in their own way—but to the benefit of nobody." This pattern, the court wrote in *Fitch* v. *Brainerd* (1805) was "at once, the cause, and the effect, of licentiousness."[16]

Despite this attorney's confident assessment, the absence of great landed estates in Connecticut cannot alone explain the failure of courts to enforce trusts for married women. Although Connecticut did not have the same class structure as England in the period studied, the region's commercial orientation created families whose interests could have been served well by a law of separate estates. Lawrence Stone noted, in fact, that the English law of separate estates developed partly in response to the needs of the rising mercantile classes in seventeenth-century England.[17] Moreover, it can be argued that the landholding systems of Pennsylvania and New York bore sufficient resemblance to that of Connecticut (and Massachusetts) to negate any arguments linking economic structure with the absence of women's trust estates, for both of those jurisdictions recognized the validity of separate property at the end of the eighteenth century.

Some jurists in Connecticut did not share their colleagues' pessimism about the ultimate effects of women's separate estates. Nor did they take a sanguine view of marriage relations in the state. They commented that private settlements were not uncommon, particularly for couples who separated without the benefit of a court-ordered divorce decree. Some even expressed their belief that marriage settlements were valid in Connecticut, despite the decision of the court on *Dibble* v. *Hutton*, because chancery precedents elsewhere were so clearly in favor of them.[18] Jurists in late eighteenth- and early nineteenth-century Connecticut who favored adopting English rules on marriage settlements used arguments stemming from their own jurisprudence as well as that of England to support their position.[19] They noted that one judicial decision in Connecticut already pointed to an acceptance of women's independent property rights. The case at issue, *Adams* v. *Kellogg* (1788), concerned the validity of a married woman's will.[20] In opposition to common law prohibitions, the Supreme Court of Errors had supported the right of Mary Kellogg to devise real estate she inherited from her former husband to her then husband, Elias. The court saw no impediments to the will, despite the arguments of the heir at law that femes coverts were disabled from devising real estate, and that his sister had been forced by her husband to favor him in her will. On an appeal to the General Assembly, the decision was upheld—an indication of legislative as well as judicial support for women's right to devise.[21]

The decision of the Supreme Court of Errors on *Adams* v. *Kellogg* ran counter to the general trend of Connecticut decisions on married women's property. How could the court refuse to recognize trusts and marital contracts, and yet allow femes coverts to devise property? The principles were contradictory, one forbidding separate estates and the other condoning a woman's act of ownership over property held in her own name. Realizing the mistake it had made, the court reversed itself in 1805, in *Fitch* v. *Brainerd.*[22] They refused at that time to recognize the will of a feme covert on the grounds that married women could not devise unless a statute appeared specifically giving them that right. Significantly, at this point the court noted its obligation to follow English law condemning feme covert wills, whereas it had refused to adopt English rules supporting separate estates just the previous year, in *Dibble* v. *Hutton.* In discussing the laws of inheritance, the court wrote, "Though the common law of England hath not, *as such*, nor ever had, any force here; yet, in the progress of our affairs, whatever was imagined at the beginning, it long since became necessary, in order to avoid arbitrary decisions, and for the sake of *rules*, which habit had rendered familiar, as well as the wisdom of ages matured, to make that law our own, by practical *adoption*—with such exceptions as diversity of circumstances, and the incipient customs of our own country, required."[23] One obvious exception was the law of separate estates. But as for devises, the court thought it clear that its earlier decision was erroneous and against all settled law on the subject, English law as well as the law of Connecticut. Once again, fear of creating separate interests within marriage guided the decision of the court, as did worries about coercion.

It is interesting to note that several years following the decision on *Fitch* v. *Brainerd,* Connecticut legislators enacted a law giving married women the right to devise.[24] The statute, enacted in 1809, has been interpreted by one historian as an attempt to ease confusion over the issue.[25] Undoubtedly this was a motivation, for over a period of seventeen years, from 1788 to 1805, women had been allowed to write wills in Connecticut. The sudden prohibition established by *Fitch* v. *Brainerd* must have created considerable anxiety. In addition, however, we must note a second factor. Since 1723, Connecticut more than any other colony and state had distinguished between the wife's property and that of the husband for purposes of inheritance. Connecticut inheritance law is discussed in the next chapter. At this point it is important to note, however, that widows possessed more extensive rights to the property they brought into marriage than to the property owned by their husbands or that acquired jointly by husband and wife. The postrevolutionary law giving women the power to devise their own estates was therefore in agreement with other Connecticut rules on inheritance. It did not indicate, however, a new attitude toward separate estates for femes coverts, as demonstrated by subsequent conservative decisions issuing from the courts.

In *Goodwin* v. *Goodwin* (1810), the Supreme Court of Errors considered the validity of a trust estate created for the wife's benefit as part of an agreement to separate.[26] Although in this case a majority of the justices on the Supreme Court of Errors still refused to support the trust estate, the court did split on the decision. Four justices favored the postnuptial settlement because the Goodwins had employed a trustee. As Justice Baldwin explained, "I have never considered the case of *Dibble* v. *Hutton*, 1 *Day* 221. as going so far as to prevent all possible provision, which a husband may be disposed to make for his wife. While such provision vests in contract between husband and wife merely, as that did, I agree it is void; but when made *bona fide*, and fairly executed by the intervention of a trustee, I know of no decision or principle that will set it aside."[27] Obviously, Baldwin believed that Connecticut courts could and should enforce trust estates created for the benefit of married women. His position did not convince a majority of his peers on the bench, however. Five justices voted against enforcing the trust. The negative decision of the majority rested not solely upon the trust but also on an attempt to sue for divorce collusively. The court learned that Mary agreed not to mention William's contraction of venereal disease when she sued for divorce, in exchange for a comfortable maintenance. Had such an attempt to deceive the court not been a factor in the trial, the majority probably would have decided in favor of the trust.

This point is demonstrated aptly by a case tried the next year, *Nichols* v. *Palmer* (1811), in which the court split five to four in favor of supporting a postnuptial agreement to separate executed through a trustee.[28] Justice Smith was the member of the court who changed his mind on the issue, and therefore it is useful to study his opinion with care. Such an investigation reveals not only his reasons for supporting the trust but also his equivocal attitude toward marriage settlements.

Smith supported the right of a husband to give his wife a separate maintenance. Although he regretted the necessity of judicial support for private separation agreements, he could not regard them as morally repugnant. In fact, he believed that they served a necessary social function as an alternative to absolute divorce. With regard to other kinds of settlements, however, Smith held a different viewpoint. He explained carefully that he favored separation agreements specifically, and not marriage settlements generally. Smith argued that the English custom of allowing femes coverts to own and control property separately from their husbands was dangerous, and he refused to countenance it. He explained his support of separate maintenances as a "middle course," one by which "the husband can form a valid, binding contract with any other person, for the support and maintenance of his wife," but a wife could have no separate legal status "either in law or chancery."[29] The key to Smith's distinction was the control exercised by the husband as opposed to the wife. As long as the decision to create a separate estate came from the man, and as long as he maintained all powers of control, Smith supported his actions.

Under Smith's arrangement, the woman who separated from her husband had no legal rights to the property held by her trustee. The trust concerned her husband only, and if the trustee proved negligent, only her husband could take legal action against him. He wrote, "It follows from these principles, that the wife can have no separate interest in the property put into the hands of a trustee for her support, and that she can have no remedy in a court of chancery to call the trustee to account; but if the trustee is guilty of a breach of trust, he must be liable to the husband for a violation of his contract, and to him, or his representatives, only." According to Smith, it was the ability of a wife to exercise independent controls over her separate estate that had proved detrimental to family interests in England. He believed that once a woman had the legal right to manage her own property, she would be more willing to abandon her husband and family. Most important, he noted that this was the principle rejected by Connecticut jurists in *Dibble* v. *Hutton* and *Fitch* v. *Brainerd*. He observed, "It was the new principle of the wife's separate property, separate rights, and her independent legal existence, which the court thought not proper to incorporate into our system."[30] Thus, as long as separate maintenances operated through husbands and trustees only, they were legitimate in Smith's eyes, because they did not grant powers of control to women.

Even after *Nichols* v. *Palmer*, both attorneys and judges continued to cite *Dibble* v. *Hutton* as proof that separate estates could not find support in Connecticut.[31] Following Smith's lead, they interpreted the decision in *Nichols* v. *Palmer* as supportive of private separation agreements, but not separate estates in general. Despite passage of the statute allowing married women the right to devise, then, Connecticut law on married women's property rights remained conservative. Although some judges acknowledged the validity of trusts designed to give married women separate estates, they still found reasons not to enforce them. In *Fitch* v. *Ayer* (1817), for example, the Supreme Court of Errors interpreted a devise from father to daughter as a devise to the daughter's husband, rather than as a separate estate for the daughter's benefit alone.[32] Had the court applied to the case either the doctrine of intentions or the wife's equity to a settlement, the woman would have received the property as a separate estate. But the judges decided against such a reading. One can almost sense a tone of relief in the words of

Zephaniah Swift, by then chief justice: "In this case there is no necessity of considering the question whether a married woman can have a separate estate; or whether we will adopt the *English* law on that subject; for upon the principles of that law, the legacy in question does not create a separate estate in the wife. . . . It is, in effect, and by law, a gift to the husband himself; and a legacy in this form has always been so considered."[33]

According to Swift's contemporary Tapping Reeve, however, the bequest in question could be interpreted as creating a separate estate. In his treatise on domestic relations Reeve wrote, "A legacy, to be paid into the proper hands of the wife, is her separate property."[34] The words of the bequest under dispute in *Fitch* v. *Ayer* indicate that it fell under the category of cases described by Reeve. It read, "I give to my loving daughter, *Thisbe Fitch*, two hundred pounds lawful money, to be paid her, by my son *Elijah Clark*, in manner following, vis. the interest thereof to be paid her annually from and after my decease, yearly, and every year, during the time of her coverture or marriage; and the principal sum of two hundred pounds to be paid her, whenever she shall become single, or to her heirs after her decease."[35] That Swift could interpret this as a legacy for the husband rather than the wife indicates a poor understanding of equitable principles among even the most distinguished members of the Connecticut bar. Even after accepting equitable principles on separate property, they continued to apply common law doctrines to the cases they heard, thereby undermining the ability of women to own property.

By the end of the period studied, the chancery reports of James Kent's New York decisions were having an effect on Connecticut law. In *Watrous* v. *Chalker* (1828), both counselors and judges cited cases from New York to bolster their arguments in favor of women's separate property rights.[36] Yet even in this case Connecticut judges decided against established equity principles and refused to grant a feme covert full powers of control over her own property. They did not allow a feme covert, Rhoda Chalker, the right to make a voluntary contract to assist her mother's husband, because, as they put it, the contract held no benefit for herself. The opinion of Chief Justice Hosmer indicates his rejection of the stands taken in New York and Maryland granting women feme sole status with regard to their separate property. He seemed instead to be supporting the position of the South Carolina courts, which held that women needed protection in the management of their property. He wrote:

Over the *separate estate* of a feme covert, through the medium of a trustee, or of her husband in that character, if no trustee is appointed, she is held competent to deal with it as if she were a feme sole. *Jaques* v. *Methodist Episcopal Church*, 17 Johns. Rep. 548. It has, likewise, been adjudged, that she may contract with her husband for a transfer of property from him to her, if it be done *bona fide* and for valuable consideration. *Lady Arundell* v. *Phipps*, 10 Ves. 139, 145. *Livingston* v. *Livingston*, 2 Johns. Chan. Rep. 537. No case, however, has been cited, nor am I aware that any exists, enforcing against a feme covert an agreement made with her husband, without either *value* or *benefit* to herself; and this I take to be the present case. Prompted by feeling, and under no legal or equitable obligation, the feme requests her husband to give his promissory note, and to make payment of it out of the avails of her land. This is the whole case; and nothing parallel to it, so far as my information extends, is to be found in the determination of any court.[37]

Yet there was an obvious emotional benefit to Rhoda Chalker in this case: if she had won, she would have succeeded in freeing her mother's husband from debtor's prison. Such a motive held no value, however, to the Connecticut Supreme Court of Errors, which sought to protect women from their feelings for their own good.

At the end of the period studied, Connecticut courts ostensibly recognized women's right to own and control property separately from their husbands. Yet not one case fully supported a gift of separate property to a married woman, or a power of control executed by a feme covert in managing her own estate. Thus despite the influence of Kent, Reeve, and even Swift, Connecticut law remained conservative on the issue of separate estates. Jurists there interpreted the law strictly. A similar, though less extreme, situation prevailed in neighboring Massachusetts—an indication of a regional bias against women's independent property rights.

MASSACHUSETTS

In Massachusetts, as in Connecticut, cases concerning trusts and marriage settlements were rare in the early reports. Those that did appear focused on the question of enforcement. Could Massachusetts common law courts enforce trust estates created to give married women the right to own and control property? Judges in Massachusetts felt unsure of their right to guarantee wives separate estates because, like Connecticut, the state had no independent equity court.[38] They believed that they could not, therefore, simply adopt the precedents of the English Chancery. In addition, no statute specifically granted common law courts jurisdiction over marriage settlements, although the General Court had taken steps to guarantee enforcement of other areas of equity law. The colonial assembly of Massachusetts gave courts of common law the power to chancer bonds and foreclose on mortgages and defeasances in 1699. In 1708 courts were empowered to handle cases of fraudulent trusts established by absconding debtors. After the Revolution, the new state moved to confirm these powers by a statute enacted in 1785.[39] In addition, the General Assembly heard petitions for relief when parties thought they could not receive justice from the common law. This practice began in the seventeenth century and continued into the nineteenth.[40]

Partly as a result of this truncated equity jurisdiction, no legal tradition on trusts for married women developed in the colony and state. In 1823 Nathan Dane commented on the confusion created by the absence of a court of chancery that could hear cases on married women's separate estates: "Though we have adopted some of the rights and obligations, especially where there is a *separation*, which are enforced only in chancery . . . yet we have no chancery court to enforce such as we have adopted. Hence, it is a subject of much uncertainty how in this state they are to be carried into effect; and for this reason too, it is very often a question which of these rights and obligations found in English books, we have, or have not adopted."[41]

Marriage settlements must have been uncommon in colonial Massachusetts, causing little legal controversy and therefore requiring no legislative or judicial clarification on enforcement. As late as 1792, for example, Chief Justice Dana of the Supreme Court could state that there was no precedent on a marriage settlement to be found in any of the Massachusetts courts.[42] In the same year, attorneys for one litigant who hoped to overthrow a settlement argued, "There is no usage of such a conveyance as the present one known in this country, so as to make it a common assurance."[43] Somewhat later, in 1809, Justice Sewall of the Supreme Court could still claim, "Here there are few marriage settlements, and consequently the wife is generally under the absolute control of the husband."[44] Given the rarity of couples who employed marriage settlements, it is hardly surprising that legal precedents on enforcement did not appear in the first reports.

In *Thatcher v. Omans* (1792) we see Chief Justice Dana of the Massachusetts Supreme Court grappling for the first time, as he claimed, with the problem of enforcing a marriage settlement.[45] The contract in question was executed in 1771 by Sarah and Moses Gill. They conveyed her real estate to a trustee, to hold for their joint lives and for the life of whoever lived longer. They retained the right to manage the estate, granting the trustee no powers of administration. After their deaths they wanted the property to descend to their heirs.

Sarah died before her husband. They had no children, and therefore under the common law Sarah's heirs should have gained title to all of her real property at her death. Unless a husband had children by his wife and could enter the lands as tenant by the curtesy, his rights ended at her death. Yet here that outcome was thwarted by the marriage settlement. As the longest liver, Moses Gill was entitled to hold the land until his death, and at that point it would descend to his heirs rather than his wife's. Sarah Gill's heir at law contested the marriage settlement. His attorney argued that under the law of Massachusetts a feme covert could not convey her estate to trustees. He contended further that under the statute of uses (1536), a conveyance to a trustee for the use of a third party was void. He argued, "The doctrine of uses is the same here as in England: it [the settlement] is void, therefore, because it creates a use upon a use, whether it be considered as a bargain and sale, or a covenant to stand seized to ùses."[46]

It is interesting to note that the counsel for Moses Gill did not base his arguments on equitable precedents supporting trust estates for married women. Either he realized that in Massachusetts such a tactic would not be successful or he was unaware of equitable precedents himself. Instead, he argued that because common law courts supported conveyances by married women, they should support the trust. In Massachusetts conveyances of feme covert property had always been allowed if the woman signed the deed. Here, then, was a conveyance to a third party, made for the valuable consideration of marriage plus twenty shillings. If the third party had then turned around and reconveyed the estate to the Gills, no one would have contested the validity of the transaction. Couples in Massachusetts often avoided the laws of inheritance in such a fashion, the counselor noted. Such a reconveyance was not attempted in this case, and yet the effect was the same. Therefore, he argued, the court should accept what amounted to a simplification of procedure, and support the trust.

His arguments convinced the court, which supported the postnuptial settlement. In writing his opinion on the case, Chief Justice Dana did not discuss equitable principles in favor of trusts. Like his colleague at the bar, he reasoned only from the common law. According to Dana, the common law could adjust its principles enough to accept arrangements like the Gills'. He observed that such a tack was essential in Massachusetts. Because there was no court of chancery to enforce the execution of trusts, courts of common law had to take unusual steps to see that justice was done. As he explained, "The objection, that this particular form of conveyance is not supported by common law, or by any statute or usage of our own, does not appear to me of great force. We know the origin of fines, recoveries, feoffments to uses, deeds of bargain and sale, covenants to uses, and leases and releases. These were all once novel, but have now become common assurances, though some of them were founded in fiction and falsehood. They were not considered void on account of their novelty, but were left to operate as far as they could, consistently with established principles of law." To support the conveyance, then, he did not rely on the statute of uses, which would have voided the whole transaction. Instead he employed the doctrine of feoffment to uses, whereby the legal title passed to the feoffee during the conveyance. The feoffees in this instance were Sarah and Moses Gill, who held as joint tenants during their lives. Whoever lived longer retained fee simple ownership. Dana agreed with Moses Gill's attorney that the arrangement under question simplified a procedure long employed in Massachusetts. He wrote, "I am unable to discern any solid reason why this mode of conveying the inheritances of femes coverts ought not to be deemed as valid as the common law mode, or our more usual one, of the husband and wife first making a deed of them to a third person, with a view only and for the intent that such third person should reconvey them to the husband and wife, to hold as shall be agreed upon between all the parties."[47]

Dana's interpretation benefited the Gills, whose intention in creating the trust was realized. But the doctrine presented by Dana was useless for women who wanted to keep their property separate from that of their husbands, and in particular to keep it from descending to their husbands' heirs. Trusts were most useful as a way of guaranteeing protection for women's property. Here, however, Dana had given Moses Gill fee simple rights in his wife's estate, thereby expanding his control over her property rather than restricting it. If such a construction were applied to all settlements, they could not serve as a protective measure for women. Instead they would be useful only for defeating the interests of wives' heirs at law in favor of husbands.

Chief Justice Dana's unusual reading of the law resulted from a failure of Massachusetts lawmakers to establish a clear equitable jurisdiction over trusts, combined with the court's desire to enforce a particular marriage settlement. In 1818 the legislature finally enacted a statute granting common law courts jurisdiction over trusts arising under deeds, which included marriage settlements.[48] The legislative action taken at that time may have been a response to rising judicial pressure, for in the years following Dana's decision on the Gill case, we see frequent remarks indicating the frustration of Massachusetts judges with their truncated equity jurisdiction. As demonstrated by cases in which courts refused to enforce trust estates, all Massachusetts judges were not willing to follow Dana's lead and revise the common law as necessity demanded. Dana himself even balked at taking this approach in all instances. Thus, in the case of *Prescott* v. *Tarbell* (1804), the Supreme Court noted its inability to compel execution of a trust owing to its limited jurisdiction.[49] Dana observed, "If the conveyance was in *trust*, this Court could not have compelled the execution of it, and, until the legislature shall think proper to give us farther powers, we can do nothing upon subjects of *that* nature."[50]

In 1813 the Supreme Court once again pointed out its inability to enforce the intent of a trust.[51] In 1765 a man had created a separate estate for his sister, Ruth, who was married to a merchant named Edward Davis. Ruth's brother wanted to protect her and her children from financial hardship in the event Edward's business failed. The settlement read, "And as for and touching the said estate, herein before limited to the said *Ruth*, it is hereby declared that the said estate is so limited to her as aforesaid in trust, that in case of the failure of the said *Edward* in business, or insolvency, whereby his estate, or effects, of any kind, shall be liable for the payment of his debts, the said hereby granted premises shall be exempt from demands of the said creditors, and be reserved by my said trustee herein before mentioned to the sole, separate use and behoof of the said Ruth, during the said natural time of her life, as aforesaid."[52]

The settlement deed further specified that the property was to descend to the "joint heirs" of Ruth and Edward after their deaths. Ruth's brother wanted to protect the family during the lifetime of the parents, and also ensure an inheritance for his nieces and nephews. His intention was not realized, however, as a result of the limited equity jurisdiction of the common law courts in Massachusetts. Instead of descending to all of the children equally, as would have been the case under equity law, the settlement property vested in the eldest son alone. According to Massachusetts law, the trust indenture created an entailed estate, under which only the eldest son could inherit.

The judiciary was not pleased with the outcome of the case, which undoubtedly offended their republican sensibilities opposing entails as well as their legal sense of what should be done regarding the intention of the donor. In writing their opinion the justices complained, "The endeavor of courts of law, in modern times, has been to give a construction, to deeds as well as wills, conformed to the intent of the parties, as far as such intent is discernible, and is consistent with rules of law." But, they admitted, "This Court has always inclined to construe an estate in trust to be an estate to uses for this reason,—that we have no Court of Chancery to compel the performance of trusts."[53] Their hands were tied in this case, despite the undemocratic result.

Even after 1818, when common law courts gained jurisdiction over trust estates in Massachusetts, justices continued to interpret the related body of law conservatively. According to historian William J. Curran, Chief Justice Isaac Parker was responsible for this development. Curran discovered that Parker adopted a policy of "the most strict interpretation" on the equity jurisdiction of Massachusetts courts.[54] In a series of important cases, the chief justice outlined his belief that courts should assume no larger equity jurisdiction than the statute expressly gave it. Parker's personal opposition to the assumption of chancery powers by common law courts in Massachusetts may have determined his conservative stand. Parker, Curran hypothesized, believed that a separate court of chancery would best serve the state. He may have opposed the assumption of equitable rules by common law courts in order to force the legislature to establish a court of chancery with full powers. Certainly there was an ongoing debate in Massachusetts at this time on the efficacy of having a separate court of chancery. It appears that during this period cases on trusts frequently fell victim to the political maneuvering of judges who favored the creation of an independent court.

Parker's conservative policy was applied to the law on trusts in *Russell* v. *Lewis* (1824).[55] Here the *cestui que trust* was indebted, and his creditors applied to the court for the right to seize the trust property. According to the principles of English equity law and the law of American states with chancery courts, trust property could be taken for the payment of debts, but the Supreme Court ruled that it was not so liable in Massachusetts. As Justice Wilde observed,

Equitable interests are only to be reached by resorting to a court of equity; and where it is clothed with sufficient powers to grant relief in all cases, creditors cannot be prejudiced. But this defect of the common law, as it certainly is, cannot be supplied in all cases by the limited powers of this Court as a court of equity. Cases may frequently occur, where property may be locked up against the just claims of creditors, and the Court would have no power to interpose and to give relief. But arguments *ab inconvenienti* are not to prevail over a well established rule of law. In such cases, the legislature alone can provide a remedy; either by enlarging the equitable jurisdiction of this Court; or by establishing a court of chancery; or if neither of these measures should be deemed expedient, provision may be made that all trusts and equitable rights and interests shall be liable to attachment and sale on execution.[56]

Thus the Massachusetts Supreme Court negated one of the benefits *cestui que trusts* could gain under equity law. The decision in *Russell* v. *Lewis* made it impossible, for example, for women with separate estates to get credit on their trust property. No one would extend credit on an estate that could not be taken for payment of debts. In light of the statute of 1818, it is difficult to understand this decision, unless it can be viewed as an example of judicial maneuvering for a separate court of chancery.

Although strong evidence indicates conservatism on trusts in Massachusetts, there is also evidence to demonstrate a more liberal attitude toward married women's property rights than existed in Connecticut. In Massachusetts, for example, couples found earlier support for their private separation agreements. Massachusetts lawmakers did not express the same fears regarding informal separations as did jurists in Connecticut. Justice Sedgwick demonstrated the difference in attitude when he observed in *Page* v. *Trufant* (1806), "Separate maintenance is lawful, and a bond given to secure it to a wife is meritorious, and therefore valid and binding."[57] Massachusetts jurists also proved more liberal than their neighbors in interpreting the doctrine of intentions for the benefit of femes coverts. The facts of a case tried in 1809, *Saunderson and Wife* v. *Stearns*, virtually duplicated those of *Fitch* v. *Ayer*, tried in Connecticut in 1817 and discussed above.[58] Although the Connecticut court refused to follow the intent of a testator and enforce a separate estate for a feme covert, the Massachusetts judges did so readily. They even appointed a trustee to manage the principal sum of ninety pounds for the *cestui que trust*, although the case appeared before passage of the statute of 1818 establishing a jurisdiction over trust estates. Clearly, then, trusts functioned on some level before the enactment of that statute.

Another case tried before 1818, *Osgood* v. *Breed* (1815), also demonstrates judicial support in Massachusetts for separate estates created through marriage settlements.[59] In his opinion on the case, Justice Jackson discussed with approval the right women had under settlements to own separate property and even to exercise powers of control over it. Here a feme covert wrote a will in which she devised real property held to her separate use under a marriage settlement. Jackson noted, "The authority of our probate courts, to approve and allow the will of a married woman, in some cases, *as a testamentary paper*, ought not, perhaps, to be questioned. . . . If a special and qualified probate be necessary to give validity to such an instrument, there seems to be no reason why the instrument should not be allowed in the probate courts, for that purpose and to that effect."[60]

Thus Massachusetts law supported the creation of separate estates for femes coverts, separate maintenances to facilitate agreements to live apart, and women's right to exercise powers over settlement property. Despite the eighteenth-century confusion over jurisdiction and the nineteenth-century judiciary's reticence to enforce equity law without a clear mandate from the legislature, some women in Massachusetts did hold separate property and find help in the courts earlier than in Connecticut. Whereas in 1817 Chief Justice Swift of Connecticut could still point to the absence of a clear precedent giving femes coverts the right to separate estates, in 1815 Justice Jackson of Massachusetts could claim, "Our laws recognize and protect the rights of married women to property given or secured to their separate use."[61] Moreover, this limited support for women's separate estates was strengthened in the 1820s under the influence of the reports of Chancellor James Kent of New York. In Massachusetts, as in Connecticut, the reports of Kent's decisions helped to clarify a confusing legal system under which, as Nathan Dane had observed, the courts followed some chancery rules while ignoring others. Kent's reports, and to a lesser extent the treatise on domestic relations published by Tapping Reeve in 1816, helped to push the states toward greater conformity in the law on marriage settlements.[62]

According to Elizabeth Warbasse, the Connecticut judiciary remained conservative on separate estates into the 1840s.[63] In fact, the first married women's property act in Connecticut may have resulted from continuing judicial refusal to enforce equitable principles on marriage settlements. Warbasse noted that in *Jones* v. *Aetna Insurance Co.* (1842), a case involving a married woman's separate estate, the chief justice of the Superior Court "airily dismissed" the applicable equity principles.[64] Similarly, in *Middleton* v. *Mather* (1843), the same court refused to enforce a postnuptial agreement between husband and wife, expressing its disapproval of separate estates.[65] At that time the court's opinion read, "If more loose or liberal views of the nature and legal effect of the marriage relation, have been entertained, in later times, either by the legislature or the public; until they shall be made to bear upon the courts, by some definite legislative act, we must abide by the rules of the common law."[66] As Warbasse observed, such a statement virtually demanded legislative action. It came in 1845 and 1849, when the General Assembly enacted statutes reserving femes coverts' real property from confiscation for the payment of husbands' debts, and granting women exclusive rights to their personal property acquired after marriage.[67] The latter statute demonstrated legislative support for the doctrine of the wife's equity to a settlement, which had never been enforced by Connecticut courts. Significantly, the Connecticut legislation applied to all women, not just to women who wrote marriage settlements. It therefore represented a radical step forward for the women of the state, who previously had experienced difficulty in obtaining even the protection of equitable principles designed primarily for use by the wealthy.

In the 1840s, Massachusetts also enacted laws clarifying women's independent property rights. Significantly, the first married women's property acts in Massachusetts simply confirmed equitable rules on female separate estates, rather than giving all women rights to own property, as was the case in Connecticut. In 1845 the legislature enacted a statute guaranteeing couples the right to use marriage settlements.[68] The statute included provisions supporting devises of separate estates to femes coverts and the right of women to contract and sue with regard to settlement property. Apparently confusion still reigned in Massachusetts courts on the subject of separate estates, for otherwise a statute such as this would have been redundant.[69] Despite some judicial support for settlements, then, the long history of opposition to chancery courts in Massachusetts finally made legislative clarification on women's separate estates a necessity.

In 1850 a married woman in Massachusetts still had to create a marriage settlement in order to protect her property from her husband's control and debts. For women in Connecticut, meanwhile, this step had become unnecessary. They all had gained property rights enjoyed by only a few of their sisters in neighboring Massachusetts. Perhaps in the long run, Connecticut women gained as a result of the conservatism of their courts. By 1850 they had more property rights than women in many other states, including Massachusetts.

Provisions for Widows

Under a legal system that defined married women as dependents, widowhood presented special problems. Bereft of financial support, widows need immediate assistance. Whereas for some women widowhood did not represent a time of economic crisis, because their husbands provided well for them by will, in the majority of families men left no wills. In these cases, and in instances when testators provided inadequately for their wives, the law stepped in, furnishing rules to determine what part of the family estate belonged to the widow, as well as the children and other heirs of the deceased.[1]

The English common law on inheritance, adopted in its basic form by all of the colonies and states, gave a widow the right to one-third of the real property owned by her husband at any time during the marriage.[2] This right was termed "dower." If the marriage were childless, the widow could claim one half of her husband's real property. Dower represented the minimal right of a woman to her husband's estate. A man could devise his wife more than the law required, or even his entire estate, but he could not give her less. If a husband did ignore the dower rule, his widow could renounce the will and demand an assignment of her thirds. This meant, however, that she could claim no part of the personal estate beyond her paraphernalia—clothing, jewelry, and personal items suitable to a woman of her social status—for dower in England and in most American jurisdictions did not include personal property in the eighteenth and early nineteenth centuries.[3] When a man died intestate, his wife received dower in the real estate and, in addition, a share of the personal estate (above her paraphernalia) owned by the husband at the time of his death. Her share of personal property was one-third the value of the whole if there was a living child or children, and one half if there were no children.

The property that did not descend to a widow as dower or as her share of an intestate estate went to the other legal heirs. By will, a man could devise his property to whomever he chose. Eighteenth-century law did not demand a provision for his children or collateral relations, as it did for his widow.[4] If a man died intestate, however, the law of England decreed that his real estate descend to his eldest son, whereas his personal property was divided equally among all the children. If there was no son in a family, the lands descended to all the daughters as coparceners. Many of the American colonies rejected the English law of primogeniture in the seventeenth century, some preferring to grant eldest sons double portions instead.[5] New York, Virginia, Maryland, and South Carolina were exceptions. New York observed the rule of primogeniture until 1774, Virginia until 1785, Maryland until 1786, and South Carolina until 1791.[6] Special treatment for eldest sons persisted until the late eighteenth century, when republican ideology made unequal distribution suspect. At that time, all the states studied here provided for the equal inheritances of children, female as well as male.[7]

According to David Narrètt, New York lawmakers may have supported primogeniture, but New Yorkers themselves avoided it. Rather than giving eldest sons exclusive rights to realty, parents provided for the distribution of their lands among all their sons, and sometimes their daughters as well. Mothers expressed their dislike of primogeniture even more firmly than fathers. The wide rejection of primogeniture among testators led Narrett to question its application in cases of intestacy. Families of both Dutch and English stock "commonly expected the eldest son to relinquish his right of primogeniture."[8] Perhaps, then, primogeniture did not determine descent in many cases of intestacy in the other colonies either. Such a custom would explain the readiness of Americans to abandon the long-standing rule at the end of the eighteenth century.

Courts guaranteed widows support from the family estate as a way of compensating women for their loss of property at marriage. Because the common law denied femes coverts the right to own property, it had a strong moral obligation to provide support during widowhood, particularly for young widows left with the care of minor children. As Blackstone explained the rationale behind dower, "The reason, which our law gives for adopting it, is a very plain and sensible one; for the sustenance of the wife, and the nurture and education of the younger children."[9]

The common law allowed a widow to remain in the main family residence for a specified period of time after her husband's death, usually one to two months in the colonies but forty days in England. During that time, the heir at law or his legal representative was obliged to assign the widow dower. If he failed to do so within the prescribed period, the widow could sue out a writ of dower against him and demand her assignment. But at the end of her quarantine, the heir also could evict a widow from her place of residence, whether or not he had assigned her dower in other property.[10]

The dower right of a widow represented a life interest only. It did not give a woman power to sell or devise dower property, only to enjoy the rents and profits from the lands during her lifetime. When a widow died, her dower estate descended to her husband's children in the same manner as the rest of the estate. If no children survived her, the property descended to her husband's heirs rather than her own. The provision for automatic descent demonstrates the primary purpose of dower, immediate support for a widow without independence. Women could use family property to maintain themselves, but they could not own it in their own names.[11]

Rules concerning the use of dower lands further delineated the position of dependency envisioned for widows by the common law. Because widows were only life tenants, they could not diminish the value of dower lands without risking a suit for waste by the ultimate heirs. "Waste" was a term signifying damage, and it included restrictions against cutting down trees, opening mines, and neglecting the upkeep of buildings and fences. Full privileges for the use of real property belonged only to fee simple owners. A man could devise real property to his wife free from restrictions against waste, but that privilege had to be stated explicitly in his will. In the absence of such a declaration, the law prohibited waste.[12]

When a man died testate, leaving his wife specific property in his will, she could choose between the devises and dower. Testamentary provisions for widows were many and various. They ranged from absolute gifts of all of the property a man owned to little or nothing at all. Some men granted their wives only their paraphernalia and then directed children to care for their mothers. Others asked their wives to raise the children and to give them a share in family property when they came of age.[13] But regardless of the kind of provision made for a widow, she could accept or reject it according to her judgment of her best interests. Each colony and state provided guidelines for administering estates, which specified the length of time given to a widow for accepting her husband's will. Generally she had from six months to a year to make her final decision.[14]

The privilege of choosing between the will and dower could be a significant one. Wives of insolvent debtors found the rule particularly advantageous, for under the common law widows received dower before debts were paid. Thus a widow's thirds could not be affected by the debts or insolvency of her husband, whereas her legacy could be claimed by creditors. Although creditors could not claim dower property for the payment of debts until after the death of the widow, the reversion could be sold during her lifetime, a practice that heightened her sense of dependency. She lived on the forced charity of her husband's creditors. Occasionally, when estates proved insolvent only after extensive investigation, courts allowed widows to claim dower even though they initially had accepted the terms of their husbands' wills.[15] Tapping Reeve noted that a wife could not be denied dower because of her husband's indebtedness, nor could a man sell or mortgage his property during the marriage if such a transaction worked to deny his wife dower.[16] Unless the woman consented to a conveyance and publicly acknowledged her willingness to renounce dower rights in the lands, the conveyance would not hold against her future claims. After the death of her husband a woman could sue the present owner for her dower and be awarded a life interest by the court as though the conveyance never had taken place. This provision was undoubtedly the most valuable aspect of the Anglo-American dower law for women.[17]

If a woman inherited real property or purchased lands in her own name before marriage, or if she and her husband inherited jointly or purchased in both their names during marriage, the woman retained title after the death of her husband. He could not bar her right by selling or mortgaging the property, unless she joined in the conveyance and underwent a private examination. Women retained fee simple title to all real property they owned or gained by right of survivorship in instances of tenancy by entireties, in addition to their dower right in their husbands' real estate.[18] Tenancy by the entirety represented one of the strongest property rights women possessed under the Anglo-American system of law. When a husband and wife held title in both their names, neither one could alienate the property without the consent of the other, and it was not liable for either spouse's debts. Although most women did not own realty in the period studied, the right of survivorship marked a significant advantage for those who did.

Yet even here husbands had the legal advantage. Just as wives retained fee simple rights in their own property during marriage, so did husbands. And whereas widows received a third, or at most a half, of their husbands' realty as dower, widowers gained life estates in all of their deceased wives' real estate. As tenants by the curtesy, men held the realty of their wives for life in their role as guardian of the children of the marriage. They could not convey the property or devise it, but they retained all the rents and profits for as long as they lived, and they made all managerial decisions. Because tenancy by the curtesy ostensibly depended on a man's role as guardian of his children, men whose wives died without giving birth to children capable of inheriting lost their right to life estates. The property descended automatically to the heirs of the wife. It was a contradiction, then, that a man's right to act as tenant by the curtesy did not end if his child died either before or after the mother. As long as a child was born alive, the husband's right accrued. No satisfactory explanation for such an inconsistency was offered by any commentator of the period, but it is clear that as tenants by the curtesy men enjoyed extensive rights not known to tenants in dower. Curtesy rights also extended to an equity of redemption or a trust, for example, whereas dower rights did not.[19]

Courts developed strict policies on releases of dower and ownership rights.[20] By requiring the formal consent of wives to all land transactions arranged by their husbands, jurists attempted to protect women's interests. When women neglected to follow statutory regulations for executing conveyances and releasing their rights, or when men conveyed land without the knowledge and consent of their wives, women could sue successfully for return of their property or dower during widowhood.

In granting one widow dower in the lands her husband conveyed without her release, Pennsylvania Supreme Court Justice Tilghman noted the absolute rights of widows: "Why should a wife stand unprotected, when the husband wishes to bar her of her dower? Dower has always been favored by the law." Tilghman's colleague, Justice Brackenridge, believed that courts of law should give dower their "most peculiar attention." He wrote with typical revolutionary flair (the year was 1810) that "the tenant in dower, is so much favored, as that it is the common by-word in the law, that the law favors three things, life, liberty, and dower."[21] Courts consistently enforced the requests of widows for dower when their husbands conveyed lands without their consent.

Given the unyielding nature of the rules on releases of dower, it is not surprising that buyers generally took pains to obtain women's consent to conveyances. For example, when Anthony Banning agreed to buy lands from John Gleaves, he asked for a release of Mrs. Gleaves's dower right. Gleaves assured Banning that the release could be obtained and executed a contract guaranteeing him all rights to the property, "without any manner of lett suit trouble or denial of the said John Gleaves and Hannah his wife."[22] Similarly, Michael Lowe demanded a release of dower from Mary Loper when he agreed to purchase lands from her husband. Mrs. Loper refused to sign the release unless Lowe agreed to pay her three guineas. He objected to the demand, offering instead "to go to the store and make her . . . a present of as fine a Gown as she ever worn."[23] A refusal by Mrs. Loper at this point caused Lowe to change his plans. He decided not to buy the property from her husband. Other men could be just as reluctant as Michael Lowe to acquire lands that might one day be encumbered by a widow's right to dower. In this

respect women possessed significant power to influence the land conveyances of their husbands.[24] The ability to keep property within the family may
have saved some women from financial hardship through the mismanagement or ill will of their spouses.

Dower was not the only form of support for widows recognized by Anglo-
American law. Jointures served as an alternative in some families, although
they probably were more common in England than in America. A jointure
was a contract between husband and wife, often made as a part of a marriage
settlement, designating what property the woman would receive if her husband died before her. When executed before marriage, a jointure barred
dower. If executed afterwards, the widow could renounce the agreement and
ask for dower instead, should such a move prove advantageous financially.
The law assumed that as a feme covert she had been under the coercion of
her husband in arranging for a postnuptial jointure; it would not, therefore,
hold her to the bargain against her will.[25]

According to Blackstone, landed families in England preferred jointures to
dower as a provision for widows. He believed, in fact, that "tenancy in dower
happens very seldom" among the elite. Apparently families of wealth in the
early modern period discovered a characteristic of dower that proved trou-
blesome to their eighteenth- and nineteenth-century American descendants
as well. As Blackstone explained it, "The claim of the wife to her dower at
common law diffusing itself so extensively, it became a great clog to alien-
ations, and was otherwise inconvenient to families."[26] As a result, families
arranged provisions for widows before marriage and thereby avoided the
disadvantages of widows' liens on entire estates. They restricted the widow's
share to certain parts of the estate, or replaced an inheritance of land with
another provision entirely, such as a maintenance and use of the mansion
house for life. In most cases, the widow's maintenance bore a direct relationship to the portion she brought into her marriage.

Jointures had the obvious advantage over dower of assuring a woman
specific property during widowhood. But if a jointure was prenuptial, it did
not allow a woman to benefit from a rise in her husband's fortunes during
marriage. It also restricted couples from selling, mortgaging, or exchang-
ing the property included in the jointure. Perhaps for both these reasons,
jointures remained uncommon in eighteenth- and early nineteenth-century
America, where family fortunes often waxed and waned within generations,
and conveyances were common.

Such were the general rules on provisions for widows. Variations on the
common law and equity themes abounded, however, in both England and the
colonies. Perhaps more than in any other area of the law, local custom in the

mother country and statutes in America served to modify the rules on inheritance. As demonstrated by George Lee Haskins and Margaret Spufford, among others, inheritance practices varied widely from one area of England to another.[27] Widows might receive all their husbands' property if they lived in one place and nothing if they lived in another, or their right to use property might be restricted to the duration of their widowhood. In addition, varying standards applied to women of different social classes. Wealthy women in England often had jointures, whereas the wives of small farmers found their rights determined more by local custom. In the absence of regional customary rights, common law dower rules prevailed.

In America, statutes that appeared early in the colonial period reformed certain aspects of the English law of inheritance. A willingness to abandon primogeniture, for example, found expression in early intestacy statutes. In addition, courts sanctioned modifications in the rules on waste, in creditors' rights, and in the method of determining dower shares, all of which affected married women. The variety of English inheritance practices may have prompted the colonists to change common law rules on dower even more readily than other areas of the common law. It may be, however, that some of the shifts we see in the colonies represented the application of standard local customs rather than innovations. Until more work has been done on English inheritance, it will be impossible to understand the extent to which American practice differed from the English in this area of the law. By comparing the colonies and states with one another over time, however, we may be able to unravel something of the story of legal change and innovation concerning inheritance in early America.

DOWER IN PERSONALTY:
THE CHESAPEAKE ADVANTAGE

When the first settlers arrived in America at the beginning of the seventeenth century, the common law of England allowed widows dower in both personal and real property.[28] At the death of her husband a widow gained a life estate in one-third to one-half of his real property, and absolute rights in one-third to one-half of the personal estate remaining after the payment of funeral expenses and debts.

During the seventeenth century, English practice on dower slowly changed. Women lost their right to dower in personal property and retained only the right to a share in real property. In writing his treatise on English law, Blackstone attempted to trace this development. He found that during the reign of Charles I, the common law still allowed widows dower in both kinds of property.[29] At that time men could bequeath only one third of their personal estates, called the "dead man's share," to persons outside their immediate families. One-third descended automatically to the widow as dower, and one-third went to the children. During the latter half of the seventeenth century, however, the rules on testamentary rights and dower began to shift. By 1700 in most areas of England, men exercised full rights to bequeath all of their personal property to whomever they pleased. The rights of their wives to dower in personal property ended as a result of the new liberal attitudes toward testamentary rights.

Blackstone wrote, "We cannot trace out when first this alteration began."[30] His difficulty in discovering the date was undoubtedly a result of the major role played by local customs in determining the dower shares of English-women. In some areas of England men long had possessed the right to bequeath personal property, and in others the shift occurred at various times, prompted by new attitudes toward devising.[31] In yet other areas the old common law rule restricting bequests persisted until changed by act of Parliament. Blackstone noted that in three areas, York, Wales, and London, the rule lasted "till very modern times." Statutes eventually unified all of English law on dower. New laws passed for York in 1693, for Wales in 1696, and for London in 1725. "Thus is the old common law now utterly abolished throughout all the kingdom of England, and a man may devise the whole of his chattels as freely, as he formerly could his third part or moiety."[32]

Although it was impossible for Blackstone to designate a single date as the time of change in the dower laws of England, it is possible to be quite specific on this point for the American colony of Connecticut, by comparing the laws enacted on dower during the seventeenth century. In Connecticut, the statutes printed in 1656 included a rule on dower that allowed widows a share of both real and personal property. After noting the rights of a widow to dower in the real property of her husband, the law read, "And it is further Ordered, That every such wife, as before expressed, immediately after the death of her husband, shall have interest in, and unto, one third part of all such Money, Goods and Chattels, of what kind soever, whereof her husband shall dye possessed, (so much as shall be sufficient for the discharge of his Funerall, and just debts, being first deducted) to be allowed, and set out to her (as before appointed) for her Dower."[33] In 1656, then, dower in Connecticut followed the general English practice of the early seventeenth century. By 1673 the law had changed, and widows no longer possessed dower rights to personal property. An edition of Connecticut laws published in that year stated that widows should receive dower in one-third the real property of their deceased husbands, with "the remainder of the Estate to be disposed according to the will of the deceased."[34] After 1673, men in Connecticut were entitled to bequeath all of their personal property to whomever they pleased, free from the dower rights of their wives.

In most of the other American colonies, dower in real property only was the rule by the beginning of the eighteenth century.[35] Two colonies did not follow England in this area of the law, however. Maryland and Virginia continued to grant dower in personal property throughout the period studied. The situation in Maryland remained fairly straightforward, but in Virginia the designation of slaves as real property for the purposes of descent created an odd twist in the law.

MARYLAND RULES

In colonial Maryland the law of inheritance developed in a manner that was particularly beneficial to widows. Wives there never lost their right to dower in personal property, including slaves. Men could bequeath only the "dead man's share," or one-third of their personal estates. In accordance with traditional common law guidelines, one-third of the personalty a man owned descended to his widow and one-third descended to his children absolutely.[36]

At the end of the eighteenth century a challenge arose to the Maryland dower law. In the case of *Griffith* v. *Griffith's Executors* (1798), the courts were asked to examine state policy concerning widows' dower rights.[37] The plaintiff, Mrs. Griffith, complained in her statement to the court that her husband had granted no part of his personal property to her in his will. Her devises consisted entirely of real property. She asked that dower in the personal estate be assigned to her. As for the real property, she claimed to be content with the will.

The heirs of Mr. Griffith disputed the request by his wife for a half-and-half disposition, and as a result there exists a detailed discussion of English and Maryland dower laws by contemporary jurists. Counsel for the widow noted that since the earliest days of settlement, Maryland courts had granted widows dower in both kinds of property. He cited several statutes, beginning in 1638 and ending in 1729, all granting widows rights to personal property. He also noted that inheritance statutes of 1704 and 1715 specifically gave the widows of testate men dower in personalty, by allowing them the right to choose between dower and bequests of chattels. Opposing counsel disagreed with this analysis, claiming that seventeenth-century Maryland statutes on dower were unclear. He argued that because the colony was required to follow English law, Maryland widows had lost their right to dower in personal property at the same time as Englishwomen. He dismissed the eighteenth-century statutes as "mistaken in the law, which is no uncommon case," and he advocated a rejection of all provisions allowing widows both kinds of dower property.[38] To recognize dower rights in personal estate would be inconsistent with the legal traditions of Maryland and the mother country, he argued.

In a key decision for women, the Court of Appeals ruled in favor of the request made by Mrs. Griffith. The justices believed that the Maryland statute of 1704 had delineated the right of widows to dower in personal property, even if common law provisions in the previous century had been equivocal. In passing judgment, however, the court expressed its belief that English common law rules of the seventeenth century had granted widows dower in personalty. Justice William Pinckney wrote that when the first settlers came to Maryland, they brought the laws of England with them. One of those laws granted widows dower in personalty, and the law was never revised in the colony, "although in England it was undergoing gradual alterations." In Pinckney's eyes, "The change of the law in England could have no influence on it here—It was not changed by an act of parliament, or suddenly changed; it altered imperceptibly and silently. The colonists being far removed from the mother country, either did not know of this change, or did not choose to follow it; and it is clear that they were not bound to follow it."[39]

The Maryland laws granting widows dower in personal property gave to women a more equitable share in family estates than they possessed elsewhere. Maryland law placed slaves in the category of personal property, and therefore the benefits were considerable.[40] Women in Maryland retained absolute control over a certain portion of the personal wealth of their families. Their ability to bequeath it gave to a certain class of Maryland matrons significant power within the family.

The benefits women derived from the Maryland dower law are demonstrated by the case of Hopewell Hebb, a resident of St. Mary's County whose husband died in 1758. Mr. Hebb wrote a will in which he divided all of his estate, both real and personal, among his wife and children. Mrs. Hebb, displeased with her share, decided to exercise her rights under the law. She accepted the devises given to her of real property, but asked for dower in the personal estate. Mr. Hebb had bequeathed certain slaves to his wife for the length of her life only, and it was this disposition that Mrs. Hebb opposed. By demanding dower she gained an absolute title to one-third of her deceased husband's slaves, including the right to bequeath them at her death. When Hopewell Hebb died in 1773, she gave three slaves to her daughter Gracy, four slaves to her daughter Ann, twenty pounds sterling to her daughter Priscilla, and the remainder of her considerable estate to her son, Vernon. The uneven nature of the bequests demonstrates the desire of the widow to control the descent of family property. She clearly favored some children over others and expressed her feelings through her will.[41]

The Maryland dower rules benefited women from the earliest years of settlement. In the Chesapeake, women possessed more rights to the estates of their deceased husbands than in any of the other colonies studied. It is particularly interesting to find this special regard for the dower rights of Maryland widows in light of research on the status of women in the Chesapeake. In a pathbreaking article, Lois Green Carr and Lorena S. Walsh demonstrated that Maryland women possessed a high status in the seventeenth century, primarily because of their small numbers. The value attached to women as wives and mothers, in combination with early death rates for men and the absence of male-dominated kinship networks, meant that husbands in Maryland were more willing to bequeath large estates to their wives than were Englishmen. Thus husbands frequently gave their widows full powers of control over both property and children.[42]

Although Carr and Walsh found that the pattern of favoring wives over children and collateral kin was weakening by the end of the seventeenth century, their conclusions are still useful for understanding the meaning of the Maryland dower law. It appears that in the Chesapeake, men willingly accorded extensive property rights to their wives, and also tailored colony laws to fit their attitudes. When the need for favoring women changed as demographic problems disappeared in the late seventeenth century, the laws remained the same. Thus Maryland wives were able to retain the right to dower in personal property when other colonial women could not. In this case, the reluctance of lawmakers to change statutory provisions worked for the benefit of women.

VIRGINIA RULES

Like their neighbors in Maryland, Virginians guaranteed widows a dower share in personal property, although in the first decades of settlement there was apparently some confusion over the exact meaning of a widow's thirds. Initially, Virginians failed to define dower by statute. They relied instead on custom or the common law to guide executors or administrators, family members, and court officials in distributing the estates of the dead. In 1664 the General Assembly acted to end the resulting confusion by enacting a law to define dower. The statute, "An Act concerning Widdows thirds," noted that doubts had arisen about the proper way of apportioning dower. To end confusion, lawmakers stated that all real and personal property was subject to dower claims. In assigning real property, cleared and wooded lands and housing were to be divided into thirds, with the widow taking her choice among the three parcels first.[43] By this definition the assembly attempted to obviate difficulties over apportioning the widow's share in cases of intestacy, when the will was unclear, or, one assumes, when the widow renounced the will and asked for her thirds instead.

Nine years later the assembly refined its definition of dower by restricting the widow's share of personal property to a child's portion if more than two children survived their father. A widow still received one-third of the real property, "to bee equally divided as to houseing, ffenced grounds, orchards, woods, and other valuable conveniences." As the statute specified, "In case the husband make a will that he hath it in his power to devise more to his wife than what is above determined, but not lesse."[44] Again, in 1705, the assembly made further refinements in its definition. At that time, lawmakers chose to make a distinction between the legal share of an intestate's wife and the minimal share a husband had to leave his widow if he wrote a will. The intestate's wife received the right to a full third of her husband's personal property, regardless of the number of surviving children. The wife of a man who devised his estate, however, still could lay claim only to a child's portion of the personal property if there were more than two living children for whom provisions had to be made. In addition, for the first time a Virginia statute on inheritance included the common law rule that a childless widow had rights to half her husband's real and personal property. Presumably, before 1705 such a division was enforced by custom only. Another important provision of the statute of 1705 for women was a clause giving widows the right to remain "in the mansion house" until heirs assigned dower, rather than for the forty days allowed by English law.[45]

Even after England's Parliament had enacted a statute to deny women dower in personal property, Virginia widows continued to benefit from the older definition of their thirds. The year 1705 did mark a decline in widows' rights, however. At that time Virginia lawmakers took the unusual step of defining slaves as real property for the purposes of inheritance.[46] They believed that the best way of preserving valuable plantations in a slaveholding economy was to allow property owners to create entailed estates of both land and slaves. Only by defining slaves as real property could such an end be realized, for personal property could not be entailed under the rules of English property law. In addition, given the existence of primogeniture in

Virginia, lawmakers also were acting to ensure that the sons who gained the land received the slaves needed to work it; the statute of 1705 gave the eldest son the right to inherit all of his father's slaves. According to C. Ray Keim, the General Assembly's motivation was to ensure the orderly transmission of essential slave labor to eldest sons along with patrimonial estates.[47] The statute did not, however, go so far as to ignore the common law rights of the younger children to distributive shares in their father's personal property. It required the eldest son to compensate his siblings for the value of their shares of the slaves.

Virginia statutes allowing widows dower in personal property also may have figured in the decision to redefine the nature of slave property. Having decided to continue the widow's thirds in personalty, the assembly still was unwilling to allow women absolute control over valuable slave property. A compromise—granting women the use of slaves for life, but not the right to sell or bequeath them—solved the lawmakers' dilemma. Perhaps most important, the law protected slaves from transfer to another family unit should a widow decide to remarry. Her new husband could use the slaves he held in right of his wife, but he could not alienate them. At the death of his wife, he had to relinquish them to the heir at law along with her dower lands. If he predeceased her, she retained control over her dower slaves as well as her lands.

Virginians approved of their experiment in defining slaves as real property. In 1727, when assemblymen enacted a second statute on the point, they observed that the law of 1705 "hath been found by experience very beneficial for the preservation and improvement of estates in this colony."[48] Despite the utility of the statute, however, numerous legal problems had arisen from the odd redefinition of slave property. With an eye toward correcting them, the assembly attempted to clarify its definition by explaining in what ways slaves were still to be regarded as personalty. The result was a rule defining slaves as realty only for the purposes of creating entails, endowing widows, and transmitting family wealth to heirs.

One apparent misunderstanding that arose from the earlier statute concerned the right of husbands to slaves brought into marriage by women marrying for the first time. Some courts claimed that men marrying single women as well as widows gained only a life estate in their wives' slaves, and not the right to sell or bequeath that property. To dispel the misconstruction, the lawmakers ordered "that where any feme sole is or shall be possessed of any slave or slaves, as of her own proper slave or slaves, the same shall accrue to, and be absolutely vested in the husband of such feme, when she shall marry."[49] The slaves bequeathed or conveyed to a feme covert also became her husband's property. That is, only dower slaves were real estate, not all slaves owned by women.

The attempt to clarify this confusing area of the law did not, ultimately, succeed. According to the Virginia assembly, its experiment eventually proved disastrous. In 1748 it enacted a law making slaves personal property for all purposes.[50] As a joint committee of the Governor's Council and members of the House of Burgesses later described the decision, "This last act [1727] being in the first part explanatory, was productive of many suits; it was thought to look back to the first law made twenty-two years before, destroyed old titles, and created new, and was attended with such doubts, variety of opinions, and confusion, that new points are even yet started, and undetermined."[51] Continuing litigation had forced Virginia lawmakers to acknowledge that their ill-advised reform created more evil than good and must be ended. Moreover, in many instances it had proved impossible to entail slaves without actually reducing the value of the settled property. Some estates became "overstocked" with slaves, and on others entailed slaves could not, over time, be distinguished from slaves held in fee simple. Resettling slaves became dangerous to owners who later needed to prove the slaves were entailed. And creditors, who still could seize entailed slaves, often were defrauded of their just debts when slaves could not be identified properly.[52]

The assembly's decision to change its definition of slave property did not affect widows' dower rights. A statute on dower enacted at the same time as the law making slaves personal property safeguarded the interest of widows.[53] But it also carefully noted that despite the redefinition of slaves as personal estate, widows would not gain absolute rights to their dower slaves, as they did to other personal property: the assembly continued to give widows only a life interest in the slaves they received as dower rather than absolute ownership. Such a distinction was essential, the lawmakers believed, "to prevent the ruin which would otherwise soon happen to some of the best estates here, by widows marrying second husbands, and carrying with them a property in so many of their first husbands slaves."[54] The statute also retained a provision giving heirs at law the right to widows' dower slaves as well as the other slaves of their fathers. Thus the assembly sought to retain what it perceived as the specific benefits of defining slaves as real property for the purpose of inheritance, while ending the disadvantageous effects of a general definition.

Despite such a goal, the English Privy Council repealed both statutes. English officials continued to believe in the efficacy of attaching slaves to land, and therefore they followed the recommendation of the Virginia lieutenant governor, William Gooch, to repeal the laws.[55] Only with the Revolution did Virginians find release from the problematical legal experiment of their ancestors. In 1776 the assembly enacted "An Act declaring tenants of lands or slaves in taille to hold the same in fee simple," and in 1792 it moved to define slaves as personal property for all other purposes.[56]

Although slaves became personal property by statute in 1792, widows did not gain absolute rights to dower slaves, as they did in neighboring Maryland. Statutes on women's inheritance rights continued to specify widows' life estates in slaves. Moreover, the new definition of slaves as personal property resulted in an adverse judicial decision on dower in *McCargo v. Callicott* (1811), in part because the revised statute on widows' rights did not state explicitly that widows had dower rights in slaves.[57] Instead, it simply gave them a life interest. The omission of the word "dower" caused the Court of Appeals to rule that upon remarriage, widows lost to their second husbands their life interests in the slaves of their first husbands. A man gained complete control over the slaves his wife brought into marriage, including the right to dispose of them by will during the life of the widow. If the second husband died intestate, his wife could take only a third share in her own dower slaves from the first marriage. The decision contradicted traditional learning on dower, for at the death of her second husband, a woman had always received her interest in the dower lands she brought to the marriage. In addition, by granting widows life interests in slaves rather than absolute rights in the first place, the colonial assembly had sought to prevent the evil of separating widows' slaves from their lands.

In *McCargo v. Callicott*, counsel in favor of the widow's dower right argued that separating slaves from lands was opposed to sound public policy. He admitted that dower in slaves presented a difficult problem to families as well as to the law. But, he claimed, defining slaves as real estate allowed second husbands certain significant rights to use slave property, without terminating the widow's interest in her former husband's estate. She retained the ability to keep the property of her deceased husband together, for her own sake and the sake of her children. He concluded forcefully, "Of what use would her dower lands (which, it is admitted, survive to her on her second husband's death) be, without slaves to work them?" The counselor refused to admit that prerevolutionary customs in widows' thirds had been changed by the statutes enacted in 1792. He claimed, "The uniform practice before the revolution was for the widow to hold her dower slaves for life, notwithstanding her second marriage. . . . Neither is the law altered in that respect." But the countering points of the opposing counselor won the unanimous approval of the Court of Appeals. He noted astutely, "Since the act declaring slaves to be personal estate, they are not, properly speaking, held as dower. The legislature has cautiously avoided using that word; instead of which its language is, that the wife shall have 'the use, for her life, of such slave as shall be in her share.' This does not prevent her disposing of such use to her second husband, which she does by the marriage."[58]

Despite such a clear delineation of the problems created for widows by the wording of the new statute, the legislature did not revise the law. It must have made the decision to remarry a more difficult one for some young widows. But ultimately more important than the postrevolutionary restrictions on remarriage in Virginia was the state's continuing commitment to granting widows a dower share of personal estate. Had either Virginia or Maryland prevented widows from claiming slaves along with land, that "great privilege" of Anglo-American law—dower—would have been reduced significantly. In a plantation society, labor-scarce except for the workers kept in bondage, women needed dower in slaves to ensure their financial security. Rules on inheritance in the early Chesapeake reflected recognition of that need by giving widows strong rights to both land and slaves.

SOUTH CAROLINA AS THE EXCEPTION

If one accepts the premise that the Chesapeake colonies granted widows dower in slaves because in a plantation society it was necessary to do so, the fact that South Carolina did not follow their example needs explanation. In South Carolina, despite a strong slaveholding tradition among the wealthier settlers and an economy based almost solely on slave labor, widows received dower only in real property, and slaves never were reclassified to fall under that category.

One reason for the difference between the South Carolina laws on dower and those of Virginia and Maryland may lie in the later settlement of the Carolinas. By the time Charles II granted a charter to the proprietors of Carolina in 1669, the Chesapeake assemblymen already were revising their first inheritance procedures. When South Carolina produced its first full code of laws in 1712, England had changed its common law rule on dower by statute everywhere except in London. Given the fact that of all the colonies studied, South Carolina was most dedicated to recreating the legal system of the mother country, it is not surprising that the colony defined dower as a one-third share of the real property owned by a husband at any time during the marriage. Because South Carolina women faced the same economic imperatives as women in the Chesapeake, however, it then fell to families to ensure widows adequate support. They did so, in part at least, by relying on wills with limitations, jointures, and marriage settlements. All of these tactics had the double advantage of ensuring support for widows while limiting husbands' rights to the personal property of their wives.

Throughout the colonial period, South Carolina experienced the high mortality and morbidity rates that have been chronicled so well for the early Chesapeake. According to John E. Crowley, a recent student of South Carolina inheritance practices, a high rate of testation resulted from the demographic disruption. He found, for example, that nearly half of all decedents with inventoried estates left wills in the early 1770s.[59] His research on the content of these wills highlights a number of points important to our understanding of dower in eighteenth-century South Carolina.

Crowley discovered unusually generous provisions for widows in South Carolina wills. Over the period from settlement to 1795, only 38 percent of all testators left their wives less than the equivalent of dower, whereas almost two-thirds allowed them a share in the estate's residue (usually the most valuable part of an estate). Significantly, four-fifths of husbands gave their wives at least some property to own outright rather than to hold for life.[60] Although initially planters were less generous to widows than merchants and tradesmen were, the three groups became more alike in their testamentary dispositions over time.[61] Demographic characteristics of the population—the young age of decedents and their wives, the absence of kin networks, and childless marriages—must have figured prominently in the creation of this testamentary pattern favoring widows. Lacking children and collateral heirs, men chose to devise their property to their wives.

In writing wills, however, testators also may have been acting to avoid the dangerous effects of intestacy. Under the English rule of primogeniture, adopted in colonial South Carolina, the eldest son inherited all of his intestate father's lands. If a man wanted to divide his estate more evenly among his children and avoid the effects of primogeniture, he had to do so either by deed during his life or by will. In addition, when a man died intestate in South Carolina, his wife received one-third to one-half of his whole estate as her widow's share. The real property she received only for her life; it descended eventually to her husband's heir at law, under the rule of primogeniture. But personal property, including slaves, she took absolutely. For a young man, looking ahead to the probable remarriage of his widow, her absolute ownership of much of his valuable estate in slaves was not attractive. He knew that his widow's second husband could take those slaves as his own and sell or bequeath them to whomever he pleased. The children of the first marriage ran the risk of losing their father's slaves unless he acted to prevent the loss by writing a will. The high rate of testation in colonial South Carolina may, then, indicate dissatisfaction with the law of intestacy, with regard to both primogeniture and widows' rights.

Although husbands in South Carolina feared the consequences of their widows' remarriages, they did not slight their wives in their wills. Generous provisions for widows attest to concern for their financial well-being and trust in their ability to care for children. But one characteristic of wills in South Carolina demonstrates that men were worried about the future distribution of property they gave to women. According to Crowley, limitations appear often in the wills of colonial South Carolina husbands, particularly those of planters. Such conditions on an inheritance might include eventual descent to a child or other heir of the legatee. Most important, a limitation prevented a second husband from gaining absolute ownership in the property; a man who contemplated his wife's remarriage could give her property, but at the same time provide for its eventual descent to his own children. The advantage of such a testamentary disposition over intestacy provisions was significant.

Fathers as well as husbands employed limitations. Crowley discovered that most daughters inherited personalty rather than land; real property usually went to sons. Moreover, daughters often inherited personal property, including slaves, equally with their brothers. Neither pattern is surprising, because they agree with what has been discovered about testator behavior elsewhere. What is significant about bequests to daughters in South Carolina wills is the high incidence of conditional terms accompanying them, particularly if the daughters were married. According to Crowley, fathers attempted to prevent their sons-in-law from gaining absolute rights to their wives' slaves by arranging for descent to the children of the marriage. This provision gave a husband the use of the slaves but not the right to sell or bequeath them. They had to be kept in the family for the benefit of the wife if she were widowed, and the children.[62]

A second and ultimately safer way of preventing daughters' husbands from alienating personal property was to place it in a trust. Trusts may have been more common in South Carolina than in other colonies, owing to the high value of slaves combined with their definition as personalty. Although it is not yet clear whether more women in South Carolina had marriage settlements and jointures than women elsewhere, preliminary evidence points in that direction. In any case, it is certain that reliance on trusts prevented some of the adverse effects of granting women bequests of slaves, and some families employed them for just that reason.

Out of a sample of 638 marriage settlements written in South Carolina between 1730 and 1830, 456 (71 percent) specified the nature of the settled property. Significantly, most settlements included personal property rather than land, and a substantial number of deeds involved slaves. Of the deeds that described settled property, fully 82 percent (372) included slaves; 28 percent (129) covered only estates in slaves. No other type of property is listed so frequently in the settlements. It also appears that women and their families saw the advantage of settling even small numbers of slaves for the separate use of wives and widows. Of settlements including only slaves, 32 percent (41/129) contained five slaves or fewer and an additional 19 percent contained six to ten slaves.[63] The families and individual women who designed these settlements realized the inherent problems in granting husbands absolute control over personal property. They acted aggressively to counteract them, and largely succeeded. With regard to widows' rights in particular, settlements could guarantee them the labor of at least their own slaves if their husbands neglected to bequeath them additional ones in their wills.

The role that marriage settlements could play in protecting the slave property of widows was recognized in Virginia by at least one individual, Justice Coalter of the Court of Appeals. In 1813, while defending the Virginia rules on widows' dower in slaves, he wrote, "I should regret an alteration in the law, so as to give a complete testamentary power, as in England. A resort to marriage settlements is the consequence there, and soon would be here. By this means, the wife is rendered more independent there, than she was under the custom: she can make the house and bed of her husband as uncomfortable as she pleases, and lose nothing by it: whereas, if he could, by absolute gifts to his children, or by seeking abroad those comforts he is denied at home, leave her pennyless at his death, she might find it her interest to conduct herself better."[64] Coalter could as easily have directed his remarks to South Carolina, where marriage settlements represented a fully developed area of the law and were employed more frequently than in Virginia, if his own remark can be taken as a guide to usage.

Although South Carolina law did not allow dower in personal property, families did develop effective ways of granting slaves to widows while protecting the property from second husbands. In fact, reliance on limitations and trusts in South Carolina may have given widows there more protection than dower provided in Maryland. In the Chesapeake colony, widows had absolute rights to dower slaves, and therefore so did their second husbands. Perhaps future investigations will reveal that women and their families in Maryland took precautionary steps similar to those used in South Carolina to protect their inheritances.

Intercolonial differences in dower and intestacy provisions for widows reflected the various social, demographic, and economic conditions of the early settlements. In some plantation societies, such as Maryland and Virginia, dower included personal property—slaves—as well as real property, whereas women in New England received dower only in real property from the seventeenth century onward. Clearly, southerners perceived a benefit in granting widows rights to slaves and farm implements that northerners did not. The distinction may reflect the demographic realities of the two regions in the first decades of settlement, because southern men died earlier than New Englanders, and left behind them young widows with minor children to support.[65] Women in the South needed to keep estates together for the good of the family. New England wives, usually widowed at middle age or later, could depend on grown children for financial assistance. Laws in Connecticut and Massachusetts therefore reflected the expectation that women would be looked after, whereas southern dower provisions demonstrated a greater commitment to women's autonomy.

DETRIMENTAL COLONIAL DOWER REFORMS

The deviation of Maryland and Virginia law from English rules on common law dower produced a beneficial effect for women. In Connecticut and Pennsylvania, seventeenth-century developments in the law on dower brought changes that were detrimental to the legal status of women rather than helpful. Attempts by lawmakers to simplify the rules of inheritance in these two colonies worked to reduce the rights of women to family property. In Connecticut and Pennsylvania women received dower only in the real property that their husbands possessed at death. In Pennsylvania all debts had to be paid before a widow received dower, and in Connecticut the courts did not recognize the right of survivorship for tenants by entireties.

Under the common law, widows received dower in all real property owned by their husbands at any time during the marriage. If a man conveyed property without the consent of his wife, she could claim dower in the lands after his death. Of the colonies studied, only Connecticut and Pennsylvania did not follow traditional guidelines for determining dower. There widows possessed rights in the lands that they brought to their husbands or inherited, but they did not have absolute rights to the lands their husbands owned before marriage or purchased during marriage. Men freely alienated or mortgaged their own real property; wives had no veto privilege over any disposition their husbands cared to make.

The oldest printed edition of Connecticut laws allowed widows dower according to common law tradition. In 1656 the courts guaranteed a widow one-third to one-half of the real property owned by her husband, "to his own use, either in possession, reversion, or remainder, within this Jurisdiction, at any time during the marriage."[66] A new statute enacted in 1673 read differently. It stated that a widow "shall immediately after the death of her Husband have right and interest by way of dower in and to one third part of the real estate of her said husband that he stood of at the time of his decease."[67] Thus widows lost on two points: their right to dower was reduced sharply, and they possessed no leverage to influence the property transactions of their spouses.

Swift discussed the restrictive dower rule briefly in his treatise on Connecticut law. He believed that the rule was necessary, practical in its elimination of widows' liens on real property. With many of his peers, Swift regarded dower as an "inconvenient encumbrance" on the alienation of lands. As such it was "repugnant to the policy of our laws."[68] Swift believed that seventeenth-century lawmakers viewed dower in a similar light, and so they enacted statutes restricting its damaging effects. The reformed dower rule may have been progressive in giving men more freedom to alienate real property, but it did not take into account the fact that women still lost all of their property rights when they married. Remember also that until 1723 Connecticut law did not recognize the separate rights women exercised over their own lands under the common law. Men gained absolute title to the realty of their wives at marriage, just as they did to personalty. After 1723, lawmakers did accept rules that allowed women to retain title to their own lands, but inheritance law remained unchanged with regard to widows' rights in their husbands' lands.

In establishing a new, more restrictive dower policy, Connecticut acted upon impulses usually associated with the nineteenth century. England, for example, did not enact a similar statute until 1833, when it finally moved to end widows' liens on the estates of their deceased husbands. The Dower Act of that year placed Englishwomen on the same footing as women in Connecticut, by allowing husbands total freedom to sell or mortgage their own property. After 1833, widows in England received dower only at the pleasure of their husbands, who could deny them that support by alienating family property before their deaths.[69] The fact that Connecticut laws long had observed the need to facilitate conveyancing and restrict the liens of widows indicates an early commercial emphasis in colonial America.

The Connecticut dower rule established itself so well that conflicts are rare in the court records of the period. A single short case note from 1772 demonstrates the attempt of one widow to gain dower in the lands her husband conveyed without her consent. The court responded to her request succinctly and negatively, noting that "the widow is entitled to her dower only in the lands and real estate of which her husband died seised and possessed, in his own right."[70]

A nineteenth-century case, *Stewart* v. *Stewart* (1824), tried before the Supreme Court of Errors, demonstrates the potential danger to widows of the Connecticut rule.[71] James Stewart executed a deed of all his real property to his six children, effective immediately upon his death. Since Stewart wrote and executed the deed during his lifetime, the effect of his action was denial of dower for his wife. Mary Stewart, left dependent on the goodwill of her children, challenged the disposition of her husband in court. She argued that because the transfer of the property occurred after the death of her husband, she was entitled to dower as though he had died seised. The Connecticut high court rejected her plea, citing the well-established doctrine on dower that favored free alienation of lands over widows' rights. It is important to note the emphasis on economic development apparent in the opinion of the court, and therefore the remarks are worth quoting at length:

> Our ancestors did not think it expedient to restrain that free transfer of real estate, which the interest of the community requires; and for this reason, the law has given to the wife no lien upon, or right, legal or equitable, to the husband's estate, during his life. Her condition, in this respect, is like that of her husband's children, or other heirs; and the only right of either, is, to such estate as he has not disposed of. The condition of creditors and purchasers, is altogether different. The law, proceeding on the equitable ground, that the estate of debtors ought not, unless for valuable consideration and *bona fide*, to be placed out of the reach of their creditors, has made all deeds made in contravention of this principle, absolutely void.[72]

In addition to restricting widows' dower shares, Connecticut courts also rejected the doctrine of survivorship for tenants by entireties. According to Swift, "In England on the death of either of the joint-tenants, his right remains, and goes to the surviving tenant. But in this state we have never adopted this odious and unjust doctrine of survivorship, but on the decease of one of the joint-tenants, his share descends to his heirs."[73] Of all the colonies studied, only Connecticut reformed the common law rule on survivorship.[74] This refusal to accept a doctrine enforced elsewhere spelled hardship for women property owners in the colony and state. Connecticut did not compensate women in any other way, and therefore elimination of the right of survivorship and of dower claims on husbands' estates made women particularly dependent on the goodwill of men and children. Only if their husbands did not alienate or mortgage property could women inherit.

In Connecticut, creditors possessed absolute rights to the property of indebted men. Their rights superseded the needs of wife and children. Family property could be seized and sold to pay debts at any time during the life of the debtor. When a man died before creditors had seized his estate, however, the property was liable to the dower claim of the widow.[75] Widows also received dower in mortgaged lands if they had not released their right at the time of the mortgage, and unlike Englishwomen, they could have dower in an equity of redemption.[76] As long as a man died in possession of realty, his widow received a life estate in one-third, even though his debts exceeded his assets. Creditors could not attach the property during her life, but after her death their claims took precedence.[77] Although Connecticut women therefore lost one privilege under the common law rules on dower, they retained another that was even more important. Pennsylvania women were not as fortunate. In that colony, as in Connecticut, widows received dower only in the property owned by their husbands at death, and in addition, the widows of insolvent debtors did not receive a dower share at all.

Pennsylvania lawmakers imitated the example of their New England predecessors in restricting dower. William Penn's original code of laws did not define the widow's share in her deceased husband's estate, but as early as March 1683, the colonial assembly enacted a law providing for a widow's thirds in the property owned by her husband "att the time of his death." The words reappeared in subsequent statutes on decedents' estates.[78] In 1706 the assembly stated explicitly that a widow could claim dower only in the lands "whereof her husband died seized."[79] At the same time, the Pennsylvania lawmakers included a clause in their new statute on conveyancing that left no doubt about their intentions regarding widows' liens on husbands' estates: "No woman shall recover her dower or thirds of any lands or tenements which have been sold, aliened or conveyed by her husband during her coverture, although she be no party to the deed nor anyways consenting to the sale or assurance of such lands or tenements, any law or usage to the contrary notwithstanding."[80] This law was repealed by the Privy Council in 1709. A new conveyancing statute appeared in 1711, but it did not include a clause restricting widows' dower rights.[81] In fact, subsequent laws on conveyancing contained no reference to feme covert property rights at all. The omission, perhaps made deliberately in an attempt to avoid repeal of the statutes in England, led to the uneven enforcement of private examinations. In any case, lawmakers knew that the statutes on decedents' estates fulfilled their desire to limit dower to a third of whatever real property a man possessed at his death. This rule prevailed in Pennsylvania during the period studied and appeared again in the postrevolutionary statute on distribution of estates enacted in 1794.[82]

Normally under the common law, executors or administrators used personal property first to meet the demands of creditors, and if that proved insufficient, then the widow received her life interest before real property was attached to pay debts. The widow retained this property until her death. Then, and only then, could it be divided among creditors. This ancient common law provision, stemming from a concern for the financially vulnerable position of married women, frequently served to keep widows off relief rolls. Of the colonies studied here, all but Pennsylvania enforced the provisions throughout the colonial and early national periods.[83]

In Pennsylvania, a concern for the rights of creditors weighed more heavily on the consciences of lawmakers than did their responsibility for protecting the incomes of married women. In the first legal code written for the colony, a provision unique to English law made lands liable to pay debts, one-third of the land if there were children and all of it if there were not.[84] The Great Law of 1683 extended this provision, for under that code one-half of the land could be taken to meet the demands of creditors if there were children. By 1688 lawmakers had decided that all of the land a man owned could be applied for the payment of his just debts, even if the widow and children, who might well have been ignorant of the financial situation of the family, were left without any means of support.[85] In 1700 the "Act for taking lands in execution for the payment of debts" revealed the attitude of the lawmakers: it stated explicitly that the purpose of the act was to protect the interests of creditors.[86]

In a primitive economy such as that of colonial Pennsylvania, the only security that could be given for a loan was land, and outside Philadelphia almost all the wealth of the colony existed in the form of real property. Mortgaged lands had to be forfeited at the death of the owner because the rents and profits they produced never were sufficient to pay off debts; forfeiture was the best way to repay creditors in a money-scarce economy. The maintenance of a strong credit base was viewed as essential to the young colony, and therefore the common law protection for widows was pushed aside quietly. Women whose husbands died solvent still could claim dower, but the right did not extend to the women who needed it the most, the wives of debtors.

The sensibility of William Penn to the rights of creditors was responsible for this variation of the common law in his proprietary colony. Before they left England the first Pennsylvania colonists agreed to make their lands liable for the payment of debts. The enlightened policies of Penn regarding imprisonment for debt have been used in the past to demonstrate his sympathy for the rights of debtors. But although Penn did maintain that it was impractical for such men to remain behind bars, where they could not possibly work to repay their debts, he may well have been considering the rights of creditors more than those of debtors when he advocated their release. Certainly the laws that made lands liable to pay debts, and the provision that denied a widow her dower, point in that direction. The proprietor's peculiar sense of responsibility toward creditors may well explain why Pennsylvania alone of all the colonies studied changed the common law in this area, even though every colony faced the pressures of an underdeveloped economy.

Although this policy was modern in principle, it was unfortunate that the laws dealing with the property rights of married women did not keep pace with the new attitudes toward debt repayment. Legal records from the eighteenth century demonstrate that women were denied support from family lands when creditors made claims on the estates.[87] For example, in 1767 Mary Jamison of Buckingham township in Bucks County petitioned the Orphans Court for assistance. As administrator of her husband's estate she had the responsibility of paying his debts, which amounted to over four thousand pounds. An inventory of the personal property showed that its value was only about five hundred pounds, and therefore the court ordered Mrs. Jamison to sell the family lands to meet her obligations.[88]

Some women received help from the courts in attempting to repay their husbands' debts without selling real property. After disposing of practically the entire personal estate of her husband and many things of her own, including a looking glass, knives and forks, bedding, her horse and saddle, and cooking utensils, Elizabeth Breese still could not repay all the debts of her husband. She petitioned the Orphans Court for help. It allowed her to assume a bond for the remainder of the debt, provided that she thought she could repay it within seven years. The judges refrained from ordering an immediate sale in this case because they "conceived the farm may be reasonably allowed her, for the nursing and taking care of the children." Elizabeth ultimately was unable to make the payments, however, and after years of struggling finally sold her land and house.[89]

In a suit for dower tried before the Supreme Court in 1791, counsel for Grace Scott made a concerted effort to overthrow this damaging aberration of the common law. Grace lost her right to dower when her husband mortgaged his lands without her consent and subsequently died insolvent.[90] The loss of dower was particularly hard for Grace. Records from the Bucks County Court of Common Pleas reveal that she had suffered from financial need for many years. In 1762, for example, she asked the court to grant her sole control over the small inheritance her father left her in his will. In her petition, Grace claimed that "for some Considerable time past, She hath been under the disagreeable Necessity, for the Safety of her Person, to absent her self both from the Bed and Board of her said Husband, and doth not Receive any Support from him."[91] Although no final decision is recorded, it is unlikely that Grace Scott received her request. A note on the case states that the court did not think this problem fell within its jurisdiction.

After the death of her husband, Grace asked for dower in his estate, despite its insolvency. She pointed out that her husband had failed to obtain her consent to his mortgage of their lands. As her attorney argued, English decisions protected women from the secret conveyances of their husbands because dower was a favored area of the law. He tried to sway the opinion of the court by noting that the laws of neighboring New Jersey allowed widows dower under similar circumstances. But the opinion of the court was strictly against him. The point was "too clear to bear an argument," for Pennsylvania law had always maintained that the right of a widow was secondary to that of creditors.[92]

The court observed that Pennsylvania had moved early in its judicial history to elevate creditors' rights above those of widows. In attempting to explain the dower law of his state, Justice Shippen wrote in 1793,

> Our ancestors in Pennsylvania seem very early to have entered into the true spirit of commerce by rejecting every feudal principle that opposed the alienation and partibility of lands. While, in almost every province around us, the men of wealth or influence were possessing themselves of large manors, and tracts of land, and procuring laws to transmit them to their eldest sons, the people of Pennsylvania gave their conduct and laws a more republican cast, by dividing the lands, as well as personal estate, among all the children of intestates, and by subjecting them, in the fullest manner, to the payment of their debts.[93]

One aspect of the Pennsylvania dower rule seems particularly harsh. When estates sold for the payment of debts left a surplus in the hands of the executor or administrator, the widow received not the entire amount, but only the interest of a third of it. Thus, even after losing her full dower share in the realty of her husband, she could not claim the full surplus, no matter how small. She had to share it with the other heirs. According to the Supreme Court, "Croston's case before the revolution, has settled this point fully, after considerable argument."[94]

The Pennsylvania dower policy gave to femes coverts a responsibility equal to their husbands' for repaying family debts, but it did not give them any commensurate power to control the accumulation of those debts. With regard to the enforcement of private examinations, for example, Pennsylvania courts were lax to the point of total ineffectiveness. Women in the Quaker colony thus encountered the inherent dangers of a developing legal system, a system that did not recognize or enforce basic common law safeguards for the protection of widows' livelihoods. In the colony of William Penn, unity of person was applied as a legal principle to the detriment of married women. Previously historians have assumed that the practices of early American courts worked to the benefit of married women, but improvement did not always accompany unconventional legal practices. In Pennsylvania—and Connecticut—the new economic conditions of colonial life did not create a liberal legal climate for femes coverts. Rather, the legal policies worked to deny women full access to one of the unquestioned privileges of the common law—dower.

The policies of Connecticut and Pennsylvania lawmakers on widows' inheritances also highlight another common assumption of early American law, the dependence of femes coverts. We must assume that the legislatures and courts of the two jurisdictions were not reducing widows' rights with the expectation of hurting women. They fully expected husbands, children, or other relatives to care for dependent matrons according to family means; the law, in fact, required children to help provide for indigent parents just as parents had a legal obligation to support their children. What is significant here is the higher degree of dependence expected of women in the two colonies and states. Women had less control over their own financial well-being in Connecticut and Pennsylvania as a result of the rule on dower; men held commensurately more power within the family. We are forced to recognize once again the relatively weak position of women under the law in regions with a history of radical Protestantism and a tradition of legal reform. Family interdependence as an ideal may have worked to the advantage of those women who found themselves respected and honored at home as well as in church, but for others the ideal became a danger. In instances of debt, financial loss, and death, greater family interdependence meant only increased hardship for women. Frequently the formal rules of law discussed here produced a harsh reality.

In economic terms, the reforms of Connecticut and Pennsylvania were unusual in their seventeenth-century origins, but they pointed in a direction that became more common by the end of the period studied. Dower as a form of support for widows worked reasonably well in an agricultural society bound together by close family and community ties. That it did not suit an expanding economy, with unusual needs for credit and the ready transfer of landed property, is demonstrated by the Connecticut and Pennsylvania examples. By the end of the eighteenth century, moreover, economic expansion had become a primary goal of the new United States. In postrevolutionary America, tenants in dower faced an increasingly uncongenial economic and legal environment, one in which their interests were perceived as a "clog" to development and thus detrimental to the goals of heirs, creditors, and society at large.[95] Although the reform of dower laws is primarily a story of the mid- and late nineteenth century, we can trace here some of the first steps toward the development of a new standard.

POSTREVOLUTIONARY REFORM IN THE SOUTH

Widows' rights to real property presented problems when estates could not be divided easily. Traditionally, courts assigned dower by "metes and bounds," that is, as a one-third or one-half share of each piece of real property owned by a deceased husband. If a man owned three farms, his widow received a share in each rather than an entire farm. Division by metes and bounds could be avoided only if all parties agreed to an alternative. Often families and creditors did reach such agreements, because it served all of their interests to do so. Sometimes commissioners who had the task of admeasuring dower shares provided alternatives themselves. If a piece of property could not be divided without damaging its sale value or the rents and profits, they ordered "special" assignments of dower. As Blackstone explained, "If the thing of which she is endowed be divisible, her dower must be set out by metes and bounds, but if it be indivisible, she must be endowed specially."[96] If a man had owned a mill, for example, his widow might gain rights to receive the income in every third month, or a third of the annual income.

The Massachusetts assembly codified this area of the common law in 1701. At that time the colony specified by statute "that of inheritance that be intire, where no division can be made by metes and bounds, so as a woman cannot be endowed of the thing itselfe, she shall be endowed thereof in a special and certain manner, as of a third part of the rents, issues or profits thereof."[97] The Massachusetts rule allowed a special kind of dower only when an estate could not be divided, but it failed to define "indivisible." In Massachusetts and the other jurisdictions studied, custom, and the opinion of individual heirs, commissioners, and judges determined assignments of dower.[98] Significantly, the Massachusetts statute did not delineate a widow's dower in land that was sold for the payment of debts or the support of the family. Sales for these purposes occurred on a regular basis, as demonstrated by the private acts passed to guarantee the rights of purchasers.[99] Because dower remained exempt from attachment for the payment of debts until after the death of a widow, it usually fell to courts of probate and the commissioners they appointed to determine, in cases of debt, just what dower was. In some instances, they set off the dower share by metes and bounds, and sold the remaining estate only. At other times they sold the reversion of the dower estate along with the rest. Occasionally they sold the entire estate, and granted the widow a share of the proceeds, generally a third of the sale price of the land or a third part of the interest from the invested proceeds of the sale. The end of every disposition was a guarantee of income for a widow from the estate of her deceased husband.[100]

In 1777 South Carolina went a step beyond the common law, as codified by Massachusetts, by allowing cash payments of lump sums to widows in lieu of dower when an estate could not be divided "without manifest disadvantage."[101] As in Massachusetts, it remained the task of the courts to determine whether a particular division was advantageous or not. In *Executor of Clifford* v. *Clifford* (1785), the master in Chancery was asked "to inquire whether it will be to the advantage of the minor to sell the land in bill mentioned, in preference to the personal estate: Also to report what will be a compensation to the widow for her dower."[102] He recommended a sale, and the Chancery ordered one.

By the end of the eighteenth century, South Carolina courts had determined that creditors' interests could make divisions sufficiently damaging to warrant granting widows cash in lieu of their traditional thirds. As a result, they began to consider the debts of an estate before admeasuring dower by metes and bounds. It became increasingly difficult for the wives of debtors, particularly insolvent debtors, to claim traditional dower shares in estates; instead, they had to accept cash payments.

The case that established a new precedent in this area of the law was *Creditors of Scott* v. *Scott* (1795).[103] The commissioners named to assign Sarah Scott her dower gave her several whole pieces of property rather than one-third of each one included in the estate. The creditors objected, claiming that the dower property included the most valuable part of the estate and therefore hurt their interests. In their suit to overthrow the assignment, they pointed out that dower could be assigned in only one of two ways, either by metes and bounds or, under the statute of 1777, as a payment in lieu of dower. Granting a dowager whole tracts of land rather than dower by metes and bounds was illegal, they claimed.

The Superior Court took time in considering its decision on the case. After hearing the arguments of counsel, Chief Justice Rutledge and Justice Bay postponed their decision overnight. They observed, "As this is a new case, and is to form a precedent, it therefore ought to be solemnly decided. We will consult the other judges, and give our opinion on the return day." They were still unresolved on the morrow, however. As the case report notes, they needed more time for studying the issue: "On the return day, the court considering the novelty and magnitude of the case, ordered the great question, to wit, whether the commissioners could assign the whole dower out of one tract, to be argued again next term."[104] Ultimately, the decision of the court favored creditors' interests. The justices decided unanimously that dower could be assigned in whole tracts only if all parties agreed. They asked the commissioners to reconsider the situation of Mrs. Scott and assign her dower either by metes and bounds or in a cash payment.

In *Creditors of Scott* v. *Scott*, the commissioners found it impossible to assign dower by metes and bounds without damaging the whole estate, which consisted of seventeen separate pieces of property. They therefore appraised the estate and ordered a cash payment to the widow. With this decision, Mrs. Scott's claim on her husband's estate ended. Freed from the encumbrance of her life estate in one-third the rents and profits, the various pieces of property could be sold more readily for the benefit of creditors.

In his discussion of the statute that instituted the new South Carolina rules on dower, Chief Justice Rutledge took care to praise its benefit for widows: "The act of assembly in this state was made, not to vary the right to dower, but to institute a more easy and certain mode of obtaining it. From the peculiar situation of this country, and the great disadvantage, sometimes to all parties, that may attend the dividing of a plantation, the commissioners are vested with powers to assess a sum of money, not as dower, but in lieu of dower."[105] Despite Rutledge's optimism, however, it is difficult to believe that a cash payment could always substitute adequately for the traditional life estate. Perhaps the selling price of a house or store did not equate with its value as a place to live or work. A cash payment in lieu of dower, moreover, ignored a widow's emotional attachment to a certain piece of property. Offsetting these disadvantages was the widow's right to take her money absolutely. Whereas a dower estate had to be turned over to her husband's creditors or heirs at her death, the cash payment was hers to employ as she saw fit while she lived, and to bequeath by last will and testament. If she died without a will, her property descended to her heirs rather than her husband's. Some women actually may have preferred a payment that carried these rights over dower.

It is clear that the shift in the dower law of South Carolina worked significantly to the advantage of creditors. No longer did widows' life estates reduce the purchase price of lands sold on execution for debt. The statute therefore indicates a commercial bias in the laws of the state. The South Carolina assembly had developed a neat means of eliminating widows' dower estates whenever they proved disadvantageous. After 1777, creditors could force a sale if they chose to do so.[106]

In addition to changing the nature of dower in cases of debt, South Carolina moved after the Revolution to reform another awkward feature of the common law rules on inheritance, the widow's life estate. In 1791, at the same time the state abolished primogeniture, the assembly ordered that henceforth in all cases of intestacy widows could take their shares of estates in fee simple rather than for life.[107] Significantly, the new rule did not replace dower; it simply served as an alternative for the widows of intestates. Widows who renounced their husbands' wills could claim only life estates, and the widows of insolvent debtors could protect their shares only by requesting dower. If an intestate's widow took a fee simple interest under the statute of 1791, it could be seized by her husband's creditors, whereas dower lands continued to be exempt until after the death of the widow.

Despite these limitations, the revised South Carolina law on intestacy marked a radical step forward for women. For the first time a state recognized the absolute rights of widows to family property. Perhaps equally important, the statute also reduced the rights husbands held as tenants by the curtesy, making them the equivalent of widows' rights. The statute read, "On the death of any married women, the husband shall be entitled to the same share of her real estate as is herein given to the widow out of the estate of the husband, and the remainder of her real estate shall be distributed among her descendants and relations in the same manner as is heretofore directed in case of the intestacy of a married man."[108] As tenant by the curtesy, then, he could claim one-third to one-half of his wife's realty in fee simple, but he lost the right to control the whole for his lifetime. He also lost his traditional right to claim all of his wife's choses in action at her death; now his right extended only to a third.[109]

After the Revolution, Maryland also moved to revise its law on widows' dower rights. Although Maryland did not duplicate the South Carolina reforms on intestate estates, it did codify rules on cash payments to widows with an eye toward protecting widows' interests. Unlike South Carolina widows, Marylanders did not have to give up dower when creditors pushed their claims on an estate. Instead, postrevolutionary Maryland courts granted widows a choice between dower and a cash sum in lieu of dower. In 1792, for example, the creditors of Thomas Howe Ridgate sued his widow for payment of the debts of her deceased husband.[110] They asked the Orphans Court to order sale of the real property belonging to the estate. Mrs. Ridgate stated that she had no objection to a sale, if it were made subject to her claim of dower. Although offered an eighth of the purchase price, Mrs. Ridgate elected to take a traditional dower share. As a result, the lands were sold subject to her dower claim, so that the final disposition was complicated and probably harmful to creditors. Mrs. Elizabeth Dowson faced the same alternative when her husband died in insolvent circumstances.[111] Like Mrs. Ridgate, she agreed to a sale of family property "if the Value of her Dower in said property is secured and paid to her."[112] Here the widow accepted a cash payment in lieu of dower. In 1796 she received one-eighth of the proceeds produced by selling her husband's real estate.

DETERMINING THE CASH VALUE
OF DOWER SHARES

A major problem remained for the courts to solve—determining what constituted an equitable cash payment. Initially, South Carolina courts followed the old common law rule and gave widows a full third of the purchase price. It did not take long, however, for judges to realize that they were being overly generous in ordering dispositions that gave women the right of absolute ownership rather than simply a life estate. In *Heyward* v. *Cuthbert* (1814), Justice Smith of the South Carolina Constitutional Court objected to a payment of one-third the purchase price of a man's lands to his widow, noting that such a payment represented an increase over the traditional dower share.[113] Increasing dower rights was not the intention of the legislature in enacting the statute of 1777, Smith claimed. Rather, the statute was designed to provide a remedy for cases in which partitioning an estate proved detrimental to the interests of heirs and creditors. As Smith saw the situation, "To give one third of the fee simple value, is a gross departure from the spirit, as well as the letter of the act. Besides it is transcending the original intention of this reasonable provision for widows. The object of this humane law was not to enrich the widow to the detriment of creditors, and the impoverishment of the rest of a man's family; but for the sustenance of the wife, and the nurture and education of the younger children; and this was to determine on the death of the widow."[114]

Courts realized that widows' thirds could vary in value considerably depending on the age and health of the woman. To a widow of twenty, a life estate signified much more than it did to a widow of sixty. Jurists needed to develop a useful system for proportioning estates between widows and other heirs or creditors. In Maryland, eighteenth-century cases involving cash payments to widows gave women one-eighth of the purchase price of their husbands' lands regardless of the age of the widow.[115] The figure probably was derived from contemporary English decisions that also placed the value of a life estate at one-eighth of the purchase price, but it was not based on sound principles. In 1799 the legislature attempted to establish a more equitable guideline. It enacted a law ordering that in selling intestates' estates, chancellors could give widows up to one-seventh of the proceeds, and not less than one-tenth, "according to the age, health and condition of such widow."[116]

Although the new statute established boundaries, it did not satisfy the needs of judges who faced the difficult task of dividing estates. In 1803 the Chancery Court of Maryland decided to confront the problem of determining widows' shares. At that time Chancellor Hanson discussed the issue in detail, noting that the General Assembly had been remiss in failing to establish more useful guidelines for determining dower. The chancellor believed that the rule outlined in the inheritance statute slighted younger women and benefited older women, for "it is plain to common sense, that the dower of an old woman cannot be equal in value to that of a young one." In an effort to equalize payments, Hanson developed a table for determining the shares of widows on the basis of age. His rules specified that "a healthy widow, not exceeding thirty years, shall be allowed one-sixth of the net amount of sales; if above thirty and not exceeding thirty-seven, one seventh; above thirty-seven and not exceeding forty-five, one-eighth; above forty-five and not exceeding fifty, one-ninth; above fifty and not exceeding fifty-five, one tenth; above fifty-five and not exceeding sixty, one-eleventh; above sixty and not exceeding sixty-five, one twelfth; above sixty-five and not exceeding seventy, one sixteenth; after that age all allowed one twentieth."[117]

Maryland jurists relied on books such as *Simpson's Algebra* and Dr. Halley's *Table of Observations* for determining the duration of life for individuals of different ages. A widow of forty-two, for example, "had an even chance of living twenty-two years," according to the courts.[118] These books were employed in England to determine the value of life and reversionary interests, but on the whole Marylanders did not respect them for their accuracy. In deciding one case, the Maryland Court of Appeals noted the unlikelihood of an English life table's applying to residents of Maryland. The probability of life varied significantly among regions according to latitude and climate. As the judicial opinion read, "Would tables, suited for the lowlands of Louisiana, furnish any index of the duration of human life in the highlands of Maryland? And, even in our own state, could any dependence be placed in the calculation of the value of an annuity, or of a reversion expectant upon a life, which would say, that as great a probability existed for the duration of human life amid the marshes of the Chesapeake Bay, as in the mountains of Allegany?"[119]

In *Williams' Case* (1827), the Chancery Court noted other problems and discrepancies in current Maryland practice.[120] The chancellors disliked in particular the continuing legislative restriction to an upper limit of one-seventh and a lower limit of one-tenth. The guidelines encompassed all women between the ages of fifteen and eighty, whose life expectancies varied from forty-seven to six years. In the mind of the Chancery the legislative formula was unreasonable and needed revision. At the same time, the chancellors also voiced their disagreement with the table developed by their predecessor in 1803. The opinion on *Williams' Case* discussed four erroneous assumptions employed by Hanson in constructing his figures and concluded that the table was so defective that it could not provide justice. Moreover, the courts faced an insurmountable problem in determining which standard, that established by the assembly in 1799 or the several developed by Hanson and his colleagues on the Court of Chancery, should be followed in determining dower shares. The various standards were "so contradictory as to be utterly irreconcilable by any ingenuity or argument; and yet being rules laid down by the Legislature, or approved by the Court of Appeals this court cannot, as in some other cases, make an election to follow any one in preference to another of them." In concluding, the court observed, "The subject can now only be extricated from the difficulties in which it has been involved by the Legislature."[121] The Maryland assembly did not accept this challenge, despite its logic. No revision of the rules on apportioning dower was enacted before the latter part of the century. Perhaps the assembly perceived what some chancellors apparently did not, the injustice in granting any widow, regardless of age, so small a proportion of her husband's estate as one-sixteenth or one-twentieth. Still propertyless under the laws of the state, few women would consent to a sale if their interests were so restricted.

Other states did not enact statutes imitating the South Carolina or Maryland models for apportioning dower shares in cash during the period studied. Presumably, in instances when parties requested sales or partitions of real property, they followed local custom in granting dower. Without a detailed study of local probate records, it is impossible to know how they handled the problem. It is clear, however, that lawmakers continued to regard a share in landed property as the surest and most equitable means of providing widows with support.

RULES ON WASTE

Although land remained the key to economic security for widows throughout the period studied, attitudes toward the use of land changed significantly over time. As the nature and value of landed estates changed, so did attitudes toward dower. A particularly useful aspect of the law for understanding the relationship between widows' rights and economic change at the end of the eighteenth century is waste. As Morton Horwitz first pointed out, dower rights in timber land became suspect in New England as more men came to view land as an investment rather than a source of present support. What Horwitz did not realize, however, was the extent to which this shift marked a change from colonial policy. Before the end of the eighteenth century, all the colonies and states studied allowed widows the right to clear woodlands for planting, but Horwitz believed that "only in the nineteenth century ... did American judges begin to argue that the English law of waste 'is inapplicable to a new, unsettled country' because of its restraint on improvement of land, even though the problem appears to have been central to eighteenth century concerns as well."[122]

In England, rules against felling trees, clearing and tilling new fields, and working mines prevented some women from enjoying the full potential of their dower estates. By enforcing these rules, the law sought to protect the interests of future heirs. Courts enforced waste provisions strictly to ensure that heirs received the full value of the property descending to them.

In the American colonies, lawmakers loosened the rules on waste to allow women additional privileges. Although widows still encountered restrictions against overworking lands and neglecting the upkeep of buildings and fences, the definition of waste changed in one significant way: most courts allowed tenants in dower to clear lands for planting. In England, the common law prohibited the felling of trees because the scarcity of timber made uncleared lands extremely valuable. Farms could be damaged by the removal of trees. In contrast, most American farms, particularly before the middle of the eighteenth century, could only be improved by clearing woodlands. In addition, colonial jurists realized that women who lived in developing areas needed to open new fields for their own use. Dower in uncleared lands could not provide women with adequate support, and many families owned woodlands almost exclusively.[123]

Jurists in America concluded that there was a significant difference between the colonial situation and that of the mother country with regard to the cultivation of farmlands. They perceived the greater availability of land in the colonies as an adequate reason for changing the law on waste. Note, for example, the words of the Pennsylvania Supreme Court in deciding the case of *Hastings* v. *Crunkleton* (1801): "There was a material difference between the local circumstances of this state and of Great Britain. It would be an outrage on common sense to suppose, that what would be deemed waste in England, could receive that appellation here. Lands in general with us are enhanced by being cleared, provided a proper proportion of woodland is preserved for the maintenance of the place. If the tenant in dower clears part of the lands assigned to her, and does not exceed the relative proportion of cleared land, considered as to the whole tract, she cannot be said to have committed waste thereby."[124]

American lawmakers still warned widows against damaging dower lands by extravagant use, sometimes through clauses inserted in statutes on dower. In 1701, for example, Massachusetts enacted a statute on assignments of dower which stated that a widow "shall be liable to action for any strip or waste by her done, committed or suffered."[125] Widows who remarried could be held responsible for waste committed by their second husbands. In *Armistead* v. *Swiney and Wife* (1732), a Virginia court held a widow responsible for the unscrupulous behavior of her second spouse.[126] As counsel argued, "This wasting is to be considered as her own Act being occasioned by her folly in Marrying such a Husband."[127]

Although statutes and legal precedents forbidding waste appeared in the records, the definition varied from case to case. Most important, in place of the strict common law provisions against clearing woodlands, American courts adopted a flexible standard more applicable to the colonial situation. An early Maryland case, *Denwood* v. *Winder* (1770), demonstrates the use of a unique American standard.[128] Here a son sued his mother and her second husband, charging waste in the clearing of woodlands for planting. Mary Winder defended her actions by pointing out to the court that all the lands granted to her as dower were woodlands. When her first husband died she had five minor children to support. There was nothing else for her to do but clear the lands assigned to her and plant them. Moreover, she argued, her efforts had improved the value of the property, not reduced it. When she took over the property it was a wilderness, with only two small log houses to provide her family with shelter. Subsequently she built a house with a separate kitchen that boasted a brick chimney, a smokehouse, cornhouse, slave quarters, and other outbuildings. Mrs. Winder claimed that she had cleared no more of the land than was necessary for her own support and the maintenance of her children. The chancellor agreed with her. He levied no charge for waste of the lands.

In Pennsylvania, lawmakers changed the law on waste by statute, thereby removing from the courts the chore of establishing a new definition. Section fourteen of "An Act for Establishing courts of Judicature" (1710) gave the courts of common pleas jurisdiction over all actions concerning waste. It also established a new standard on waste: "No falling or destroying of timber trees for the necessary improvement of land or making plantations, nor the falling of timber trees for building or repairing any houses upon such plantations, nor the felling and cutting of wood and timber for any other use, unless the same be sold or carried off from the land it grew on, shall be adjudged waste, punishable within this province."[129] These provisions imply the rationale behind modifying the common law rule on waste. The assembly approved of clearing farmlands, but not of selling timber for a profit. The distinction meant a great deal in Pennsylvania in 1710, when most lands were undeveloped and the need for farmlands was great.

In *Hastings* v. *Crunkleton* we see the Pennsylvania Supreme Court applying the state's definition of waste. The case report reveals that the heir assigned Elizabeth Crunkleton her thirds, "and on her taking possession, she cut down timber and cleared lands, part of what was allotted to her."[130] Although the widow's behavior constituted waste under the common law, the Pennsylvania court sanctioned her action. In Pennsylvania, when courts determined cases on waste they had to give consideration to the type of land assigned to a widow as dower. Here the land was all uncleared, and worthless for providing support unless it could be converted into farmland. To restrict her was absurd, and therefore the court ruled that a "tenant in dower may clear woodland assigned to her in dower, provided she does not exceed a just proportion of the whole tract."[131]

Like *Hastings* v. *Crunkleton*, most early nineteenth-century cases continued to turn upon a revised definition of waste established in the colonial period. James Kent believed that most states enforced a flexible standard on waste. In his *Commentaries* he cited cases from Pennsylvania, New York, Virginia, and North Carolina to demonstrate the point, and concluded, "If the land be wholly wild and uncultivated, it has been held, that the tenant may clear part of it for the purpose of cultivation; but he must leave wood and timber sufficient for the permanent use of the farm." In determining exactly what constituted waste, Kent noted, "It is a question of fact for a jury, what extent of wood may be cut down, in such cases, without exposing the party to the charge of waste." In the United States, he concluded, the rules on waste had been "enlarged" to make them "better accommodated to the circumstances of a new and growing country."[132]

Kent's analysis applied even in a state like South Carolina, where the use of slaves presented special problems to jurists charged with defining waste. *Paslay* v. *Byrd* (1822), tried by the South Carolina Court of Chancery, concerned a situation similar to that seen in the Maryland case of *Denwood* v. *Winder*.[133] Here a man wrote a will in which he gave his plantation to his wife for her life. He charged her with raising their children, who were the residuary legatees. The widow remarried, and her children subsequently sued her and her second husband for waste. They charged their mother with clearing lands for planting and keeping improper accounts. In her defense, Mrs. Byrd argued that although she had cleared new fields on the farm, doing so was necessary for the support of the family. The chancellor agreed, and despite his belief that waste had been committed by the mother, he supported her actions. He wrote, "The rule of our Law, borrowed from the English Common Law and not altered by any Statute, certainly is that a tenant for life is at liberty to cut down timber for fire wood, fencing & such ordinary uses: But is not permitted to clear bodies of woodland for planting." There were "peculiarities" in this case, however, which prevented him from enforcing the common law rule. The husband had charged his wife to keep the estate together for her own and the children's support. The family estate in slaves required extension of the fields available for planting. If new fields were not cleared, the slaves who were reaching adulthood and their greatest capacity for labor could not be employed fully. The chancellor's remarks reveal his belief that waste in South Carolina meant something very different from waste in England, owing partly to the nature of slave property. He explained, "His [the testator's] Estate in Slaves was increasing & more labourers growing up, who would require more land to be cleared, if the open land were not sufficient, for them; or if part of the cleared lands was so much worn out as to render it expedient that more land should be cleared for the benefit of the family such clearing cannot reasonably come under the denomination of waste."[134]

South Carolina courts allowed widows to plant whatever dower lands they required for the full employment of their slaves, both the slaves they inherited from their husbands and the slaves they owned in their own right. If women cut down timber and cleared lands to do so, the courts supported them, even though they recognized the damage rendered to lands by over-planting. For example, in the case of *Mackie* v. *Alston* (1806), a widow owned slaves under a marriage settlement in addition to the slaves bequeathed to her by her husband.[135] When she attempted to employ all the slaves on her dower lands, the heirs of her husband objected, claiming that she could use only the slaves granted to her by her husband. Any other action constituted waste. But the South Carolina judiciary supported the right of Mrs. Mackie to employ all her slaves. They noted that the will written by her husband did not restrict her ability to farm the land with her own slaves. Until her death, the court ordered, Mrs. Mackie must be permitted to work the lands assigned to her as dower in whatever manner she pleased.

Although most state courts continued to apply a liberal interpretation on waste in the nineteenth century, courts in Connecticut and Massachusetts became more restrictive.[136] They began to distinguish between woodland and cleared land in their decisions on admeasurements of dower, and to rule against widows' rights to cut timber. The shift in attitude toward waste indicates the increasing value of uncleared lands in the two states, and perhaps a dislike of widows' liens on real estate as well.

In *Crocker* v. *Fox and Wife* (1791), the Connecticut judiciary first applied its more restrictive interpretation of waste to a case on dower.[137] The case involved a suit by an heir in reversion against a widow for "cutting and destroying" the trees standing on her dower lands. The widow, Mrs. Fox, argued that an action of waste could not be brought against a tenant in dower in Connecticut. No precedent existed, and therefore the English rule on waste could not be regarded as a part of the common law of the state, as the appellant claimed. Although the court admitted that the English rule "does not extend here," it found against Mrs. Fox's right to clear her lands.[138] And for the future, a remedy in all cases of waste would be available.

In Massachusetts, the law of waste agreed with that of Connecticut. Cases decided in the early nineteenth century established the rule that widows could not have dower in timber lands. As in Connecticut, earlier decisions were not similarly harsh. In *Nash* v. *Boltwood* (1783), a widow had received dower in uncultivated lands her husband conveyed without her consent. As reported in a later case, "In the action of *Nash* v. *Boltwood*, the land in which dower was demanded had been conveyed, by the husband of the demandant, when it was in a wild and unimproved state, incapable of any yearly rent or profit; and although, after the conveyance, great improvements had been made by the grantee, and those claiming under him, the demandant had judgment."[139]

By 1808 the Massachusetts courts were reevaluating their rules on dower. Lands in the state continued to increase in value, and many men bought woodlands not to clear and farm but to hold for investment. If dower accompanied by the right to clear land for cultivation were granted in such property, the intent of the purchasers would not be realized. Children or other heirs might inherit farmland valued lower than the equivalent estate in timberland. Thus changing economic conditions in the state had made a new dower rule essential. In Massachusetts, the first movement toward developing a new standard on dower and waste appeared in the decision on *Leonard* v. *Leonard* (1808).[140]

In admeasurements of dower, Massachusetts courts took care to give widows land that could produce one-third of the yearly rents and profits of the whole estate. They did not give widows a third of the quantity of the land, without attention to its productive value. In this way they could be sure that widows received property capable of providing them with support. In *Leonard* v. *Leonard*, the court ruled that because woodlands yielded no income at all, they should not be considered in admeasurements of dower. Instead, widows should receive their thirds only in lands that produced annual income. Although such an interpretation would benefit some women, it reduced the dower share of Desire Leonard because "a considerable part" of her husband's estate was woodland and therefore unproductive. In defending its decision, the court claimed, "This rule is adopted equally to protect widows from having an unproductive part of estate assigned to them, and to guard heirs from being left, during the life of the widow, without the means of support."[141]

In *Conner* v. *Shepherd* (1818), the Supreme Judicial Court of Massachusetts confirmed its earlier ruling.[142] It decreed that a widow could not have dower in timberlands at all, and explained its reasoning more carefully than in the case of Desire Leonard. According to Chief Justice Parker, there were several important reasons for denying widows dower in uncultivated land. First, such land was not useful to widows because it could not produce a yearly income. Tenants in dower could not clear it because doing so would make them vulnerable to a charge of waste. Parker realized that he was invoking the technical, common law definition of waste when he made this argument; he undoubtedly also knew that other states rejected that definition and allowed widows to clear dower lands, just as Massachusetts had done in the past. But according to Parker, "It is not an extravagant supposition that lands actually in a state of nature may, in a country fast increasing in its population, be more valuable than the same land would be with that sort of cultivation which a tenant for life would be likely to bestow upon it; and that the very clearing of the land, for the purpose of getting the greatest crops with the least labor, which is all that could be expected from a tenant in dower, would be actually, as well as technically, waste of the inheritance." Second, granting widows dower in woodlands might obviate the speculative end of the purchasers who had intended the property "as a future fund for their posterity, increasing in value with the population and improvement of the country." Third, Parker expressed his fear that dower in woodland would serve as a burden both to heirs and to society at large, because it would make the property inalienable for the life of the widow. Lands purchased for speculative purposes had to be transferable, or the investment might fail. In such a situation, dower served only "as a clog upon estates designed to be the subject of transfer." It is interesting that Parker employed the same term used by Blackstone to explain the replacement of dower by jointures among wealthy English families in a much earlier period.[143] Dower, apparently, was regarded as a "clog" for centuries before lawmakers finally gave widows the right to fee simple interests rather than life estates.

Morton Horwitz, who discussed the Conner suit in his study of nineteenth-century American courts, believed that the case marked an attempt to reduce the dower rights of widows generally. He emphasized Parker's observation that a widow's thirds often became an awkward encumbrance on the transfer of property. In Massachusetts, according to Horwitz, the courts tried to reduce the damaging effects of dower by establishing precedents such as *Conner v. Shepherd* that worked to reduce dower rights.[144] Thus they followed in the footsteps of their colonial predecessors, who also did damage to dower in an attempt to promote ease of alienation.

Horwitz's perspective has validity. Courts in the nineteenth century did regard dower as a barrier to economic development in many cases. Dower also complicated conveyances and produced suits at law over admeasurements and the use of the property. Dower hampered the partitioning of estates, and perhaps most dangerous, it denied creditors payment of debts for long periods of time. Massachusetts and Connecticut courts therefore attempted to reduce the problems associated with dower by restricting the rights of widows to the estates of their husbands. Their action fit the pattern already traced for New England law on women's property. Beginning early in the colonial period, lawmakers had not hesitated to reduce women's rights in order to reach social, economic, or legal goals. In the postrevolutionary period, the conservative tradition of the New England courts may have made it easier for them to deny widows dower in uncultivated lands. Dower was not an inviolate area of the law to reformers in Connecticut and Massachusetts; women's rights in all areas of the law had yielded to the goals of policymakers from the earliest days of settlement.

Other states were more generous to widows, including New York. Although the state assembly enacted a statute in 1787 forbidding waste by both dowagers and tenants by the curtesy, it did not interpret the law as closely as the New England courts.[145] In New York, widows continued to receive dower shares in unimproved lands, although courts recognized the difficulty in determining a proper admeasurement in property that did not produce a yearly rent or profit, and therefore technically could not contribute to a widow's support. In such a case, however, the widow's share could be apportioned according to the purchase value of the land, rather than its productive value. In *Shaw* v. *White* (1816), the state Supreme Court ordered such a payment to one widow, whose husband had conveyed woodlands without the consent of his wife.[146]

The difference between New York and Massachusetts law on this point is demonstrated well by comparing the decision on *Webb* v. *Townsend*, heard by the Massachusetts Supreme Court in 1822, with that of the New York Supreme Court on *Shaw* v. *White*.[147] The circumstances of the widows in the two cases were identical; both their husbands had conveyed unimproved lands without their consent. Counsel for the Massachusetts woman even referred to New York decisions in an attempt to convince the court of her right to dower, arguing, "In New York it is settled, that a tenant for life may cut down trees in order to put wild land in a state of cultivation . . . and that there may be tenant by the curtesy of wild land." He observed that because tenants in dower and by the curtesy were entitled to estates in the same kind of land, it would be illogical to grant widowers tenancy by the curtesy in woodlands, and at the same time deny widows dower.[148] His reference to the law of neighboring New York did not move the high court in his own state, however. Justices there believed that the point was settled by the decision on *Conner* v. *Shepherd*. Dower in Massachusetts was defined not as a share in the value of land but rather as a share in its rents and profits. The court refused to retreat from its new definition.

By supporting the right of widows to dower in uncultivated land, the New York judiciary was not necessarily expressing anticommercial attitudes. The middle and southern states were just as anxious as those of New England to promote easy transfer of property and the rights of creditors. Unlike the New Englanders, however, they sought ways to encourage expansion without reducing the rights of widows. The legal developments on dower in Maryland and South Carolina, for example, may have improved the position of widows while promoting the interests of creditors, purchasers, and future heirs. Reforms in those jurisdictions stand in contrast to the restrictive actions of the New England states.

Although inheritance laws and practices varied considerably from place to place and over time in colonial and early national America, one characteristic remained constant, the enforced dependency of widows. Provisions governing the transfer of family property, both those fashioned by the common law and those resulting from legislative enactments, assumed that economic dependency for widows was a norm to be enforced. Lawmakers apparently saw nothing inconsistent in their principles governing wives and widows. They made wives economically dependent on husbands during marriage, arguing under the principle of unity of person that this action was fair because the husband had the legal obligation to support them both. Once the husband had died, the courts did make his estate liable for the continued support of his widow, but only at a level far below the standard of living enjoyed by the two of them during marriage. Unless a woman owned land, she had no guarantee that her share of the family estate would equal what she had put into it. Thus, after a widow's source of support had vanished, the law continued to deny her the property she needed to maintain her standard of living, despite the fact that there no longer existed a rationale comparable to unity of person for doing so.

When wives died, widowers did not encounter an enforced reduction in their standard of living. Instead, they exercised the right to control all of their wives' property for life as tenants by the curtesy. In addition, of course, they retained all their own property until death. Lawmakers ignored children's interests as long as fathers lived, but children and mothers had to share family property immediately upon the death of the patriarch.

Different social policies on the property rights of widows and widowers evolved in response to different attitudes toward the roles of men and women. Early American society envisioned a dependent, subservient position for women of all ages, but not for men at any point in their adult lives. Inheritance rules reflected social realities. Obviously, lawmakers felt comfortable enforcing a system that made elderly mothers more likely to ask for help from children than elderly fathers. Children, in turn, may have responded to the needs of mothers more generously than to the needs of fathers.

When widows of small means could not turn to adult children or other close relatives for assistance, their options were limited. If young enough, they might remarry. The decision to take a new spouse might occur even when a widow controlled the entire family estate during the minority of her children. For women—and men—in early America, running a household alone was difficult; the labor of a helpmate could mean the difference between a competent livelihood and financial need.

Far too often impoverished widows without family connections simply could not get along. They needed public assistance. In many communities, widows and single women living alone constituted the largest segment of recipients of poor relief. They turned up in almshouses as well. In the postrevolutionary period, some communities began to establish institutions designed specifically to assist these members of the deserving poor. Women in New York City sought incorporation for their Society for the Relief of Poor Widows with Small Children in 1802. Other New York women incorporated "an Association for the Relief of respectable, aged, indigent females" in 1815.[149] As early as 1810, women on the frontier in Whitestown, New York, sought incorporation for their "Female Charitable Society," one of only four "Village Corporations." Mary P. Ryan posits that by mid-century women in upstate New York provided vital assistance to the poor, orphans, and women in need.[150] Suzanne Lebsock has documented women's charitable activities on behalf of members of their sex in Petersburg, Virginia, and she has suggested that Petersburg women represented a national movement.[151] Men's charitable activities in the early nineteenth century also frequently focused on widows and orphans.[152] Among the poor, widows met the qualifications necessary to excite public sympathy and assistance.

If a widow owned enough property, she might choose to remain single no matter what her age. Lebsock's research indicates that women with property adequate for their support remarried less often than those of lower economic standing. This finding, in combination with evidence demonstrating that South Carolina widows entering into new unions made marriage settlements more often than other women, points toward an intriguing conclusion. Although men continued to enforce common law rules on marital property, women disliked the limited nature of their property rights under coverture. When possible, they expressed their dissatisfaction actively, in forms ranging from a refusal to remarry to reliance on marriage settlements. Somewhat later, by the middle of the nineteenth century, women were taking even more active steps. They were agitating for passage of the married women's property acts and reforms in inheritance statutes that spelled increased financial independence for all women.

Conclusion

The tremendous variation evident in early American rules on married women's property rights teaches us to be wary of easy generalizations. Each jurisdiction developed its own system of complex and changing rules for governing the legal status of women. As a result, only by studying several areas of the law in a number of colonies and states is it possible to gain a general understanding of the relationship between property and women's rights. Past studies have suffered from a failure to cast the net widely enough. Given the complexity of American law, one or two examples of autonomy or dependence cannot produce an accurate definition; they can only mislead.

The evidence presented in this study indicates that regional differences in women's rights resulted from ideological considerations as well as social and economic factors. For women living in the late colonial and early national periods, the structure of a legal system became significant for determining their property rights. In particular, the presence of a separate court of chancery spelled access to a set of rules and precedents favoring greater independence for women. In New York, Maryland, Virginia, and South Carolina, chancellors applied and developed a body of law allowing femes coverts to own separate property. Over time, the degree of independence granted to women in these jurisdictions increased, and by the end of the period studied, the right to separate property was exercised with relative ease.

Given the historical relationship between the common law and women's property rights, colonies and states without separate courts of chancery could not offer women the privileges they enjoyed under equity law. In Connecticut and Massachusetts, courts struggled with the question of the legality of separate estates in the early decades of the nineteenth century. Without either a chancery court or a legislative assignment of specific jurisdiction over trusts, the New England judiciary felt unable to assist women in holding property free from the control of their husbands. In addition, women in early nineteenth-century Massachusetts became pawns in a political battle for the establishment of an independent chancery. In Pennsylvania, common law courts held an equitable jurisdiction allowing them to enforce trusts for married women, but evidence indicates that the judiciary felt uncomfortable in exercising the full panoply of equitable rules and precedents. As a result, Pennsylvania wives with marriage settlements did not enjoy the same protections as women in jurisdictions with independent chancery courts.

As the situation in Pennsylvania reveals, however, ideological opposition to chancery courts cannot alone account for the failure of a colony to enforce separate estates. The structure of any legal system could be shaped to meet local needs. Apparently, then, Connecticut and Massachusetts jurists opposed separate estates for causes other than their connection with the English Chancery. It becomes important to note that women in Connecticut, Massachusetts, and Pennsylvania also faced liabilities under the common law not known to women in the other jurisdictions studied. Rules on private examinations and inheritance rights contributed to the comparatively weak legal status of women in these jurisdictions.

Pennsylvania authorities remained negligent on the subject of private examinations throughout the period studied. The legislative assembly did not require them until just before the Revolution, and even after that time enforcement did not match that of Maryland, Virginia, or South Carolina. Massachusetts lawmakers, by never requiring private examinations at all, ignored the possibility of coercion in this area of the law while upholding it in others. In Connecticut before 1723, women lost all rights to real and personal property when they married. They did not join in land conveyances, as did women in other colonies, because they had nothing to convey, not even a dower right. Reformers in Connecticut restricted a widow's thirds to the real property owned by her husband at his death, rather than during the marriage. Pennsylvania imitated the example of Connecticut jurists in limiting the dower shares of widows. In William Penn's colony, widows could claim dower only in the property owned by their husbands at death, and in addition, creditors' rights superseded those of widows. During the period emphasized in this study, women in Connecticut gained the right to participate in conveyances of real estate, but their dower shares remained as defined in the first decades of settlement. Eighteenth-century innovations further reduced the dower share of widows as jurists "exploded" the rule of survivorship for tenants by entireties and restricted the legal right of widows to clear woodlands for planting. Like Connecticut, Massachusetts adjusted its view of waste in the late eighteenth century to prevent widows from developing uncleared lands.

With one exception, similar damaging rules did not appear in New York, Maryland, Virginia, or South Carolina. The exception concerned the enforcement of private examinations in New York, where lawmakers remained as careless as in neighboring Pennsylvania. The other colonial assemblies all recognized the importance of the procedure early in the colonies' development, however, and enacted statutes requiring it. Dower shares remained intact according to the common law definition. Even more important, Maryland and Virginia continued to guarantee widows a share of personal property along with their thirds in realty. After the Revolution, waste rules did not change in these states, as they did in Connecticut and Massachusetts. In fact, postrevolutionary widows in South Carolina witnessed passage of the most egalitarian inheritance statute in the United States. During the same period, Maryland and South Carolina also took steps to delineate the rights of widows in cases concerning the partitioning of estates.

In one area of the law, women in the New England colonies enjoyed an advantage unknown elsewhere. Puritan lawmakers in the seventeenth century deviated from English tradition and enacted statutes allowing absolute divorce. Although it is not yet clear how many colonial women profited from the availability of absolute divorce, the appearance of the first statutes marked an important theoretical advance that found wider expression immediately after the Revolution. And as Cott and Kerber have shown, by that time at least, New England women were reaping the benefits of state divorce provisions. Although Pennsylvania and New York moved to allow absolute divorce in the late eighteenth century, the southern states remained conservative in declining to recognize a judicial authority for dissolving marriages. South Carolina, moreover, refused to allow absolute divorce at all throughout the period studied.

In spite of the obvious benefits of absolute divorce accompanied by property divisions or payments of alimony, women in jurisdictions with chancery courts enjoyed more property rights than women in Connecticut, Massachusetts, and Pennsylvania. Few women felt the effects of divorce legislation, but many engaged in land conveyances and even more lived part of their lives as widows. Moreover, the benefits enjoyed by the privileged women in New York, Maryland, Virginia, and South Carolina with separate estates could be counterpoised against the ill effects experienced by the women who would have sought absolute divorces if they had been available. In addition, the availability of legal separations enforced by chancery courts in these jurisdictions helped to mitigate the harshest effects of the rules on divorce.

The examples from divorce, inheritance, and conveyancing law demonstrate that differing rules on women's rights did not depend solely on the presence or absence of chancery courts, despite the importance of equity law to femes coverts. It appears that differences in the property rights of American women resulted as much from the negative influence of ideological reforms in Connecticut, Massachusetts, and Pennsylvania as from the positive influence of equity principles in New York, Maryland, Virginia, and South Carolina. Until further work is done in seventeenth-century law, this conclusion must necessarily remain tentative, but at this point it seems likely that the New England settlers' ideological and political opposition to chancery courts and the complications of English land law resulted in early reforms that proved detrimental to women. Although Pennsylvania law developed during a later period, the radical Protestant reform tradition continued to encourage legal change and simplification. As a result, Pennsylvania introduced several of the changes instituted by the Puritans earlier in the seventeenth century, and added some reforms of its own.

There can be no doubt that private examinations, wives' signatures on land deeds, widows' liens on family property and lifetime shares in insolvent estates, and marriage settlements delineating separate property created complications in the law. They introduced additional procedures, operated as bars to development, and required a special jurisdiction to guarantee enforcement. As reformers foresaw, the law became simpler when women lost protection for their property rights. Unity of person worked well in communities that wanted to simplify land law, courts, and procedures. We cannot ignore the fact, however, that although simplification may have been the primary goal of the reformers, they also readily abandoned rules designed to offer women protection for their property rights. Although dower, for example, acted as a deterrent to economic development, it also provided essential financial security to widows. It is significant that colonial reformers eliminated procedures designed to promote widows' interests without replacing them with other kinds of protections. Instead of granting women the property rights necessary to look after their own interests, as nineteenth-century reformers would do, they strengthened the concept of unity of person.

Connecticut, Massachusetts, and Pennsylvania were advanced in their efforts to improve the land law, but they also acted conservatively in upholding and strengthening traditional patriarchal ideals. Ultimately, their reforms proved dangerous for women because they denied wives the autonomy necessary to safeguard their own interests. Puritans' opposition to chancery and their desire to simplify the land law fed into negative feelings about certain aspects of English family law that condoned separate and conflicting interests between spouses. To eliminate potential sources of conflict and remain true to their belief in male dominance within the family, legal reformers increased

a husband's ability to control his wife's estate. In other words, when simplification of the law required either more or less independence for women,
seventeenth- and eighteenth-century reformers invariably chose the latter.
This remained the case even as late as the end of the eighteenth century,
when the New England states revised the traditional American rules on waste
without making commensurate changes in the law of dower. By the middle of
the nineteenth century, when even New Englanders' attitudes toward the
family had shifted considerably, the solution would be different.

In contrast to lawmakers in Connecticut, Massachusetts, and Pennsylvania, those in the southern colonies and New York remained committed to
recreating the common law and equity law systems of England. When they
deviated from established rules and precedents, it was in response to considerations peculiar to the colonial situation that required action. Revision in the
law of waste stemmed from a need to promote agricultural development as
well as to provide for widows in a new land. The absence of ecclesiastical
courts necessitated a wider jurisdiction for chancery over questions of marriage and separation. A continuation of dower in personal property arose in
response to the demands of the plantation labor system. None of these
changes grew out of an ideological commitment to promoting simplification.
Instead, they resulted from a need to adjust Old World definitions to New
World circumstances. In most cases this conservatism worked to the advantage of women. Where legal rules are concerned, no generalization is completely apt, however. The adherence of New York, Maryland, Virginia, and
South Carolina to primogeniture, for example, placed daughters in these jurisdictions at a disadvantage compared to their counterparts in more reform-
minded colonies.

In the past, historians have argued that the early national period did not
witness an extension of women's proprietary capacity, but rather that women
lost privileges enjoyed by their colonial mothers and grandmothers. Such an
argument now seems out of line with the evidence. In the colonial period,
women did not experience a significant improvement in their legal rights, and
although certain postrevolutionary developments did result in losses—the
waste rules of New England and the North Carolina intestacy statute, for
example—many more marked an increase in women's autonomy. The most
significant changes appeared in the area of equitable separate estates, but
some new common law rules also marked improvements for women, including the Pennsylvania and New York acceptance of private examinations, the
Connecticut statute on women's wills, the Massachusetts feme sole trader
law, the Maryland and South Carolina rules on cash payments in lieu of
dower, the end of primogeniture and double shares for eldest sons in inheri-

tance law everywhere, and the South Carolina intestacy statute, as well as the new availability of divorce in several states. Viewed together, these reforms indicate a growing awareness of the benefits that society could derive from expanding the property rights of married women.

Immediate postrevolutionary legal changes favoring women were rare, but republican ideology did foster at least three developments of considerable importance. Most significant was the abolition of primogeniture and eldest sons' double shares. After the Revolution, daughters and sons were regarded as equals in intestacy statutes. In addition, South Carolina went even further than her sister states in enacting an intestacy statute that made wives more nearly the equals of husbands for purposes of inheritance. Although no revolutionary code elevated the status of women above the traditional one of helpmate, these two developments in inheritance law demonstrated the possibilities for legal reform that might flow from a republican commitment to human equality. In addition, the rapid revision of divorce law in Pennsylvania and New York, and the gradual loosening of standards in Maryland and Virginia, signified the end of English control over colonial legislation. Now Americans were free to write their own marriage laws, and the ones they advocated gave many women the freedom to divorce for the first time. At this point it is impossible to know whether later nineteenth-century changes represented a delayed response to republican ideals, but that possibility should not be overlooked by future researchers. Current historians' emphasis on the exclusive role of industrialization in fostering change in the status of nineteenth-century women has created a perspective that ignores other significant forces, including ideological ones.

The evidence presented in this study demonstrates, in fact, the close relationship between economic and ideological forces in promoting legal change. At several points in early American history, changing economic conditions produced a need for legal reform. Therefore changes in the law did occur as a result of changes in the economy, as is commonly believed. But economic change could foster legal rules that both benefited and harmed married women. There was no direct correlation between economic change and an expansion of women's rights. The nature of a specific legal reform, whether it improved the position of women or not, depended on forces other than economic ones. The most important determining forces were ideological and social.

Early colonial lawmakers and jurists in the age of early industrialization had a great deal in common. Both groups faced a situation that called for legal reform in light of economic conditions. The colonists found themselves freed from the rigid, slow-moving mechanisms of English law. They seized an advantage unavailable to contemporaries in the mother country, and shaped their American legal systems according to their needs. Similarly, nineteenth-century lawmakers realized that rules of property designed for agricultural communities no longer fit circumstances in industrializing America. They, too, set out on a course of legal reform.

The two groups of reformers held very different ideas about women's roles and family life. Colonialists lived in a patriarchal age; they developed protective strategies for women's property rights but did not believe in the need for women's financial autonomy. When reforms were instituted to improve property law in light of colonial economic conditions, they often resulted in a loss of rights for women, particularly in regions where patriarchal families were strongest. For this reason, colonies that lacked a radical reform tradition produced legal systems offering women more protection for their property rights.

In the early decades of settlement, simplification of the law, or even improvement, could be dangerous for women. By 1800, however, families were becoming increasingly egalitarian. Male dominance in the family circle was yielding to an emphasis on spouses' equality, albeit an equality based on the idea of separate spheres. Women's ability to manage property was increasing with improvements in self-image and education. The United States also had established a government based on the idea of individual liberty. Women themselves were starting to ask for an expansion of their property rights, and threatening to rebel against tyrannical rule if they did not get what they wanted. Ideas about what women could and should do, in short, had changed, and therefore nineteenth-century lawmakers' responses to economic forces were quite different from the responses of men in the seventeenth and early eighteenth centuries. As we have seen, the law became more willing to grant women independent rights to property. This was a trend that became even more pronounced in the years following 1830.

Thus, when Connecticut law on married women's testamentary capacity became confused in the decades following the Revolution, the legislative assembly ultimately decided in favor of granting wives the power to write wills, rather than denying it as had earlier lawmakers. In cases of insolvent estates, Maryland and South Carolina favored granting widows cash payments over which they had absolute control, instead of eliminating the dower right altogether; the solution of early Pennsylvania no longer held much attraction. And rather than restricting life estates in an attempt to spur economic development, as colonial lawmakers in Connecticut, Massachusetts, and Pennsylvania had done, postrevolutionary South Carolina gave widows fee simple interests in the lands of intestate husbands. Finally, divorce laws necessitated a clear definition of the property rights granted to both parties, particularly in divorces from bed and board that gave a wife feme sole trader status. In the nineteenth century, when more women exercised the ambiguous rights of feme sole traders, the position needed redefinition. It became a more powerful one.

In the early national period, one force for legal change that occasionally worked to the advantage of women was neither strictly ideological nor economic. It concerned the desire of jurists to eliminate blatant local deviations from widely accepted principles and procedures. Thus Pennsylvania and New York acknowledged the usefulness of private examinations, and Connecticut and Massachusetts accepted the validity of separate estates. As lawyers became more aware of the quality of law administered in other states, largely through the first published American reports, they turned a more critical eye on local conditions. Anglicization of the law in the eighteenth century had begun this process of critical self-assessment, and the increasing sophistication of the legal profession in the early national period continued it.[1]

It also appears that in the late eighteenth and early nineteenth centuries, jurists and the communities they represented no longer sought simplification of the law as an end in itself. Clarification became increasingly important, but the utopian ideals of the early colonists had lost their appeal by the end of the eighteenth century, even in those jurisdictions that had attempted the most experiments. Some historians argue, in fact, that nineteenth-century jurists did their best to make the law as incomprehensible to the public as possible.[2] Complications in the law increased the respect accorded to those individuals charged with administering it. In this context, simplification had value only if it served particular goals important to the legal profession.

Increasing legal and legislative business after the Revolution had an indirect effect on women's rights in some areas of the law. As more women and men sought absolute divorces, for example, legislative assemblies had to give up their jurisdiction and turn it over to the courts.[3] The same pattern occurred for certain kinds of private bills commonly sought by women, including the right of a widow to sell real property belonging to a deceased husband's estate, or the right of a woman to act as a feme sole trader. Statutes such as the one governing feme sole traders in Massachusetts represented an attempt to ease the burden of the legislature in hearing individual requests. More women benefited when a general rule appeared. Thus the increase in business that accompanied population growth and urbanization forced lawmakers to extend to many women the privileges previously known to only a few.

Unlike their colonial predecessors, nineteenth-century Americans were prepared to revise the relationship between husband and wife. An important intellectual shift had occurred. Lawmakers no longer sought to promote economic development and to clarify the respective roles of husband and wife by clinging to unity of person. Rather than limiting the rights exercised by women, they frequently took steps to expand them. During the period emphasized in this study only the beginnings of the shift toward greater independence for women are visible, but the early reforms point toward the more radical changes of the mid- and late nineteenth century. At that point women would gain the right to own property whether or not they had marriage settlements or the consent of their husbands. They would enjoy the protection of the law in keeping their wages as separate property, and in making contracts and writing wills. Revised laws of inheritance would give them absolute rights to their shares in the estates of deceased husbands. All of these rights were foreshadowed by legal changes in the late colonial and early national periods.

Reform in the property rights of married women occurred at a painfully slow rate, hampered by the strength of old legal concepts such as coercion and unity of person. Even as these ideas disappeared or lost influence in some areas of the law, they reappeared in others. The legal profession clung with tenacity to its role as protector of women, as society shrank from the implications of changing family life. But the prejudices of an earlier generation were weakening before the influence of new attitudes toward women and the family. An emphasis on individual freedom, increased education for women, and the role of women's rights groups in agitating for compliance with the ideals of the Revolution all marked the nineteenth century as a period of new directions for women. Their world differed dramatically from the world of their colonial ancestors. It required an entirely new definition of women's legal rights, a definition that women themselves would help to shape for the first time in American history.

Notes

Abbreviations used in the notes:
MHR   Maryland Hall of Records, Annapolis
SCA   South Carolina Department of History and Archives, Columbia
HSP   Historical Society of Pennsylvania, Philadelphia
BCHS   Bucks County Historical Society, Doylestown, Pa.

PREFACE

1. William E. Nelson, *Americanization of the Common Law: The Impact of Legal Change on Massachusetts Society, 1760–1830* (Cambridge, Mass., 1975); Morton J. Horwitz, *The Transformation of American Law, 1780–1860* (Cambridge, Mass., 1977); Michael Hindus, *Prison and Plantation: Crime, Justice, and Authority in Massachusetts and South Carolina, 1767–1878* (Chapel Hill, N.C., 1980); David Thomas Konig, *Law and Society in Puritan Massachusetts: Essex County, 1629–1692* (Chapel Hill, N.C., 1979). The move to study law and social forces together began, of course, under the direction of Willard Hurst at the University of Wisconsin Law School. But for early Americanists in particular, the emphasis on community studies and other forms of social history beginning in the 1960s was essential for encouraging interdisciplinary work in legal and social history.

2. I was able to reach this understanding as a result of reading three historiographical papers delivered at the Sixth Berkshire Conference on the History of Women, Smith College, Northampton, Mass., 1 June 1984: Norma Basch, "Problems and Possibilities in the Legal History of Women: From the American Revolution to the Progressive Era"; Janet Senderowitz Loengard, "Legal History and the Medieval Englishwoman: A Fragmented View"; and Mary Lyndon Shanley, "Lawyers and Feminists: The Historiography of Women and the Law in Victorian England."

3. In 1924 Elisabeth Anthony Dexter argued that colonial women enjoyed greater occupational freedom than did women who lived in the postrevolutionary decades. Dexter's thesis of decline, espoused in *Colonial Women of Affairs* (1924; rev. ed., Boston, 1931), was reinforced by a highly influential study of women's legal status that emphasized married women's relative freedom to own and control property in the early colonial period: Richard B. Morris, *Studies in the History of American Law: With Special Reference to the Seventeenth and Eighteenth Centuries* (1930; reprint ed., New York, 1959). Because historians of the nineteenth century were confronted with evidence of women's enforced economic dependence under the law, the colonial system, as presented by Dexter and Morris, looked bright by comparison. The thesis of decline, then, was picked up by the historians of the nineteenth century who wrote

the first overviews of women in American history. In *Womanhood in America* (New York, 1975), Mary P. Ryan discussed the declining status of women after the Revolution, as did Ann D. Gordon and Mari Jo Buhle in "Sex and Class in Colonial and Nineteenth-Century America," in Berenice Carroll, ed., *Liberating Women's History* (Urbana, Ill., 1976), 278–300. Women's declining legal status after the Revolution (as opposed to their status in general) has been discussed in two influential works: Joan Hoff Wilson, "The Illusion of Change: Women and the American Revolution," in Alfred H. Young, ed., *Explorations in the History of American Radicalism* (DeKalb, Ill., 1976), 383–445; and Linda K. Kerber, *Women of the Republic: Intellect and Ideology in Revolutionary America* (Chapel Hill, N.C., 1980). Kerber is more optimistic on women's status in general, apart from the law. Wilson reiterated her position in a subsequent article, "Hidden Riches: Legal Records and Women, 1750–1825," in Mary Kelley, ed., *Woman's Being, Woman's Place: Female Identity and Vocation in American History* (Boston, 1979), 7–25. Revisionist interpretations of women's social status after the Revolution are Mary Beth Norton, *Liberty's Daughters: The Revolutionary Experience of American Women, 1750–1800* (Boston, 1980); and Suzanne Lebsock, *The Free Women of Petersburg: Status and Culture in a Southern Town, 1784–1860* (New York, 1984). Lebsock extends her argument to include certain aspects of women's legal status as well.

4. In studying women's legal status, I entered into the historical debate over the relative status of women in colonial and early national America. During the years of research on this book, historians became increasingly sophisticated in their discussions of the meaning of women's status. Initially, Ryan (*Womanhood in America*), Gordon and Buhle ("Sex and Class"), and others, including Gerda Lerner ("The Lady and the Mill Girl: Changes in the Status of Women in the Age of Jackson, 1800–1840," *Midcontinent American Studies Journal* 10 [1969]: 5–14), argued for the thesis of decline. Although advertised primarily by nineteenth-century historians, the golden-age thesis, as it was called, was employed by colonial historians as well. For the clearest exposition of the argument, see Roger Thompson, *Women in Stuart England and America: A Comparative Study* (Boston, 1974). See also Joan R. Gundersen and Gwen Victor Gampel, "Married Women's Legal Status in Eighteenth-Century New York and Virginia," *William and Mary Quarterly*, 3d ser. 39 (1982): 114–34; and C. Dallett Hemphill, "Women in Court: Sex-Role Differentiation in Salem, Massachusetts, 1630–1683," *William and Mary Quarterly*, 3d ser. 39 (1982): 164–75. Their arguments echo the work of earlier historians such as Morris (Mary Sumner Benson (*Women in Eighteenth-Century America: A Study of Opinion and Social Usage* [New York, 1935; reprint ed., Port Washington, N.Y., 1966]), and Mary R. Beard (*Woman as Force in History: A Study in Traditions and Realities* [New York, 1946; reprint ed., 1962]). Recently historians of women have come to agree that the perspective emphasized by the golden-age thesis is overly simplistic and restricts discussion. Elsewhere I have attempted to demonstrate the shortcomings of the thesis, as posited in particular by Morris and Beard, with regard to the property rights of colonial women (see Marylynn Salmon, "The Legal Status of Women in Early America: A Reappraisal," *Law and History Review* 1 [1983]: 129–51). In a much-needed synthesis of the work on early American women, Mary Beth Norton argued against continued reliance on the outdated framework (see "The Evolution of White Women's Experience in Early America," *American Historical Review* 89 [1984]: 593–619). It appears that we can now

put the golden-age thesis to rest. Other revisionist interpretations of women's general status in the colonial period are Lyle Koehler, *A Search for Power: The "Weaker Sex" in Seventeenth-Century New England* (Urbana, Ill., 1980); and Laurel Thatcher Ulrich, *Good Wives: Image and Reality in the Lives of Women in Northern New England, 1650–1750* (New York, 1982).

5. One reason historians accepted the thesis of a colonial improvement in women's rights and a postrevolutionary decline was that little original research had been done in the field of early American women's history, and yet teachers and writers felt a need to make generalizations. Morris's innovative study of women's rights in colonial America was one of only a handful of discussions based on primary research. Beard's *Woman as Force in History* focused on the question of equity law in the Anglo-American legal tradition. In *Women's Life and Work in the Southern Colonies* (Chapel Hill, N.C., 1938; reprint ed., New York, 1972), Julia Cherry Spruill included a chapter entitled "Under the Law" (pp. 340–66). Sophie Drinker wrote two articles on women and the law: "Women Attorneys in Colonial Times," *Maryland Historical Magazine* 56 (1961): 335–51; and "Votes for Women in Eighteenth-Century New Jersey," *New Jersey Historical Society Proceedings* 80 (1962): 31–45. Mary Philbrook also discussed suffrage in "Women's Suffrage in New Jersey Prior to 1807," *New Jersey Historical Society Proceedings* 57 (1939): 87–98. Increased interest in women's history in the 1970s led to new work on the rules governing women's rights. Historians turned to a variety of legal sources to discover new material on the legal status of women. Creative studies on various aspects of women's rights now include such classics as Lois Green Carr and Lorena S. Walsh, "The Planter's Wife: The Experience of White Women in Seventeenth-Century Maryland," *William and Mary Quarterly*, 3d ser. 34 (1977): 542–71; Nancy F. Cott, "Divorce and the Changing Status of Women in Eighteenth-Century Massachusetts," *William and Mary Quarterly*, 3d ser. 33 (1976): 586–614; and Alexander Keyssar, "Widowhood in Eighteenth-Century Massachusetts: A Problem in the History of the Family," *Perspectives in American History* 8 (1974): 83–119.

6. Although the educational and lobbying efforts of women's rights activists beginning in the mid-nineteenth century cannot explain the earliest reforms in women's property rights, there can be no doubt that reformers played a pivotal role in promoting later legislation. The stage had been set for legal change by a multitude of forces, but the impact of women's rights advocates in bringing about reforms at specific times should not be underestimated. An excellent study demonstrating the relationship between long- and short-range causes of nineteenth-century reforms in women's rights is Norma Basch, *In the Eyes of the Law: Marriage and Property in Nineteenth-Century New York* (Ithaca, N.Y., 1982). A pathbreaking study of the early women's rights movement that was never published is Elizabeth Bowles Warbasse, "The Changing Legal Rights of Married Women, 1800–1861" (Ph.D. dissertation, Radcliffe College, 1966). A more recent study of married women's property law in the first half of the nineteenth century is Richard H. Chused, "Married Women's Property Law: 1800–1850," *Georgetown Law Journal* 71 (1983): 1359–1425. In "Law and the Family in Nineteenth Century America" (Ph.D. dissertation, Brandeis University, 1979), Michael Grossberg provides a valuable analysis of the relationship among legal change, social change, and the family. Through discussions of courtship, marriage procedures and prescriptions, contraception, abortion, illegitimacy, and child custody,

he attempts to uncover the roots of legal change during a pivotal period in American family history. His work provides a useful companion to this study of married women's property rights. Because Grossberg studied the entire nineteenth century, however, he was able to follow through on legal issues only indicated here. See also Grossberg's "Who Gets the Child? Custody, Guardianship, and the Rise of a Judicial Patriarchy in Nineteenth-Century America," *Feminist Studies* 9 (1983): 235–60.

CHAPTER ONE

1. On diversity in English inheritance practices, the most widely studied area of property law, see George Lee Haskins, *Law and Authority in Early Massachusetts: A Study in Tradition and Design* (New York, 1960), 180–82; Margaret Spufford, *Contrasting Communities: English Villagers in the Sixteenth and Seventeenth Centuries* (London, 1974), 85–90, 104–18, 159–64; and Margaret Spufford, "Peasant Inheritance Customs in the Midlands, 1280–1700," and E. P. Thompson, "The Grid of Inheritance: A Comment," both in Jack Goody, Joan Thirsk, and E. P. Thompson, eds., *Family and Inheritance: Rural Society in Western Europe, 1200–1800* (Cambridge, England, 1976), 156, 328. On regional variation in rules governing women's contracts and conveyancing, see *The Laws Respecting Women*, reprint ed. with a foreword by Shirley Raissi Bysiewicz (London, 1777; reprint ed., Dobbs Ferry, N.Y., 1974), 172–77. On diversity in English local law and custom generally, see David Grayson Allen, *In English Ways: The Movement of Societies and the Transferal of English Local Law and Custom to Massachusetts Bay in the Seventeenth Century* (New York, 1982); and Julius Goebel, Jr., "King's Law and Local Custom in Seventeenth-Century New England," *Columbia Law Review* 31 (1931): 416–48.

2. On lax colonial administration in the seventeenth century, see Michael Kammen, *Empire and Interest: The American Colonies and the Politics of Mercantilism* (Philadelphia, 1970); Viola F. Barnes, *The Dominion of New England: A Study in British Colonial Policy* (New Haven, Conn., 1923); and I. K. Steele, *Politics of Colonial Policy: The Board of Trade in Colonial Administration* (Oxford, 1968). On the independent development of colonial legal systems, see Haskins, *Law and Authority in Early Massachusetts*; Morris, *Studies in American Law*; Konig, *Law and Society in Puritan Massachusetts*, especially chaps. 1–2; and Marylynn Salmon, "The Court Records of Philadelphia, Bucks, and Berks Counties in the Seventeenth and Eighteenth Centuries," *Pennsylvania Magazine of History and Biography* 107 (1983): 249–62.

3. Haskins, *Law and Authority in Early Massachusetts*, 6.

4. As Konig puts it, "In the establishment of a society at Massachusetts Bay in 1629, two concepts had paradigmatic force: the gathered church with its congregationally ordained leader and the compact community of neighbors and families. While the colonial leadership had recognized the realistic limitations of those ideals and had set up powerful legal institutions to support them, the ideals themselves had possessed a strong exhortatory and symbolic quality" (*Law and Society in Puritan Massachusetts*, 89). See also Haskins, *Law and Authority in Early Massachusetts*, especially chaps. 8, 9, and 11.

5. Puritans were active in the English movement for law reform in the seventeenth century as well (see Konig, *Law and Society in Puritan Massachusetts*, 16–18; Donald

Veall, *The Popular Movement for Law Reform, 1640–1660* [Oxford, 1970]; and Stuart E. Prall, *The Agitation for Law Reform during the Puritan Revolution* [The Hague, 1966]).

6. Edmund S. Morgan, *The Puritan Family: Religion and Domestic Relations in Seventeenth-Century New England* (1944; reprint ed., New York, 1966), 17–21; Ulrich, *Good Wives*, 6–8.

7. Quoted in Koehler, *A Search for Power*, 38.

8. Quoted in Gail Sussman Marcus, "'Due Execution of the Generall Rules of Righteousness': Criminal Procedure in New Haven Town and Colony, 1638–1658," in David D. Hall, John M. Murrin, and Thad W. Tate, eds., *Saints and Revolutionaries: Essays on Early American History* (New York, 1984), 100–101.

9. Quoted in Koehler, *A Search for Power*, 31.

10. On the reform tradition of early Pennsylvania, see Mary Maples Dunn, *William Penn: Politics and Conscience* (Princeton, N.J., 1967); and Edwin B. Bronner, *William Penn's "Holy Experiment": The Founding of Pennsylvania, 1681–1701* (New York, 1962). As Bronner quotes William Penn, "For my country, I eyed the Lord, in obtaining it; and more was I drawn inward to look to him, and to own it to his hand and power, *than to any other way; I have so obtained it, and desire to keep it;* that I may not be unworthy of his love; but do that, which may answer his kind Providence, and serve his truth and people: *that an example may be set up to the nations;* there may be room there, though not here, for such an *holy experiment*" (p. 6).

11. Maryland, Virginia, and South Carolina all established independent courts of chancery, for example. Lawmakers tended to follow English law on divorce as well.

12. On English colonists' feelings of provincialism, see Bernard Bailyn, "Politics and Social Structure in Virginia," in James Morton Smith, ed., *Seventeenth-Century America: Essays in Colonial History* (Chapel Hill, N.C., 1959), 90–115; John Clive and Bernard Bailyn, "England's Cultural Provinces: Scotland and America," *William and Mary Quarterly*, 3d ser. 11 (1954): 200–213; Jack P. Greene, "Search for Identity: An Interpretation of the Meaning of Selected Patterns of Social Response in Eighteenth-Century America," *Journal of Social History* 3 (1969–70): 189–220; and Carole Shammas, "English-Born and Creole Elites in Turn-of-the-Century Virginia," in Thad W. Tate and David L. Ammerman, eds., *The Chesapeake in the Seventeenth Century: Essays on Anglo-American Society and Politics* (New York, 1979), 274–96.

13. Shammas, "English-Born and Creole Elites in Virginia," 279.

14. Quoted in ibid., 284. Shammas comments on Virginia planters' attitudes toward improving their estates on p. 283.

15. On the effects of demographic disruption on women and men in early colonial Maryland, see Carr and Walsh, "The Planter's Wife," 542–71.

16. Norton, "Evolution of White Women's Experience," 597–98.

17. Stanley N. Katz, "The Politics of Law in Colonial America: Controversies over Chancery Courts and Equity Law in the Eighteenth Century," *Perspectives in American History* 5 (1971): 257–58.

18. Cott, "Divorce in Massachusetts," 588–89.

19. Ibid., 589.

CHAPTER TWO

1. As Blackstone phrased it, "By marriage, the husband and wife are one person in law: that is, the very being or legal existence of the woman is suspended during the marriage, or at least is incorporated and consolidated into that of the husband: under whose wing, protection, and *cover*, she performs every thing. . . . Upon this principle, of an union of person in husband and wife, depend almost all the legal rights, duties, and disabilities, that either of them acquire by the marriage" (William Blackstone, *Commentaries on the Laws of England*, 4 vols. [Oxford, 1765–69], 1:430).

2. On the legal rights of single women, see ibid., 2:213–16, 497–99; *The Laws Respecting Women*, 117–36; Tapping Reeve, *The Law of Baron and Feme, of Parent and Child, of Guardian and Ward, of Master and Servant, and of the Powers of Courts of Chancery* (New Haven, Conn., 1816), 3, 8, 160, 192–93; and Zephaniah Swift, *A System of the Laws of the State of Connecticut: In Six Books*, 2 vols. (New Haven, Conn., 1795–96), 1:194, 200.

3. *The Laws Respecting Women*, 153–54; Reeve, *Baron and Feme*, 126–36. The clearest discussions of eighteenth-century law on husbands and wives appear in Blackstone, *Commentaries*, vol. 1, chap. 15, and vol. 2, chap. 23; *The Laws Respecting Women*, especially book 2; Reeve, *Baron and Feme*, part 1; and Swift, *System of the Laws of Connecticut*, vol. 1, book 2. The points discussed here are taken from these authorities.

4. On property law, see generally Blackstone, *Commentaries*, 1:430–32, 2:433–36; *The Laws Respecting Women*, 148–63; Reeve, *Baron and Feme*, 1–8, 22–30, 60–63, 192–93; Swift, *System of the Laws of Connecticut*, 1:194–95; and James Kent, *Commentaries on American Law*, 4 vols. (New York, 1826–30), 2:129–43.

5. On widows' property rights, see generally Blackstone, *Commentaries*, 2:129–39; *The Laws Respecting Women*, 197–99; Reeve, *Baron and Feme*, 37–59; and Swift, *System of the Laws of Connecticut*, 1:254–57.

6. Blackstone, *Commentaries*, 2:132, 136, 293, 355; Leonard Alston, ed., *De Republica Anglorum: A Discourse on the Commonwealth of England by Sir Thomas Smith* (Cambridge, England, 1906), 127; William Searle Holdsworth, *A History of English Law*, 16 vols. (London, 1903–66), 3 (5th ed., 1942): 193, 195–96; Kent, *Commentaries*, 2:150–51.

7. Holdsworth, *A History of English Law*, 3:236–40; *An Essay on the Nature and Operation of Fines* (London, 1783), 2–3.

8. *Essay on Fines*, 68–69; Blackstone, *Commentaries*, 2:355; *The Laws Respecting Women*, 181; Holdsworth, *A History of English Law*, 3:245.

9. Holdsworth, *A History of English Law*, 3:236.

10. *The Laws Respecting Women*, 133.

11. Holdsworth, *A History of English Law*, 7 (1st ed., 1925): 361. Blackstone discussed the procedure in *Commentaries*, 2:338–39.

12. Reeve, *Baron and Feme*, 90–91; Kent, *Commentaries*, 2:151–52 and cases there cited. Blackstone approved of the colonists' use of simple conveyancing forms. See his remarks in *Commentaries*, 2:360–61. I would like to thank Clive Holmes for pointing out this reference.

13. Reeve, *Baron and Feme*, 98; *The Laws Respecting Women*, 70–72, 393. Blackstone

discussed the principle of coercion as it related to criminal law in *Commentaries*, 4:28–29.

14. William Waller Hening, ed., *The Statutes at Large: Being a Collection of all the Laws of Virginia, from the First Session of the Legislature, in the Year 1619*, 13 vols. (Richmond, Va., 1809–23; reprint ed., Charlottesville, Va., 1969), 2:317.

15. Thomas Bacon, ed., *Laws of Maryland at Large, with Proper Indexes: Now First Collected into One Compleat Body* . . . (Annapolis, Md., 1765), chap. 2.

16. John D. Cushing, ed., *The Earliest Printed Laws of North Carolina, 1669–1751*, 2 vols. (Wilmington, Del., 1977), 2:35.

17. Thomas Cooper, ed., *The Statutes at Large of South Carolina*, 5 vols. (Columbia, S.C., 1836–39), 3:302–3.

18. Carroll v. Warren (1736), Chancery Records, 7:100, MHR.

19. Ibid., 106.

20. Ibid., 131.

21. Jones et al. v. Porters (1740), in R. T. Barton, ed., *Virginia Colonial Decisions: The Reports by Sir John Randolph and by Edward Barradall of Decisions of the General Court of Virginia, 1728–1741*, 2 vols. (Boston, 1909), 2:93.

22. "An Act for amending the Act, intituled, An Act for settling the Titles and Bounds of Lands; and for preventing unlawful Shooting and Ranging thereupon," in Hening, *Laws of Virginia*, 4:401.

23. Harvey and Wife v. Pecks, 15 Munford 518 (1810).

24. Ibid., 524, 528.

25. Countz v. Geiger, 1 Call 193 (1797).

26. Ann Bissett v. James Bissett (1761), Chancery Records 10:60, MHR; Ann Bissett v. James Bissett, heir of David Bissett, 1 Harris and McHenry 211 (1762).

27. Bissett v. Bissett, Chancery Records, 10:61–62, MHR.

28. Ibid., 71.

29. Ibid., 62.

30. Swift, *System of the Laws of Connecticut*, 1:194–95.

31. The statute read, "For the future, any real Estate, whereof any Woman at the Time of her Marriage, is seised as her Estates of Inheritance, or does during such Coverture, become so, either by Descent or otherwise, shall not be Alienable by her Husband's Deed, without her Consent, testified by her Hand and Seal to such Deed and Acknowledgment of the same before an Assistant or Justice of the Peace" (in *Acts and Laws of His Majesty's English Colony of Connecticut in New-England in America* [New London, Conn., 1750]), 119).

32. Peter Butler and William Atwater v. Juliana Buckingham, 5 Day 496 (1813). In this case, the conveyance of a feme covert was adjudged void because she did not have a private examination.

33. Statutes on conveyancing in Massachusetts specified that deeds of conveyance had to be acknowledged and recorded. None mentioned private examinations. The earliest statute on conveyances, enacted in 1652, implies that men alone conveyed family property, as in Connecticut. It read, "No sale or alienation of houses & lands in this jurisdictio [*sic*], shal be holde good in Law except the same be done by deed in writing, under hand & seal, and delivered & possession given upon part, in the name of the whole, by the seller, or his atturney, so authorized under hand & seal, unles the

sayd deed be acknowledged & recorded according to Law" (John D. Cushing, comp., *The Laws and Liberties of Massachusetts, 1641–1691: A Facsimile Edition*, 3 vols. [Wilmington, Del., 1976], 1:20). In 1697 the law stated explicitly that a single grantor could establish the validity of a conveyance in court by acknowledging it alone. Once the document was recorded, it was good against all claims "without any other Act or Ceremony in the Law whatsoever" (John D. Cushing, ed., *Massachusetts Province Laws, 1692–1699* [Wilmington, Del., 1978], 99). The same wording made its way into the first postrevolutionary statute on conveyancing, "An Act directing the Mode of transferring Real Estates by Deed, and for preventing Fraud therein," enacted in 1784 (in *The Laws of the Commonwealth of Massachusetts from November, 1780 . . . to February 28, 1807*, 3 vols. [Boston, 1807], 1:131–34). The practice was confirmed again in the revised statutes of 1835 (Theron Metcalf and Horace Mann, eds., *The Revised Statutes of the Commonwealth of Massachusetts Passed November 4, 1835* [Boston, 1836], 404–6).

34. John Fowler v. Daniel Shearer, 7 Tyng 14 (1810).

35. Abigail Catlin v. Samuel Ware, 9 Tyng 218 (1812).

36. Ibid., 220.

37. Joseph Dudley v. Elizabeth Sumner, 5 Tyng 438 (1809). He voiced some of the same concerns in Arthur Lithgow v. James Kavenagh, 9 Tyng 172–73 (1812).

38. Dudley v. Sumner, 5 Tyng 480.

39. Gail McKnight Beckman, ed., *The Statutes at Large of Pennsylvania in the Time of William Penn* (New York, 1976), 86, 133, 147; *Laws of the Commonwealth of Pennsylvania*, 10 vols. (Philadelphia, 1810–44), 1:94–98.

40. Hugh Davey et ux. v. Peter Turner, 1 Dallas 11 (1764).

41. Ibid., 13.

42. Ibid.

43. Ibid., 14.

44. The Lessee of Thomas Lloyd v. Abraham Taylor, 1 Dallas 17 (1768). The conveyance apparently was a successful attempt by a husband to defeat the inheritance rights of his wife and children. The Lloyds conveyed land held in fee by Mercy to a third party, who immediately reconveyed to the husband alone. Several years later the husband went into debt and lost the lands on an execution.

45. Ibid.

46. *Laws of Pennsylvania*, 1:307–9.

47. Kirk v. Dean, 2 Binney 345 (1810).

48. John M. Murrin, "Anglicizing an American Colony: The Transformation of Provincial Massachusetts" (Ph.D. dissertation, Yale University, 1966); John M. Murrin, "The Legal Transformation: The Bench and Bar of Eighteenth-Century Massachusetts," in Stanley N. Katz and John M. Murrin, eds., *Colonial America: Essays in Politics and Social Development*, 3d ed. (New York, 1983), 540–71.

49. Matthew Crips to John Dickinson, John Dickinson Papers, Box 9, Folder 10, Library Company of Philadelphia.

50. Thomas McKean to Sally McKean, McKean Papers, Letterbook vol. 6, fols. 23–27, HSP. It is ironic that the man involved in this illegal conveyance sat on the Supreme Court. His action also demonstrates the ease with which men could sell lands without their wives. I would like to thank Mary Beth Norton for pointing out this reference.

51. In the earliest days of control by the English, New York followed the southern

pattern of granting immediate recognition to women's property rights. The Charter of Liberties ordered "that Noe Estate of a feme Covert shall be sold or conveyed But by Deed acknowledged by her in Some Court of Record the Woman being secretly Examined if She doth it freely without threats or Compulsion of her husband" (Charles Z. Lincoln, ed., *The Colonial Laws of New York from the Year 1664 to the Revolution* . . ., 5 vols. [Albany, N.Y., 1894], 1:114). Assemblymen never included this provision in any statute on conveyancing, however. Thus, although occasionally buyers and sellers requested examinations for married women, the law did not require them. See, for example, "A Bill to prevent deceit & Forgerys," enacted in 1684 to strengthen the rules on conveyancing (in ibid., 1:148–49).

52. "An Act to confirm certain ancient Conveyances and directing the Manner of proving Deeds to be recorded," in ibid., 5:202–3.

53. Jackson, ex dem. Woodruff and others v. Gilchrist, 15 Johnson's Supreme Court Reports 89 (1818).

54. Ibid., 110–11.

55. Garlick v. Strong and Garlick, 3 Paige's Chancery Reports 440 (1832).

56. Ibid., 452.

57. Martha Humphrey, Widow v. Phinney, 2 Johnson's Supreme Court Reports 484 (1807). See also Bancroft and Wife v. White, 1 New York Common Law Reports (1 Caines Reports) 185 (1803); and Shaw, Widow v. White, 15 Johnson's Supreme Court Reports 179 (1816).

58. Jackson, ex dem. Corson and Sebring v. Cairns and Coles, 20 Johnson's Supreme Court Reports 301 (1822). See also Jackson, ex dem. E. Stevens v. T. Stevens, 16 Johnson's Supreme Court Reports 110 (1819), and Jackson ex dem. Clowes v. Catharine Vanderheyden, 17 Johnson's Supreme Court Reports 167 (1819), which focused on the same points of law.

59. Two cases, one early in the eighteenth century and one from the end of the century, offer some contradictory evidence. In Robins' Lessees v. Bush, tried in 1723, the Provincial Court voided a deed made without a proper acknowledgment. The Appeals Court reversed this decision. A second appeal, this time to the lord proprietor, was demanded, but no record survives of the result (see 1 Harris and McHenry 50 [1723]). Similarly, in Richard Hoddy's Lessee v. William Harryman the Maryland Court of Appeals admitted a defective deed as evidence in a dispute over property, acting against the arguments of the attorney general (see 3 Harris and McHenry 581 [1797]). Thus, even in a colony that enforced procedures to protect women's property rights, occasional lapses occurred.

60. Hawkins's Lessee v. Gould, 3 Harris and Johnson 243 (1804).

61. The Corporation of the Roman Catholic Clergymen's Lessee v. Hammond, 1 Harris and Johnson 580 (1805).

62. Ibid., 588.

63. Hawkins, et al. Lessee v. Burress et al., 1 Harris and Johnson 513 (1804); Heath's Lessee v. Eden's Guardian, 1 Harris and Johnson 751 (1805).

64. The first statement read, "And the said *Susanna Trueman* being examined privately by us and out of the hearing of her said husband, acknowledged that she did the same *of her own free will, and not through any threats of her said husband, or fear of his displeasure*" (Hawkins v. Burress, 1 Harris and Johnson 517). The emphasis is in the original. The second was similar, reading, "And at the same time came *Mary Heath*,

who being by us privately examined out of the hearing of her husband, *acknowledged her right of dower to the within* land and premises, and declared she did freely and voluntarily, without threats or fear of her said husband displeasure" (Heath v. Eden, 1 Harris and Johnson 751). The emphasis is in the original. In both cases, the court refused to read "ill-usage" into the acknowledgments; jurists in Maryland viewed this wording as essential.

65. See also the discussion on wording in John Lee Webster's Lessee v. William Hall, 2 Harris and McHenry 19 (1782). Other late eighteenth- and early nineteenth-century cases confirm the pattern. See Abraham Lewis's Lessee v. William Waters, 3 Harris and McHenry 430 (1796); Jacob's Lessee v. Kraner, 1 Harris and Johnson 291 (1802); and Peddicoart's Lessee v. Rigges, 1 Harris and Johnson 292 (1802).

66. Edward Flanagan and Wife's Lessee v. John Tully Young, 2 Harris and McHenry 38 (1782).

67. Ibid., 45.

68. See "An Act for amending the Act, intituled, An Act for settling the Titles and Bounds of Lands; and for preventing unlawful Shooting and Ranging thereupon," in Hening, *Laws of Virginia*, 4:397–401.

69. Ibid., 401.

70. Jones et al. v. Porters (1740), in Barton, *Virginia Colonial Decisions*, 2:93.

71. Harvey and Wife v. Pecks, 15 Munford 518 (1810).

72. Ibid., 523–24.

73. Robert Ewing v. Mrs. Ann Smith and Thomas R. Smith, 3 Desaussure 417 (1811).

74. Ibid., 456. A prerevolutionary case, Sir Thomas Frankland, Complainant v. Thomas Smith and Sarah his wife, et al., demonstrates earlier adherence to the rules on feme covert acknowledgments and private examinations (in Anne King Gregorie, ed., *Records of the Court of Chancery of South Carolina, 1671–1779*, with an introduction by J. Nelson Fierson [Washington, D.C., 1950], 623).

75. *Laws of Pennsylvania*, 1:308.

76. Shaller and another, administrators of Shaller v. Brand, 6 Binney 442 (1814).

77. Watson v. Mercer and another, 6 Sergeant and Rawle 51 (1820).

78. Lessee of Watson and Wife v. Bailey and others, 1 Binney 470 (1808).

79. Ibid., 471. The emphasis is in the original.

80. Ibid., 479.

81. Lessee of McIntire v. Ward, 5 Binney 296 (1812).

82. Ibid., 301–2.

83. Ibid., 302–3.

84. Evans v. The Commonwealth, 4 Sergeant and Rawle 272 (1818).

85. Brackenridge argued his point in Shaller v. Brand, 6 Binney 445–47 (1814), and Lessee of McIntire v. Ward, 5 Binney 302–3 (1812).

86. Watson v. Mercer, 6 Sergeant and Rawle 50 (1820).

87. *Laws of Pennsylvania*, 9:129.

88. Tate and Wife v. Stooltzfoos and others, 16 Sergeant and Rawle 35 (1827).

89. Ibid.

90. Jackson v. Gilchrist, 15 Johnson's Supreme Court Reports 111 (1818). The emphasis is in the original.

91. Quoted in Charles Biddle, *The Autobiography of Charles Biddle* (Philadelphia, 1883), 2–3. I would like to thank Mary Beth Norton for pointing out this reference.

CHAPTER THREE

1. For a general discussion of femes coverts' contractual disabilities see Blackstone, *Commentaries*, 1:430–31; John Joseph Powell, *Essay upon the Law of Contracts and Agreements: In Two Volumes* (London, 1790), 1:59–112; *The Laws Respecting Women*, 148, 170–72; Reeve, *Baron and Feme*, 89, 98; Samuel Church, Notebook, "Lectures on Law by Tapping Reeve," 1806, p. 187, Myron Taylor School of Law, Cornell University, Ithaca, N.Y.; Kent, *Commentaries*, 2:168–69; Holdsworth, *A History of English Law*, 3 (5th ed., 1942): 528, 542, 8 (1st ed., 1925): 51; Marshall D. Ewell, *Cases on Domestic Relations* (Boston, 1891), 178–79.

2. Blackstone, *Commentaries*, 1:430.

3. Church, "Lectures," 192.

4. Ibid., 192–93. In *Baron and Feme*, Reeve wrote, "It is a maxim of the common law, that the husband and wife cannot contract with each other, during the coverture. The reason assigned is, that they are one person in the eyes of the law, and that it would be absurd for any person to contract with himself. The maxim is generally correct, that an husband and wife cannot contract with each other; but the reason assigned has no foundation in truth. The law does not view the husband and wife as one person; for a deed or devise of land to a wife, vests in her, and not in the husband. As to real property, then, they are two distinct persons" (p. 29).

5. Reeve, *Baron and Feme*, 90–91, 98; the quotation is from p. 98. See also the discussions in Church, "Lectures," 187; and in *The Laws Respecting Women*, 148. The principle of coercion had particular significance for contracts made directly between spouses, which were seldom condoned by the common law under any circumstances. These were the contracts emphasized by Blackstone in his discussion in *Commentaries*, 1:430. See also Ewell, *Cases on Domestic Relations*, 150–52.

6. Reeve, *Baron and Feme*, 98, 165, 171; the quotation is from p. 98. See also Church, "Lectures," 187, 189; and Ewell, *Cases on Domestic Relations*, 148–49.

7. Reeve, *Baron and Feme*, 79; Kent, *Commentaries*, 2:179; Holdsworth, *A History of English Law*, 3:528–30; *The Laws Respecting Women*, 170.

8. Blackstone, *Commentaries*, 1:430. Tapping Reeve wrote, "It is an indisputable rule, that a wife can act as attorney to her husband" (*Baron and Feme*, 79).

9. If a husband entrusted his wife with a power of attorney, she could conduct his business affairs to the extent specified in that document. To cite one example, Deborah Logan received extensive powers from her husband by a letter of attorney executed in 1798. See the Letter of Attorney from George Logan to his Wife, Deborah Logan (1798), John Dickinson Papers, Box 9, Folder 15, Library Company of Philadelphia.

10. The statement appears in Justice Yeates's opinion on Webster v. McGinnis, 5 Binney 236 (1812). See also Blackstone, *Commentaries*, 1:418, where he wrote, "A wife, a friend, a relation, that use to transact business for a man, are *quoad hoc* his servants; and the principal must answer for their conduct: for the law implies, that

they act under a general command; and, without such a doctrine as this, no mutual intercourse between man and man could subsist without any tolerable convenience." Blackstone's point was reiterated in *The Laws Respecting Women*, 170.

11. Webster v. McGinnis, 5 Binney 235 (1812).

12. Ibid., 236.

13. Ibid., 237.

14. Relevant decisions include Executors of Willingham v. Executors of Simons, 1 Desaussure 272 (S.C., 1792); Spencer v. Tisue, 1 Addison 316 (Pa., 1796); and Bioren's Lessee v. Keep, 1 Yeates 576 (Pa., 1795).

15. Spencer v. Tisue, 1 Addison 319 (1796).

16. Willingham v. Simons, 1 Desaussure 272 (1792).

17. Ibid., 273. The chancellor emphasized his point, saying, "One thing however we would wish to be particularly attended to, which is, that we are decidedly of opinion the payment to Mrs. Simons was to all intents illegal.—Nor can any payment to a wife, of money owing to the husband, ever be made legal but by some subsequent act, or some very strong presumptive consent of the husband, which is so in the present case."

18. See, for example, Baxter v. Smith and Wife, 6 Binney 427 (Pa., 1814).

19. The rule is explained in *The Laws Respecting Women*, where it is written, "This restricted right of purchasing lands which the law allows to femes-covert is granted, because it does not make the property of the husband liable to any disadvantage, nor does it support a separate will, or power of contracting in the wife, but here the will of the wife is supposed concurrent with that of the husband" (p. 172). See also, Blackstone, *Commentaries*, 2:292; and Kent, *Commentaries*, 1:150.

20. Swift, *System of the Laws of Connecticut*, 1:200; Kent, *Commentaries*, 2:136; Holdsworth, *A History of English Law*, 2 (4th ed., 1936): 387. It seems odd that Tapping Reeve, generally so thorough in his discussion of the legal rights of wives, did not mention feme sole traders. He did include a discussion of the right of women to hold and control property separately from their husbands, however. The rules he explained there encompassed those for independent businesswomen, although Reeve did not say so explicitly (see *Baron and Feme*, 161–83).

21. *The Laws Respecting Women*, 172–73; Blackstone, *Commentaries*, 2:450; Powell, *Essay upon Contracts*, 1:109–10.

22. *The Laws Respecting Women*, 172–77; Powell, *Essay upon Contracts*, 1:77.

23. *The Laws Respecting Women*, 177.

24. For discussions of early American businesswomen, see Mary Beth Norton, "A Cherished Spirit of Independence: The Life of an Eighteenth-Century Boston Businesswoman," in Carol R. Berkin and Mary Beth Norton, eds., *Women of America: A History* (Boston, 1979), 138–51; Spruill, *Women in the Southern Colonies*, 276–92; and Kerber, *Women of the Republic*, 148–52. Two older accounts attempted to estimate the number of women employed outside the home in colonial and revolutionary America; although the figures now are being questioned, the books still include important information on women in business: Dexter, *Colonial Women of Affairs*; and Elizabeth Anthony Dexter, *Career Women of America, 1776–1840* (Francestown, N.H., 1950).

25. Cases in which married women's rights to operate independent business establishments were challenged include Commonwealth v. Cullins, 1 Williams 116 (Mass.,

1804); James Russell, Administrator, et al., v. Nathan Brooks, 7 Pickering 65 (Mass., 1828); T. Howard and Maria his Wife v. Moffatt, 2 Johnson's Chancery Reports 206 (N.Y., 1816); Catharine Megrath v. Administrators of John Robertson and Ann Robertson, 1 Desaussure 445 (S.C., 1795).

26. Cooper, *South Carolina Statutes*, 2:593. The full title of the act was "An Act for the better securing the payment of debts due from any person inhabiting and residing beyond the sea or else where without the limits of this Province of South Carolina, and to subject a Feme Covert that is a Sole Trader to be arrested and sued for any Debt contracted by her as a Sole Trader."

27. Ibid., 3:616–61; the quotation is from p. 621. The full title of the act was "An Act for the better securing the payment and more easy recovery of debts due from any person or persons inhabiting residing or being beyond the seas, or elsewhere without the limits of this Province, by attaching the moneys, goods, chattels, debts and books of account of such person or persons, if any he, she or they shall have within this Province; and to sue for and recover such debts as shall be contracted with her as a sole trader, and to subject such feme covert to be arrested and sued for any debt contracted by her as a sole trader."

28. David J. McCord, ed., *Statutes at Large of South Carolina*, vol. 6 (Columbia, S.C., 1839), 212.

29. Ibid.

30. Ibid., 236. This provision appeared in an amendment to the original law, added only a few days later.

31. Records of the Secretary of State, Miscellaneous Records, Charleston Series, SCA. See, for example, agreements executed in 1754 (vol. KK: 263–64), 1767 (vol. MM: 629, 691), 1774 (vol. RR: 13, 35, 80, 112, 130), and 1784 (vol. UU: 252, 371, 396, 424).

32. Catharine Magrath v. Jno. and Ann Robinson['s] Administrators (1795), Charleston District Court of Chancery Decrees, 1:1, SCA. The case also is reported as Catharine Megrath v. Administrators of John Robertson and Ann Robertson, 1 Desaussure 445 (1795).

33. Magrath v. Robinson, 1:2, SCA.

34. Megrath v. Administrators of Robertson, 1 Desaussure 446.

35. Magrath v. Robinson, 1:5, SCA.

36. *Laws of Pennsylvania*, 1:99–100.

37. Ibid., 99.

38. On the issue of consent, see the citations at n. 20, above.

39. "An Act authorizing the Justices of the Supreme Judicial Court, to licence the Sale of Real Estate by married Women in certain Cases, and for other Purposes in the Act mentioned," in *The Perpetual Laws of the Commonwealth of Massachusetts*, 3 vols. (Boston, 1801), 1:404.

40. Lydia Bachelor v. Her Husband, William Bachelor, 1 Williams 256 (1804).

41. Commonwealth v. Cullins, 1 Williams 116 (1804). See also King and Mead v. Mary Paddock, 18 Johnson's Supreme Court Reports 141 (N.Y., 1820). Here a woman was adjudged a feme sole trader and capable of answering a suit in her own name because her husband had not returned from a trading voyage on which he had embarked twelve years earlier. He was presumed dead.

42. Russell v. Brooks, 7 Pickering 65 (1828).

43. Ibid., 66.

44. Ibid., 67.

45. Deborah Gregory v. Thomas Paul, Executor, et al., 15 Tyng 31 (1818); Phebe Abbot v. John Bayley, 6 Pickering 89 (1827).

46. *The Laws Respecting Women*, 171; Kent, *Commentaries*, 2:154–57. English precedent on the point is discussed at length in Gregory v. Paul, 15 Tyng 32–35.

47. Gregory v. Paul, 15 Tyng 34.

48. Powell, *Essay upon Contracts*, 1:75, 97.

49. Ibid., 34–35.

50. Blackstone, *Commentaries*, 1:430; *The Laws Respecting Women*, 152–53; Reeve, *Baron and Feme*, 79–82; Swift, *System of the Laws of Connecticut*, 1:197; Kent, *Commentaries*, 2:146; Holdsworth, *A History of English Law*, 3:529–30.

51. Reeve, *Baron and Feme*, 79–80. See also Powell, *Essay upon Contracts*, 1:93–94.

52. Reeve, *Baron and Feme*, 80–81; Swift, *System of the Laws of Connecticut*, 1:197.

53. Swift, *System of the Laws of Connecticut*, 1:197. See the discussion by Spruill on the use of such advertisements in the colonial South in *Women in the Southern Colonies*, 178–84.

54. In Ann Govane v. William Govane (1757), a wife complained to the Court of Chancery that "The said William Govane hath forewarned Several Store Keepers (as your Oratrix hath heard and verilly believes to be true) to [not] let your Oratrix have any thing whatever on his Account and that if they do he will not pay for the same." Here the chancellor decided the prohibition was unreasonable, because William had forced his wife to leave their home and refused to support her. The court ordered a separation with alimony for the wife (Chancery Records, 8:820–948, MHR; the quotation is from p. 821).

55. Jane Pattison v. Jeremiah Pattison (1736–37), Chancery Records, 6:207, MHR.

56. Ibid., 235.

57. Ibid. See also McGahay v. Williams, 12 Johnson's Supreme Court Reports 293 (1815), in which the court ordered a husband to pay for his wife's board and lodging, even though she originally left him, because she wanted to return home and he would not allow her to do so. "If a husband turns away his wife, he gives her a credit wherever she goes, and must pay for necessaries furnished her" (p. 295).

58. The Pennsylvania law stated that the "lands, tenements and estate" of deserting husbands "shall be and are hereby made liable and subject to be seized and taken in execution, to satisfy any sum or sums of money, which the wives of such husbands, or guardians of their children, shall necessarily expend or lay out for their support and maintenance" (*Laws of Pennsylvania*, 1:100).

59. Rotch, administrator of Elam v. Miles, 2 Connecticut Reports 638 (1818).

60. Private bills are discussed in Kerber, *Women of the Republic*, 150–51, and Spruill, *Women in the Southern Colonies*, 361–62. See also the discussion below and the references at n. 63.

61. "An Act, to enable Susannah Cooper, to sell and dispose of her personal estate, by deed or will, notwithstanding her husband, Isles Cooper, shall happen to be living; and for other purposes therein mentioned," in Hening, *Laws of Virginia*, 5:294. Spruill discussed a similar bill enacted by the Virginia House of Burgesses for Frances Greenhill in 1752. Greenhill's bill was disallowed in England, but Cooper's apparently died in the Board of Trade. Because it contained a suspending clause, we cannot

know whether Cooper—and her son—ever benefited from her private act (*Women in the Southern Colonies*, 362; *Journal of the Commissioners for Trade and Plantations from April 1704* ... , 27 vols. [London, 1920–], 10:33). I would like to thank John M. Hemphill for his generosity in providing information on the Cooper bill.

62. Hening, *Laws of Virginia*, 5:294.

63. On the Chancery action, see James Heath v. Susannah and Thomas Tracy (1705), Chancery Records, 2:538, MHR. The private bill is discussed in Spruill, *Women in the Southern Colonies*, 361–62.

64. Abner C. Goodell, ed., *Acts and Resolves, Public and Private, of the Province of Massachusetts Bay*, 18 vols. (Boston, 1869–1912), 2 (1874): 123, 6 (1896): 209. The Evans bill was enacted in 1718 and Conqueret's in 1767.

CHAPTER FOUR

1. The focus of the discussion of early American divorce law in this study concerns the relationship between divorce or separation and women's property rights. Important studies focusing on the social and religious implications of divorce in early America, and the evolution of the grounds for divorce, include Cott, "Divorce in Massachusetts"; Nancy F. Cott, "Eighteenth-Century Family and Social Life Revealed in Massachusetts Divorce Records," *Journal of Social History* 10 (1976): 20–43; Henry S. Cohn, "Connecticut's Divorce Mechanism, 1636–1969," *American Journal of Legal History* 14 (1970): 35–55; J. D. Sumner, Jr., "The South Carolina Divorce Act of 1949," *South Carolina Law Quarterly* 3 (1951): 253–59; William Renwick Riddell, "Legislative Divorce in Colonial Pennsylvania," *Pennsylvania Magazine of History and Biography* 57 (1931): 175–80; Thomas R. Meehan, " 'Not Made Out of Levity': Evolution of Divorce in Early Pennsylvania," *Pennsylvania Magazine of History and Biography* 92 (1968): 441–64; Matteo Spalletta, "Divorce in Colonial New York," *New York Historical Society Quarterly* 39 (1955): 422–40; James S. Van Ness, "On Untieing the Knot: The Maryland Legislature and Divorce Petitions," *Maryland Historical Magazine* 67 (1972): 171–75; and D. Kelly Weisberg, "Under Great Temptations Here: Women and Divorce Law in Puritan Massachusetts," and Michael S. Hindus and Lynne E. Withey, "The Law of Husband and Wife in Nineteenth-Century America: Changing Views of Divorce," both in D. Kelly Weisberg, ed., *Women and the Law: The Social Historical Perspective*, vol. 2: *Property, Family, and the Legal Profession* (Cambridge, Mass., 1982), 117–32, 133–54.

2. Agreements to separate and divide property that were executed through trustees came under virtually the same rules as prenuptial marriage settlements creating female separate estates. Blackstone noted the jurisdiction of chancery courts over trusts in *Commentaries*, 3:439–40. On marriage settlements, see chap. 5 herein and Marylynn Salmon, "Women and Property in South Carolina: The Evidence from Marriage Settlements, 1730–1830," *William and Mary Quarterly*, 3d ser. 39 (1982): 655–59.

3. On common law contracts between husbands and wives, see chap. 3. On judicial support of private separation agreements, see *The Laws Respecting Women*, 184; Reeve, *Baron and Feme*, 91–97, 166, 213–15; Swift, *System of the Laws of Connecticut*, 1:200–201; Kent, *Commentaries*, 2:178; Ewell, *Cases on Domestic Relations*, 148–49, 152–57,

178; and Holdsworth, *A History of English Law*, 6 (1st ed., 1924): 646. All American jurists did not approve of the harsh injunctions against common law contracts between husbands and wives. Reeve disdained the rule as impractical and unnecessary; he wrote sarcastically of conveyancing law, "A, the husband of B, cannot convey real property to B. Yet if A conveys to C, a third person, who, by agreement, immediately conveys to B, A does in fact convey to B through C, who is only a conduit pipe, through which the title is conveyed to B. Can any good reason be assigned why A should not convey directly to B, instead of pursuing such a circuitous route?" (*Baron and Feme*, 90–91).

4. Relevant Connecticut cases include Dibble v. Hutton, 1 Day 221 (1804); Humphrey v. Humphrey, 1 Day 271 (1804); Mary Goodwin v. William Goodwin, Jun., 4 Day 343 (1810); and Watrous et al. v. Chalker, 7 Connecticut Reports 224 (1828).

5. On wife sales, see Samuel Pyeatt Menefee, *Wives for Sale: An Ethnographic Study of British Popular Divorce* (New York, 1981).

6. Fry v. Derstler, 2 Yeates 278 (1798).

7. Cott, "Divorce in Massachusetts," 588–89; Blackstone, *Commentaries*, 1:428–29, 3:93–94; *The Laws Respecting Women*, 92–98, 186–88. Reeve discussed English law in *Baron and Feme*, 202–5.

8. Reeve, *Baron and Feme*, 205; *The Laws Respecting Women*, 92.

9. Joseph Henry Smith, *Appeals to the Privy Council from the American Plantations* (New York, 1950; reprint ed., New York, 1965), 583.

10. Cott's discussion focuses on the issue of changing grounds for divorce in "Divorce in Massachusetts," 586–614. For the particular points made here, see especially pp. 589–90, 599–608.

11. Swift, *System of the Laws of Connecticut*, 1:191, 200–201.

12. Cohn, "Connecticut's Divorce Mechanism," 39. On the practice of giving legislative divorces for cruelty, see Swift, *System of the Laws of Connecticut*, 1:193.

13. Cott, "Divorce in Massachusetts," 589. Cohn also mentioned the influence of the Puritan treatise in "Connecticut's Divorce Mechanism," 37, as did the predecessor of both Cott and Cohn, George Elliott Howard. See his *History of Matrimonial Institutions, Chiefly in England and the United States*, 3 vols. (Chicago, 1904), 2:77–79.

14. Morris, *Studies in American Law*; Haskins, *Law and Authority in Early Massachusetts*; Konig, *Law and Society in Puritan Massachusetts*.

15. Meehan, " 'Not Made Out of Levity,' " 442–43.

16. Ibid., 443–46. See also Riddell, "Legislative Divorce in Colonial Pennsylvania," 175; and Smith, *Appeals to the Privy Council*, 585–86.

17. Spalletta, "Divorce in Colonial New York," 422.

18. Spruill, *Women in the Southern Colonies*, 342–44; Sumner, "The South Carolina Divorce Act," 254–55; Nelson Manfred Blake, *The Road to Reno: A History of Divorce in the United States* (Westport, Conn., 1962), 40–45. Blake based his work largely on other authors' research; he relied heavily on Howard's *History of Matrimonial Institutions*, 2:348–76.

19. Gregorie, *Records of South Carolina*, 326–30.

20. Ibid., 381–82.

21. Margaret Macnamara v. Thomas Macnamara (1707), Chancery Records, 2: 579, MHR.

22. Ibid., 580.

23. The Macnamara case appears to have been an extreme one. Thomas's abhorrent behavior undoubtedly prompted Seymour to act aggressively even though he realized the legal correctness of the defendant's argument. The case report explained the court's position: "His Excy being Convinced not only by undeniable Testimonies but Even by his own Knowledge of the Inhumanity and barbarity of ye sd thos. towards his Wife manifested not only to his Excy but to All her Majestys noble Councill in Assembly before whom Appeared not long since the sd Margaret so battered, bruised and Inhumanly beaten in most parts of her body that had she not been of a Constitution more than ordinary strong she Could hardly have recovered it" (ibid.). The validity of Margaret's accusation of sexual misconduct was confirmed again years later. Thomas's petition "to restore him to his practice in the Several Courts of this province," a statement that reveals his knowledge of the law and therefore explains his earlier request for an ecclesiastical court trial, was rejected. The attorney general objected because Thomas "lyes under an Indictment found by the Grand Jury of the province for Attempting to Bugger a Certain Benja. Allen" (ibid., 833).

24. Jane Pattison v. Jeremiah Pattison (1736–37), Chancery Records, 6:207, MHR; Ann Govane v. William Govane (1752), Chancery Records, 8:820, MHR.

25. *Laws of Pennsylvania*, 2:343.

26. "An Act for regulating Marriage and Divorce," in Theron Metcalf, ed., *The General Laws of Massachusetts, from the Adoption of the Constitution, to February 1822*, 2 vols. (Boston, 1823), 1:301.

27. "An Act directing a mode of trial, and allowing of divorces in cases of adultery," in *Laws of the State of New York Passed at the Sessions of the Legislature Held in the Years 1777 ... 1784 ...* , 2 vols. (Albany, N.Y., 1886), 2:494; Spalletta, "Divorce in Colonial New York," 439.

28. Samuel Torbert and Beulah his Wife v. Jacob Twining and Thomas Story, 1 Yeates 440 (1795). Henry Cohn discussed the Connecticut statute of 1796 in "Connecticut's Divorce Mechanism," 43–44.

29. The first private divorce act in Maryland was granted to John Sewell in 1790. The fact that his wife had born a mulatto child prompted the assembly to take such a drastic step (see *Laws of Maryland* [Annapolis, Md., 1791], chap. 25). The same reason forced the Virginia legislative body to enact its first divorce bill in 1803 (see *Acts Passed at a General Assembly of the Commonwealth of Virginia* [Richmond, Va., 1803], 20–21). See also Blake, *The Road to Reno*, 51; and Howard, *History of Matrimonial Institutions*, 3:31–32.

30. "An Act to prescribe the method of proceeding in suits, and on petition for divorces," in *Acts Passed at a General Assembly of the Commonwealth of Virginia* (Richmond, Va., 1827), 21–22; "An Act prescribing general regulations to govern applications for divorces *a vinculo matrimonii*, and divorcing Robert Moran from his wife Lydia," in *Acts of the General Assembly of Virginia* (Richmond, Va., 1848), 165–67.

31. "An Act to give to the Chancellor and the County Courts as Courts of Equity, jurisdiction in cases of Divorce," in *Laws Made and Passed by the General Assembly of the State of Maryland* (Annapolis, Md., 1842), chap. 262.

32. Elizabeth Vaigneur, David Strobhart and Margaret his Wife v. W. J. Kirk, Survivor of his late Wife, Mary Jane Kirk, 2 Desaussure 664 (1808).

33. Cases include Anonymous, 1 Desaussure 113 (1785); Jennet Prather by her

next friend v. William Prather, 4 Desaussure 33 (1809); Harriet Devall by her next friend v. Michael Devall and Others, 4 Desaussure 79 (1809); Ann Taylor per prochein ami v. Walter Taylor, 4 Desaussure 167 (1811); Judith Williams per prochein ami v. Josiah Williams, 4 Desaussure 183 (1811); Catharine Threewits by her next friend v. Lewellyn Threewits, 4 Desaussure 560 (1815); Maria Lady Nisbett v. Sir John Nisbett (1816), Charleston District Court of Chancery Decrees, 3:164, SCA; Margarett Summers by her next friend v. Elijah Summers (1817), Washington District Equity Decrees, 1807–21, 54, SCA; and Margaret Gilliam by her next friend v. John Gilliam (1817), Washington District Equity Decrees, 1807–21, 51, SCA.

34. Winthrop D. Jordan, *White over Black: American Attitudes toward the Negro, 1550–1812* (Chapel Hill, N.C., 1968), 140–49. In "The Law of Husband and Wife," Hindus and Withey interpret the absence of divorce as an attempt to offer women security within marriage despite the sexual double standard. They also argue that South Carolina lawmakers defined marriage as a union made for interest rather than love, and that therefore they "refused to permit divorce where the logical accompaniment would have been to return a woman's previously separate property" (p. 150). The authors' emphasis on nineteenth-century courts' interpretation of marriage as a contractual arrangement, albeit one of a special nature, is productive, but their discussion of South Carolina law on this point is contradictory. If courts were hesitant to divorce couples and return women's property to them, then it was men's security within marriage that concerned them, not women's.

35. Jordan, *White over Black*, 148.

36. Bertram Wyatt-Brown, *Southern Honor: Ethics and Behavior in the Old South* (New York, 1982), 293–97, 300–308.

37. Ibid., 283–89, 300–307; the quotation is from p. 286. Wyatt-Brown states incorrectly that in South Carolina "even legal separations were forbidden" (p. 300). As we have seen, courts of chancery in the state approved of separations when wives were abused physically or deserted by their husbands. In *The Plantation Mistress: Woman's World in the Old South* (New York, 1982), Catherine Clinton includes a brief account of divorce (pp. 79–85). She notes that divorce was rare in the antebellum years and decided on a case-by-case basis, with legislators demonstrating a bias in favor of requests made by wealthy planters or their wives. Clinton notes that in South Carolina the legislature considered only eight petitions for divorce before 1830. She claims that the lawmakers refused one request; she says nothing about the outcome of six of the cases; and she implies that one petitioner was successful. The prose, however, is ambiguous: she writes, "A wife's adultery was in this case concrete and irrefutable grounds for divorce" (p. 83). Does she mean that the husband actually got his divorce? If so, this is the only such case on record for South Carolina.

38. *Laws of Maryland*, chap. 25; *Acts Passed at a General Assembly of the Commonwealth of Virginia* (1803), 20.

39. Statutes included guidelines for determining alimony in cases of divorce. Sometimes they stated explicitly that alimony should be equal to what a woman would receive at her husband's death. The Massachusetts statute of 1786 read, "When the divorce shall be for the cause of adultery committed by the husband, the wife shall have her dower assigned to her in the lands of her husband, in the same manner as if such husband was naturally dead" (see Metcalf, *General Laws of Massachusetts*, 1:302).

In the jurisdictions that had no divorce statutes, alimony provisions were made at the discretion of lawmaking bodies or, more generally, chancellors.

40. Peckford v. Peckford, 1 Paige's Chancery Reports 275 (1828). In C. Miller v. A. Miller, 6 Johnson's Chancery Reports 91 (1822), the chancellor wrote, "The general rule, in such cases, seems to be, to allow the wife a *third*, or, at least a fourth part of the annual income of the husband's real estate; but it is in the power and discretion of the Court to vary the allowance from time to time, according to the circumstances of the parties."

41. Galwith v. Galwith, 4 Harris and McHenry 477 (1689); Crane v. Meginnis, 1 Gill and Johnson 463 (1829).

42. The statute read, "That after such sentence, nullifying or dissolving the marriage, all and every the duties, rights and claims, accruing to either of the said parties, at any time theretofore, in pursuance of the said marriage, shall cease and determine." Presumably this clause provided for restitution of the property each party had owned at the time of the marriage (*Laws of Pennsylvania*, 2:345–46).

43. Smith v. Smith, 3 Sergeant and Rawle 248 (1817); Light v. Light, 1 Watts 263 (1832); *Acts of the General Assembly of the Commonwealth of Pennsylvania* (Harrisburg, 1815), 150–54; *Acts of the General Assembly of the Commonwealth of Pennsylvania* (Harrisburg, Pa., 1817), 67.

44. Klingenberger v. Klingenberger, 6 Sergeant and Rawle 187 (1820).

45. Ibid., 188.

46. Cott, "Divorce in Massachusetts," 609–11; the quotation is from p. 611.

47. Ibid., 599–604, 606–7.

48. Ibid., 594.

49. Swift, *System of the Laws of Connecticut*, 1:192–93; Zephaniah Swift, *A Digest of the Laws of the State of Connecticut*, 2 vols. (New Haven, Conn., 1822–23), 1:21; *Acts and Laws of His Majesty's Colony of Connecticut*, 43.

50. Swift, *System of the Laws of Connecticut*, 1:200–201.

51. Kerber, *Women of the Republic*, 162.

52. Cott, "Divorce in Massachusetts," 610–11.

53. The first English case supporting a marriage settlement executed without trustees was Rippon v. Dawding, Ambler 565, tried in 1769. The case was cited to support similar decisions in America. By 1816 Reeve could write that settlements without trustees were "no uncommon thing" (*Baron and Feme*, 163).

54. In Carson v. Murray et al., 3 Paige's Chancery Reports 501 (N.Y., 1832), the chancellor wrote regarding support of private separation agreements, "As many of the decisions which have gone the greatest length on this subject took place previous to the revolution, they have been recognized here as settling the law in this state to the same extent. I do not, therefore, feel myself at liberty to follow the opinions of the judges of the present day, as to the policy of supporting such agreements, in opposition to the law as settled by their predecessors; though I would not consent to extend the principle beyond adjudged cases."

55. Carson v. Murray, 3 Paige's Chancery Reports 483 (1832); Rogers by her next friend v. Rogers, 4 Paige's Chancery Reports 516 (1834). See also Baker v. Barney, 8 Johnson's Supreme Court Reports 72 (1811); and Fenner v. Lewis, 10 Johnson's Supreme Court Reports 38 (1813). James Kent discussed the history of private

separation agreements in New York in his *Commentaries*, 2:161–62.

56. Rogers v. Rogers, 4 Paige's Chancery Reports 517.

57. Carson v. Murray, 3 Paige's Chancery Reports 487.

58. John Nichols v. Allyn Palmer, executor of Noyes Palmer, deceased, 5 Day 47 (1811).

59. Ibid., 58.

60. Ibid., 60.

61. Ibid., 56.

62. Ibid., 52.

63. Ann Purcell v. Charles Purcell, 4 Hening and Munford 507 (1810).

64. Ibid., 511.

65. Ibid., 518–19.

66. The case report of Jellineau v. Jellineau appears only in summary form in the report for a later case, Threewits v. Threewits, 4 Desaussure 560 (1815). As the chancellor explained, "In the case of Elizabeth Jellineau, suing by her next friend, against her husband, Francis Jellineau, the Court upon full argument made a decree so full and clear to the points in question that I will, for the benefit of the profession, state it fully, as it is not in print" (p. 570).

67. Ibid., 570.

68. Prather v. Prather, 4 Desaussure 34 (1809). The Prather case was heard in February, and apparently it settled the issue of Chancery's jurisdiction over separate maintenances. In a case tried in the following term of the court, the point on jurisdiction was not raised by the defendant's counsel. The chancellor apparently had been prepared for an argument. He noted, "Although the Court could furnish abundant reasons for entertaining the cause, and decreeing alimony, it is deemed unnecessary so to do, inasmuch as the defendants by their answer have admitted the jurisdiction of the Court" (see Devall v. Devall, 4 Desaussure 82 [1809]).

69. Prather v. Prather, 4 Desaussure 35.

70. Taylor v. Taylor, 4 Desaussure 167 (1811); the quotation is from p. 174.

71. Ibid., 174–75.

72. Rebecca Rhame v. Bradley Rhame, 1 McCord's South Carolina Chancery Reports 205 (1826).

73. Jellineau v. Jellineau (n.d.), as reported in Threewits v. Threewits, 4 Desaussure 570 (1815); Prather v. Prather, 4 Desaussure 32 (1809); Williams v. Williams, 4 Desaussure 183 (1811); Nisbett v. Nisbett (1816), Charleston District Court of Chancery Decrees, 3:164, SCA.

74. Nisbett v. Nisbett (1816), Charleston District Court of Chancery Decrees, 3:164, SCA; Summers v. Summers (1817), Washington District Equity Decrees, 1807–21, 54, SCA.

75. Deborah Gregory v. Thomas Paul, Executors, et al., 15 Tyng 32 (1818).

76. Kent, *Commentaries*, 2:126. As he explained it, "The danger or injury must be serious, and the slightest assault or touch in anger was not, in ordinary cases, sufficient."

CHAPTER FIVE

1. On the issue of interpretation, see Salmon, "Women and Property in South Carolina," 657–59, and Marylynn Salmon, "The Property Rights of Women in Early America: A Comparative Study" (Ph.D. dissertation, Bryn Mawr College, 1980), 1–11, 150–55.

2. Historians' emphasis on nineteenth-century developments over those of the sixteenth century perhaps is demonstrated best by pointing to the imbalance in our knowledge of the events of the two eras. Despite the burgeoning interest in women's history over the past twenty years, Maria L. Cioni is the only historian to approach the question of English chancery developments since Mary R. Beard's exploratory study, *Woman as Force in History*, published in 1946. Cioni's study, "The Elizabethan Chancery and Women's Rights," appears in Delloyd J. Guth and John W. McKenna, eds., *Tudor Rule and Revolution: Essays for G. R. Elton from His American Friends* (Cambridge, England, 1982), 160. It is taken from her unpublished dissertation, "Women and the Law in Elizabethan England with Particular Reference to the Court of Chancery" (Ph.D. dissertation, University of Cambridge, 1974). Meanwhile, numerous studies of the married women's property acts in the United States have appeared, including Basch, *In the Eyes of the Law*; Chused, "Married Women's Property Law"; Peggy A. Rabkin, *From Fathers to Daughters: The Legal Foundations of Female Emancipation* (Westport, Conn., 1980); Kay Ellen Thurman, "The Married Women's Property Acts" (L.L.M. dissertation, University of Wisconsin Law School, 1966); and Warbasse, "Legal Rights of Married Women."

3. Most recently, Lebsock has argued that in Virginia the first married women's property act was passed because of a legislative desire to preserve some family property from confiscation for husbands' debts during periods of economic crisis (*Free Women of Petersburg*, 84–86). The first historian to observe the relationship between debtor-creditor relations and passage of early married women's property acts was Warbasse ("Legal Rights of Married Women," 143–50, 203–5). See also the excellent discussion by Basch in *In the Eyes of the Law*, 113–35; and the apt commentary of Chused in "Married Women's Property Law," 1398–1404. This point is discussed further below.

4. Lebsock, *Free Women of Petersburg*, 57–60.

5. Holdsworth, *A History of English Law* 1 (7th rev. ed., 1956): 454, 5 (1st ed., 1924): 303; Blackstone, *Commentaries*, 3:431–32, 439.

6. Holdsworth, *A History of English Law*, 5:310–31.

7. Cioni, "The Elizabethan Chancery," 174.

8. Holdsworth, *A History of English Law*, 5:312.

9. Ibid., 313–14.

10. Ibid., 310–15.

11. Lloyd Bonfield, *Marriage Settlements, 1601–1740: The Adoption of the Strict Settlement* (Cambridge, England, 1983), 102–22; Lawrence Stone, *The Family, Sex and Marriage in England, 1500–1800* (London, 1977), especially chaps. 6 and 8. On egalitarian marriages, see R. Trumbach, *The Rise of the Egalitarian Family: Aristocratic Kinship and Domestic Relations in Eighteenth-Century England* (London, 1978).

12. Cioni, "The Elizabethan Chancery," 160.

13. Ibid., 172–74.

14. Bonfield, *Marriage Settlements*, 120.

15. Ibid., 121.

16. Stone, *The Family in England*, 332, 330. Bonfield also posits a correlation between changes in forms of marriage settlements employed by the propertied classes for distributing family wealth and the changing nature of family ties in early modern England (see his "Marriage, Property and the 'Affective Family,'" *Law and History Review* 1 [1983]: 297–312). Bonfield notes the connection in *Marriage Settlements*, but writes that it is still "a matter for speculation" (p. 120).

17. Blackstone, *Commentaries*, 2:137. See also Cioni, "The Elizabethan Chancery," 175–78; and *The Law of Baron and Feme* (London, 1734), 150.

18. Cioni, "The Elizabethan Chancery," 178. On jointures as an alternative to dower, see Lloyd Bonfield, "Marriage Settlements, 1660–1740: The Adoption of the Strict Settlement in Kent and Northamptonshire," in R. B. Outhwaite, ed., *Marriage and Society: Studies in the Social History of Marriage* (London, 1981), 106–8. Blackstone discussed the comparative advantages of the two forms in *Commentaries*, 2:138–39.

19. Holdsworth, *A History of English Law*, 5:312.

20. Ibid., 5:311, 314–15, 7 (1st ed., 1925): 376–80. Blackstone discussed the history of uses and trusts in *Commentaries*, 2:327–37. Cioni remarks that although the Elizabethan Chancery began improving women's legal rights, the process of change did not end there. She writes, "The unquestioned improvements in the status of propertied women, which are so marked a feature of English society in the seventeenth and eighteenth centuries, rested upon the consideration given to their needs by the Elizabethan Chancery" ("The Elizabethan Chancery," 182).

21. Holdsworth, *A History of English Law*, 5:314; *The Law of Baron and Feme*, 222–23; *The Laws Respecting Women*, 179. Because no historian has attempted a study of English law on married women's separate estates in the seventeenth and eighteenth centuries, our knowledge of the development of various principles and precedents of law is slight. In particular, it is difficult to discover exactly when chancery made certain decisions. Because American jurists based their decisions regarding marriage settlements almost exclusively on English decisions, their discussions of English law can provide some information, but it is not clear how accurate their interpretations were. We need a detailed study of English precedent law on separate estates before we can be precise on the chronological development of this area of the law.

22. On the use of marriage settlements to protect and control family estates, see Bonfield, *Marriage Settlements*, especially chap. 6; Lloyd Bonfield, "Marriage Settlements and the 'Rise of Great Estates': The Demographic Aspect," *Economic History Review*, 2d ser. 32 (1979): 483–93; H. J. Habakkuk, "Marriage Settlements in the Eighteenth Century," *Transactions of the Royal Historical Society*, 4th ser. 32 (1950): 15–31; Christopher Clay, "Marriage, Inheritance, and the Rise of Large Estates in England, 1660–1815," *Economic History Review*, 2d ser. 21 (1968): 503–18; and Lawrence Stone, *The Crisis of the Aristocracy, 1558–1641* (Oxford, 1965), 632–49.

23. Reeve, *Baron and Feme*, 162–63, 170–73; Kent, *Commentaries*, 2:164–67. The author of *The Laws Respecting Women* wrote, "The trustee is considered as merely the instrument of the conveyance, and can in no shape affect the estate, unless by alienation for a valuable consideration, to a purchaser without notice; which as *cestuy*

que use is generally in possession of the land, is a thing that can rarely happen" (p. 161).

24. According to Cioni, the wife's equity first appeared as an attempt to guarantee widows support ("The Elizabethan Chancery," 175). See also Reeve, *Baron and Feme*, 9, 178–79.

25. Morris cited agreements between Peter Gordon and Jane Moore (1654) and John Philips and Faith Dotey (1667) in *Studies in American Law*, 135–38, 163. On seventeenth-century settlements, see Salmon, "The Legal Status of Women in Early America," 146–50.

26. The establishment of an independent royal government in South Carolina in 1729 undoubtedly affected the regularization of recording deeds in the 1730s. Settlements appear in a significant number beginning at that time. For a study of marriage settlements in South Carolina I employed a sample of 638 settlements created between 1730 and 1830 (see Salmon, "Women and Property in South Carolina," 659–60).

27. Ibid., 655–85.

28. Rippon v. Dawding, Ambler 565 (1769).

29. Reeve noted in 1816 that settlements without trustees had become "no uncommon thing" (*Baron and Feme*, 163).

30. In my sample of 638 South Carolina settlements, 552 (83 percent) were prenuptial (Salmon, "Women and Property in South Carolina," 661). There was no change in this pattern over time, an indication that women continued to secure separate property at the time when they held the greatest bargaining power over men. Women acting alone did not always make the decision for a settlement, of course. Reeve noted the role of parents and guardians in bargaining with the suitors of young women in *Baron and Feme*, 174. On the validity of postnuptial settlements, see Hugh Davey et ux. v. Peter Turner, 1 Dallas 11 (Pa., 1764), in which the court supported the right of a married woman to contract with her husband for the purpose of creating a separate estate.

31. Richard Francis, *Maxims of Equity* (London, 1728), 5.

32. Holdsworth, *A History of English Law*, 5:313; George W. Keeton and L. A. Sheridan, *Equity* (London, 1969), 442–43; *The Law of Baron and Feme*, 236; Reeve, *Baron and Feme*, 182–83. In the South Carolina case of Thomas Cape and Wife v. B. Adams and Others (1797), a man tried to create a settlement of his wife's property for his own benefit without her knowledge or consent (1 Desaussure 567). The court disallowed his deed.

33. In my sample of South Carolina settlements, an unusually high proportion were created by widows upon remarriage: 56 percent before 1780 and 40 percent from 1780 to 1830 were widows' settlements. Even more significant, perhaps, is the fact that widows wrote settlements reserving powers of control for themselves more frequently than did women marrying for the first time. Such a discrepancy indicates that widows did not create settlements simply because they had property, but also because they wanted to control that property (see Salmon, "Women and Property in South Carolina," 679–83). Moreover, there is no evidence to indicate that widows in South Carolina had more wealth than single women generally. It was the custom for fathers to give their daughters portions at marriage, and therefore single women from

propertied families generally did possess some wealth that could be settled upon them as a separate estate at marriage (see John E. Crowley, "Family Relations and Inheritance in Early South Carolina," *Histoire Sociale* 17 [1984]: 46–50).

34. Reeve, *Baron and Feme*, 42–47, 162.

35. See, for example, the Connecticut dower statute of 1656 in John D. Cushing, ed., *The Earliest Laws of the New Haven and Connecticut Colonies, 1639–1673* (Wilmington, Del., 1977), 28–29; and the Massachusetts dower statute of 1647 in Cushing, *Laws and Liberties of Massachusetts*, 1:26. In both colonies and states throughout the period studied, women with jointures could not also claim dower.

36. Reeve, *Baron and Feme*, 178–79. American cases on the principle of the wife's equity to a settlement include Philip Verplank v. Robert Sterry and Louisa Ann his Wife, 12 Johnson's Supreme Court Reports 536 (N.Y., 1815); T. Howard and Maria his Wife v. Moffatt, 2 Johnson's Chancery Reports 206 (N.Y., 1816); E. Turrel v. P. Turrel and Jones, 2 Johnson's Chancery Reports 391 (N.Y., 1817); E. S. Kenny v. Udall and Kenny, 5 Johnson's Chancery Reports 464 (N.Y., 1821); Glen and Wife v. D. Fisher, 6 Johnson's Chancery Reports 33 (N.Y., 1822); Haviland v. Myers, 6 Johnson's Chancery Reports 25 (N.Y., 1825); S. Haviland, by her next friend v. Bloom and Myers, 6 Johnson's Chancery Reports 178 (N.Y., 1822); Fabre and Wife v. Colden, 1 Paige's Chancery Reports 166 (N.Y., 1828); F. Carter, by her next friend v. J. K. Carter, 1 Paige's Chancery Reports 463 (N.Y., 1829); Mumford and Others v. Murray, 1 Paige's Chancery Reports 620 (N.Y., 1829); Mathewes and Others v. The Executors of Mathewes et al. (1762), in Gregorie, *Records of the South Carolina Chancery*, 507; Josiah Tatnell and Wife v. Executors of Fenwick, 1 Desaussure 143 (S.C., 1786); Elizabeth Greenland alias Brown v. Cornelius Brown, 1 Desaussure 196 (S.C., 1789); Postell and Wife and Smith and Wife v. Executors of James Skirving, 1 Desaussure 158 (S.C., 1789); McPike v. Hughes and Rumph, Charleston District Court of Chancery Decrees, 3:175 (S.C., 1816), SCA; Stephen Rogers et al. v. R. Curloss, Administrator of Bretton, Marlboro County Equity Decrees, 30 (S.C., ca. 1825), SCA; and Helms v. Franciscus, 2 Bland 544 (Md., 1818). No case directly on point appears in the early Virginia reports, although in one case report the Supreme Court of Appeals acknowledged that "the wife may take a separate estate from her husband, and even have a decree against him in respect of such estate" (Moore's Executrix v. Ferguson and Other, 2 Munford 422 [1811]). Cases do demonstrate the commitment of the Virginia Chancery to supporting female separate estates, including Ward and Other v. Webber and Wife, 1 Washington 274 (1794); and Moore's Administrator v. Dawney and Another, Administrator of Bell, 3 Hening and Munford 127 (1808).

37. Helms v. Franciscus, 2 Bland 576 (1818).

38. Postell and Smith v. Skirving, 1 Desaussure 158 (1789).

39. Helms v. Franciscus, 2 Bland 576 (1818).

40. Ibid.

41. Rogers v. Curloss, Marlboro County Equity Decrees, 30 (ca. 1825), SCA.

42. Kenny v. Udall and Kenny, 5 Johnson's Chancery Reports 464 (1821).

43. Ibid., 477.

44. Jacob Yohe v. William and John Barnet, Administrators of Henry Barnet, 1 Binney 358 (1808). An earlier case in which the Supreme Court refused to enforce

the doctrine of the wife's equity was Samuel Torbert and Beulah his Wife v. Jacob Twining and Thomas Story, 1 Yeates 432 (1795).

45. Yohe v. Barnet, 1 Binney 365.

46. Chief Justice McKean commented on Pennsylvania's attitude toward equity law in Walter White, Lessee of Earles Barnes v. Solomon Hart, 1 Yeates 226 (1793). Few studies of equity law in Pennsylvania are available, and nothing has been written for many years. See William Henry Rawle, *Equity in Pennsylvania* (Philadelphia, 1868), and Spencer R. Liverant and Walter H. Hitchler, "A History of Equity in Pennsylvania," *Dickinson Law Review* 37 (1932–33): 156–83. The records of Pennsylvania's short-lived Chancery Court are available in Albert Smith Faught, ed., *The Registrar's Book of Governor Keith's Court of Chancery of the Province of Pennsylvania, 1720–1735* (Harrisburg, Pa., 1941).

47. Evidence from South Carolina demonstrates, however, that couples designed settlements to benefit wives rather than husbands (see Salmon, "Women and Property in South Carolina," 662).

48. The Pennsylvania dower rule is discussed in chap. 7.

49. For Maryland, see "An Act for the enrolling of Conveyances, and securing the Estates of Purchasers," in Bacon, *Laws of Maryland*, chap. 2. Maryland courts enforced the law strictly, as demonstrated in Richard Ponsonby v. Robert, Sarah and Gerard Briscoe (1780–88), Chancery Records, 16:96, MHR. For Virginia, see "An act for settling the Titles and Bounds of Lands: and for preventing unlawful shooting and Ranging thereupon," in Hening, *Laws of Virginia*, 3:517. On enforcement of recording in Virginia, see Anderson v. Anderson, 2 Call 198 (1799). For South Carolina, see "An Act to oblige persons interested in Marriage Deeds and Contracts, to record the same in the Secretary's office of this state," in Cooper, *South Carolina Statutes*, 4:656. In Ann Garner and her Children v. Executors and Creditors of Melcher Garner, deceased, 1 Desaussure 437 (1795), Chancery supported an unrecorded settlement because of the "obscurity" of the act. In Lennox and Wife v. W. H. Gibbes, 1 Desaussure 305 (1792), Chancellor Hutson ruled, "The act for recording marriage settlements is so obscurely worded that the court would not enlarge its application but restricted it to the very terms used in the law, and pronounced that part of the act was unintelligible and inoperative." The law was revised in 1792 (see Cooper, *South Carolina Statutes*, 5:203). By 1794 courts were enforcing the recording rule strictly. See John Ward, Administrator of John Wilson v. Leighton Wilson and K. Simons and Wife, 1 Desaussure 401 (1794). Later cases are Archibald Taylor v. Robert Heriot, Executor of William Heriot, 4 Desaussure 227 (1812); Philip Givens v. S. T. Branford, 2 McCord's South Carolina Law Reports 152 (1822); Charity Forest, by Thomas Karwon, her Trustee v. James Warrington, 2 Desaussure 254 (1804); Edward Croft v. George Arthur, James Hibben and Benjamin Harvey, Administrators of Stephen Townsend, 3 Desaussure 223 (1811); and Boatright and Glaze v. S. E. M. Wingate, Survivor and Administrator of Edward Wingate, Brevard's South Carolina Law Reports, Part 2, 423 (1814). For Pennsylvania, see "An Act for acknowledging and recording of deeds," in *Laws of Pennsylvania*, 1:422; and Lessee of Samuel B. Foster v. Robert Whitehill, 2 Yeates 259 (1797).

50. Cooper, *South Carolina Statutes*, 4:656.

51. Foster v. Whitehill, 2 Yeates 259 (1797).

52. Ibid., 260.

53. Before 31 December 1780, 327 settlements were recorded in the colonial offices in Charleston (see Salmon, "Women and Property in South Carolina," 659–60). In Pennsylvania, see for example the deeds of settlement for Sarah Cawley and Sarah Morgan, Bucks County Deed Books, 10:69 and 19:139 (1779), BCHS; and Davey v. Turner, 1 Dallas 11 (1764). Significantly, England did not require the recording of trust instruments, a policy in line with its failure to record deeds.

54. John Hall v. William Holland and Francis Holland (1726), Chancery Records, 5:159, MHR.

55. Rebecca Drayton v. William Pritchard et al. (1816), Charleston District Court of Chancery Decrees, 3:161, SCA. Related cases include Peigne v. Snowden, 1 Desaussure 591 (1800); Joseph Peace, Assignee of James Kiernan v. Thomas P. Spierin and Others, 2 Desaussure 460 (1807); and Croft v. Townsend's Administrators, 3 Desaussure 223 (1811).

56. Kipp v. Hanna, 2 Bland 26 (1820).

57. Ibid., 27. Related Maryland cases include Ponsonby v. Briscoe (1780–88), Chancery Records, 16:96, MHR; and Jones v. Slubey, 5 Harris and Johnson 372 (1822).

58. Reeve, *Baron and Feme*, 176.

59. Coutts and Others v. Greenhow, 2 Munford 363 (1811).

60. Ibid., 363, 371.

61. Basch, *In the Eyes of the Law*, 122–26; the quotations are from pp. 122 and 125–26.

62. Coutts v. Greenhow, 2 Munford 363–64. Support for marriage settlements in South Carolina also is demonstrated by the official attitude toward those created by Loyalists' wives at the time of the Revolution. For a full discussion of this point, see Salmon, " 'Life, Liberty, and Dower,' " 86–88.

63. Reeve, *Baron and Feme*, 164. Reeve wrote, "Technical terms are not necessary to create this separate property. If it can be inferred from the words of the conveyance, that it was the intention of the grantor, that she should have the things granted to her separate use, that is sufficient."

64. Ibid., 163–65, 190–92; Kent, *Commentaries*, 2:165. For a case in which the court interpreted poor wording in a settlement for the benefit of a widow, see Roane's Executors v. Hern et al., 1 Washington 47 (Va., 1791).

65. David Johnson and Others v. L. Thompson, 4 Desaussure 458 (1814).

66. Ibid., 458–59.

67. Lowndes Trustee v. Executors of Champneys (1821), Charleston District Court of Chancery Decrees, 3:354, SCA.

68. Ibid., 355.

69. Torbert v. Twining and Story, 1 Yeates 432 (1795).

70. Ibid., 433–34.

71. Ibid., 439, 440.

72. Ibid., 440.

73. Reeve, *Baron and Feme*, 162–63, 170–73; Kent, *Commentaries*, 2:165.

74. Salmon, "Women and Property in South Carolina," 668–69; Thomas Attaway Reeder v. John Cartwright, 2 Harris and McHenry 469 (Md., 1790); Price v. Michel (1821), Charleston District Court of Chancery Decrees, 3:377, SCA.

75. Related cases include Robert Wright v. Richard Wright and Thomas Wright (1737), and William Raven v. Col. John Gibbes and Henry Bedon (1760), both in Gregorie, *Records of South Carolina*, 389, 502; Richardson v. Mountjoy, Barradall's Reports 194 (Va., 1739); Robinson's Administrator v. Brock, 1 Hening and Munford 212 (Va., 1807); Pickett and Wife and Others v. Chilton, 5 Munford 467 (Va., 1817); Administrators of Elizabeth Stone v. Charles Massey, 2 Yeates 363 (Pa., 1798); and Price and Nisbet v. Bigham's Executors, 7 Harris and Johnson 296 (Md., 1826).

76. As in England, each power of control had to be granted separately (see Kent, *Commentaries*, 2:164–65). In a Pennsylvania case, a woman devised both real and personal property despite the fact that her settlement granted her the right to bequeath personal estate only. The court ruled that her disposition of real estate was void, and awarded it to her heir at law in opposition to her wishes (James Haldane and Elizabeth his Wife v. Miers Fisher and Joseph Swift, 1 Yeates 121 [1792]).

77. Even though women had separate estates, husbands still had a legal obligation to support their wives, and the trust property was not allowed to become a fund for everyday expenses. The situation was different if a couple separated, however. Then a woman's separate estate could, by court order, become liable for necessaries. In a New York case tried in 1811, Baker v. Barney, the court ruled, "If the husband and wife part by consent, and he secures to her a separate maintenance suitable to his condition and circumstances in life, and pays it according to agreement, he is not answerable even for necessaries; and the general reputation of the separation will, in that case, be sufficient" (8 Johnson's Supreme Court Reports 73). See also A. Bethune and William Cook v. Beresford and Wife, and Saunders and Others, 1 Desaussure 180–81 (S.C., 1790); and Chanet v. Clement (1821), Charleston District Court of Chancery Decrees, 3:414, SCA.

78. Reeve, *Baron and Feme*, 171; Kent, *Commentaries*, 2:164. I have found no case to prove the point.

79. Petition of Ann Slann (1752), in Gregorie, *Records of South Carolina*, 452.

80. Bethune v. Beresford, 1 Desaussure 174 (1790).

81. Ibid.

82. Ibid., 177, 181.

83. Lowry et ux. v. Tiernan and Williamson, 2 Harris and Gill 34 (1827).

84. Ibid., 40.

85. Reeve, *Baron and Feme*, 162–63; Catharine Harrison v. David Crawford and Thomas Contee (1794–95), Chancery Records, 34:528, MHR; Petition of Ann Slann (1752), in Gregorie, *Records of South Carolina*, 452. This was not a privilege extended to minors, however, as demonstrated by Curtis v. Duncan (1821), Charleston District Court of Chancery Decrees, 3:428, SCA.

86. Reeve, *Baron and Feme*, 168, 172. In Price v. Michel (1821), the court determined that a feme covert who was separated from her husband did not need to inform her trustee of the dispositions she made of her own separate estate. Because she no longer lived with her husband, she was not under his coercion, and therefore the trustee's intermediary role of protector was unnecessary (Charleston District Court of Chancery Decrees, 3:377, SCA).

87. Stone v. Massey, 2 Yeates 365 (1798).

88. Ibid., 366.

89. Charlotte Poaug made such a change in her marriage settlement (Marriage

Settlement between Charlotte Poaug and John Poaug [1771], Marriage Settlements, 1:78, SCA).

90. Reeve, *Baron and Feme*, 172.

91. English cases beginning in 1723 were discussed by Chancellor Desaussure in Robert Ewing v. Mrs. Ann Smith and Thomas R. Smith, 3 Desaussure 427–45 (1811).

92. Ibid., 417.

93. For discussions of the effect of the American Revolution on South Carolina law, see James W. Ely, Jr., "American Independence and the Law: A Study of Post-Revolutionary South Carolina Legislation," *Vanderbilt Law Review* 26 (1973): 939–71; and Salmon, " 'Life, Liberty, and Dower,' " 85–106.

94. Ewing v. Smith, 3 Desaussure 456.

95. Ibid., 459.

96. Tiernan v. Poor et ux. et al., 1 Gill and Johnson 216 (1829).

97. Ibid., 229. The Pennsylvania case of Smith v. Brodhead's Executors (1792) discusses the issue of conveyancing law and separate estates, but has no recorded decision (4 Dallas 155).

98. Trustees of the Methodist Episcopal Church et al. v. John D. Jaques et al., 3 Johnson's Chancery Reports 77 (1817). Two earlier cases involving the same parties are reported in 1 Johnson's Chancery Reports 65 and 450 (1814, 1815).

99. The New York Court of Errors heard the appeal: John D. Jaques and Robert Jaques, appellants v. Trustees of the Methodist Episcopal Church et al., 17 Johnson's Supreme Court Reports 548 (1820). Norma Basch discussed the cases in *In the Eyes of the Law*, 76–77.

100. Kent, *Commentaries*, 2:166.

101. Related American cases on the issues of coercion and women's right to convey their estates to help their husbands include Andrew Kerr and Wife v. Charles P. Butler, 2 Desaussure 279 (S.C., 1804); Price v. Michel (1821), Charleston District Court of Chancery Decrees, 3:377, SCA; Demarest and Wife v. Wynkoop and Other, 3 Johnson's Chancery Reports 129 (N.Y., 1817); Bradish v. Gibbes and Others, 3 Johnson's Chancery Reports 523 (N.Y., 1818); and Darne and Gassaway v. Catlett et ux., 6 Harris and Johnson 475 (Md., 1825).

102. Elizabeth Wilson v. Vernon Hebb, Chancery Court Papers No. 5668 (1791–96), MHR. I would like to thank Lois Green Carr for alerting me to this source.

103. "Letters of Elizabeth and Vernon Hebb," *Chronicles of St. Mary's* 11 (1963): 2.

104. Ibid., 3–4.

105. Wilson v. Hebb, Chancery Court Papers No. 5668 (1791–96), MHR. Related cases include Henderson and Wife v. Laurens, 2 Desaussure 170 (S.C., 1803); and Jones v. Stockett, 2 Bland 409 (Md., 1823).

106. William Cater v. Thomas Eveleigh and Ann his Wife, 4 Desaussure 19 (1809). For a related case concerning trustee mismanagement and fraud, see Darne and Gassaway v. Catlett, 6 Harris and Johnson 476 (Md., 1825).

107. Cater v. Eveleigh, 4 Desaussure 20.

108. Mary Hibben v. John Scott and John Brockington and Martha his Wife, Chancery Court Case Papers, Bundle 1780–88, Folder No. 1 (1788), SCA. A Mary-lander, Eleanor Dorsey, lost her trust estate when her trustee's son took over its management after the death of his father and then died in insolvent circumstances

shortly thereafter. See Eleanor Dorsey, Jeremiah Townley Chase et al. v. Charles Ridgely's Executors (1788), Chancery Records, 24, Part 2, 342, MHR.

109. Administrator of Charles M. Picton v. Angus Graham and J. Walker, 2 Desaussure 592 (1808); Wm. Rutherford v. John Henry Ruff, 4 Desaussure 350 (1812); Dalilah Freeman v. Robert Cochran (ca. 1812), Marlboro County Equity Decrees, 23, SCA. For a case of deceit perpetrated by an entire family, see Nicholas Lowe Darnall v. Benjamin Hall and Richard Bennett Hall (1780–96), Chancery Records, 33:312, MHR.

110. Philips v. Snowden and Jenings (1790), Chancery Records, 22:419, MHR.

111. Ibid.

112. Out of my sample of 638 settlements, only 16 (3 percent) gave trustees exclusive control over settled property. In 591 settlements (90 percent), trustees held only minimal powers or were not employed at all. In 31 of the settlements (5 percent), the trustee and couple shared control or the arrangement is unknown (Salmon, "Women and Property in South Carolina," 669).

113. Rippon v. Dawding, Ambler 565 (1769).

114. Barnes v. Hart, 1 Yeates 221 (1793). The case also is reported in 2 Dallas 199 (1793).

115. Barnes v. Hart, 1 Yeates 230.

116. Ibid., 227, 233.

117. Beall v. King and Woolford (1792–97), Chancery Records, 39:30, MHR. A second case demonstrating support for simple marriage settlements was decided at about the same time: Davis v. Davis and Welsh (1797), Chancery Court Papers, No. 1310, MHR.

118. Beall v. King and Woolford (1792–97), Chancery Records, 39:68, MHR.

119. Helms v. Franciscus, 2 Bland 562 (1818).

120. On New York law, see Kent, Commentaries, 2:162–63; D. Livingston v. M. and E. Livingston, 2 Johnson's Chancery Reports 537 (1817); and Garlick v. Strong and Garlick, 3 Paige's Chancery Reports 440 (1832).

121. Judith Barrett by her next Friend v. Judah Barrett, 4 Desaussure 454 (1814). The chancellor also revealed his negative attitude toward simple agreements when he observed, "As the intended husband undertook to get a proper deed drawn, the Court will attribute its imperfections to him, and supply all its defects. A trustee will be appointed on her behalf" (p. 454). In 1802 the South Carolina Chancery refused to enforce a simple contract (see Executors of Mary Smelie v. Benj: Reynolds and Others, 2 Desaussure 66). See also Thomas I. I. Dupree v. McDonald, 4 Desaussure 209 (1812).

122. Price v. Michel (1821), Charleston District Court of Chancery Decrees, 3:380, SCA.

123. Tabb and Others v. Archer and Others, and Randolph and Others v. Randolph and Others, 3 Hening and Munford 400 (1809).

124. Ibid., 405–6.

125. Kent, Commentaries, 2:162.

126. The rise of the companionate ideal in the United States is chronicled by Norton in Liberty's Daughters (see especially chap. 8).

127. Reeve, Baron and Feme, 165–66.

128. Lebsock, Free Women of Petersburg; Norton, Liberty's Daughters.

129. Kerber, *Women of the Republic*.

130. Horwitz, *The Transformation of American Law*, 160–210; Nelson, *Americanization of the Common Law*, 54–63, 136–44, 154–58.

CHAPTER SIX

1. Quoted in Katz, "The Politics of Law in Colonial America," 260.

2. On Puritan opposition to the High Court of Chancery, see Prall, *The Agitation for Law Reform*; and Veall, *The Popular Movement for Law Reform*.

3. Katz, "The Politics of Law in Colonial America," 261.

4. Koehler's study of the status of women in early New England, *A Search for Power*, is particularly critical of the earlier interpretation. Most recently, Mary Beth Norton has emphasized the strength of patriarchal authority in Puritan families ("Evolution of White Women's Experience," 598).

5. Ulrich, *Good Wives*.

6. Bacon v. Taylor, 1 Kirby 368 (1788). Swift noted that this was the only case on trusts heard by the Superior Court of the state before 1795. He wrote, "If the decision of the superior court in the only case which has come before them, be considered as law, the business of uses and trusts, is at an end" (see *System of the Laws of Connecticut*, 1:321).

7. Swift, *System of the Laws of Connecticut*, 1:321–24.

8. Ibid., 324.

9. See, for example, the comments of attorneys and judges in Dibble v. Hutton, 1 Day 224, 233 (1804); Elizabeth Mary Fitch v. Jehu Brainerd, 2 Day 173, 184 (1805); and John Nichols v. Allyn Palmer, executor of Noyes Palmer, deceased, 5 Day 51 (1811).

10. Fitch v. Brainerd, 2 Day 184 (1805).

11. Mehitable Parsons v. S. Titus Hosmer, 2 Root 1 (1793).

12. Dibble v. Hutton, 1 Day 221 (1804).

13. Ibid., 221, 222.

14. Ibid., 236–37.

15. Ibid., 224.

16. Fitch v. Brainerd, 2 Day 173, 194 (1805).

17. Stone, *The Family in England*, 331.

18. Nichols v. Palmer, 5 Day 56 (1811); Fitch v. Ayer, 2 Connecticut Reports 146 (1817); Mary Goodwin v. William Goodwin, Jun., 4 Day 357 (1810).

19. In Dibble v. Hutton, 1 Day 228, counsel for Mary Hutton argued, "The principle of a separate interest between husband and wife, has been recognized, by our own courts, in the case of *Parsons v. Hosmer*. And, in another case, without attending to the English decisions so fully as we ought, it has been decided, that a married woman may devise her estate to her husband, without a power; and thus, a separate interest has been recognized."

20. Adams v. Kellogg, 1 Kirby 195, 438 (1786–88).

21. Fitch v. Brainerd, 2 Day 186 (1805).

22. Ibid., 163.

23. Ibid., 189.

24. Connecticut, *Session Laws*, May 1809, 15.

25. Warbasse, "Legal Rights of Married Women," 15–16.

26. Goodwin v. Goodwin, 4 Day 343 (1810).

27. Ibid., 352.

28. Nichols v. Palmer, 5 Day 47 (1811).

29. Ibid., 57.

30. Ibid., 57, 58.

31. Peter Butler and William Atwater v. Juliana Buckingham, 5 Day 496, 505 (1813).

32. Fitch v. Ayer, 2 Connecticut Reports 143 (1817).

33. Ibid., 145–46.

34. Reeve, *Baron and Feme*, 163.

35. Fitch v. Ayer, 2 Connecticut Reports 143 (1817).

36. Watrous et al. v. Chalker, 7 Connecticut Reports 224 (1828).

37. Ibid., 226–27.

38. According to Katz, "From 1675 the General Court empowered the county courts of the province to act as courts of equity, and they retained this authorization throughout the colonial period" ("The Politics of Law in Colonial America," 265). Haskins also reported that "equity jurisdiction was expressly provided for, but it was to be exercised in the course of an action at law rather than in a separate suit, as in England" (*Law and Authority in Early Massachusetts*, 183). Apparently, then, there was recognition of a person's right to sue according to general equitable principles. Only work in county court records will reveal if any women or their families took advantage of this option to enforce the terms of marriage settlements. On the history of chancery in Massachusetts, see Edwin H. Woodruff, "Chancery in Massachusetts," *Boston University Law Review* 9 (1929): 168–92; and William J. Curran, "The Struggle for Equity Jurisdiction in Massachusetts," *Boston University Law Review* 31 (1951): 269–96.

39. "An Act for hearing and determining of Cases in Equity" (1699), in Cushing, *Massachusetts Province Laws*, 153; "An Act to Enable Creditors to Receive Their Just Debts" (1708), in Goodell, *Acts and Resolves of Massachusetts Bay*, 1:629; "An Act giving Remedies in Equity," in *Perpetual Laws of the Commonwealth of Massachusetts*, 1:251.

40. There are twelve volumes of "resolves" passed between 1692 and 1774 published in Goodell, *Acts and Resolves of Massachusetts Bay*, vols. 7–18.

41. Nathan Dane, *A General Abridgment and Digest of American Law*, vol. 1 (Boston, 1823), 332, quoted in Warbasse, "Legal Rights of Married Women," 45.

42. Samuel Thatcher v. Thomas Omans et al., 3 Pickering 522 (1792).

43. Ibid., 523.

44. Joseph Dudley v. Elizabeth Sumner, 5 Tyng 480 (1809).

45. Thatcher v. Omans, 3 Pickering 521 (1792).

46. Ibid., 523.

47. Ibid., 531.

48. "An Act for giving further remedies in Equity," in Metcalf, *General Laws of Massachusetts*, 2:431.

49. Oliver Prescott, Jr. et al. v. Mary Tarbell et al., 1 Williams 204 (1804).

50. Ibid., 208.

51. John Davis v. William Hayden et al., 9 Tyng 514 (1813).

52. Ibid., 515.

53. Ibid., 518–19.

54. Curran, "Equity Jurisdiction in Massachusetts," 276.

55. Benjamin Russell v. John Lewis, 2 Pickering 508 (1824).

56. Ibid., 511.

57. Benjamin Page v. Colson Trufant et al., 2 Tyng 162 (1806).

58. Samuel Saunderson and Eunice, his Wife v. Thomas Stearns, 6 Tyng 37 (1809).

59. David Osgood v. Ebenezer Breed, 12 Tyng 525 (1815).

60. Ibid., 533.

61. Fitch v. Ayer, 2 Connecticut Reports 145 (1817); Osgood v. Breed, 12 Tyng 533 (1815).

62. On the influence of Kent and Reeve, see for example the citations in Jabez Bullard v. Deborah Briggs, 7 Pickering 535, 541 (1829).

63. This discussion of Connecticut and Massachusetts law in the 1840s relies heavily on Warbasse, "Legal Rights of Married Women," 186–91.

64. Ibid., 186. The case reference is Jones v. Aetna Insurance Co., 14 Connecticut Reports 501 (1842).

65. Fourth Ecclesiastical Society in Middletown v. Mather, 15 Connecticut Reports 587 (1843).

66. Ibid., 599.

67. Connecticut, *Session Laws*, 10 June 1845, 36, and 22 June 1849, 16.

68. Massachusetts, *Session Laws*, 25 March 1845, 531.

69. As late as 1835, Justice Wilde of the Supreme Court was still discussing the effect of the statute of uses on trusts created for married women, and counsel for one husband who sought to overthrow his wife's marriage settlement could argue, "By the deed of Sally Humphrey, Hobbs [her trustee] took an estate in the premises for the life of the plaintiff, for her use, which use, by operation of law, was immediately executed, and gave to her a freehold estate therein in possession for her life, that the respondent [her husband] and the plaintiff, in her right, became rightfully seised and possessed of the premises.... The right to receive the rents and profits of the premises belongs to him alone, as husband of the plaintiff." Such statements indicate that jurists in Massachusetts continued to possess only a poor understanding of the law of women's separate estates well into the 1830s (see Harriet Ayer v. Samuel W. Ayer, 16 Pickering 328, 330).

CHAPTER SEVEN

1. An individual who provided for his heirs by will died "testate." An individual without a will died "intestate."

2. The general definition of common law dower and provisions for the widows of intestates included here is based on Blackstone, *Commentaries*, 2:129–39; *The Laws Respecting Women*, 188–292; Swift, *System of the Laws of Connecticut*, 1:254–57; and Reeve, *Baron and Feme*, 37–59.

3. Women could claim their paraphernalia even when an estate was insolvent, but in such a case the right was reduced sharply; then they could take only what was deemed

"necessary." In a Massachusetts case, Hanlon v. Thayer (1764), a jury supported the action of a sheriff who attached a widow's clothing for the payment of her deceased husband's debts. The chief justice disagreed with the decision, however. He wrote, "I always took it to have been the Custom in such Cases as this, for the Wife to have her Cloaths; in Cases that have come before me as a Judge of Probate I never knew it denied to the Wife where the Estate was insolvent" (Quincy's Reports, 102). In addition to clothing, the widows of insolvents usually kept bedding and cooking utensils.

4. In the seventeenth century and until 1724 in London, men could devise only the "dead man's share," a third of their estates. One-third of the residue went to their wives as dower, and one-third to their lineal descendants (see *The Laws Respecting Women,* 221–24; and Blackstone, *Commentaries,* 1:437–38).

5. In March 1683 the General Assembly of Pennsylvania provided for the equal distribution of an intestate's estate among his children, but the next year double portions for eldest sons found approval among lawmakers (see Staughton George, Benjamin M. Nead, and Thomas McCamant, comps., *Charter to William Penn and Laws of the Province of Pennsylvania* [Harrisburg, Pa., 1879], 141, 174). Eldest sons received double portions in Massachusetts beginning in 1641 (see Thomas G. Barnes, ed., *The Book of the General Lawes and Libertyes Concerning the Inhabitants of the Massachusets* [San Marino, Cal., 1975], 53–54), and in Connecticut, in 1656 (see Cushing, *Earliest Laws of Connecticut,* 56). On partible inheritance generally, see George Lee Haskins, "The Beginnings of Partible Inheritance in the American Colonies," *Yale Law Journal* 51 (1942): 1280–1315.

6. Lincoln, *Colonial Laws of New York,* 1:9, 114, 5:616–17; Hening, *Laws of Virginia,* 12:156–57; Virgil Maxy, comp., *The Laws of Maryland,* 3 vols. (Baltimore, 1811), 2:16; Cooper, *South Carolina Statutes,* 5:162.

7. On the effect of republican ideology on inheritance law, see Stanley N. Katz, "Republicanism and the Law of Inheritance in the American Revolutionary Era," *Michigan Law Review* 76 (1977–78): 1–29.

8. David Evan Narrett, "Patterns of Inheritance in Colonial New York City, 1664–1775: A Study in the History of the Family" (Ph.D. dissertation, Cornell University, 1981), 221–39; the quotation is from p. 227. Linda E. Speth's findings for Southside Virginia echo those of Narrett. She concluded that "as the male testators disposed of the land, cattle, and slaves they had taken a lifetime to accumulate, their primary concern was that when possible, all members of the family, male and female, receive a share of the estate. The testators ignored primogeniture, tried to give all of their sons land, and proved generous in their treatment of the women in their families" ("More Than Her 'Thirds': Wives and Widows in Colonial Virginia," *Women and History,* no. 4 [1982]: 15).

9. Blackstone, *Commentaries,* 2:130.

10. See, for example, Jackson ex dem. Clark v. O'Donaghy, 7 Johnson's Supreme Court Reports 247 (1810).

11. According to the Massachusetts Supreme Court, in the early nineteenth century it was "not uncommon" for a widow's children to sell their reversionary interests in their mother's dower lands before her death, thereby undoubtedly increasing her sense that the property was hers in no sense (see Simon Hunt v. Abraham Hapgood and Another, 4 Tyng 120 [1808]).

12. Blackstone, *Commentaries*, 2:122, 281–83; *The Laws Respecting Women*, 203; Holdsworth, *A History of English Law*, 3 (5th ed., 1942): 122–24. In the Connecticut case of Wilford v. Rose (1793), the widow was allowed to clear lands devised to her for life because her husband stated in his will that she was free to "improve" the lands (2 Root 20).

13. Work on inheritance practices in early America is of high quality. See Linda Auwers, "Father, Sons, and Wealth in Colonial Norwich, Connecticut," *Journal of the History of the Family* 3 (1978): 136–49; Lois Green Carr, "Women and Inheritance in the Colonial Chesapeake," paper presented at the 8th annual symposium of the United States Capitol Historical Society, "Women in the Age of the American Revolution," Washington D.C., 28 March 1985; Carr and Walsh, "The Planter's Wife"; Crowley, "Inheritance in South Carolina"; James W. Deen, Jr. [Jamil Zainaldin], "Patterns of Testation: Four Tidewater Counties in Colonial Virginia," *American Journal of Legal History* 16 (1972): 154–76; John Demos, *A Little Commonwealth: Family Life in Plymouth Colony* (New York, 1970); Toby L. Ditz, *Ownership and Obligation: Family and Inheritance in Five Connecticut Towns, 1750–1820* (Princeton, N.J., forthcoming); Philip J. Greven, Jr., *Four Generations: Population, Land, and Family in Colonial Andover, Massachusetts* (Ithaca, N.Y., 1970); C. Ray Keim, "Primogeniture and Entail in Colonial Virginia," *William and Mary Quarterly*, 3d ser. 25 (1968): 545–86; Keyssar, "Widowhood in Massachusetts"; Lebsock, *Free Women of Petersburg*, chaps. 2, 5; Narrett, "Patterns of Inheritance in Colonial New York City"; Kim Lacy Rogers, "Relicts of the New World: Conditions of Widowhood in Seventeenth-Century New England," in Kelley, *Woman's Being, Woman's Place*, 26–52; Daniel Blake Smith, *Inside the Great House: Planter Family Life in Eighteenth-Century Chesapeake Society* (Ithaca, N.Y., 1980), chap. 6; Speth, "More Than Her 'Thirds,'" 5–41; Lorena S. Walsh, "'Till Death Us Do Part': Marriage and Family in Seventeenth-Century Maryland, 1658–1705," in Tate and Ammerman, *The Chesapeake in the Seventeenth Century*, 126–53; and John J. Waters, "Patrimony, Succession, and Social Stability: Guilford, Connecticut in the Eighteenth Century," *Perspectives in American History* 10 (1976): 131–60.

14. For cases concerning a widow's choice between dower and a devise, see Noel and Wife v. Garnett, 4 Call 92 (Va., 1786); Blunt et al. v. Gee et al., 5 Call 481 (Va., 1805); Bernard v. Hipkins, 6 Call 101 (Va., 1806); Elizabeth Upshaw v. LeRoy Upshaw et al., 2 Hening and Munford 381 (Va., 1808); Thomas Ogle's Creditors v. Sybilla Ogle (1793–94), Chancery Records, 30:87, Papers No. 5326, and Chancery MHR; Charles Carroll of Carrollton v. Achsah Howard et al. (1794–1820), Chancery Records, 30:430, and Chancery Papers No. 7257, MHR; Richard Quarles et al. v. S. Garrett et al., 4 Desaussure 145 (S.C., 1810); Henry Snelgrove et al. v. William Snelgrove et al., 4 Desaussure 292 (S.C., 1812); Joseph Craecraft and Wife v. Benjamin Wions, 1 Addison 350 (Pa., 1798); Mary Hamilton, late wife of Joseph Hamilton, late wife of Alexander Adams, and formerly wife of John Patten v. Abraham Buckwalter, 2 Yeates 389 (Pa., 1798); Christiana Evans v. Joshua Evans, Jr., 3 Yeates 507 (Pa., 1803); Jones v. Powell et al., 6 Johnson's Chancery Reports 194 (N.Y., 1822); Hildreth v. Jones, 13 Tyng 525 (Mass., 1816); and Phineas N. Crane, Executor v. Kezia Crane, 17 Pickering 422 (Mass., 1835).

15. Cases in which widows first accepted the provisions in their husbands' wills and then had to accept dower when the estates proved insolvent or heavily indebted

include John Orchard et al. v. Smith and Wife (1738–39), Chancery Records, vol. 7, part 1, 89, MHR; Hercules Courtenay et al. v. Isabella Neill and Thomas McIntire (1788–90), Chancery Records, 19:492, and Chancery Papers No. 1271, MHR; Jeremiah Yellott v. Deborah Sterrett et al. (1788–1810), Chancery Records, 29:154, and Chancery Papers Nos. 5893, 3986, MHR; Brown and Wife v. Executors of William Cattell, 1 Desaussure 112 (S.C., 1785); and Mary Gist et al. v. The Heirs and Representatives of Col. W. Cattell, 2 Desaussure 53 (S.C., 1801). For a related Massachusetts case, see Hannah Currier, Appellant, 3 Pickering 375 (1825). In New York the statute of limitations did not apply to tenants in dower, according to Hitchcock v. Harrington, 6 Johnsons' Supreme Court Reports 290 (1810). A widow who assumed that her husband's estate was insolvent and asked for dower rather than accepting a devise had no remedy if the estate later proved solvent. See, for example, the decision of the Massachusetts Supreme Court on Hannah Currier, Appellant, 3 Pickering 375 (1825).

16. Reeve, *Baron and Feme*, 39, 52. An early nineteenth-century Virginia case, Blanton v. Taylor (1820), demonstrates the lengths to which courts were willing to go to give widows dower. Here a husband and his wife created a fraudulent trust in an attempt to protect their slaves from creditors. In exchange for the use of the slaves, Mrs. Langhorne renounced her dower right. When the trust was overthrown in court, her dower right was restored, because the court assumed that she had been under the coercion of her husband in creating the fraudulent trust (Gilmer 209).

17. For cases in which widows did not join in conveyances and later successfully sued for dower, see Charles Ridgely of Hampton v. Mary Nicholson et al. (1792–94), Chancery Records 27, part 2, 325, and Chancery Papers No. 4352, MHR; Benjamin Chew and Catherine his Wife et al. v. John Gleaves' Heirs (1793–97), Chancery Records, 40:228, and Chancery Papers No. 893, MHR; Handy v. The State, 7 Harris and Johnson 42 (Md., 1826); Mary Bentham v. J. B. Richardson et al. (1821), Charleston District Court of Chancery Decrees, 3:398, SCA; Braxton v. Coleman, 5 Call 433 (Va., 1805); Jane Sharp v. William Pettit, 1 Yeates 389 (Pa., 1794); Colvin v. Morris et al., 2 Yeates 518 (Pa., 1799); Thompson v. Morrow, 5 Sergeant and Rawle 289 (Pa., 1819); Constant Crocker v. Grace Fox, 1 Root 227 (Conn., 1790); Peter Butler and William Atwater v. Juliana Buckingham, 5 Day 492 (Conn., 1813); and Zerviah Perry v. Joseph Goodwin, 6 Tyng 498 (Mass., 1810).

18. Blackstone, *Commentaries*, 2:182; *The Laws Respecting Women*, 118–21, 183; Reeve, *Baron and Feme*, 27–28; Kent, *Commentaries*, 2:130–33.

19. On tenancy by the curtesy, see Blackstone, *Commentaries*, 2:126–28; *The Laws Respecting Women*, 163–66; Reeve, *Baron and Feme*, 28–30; and Kent, *Commentaries*, 2:130–31. On the rights of widows versus those of widowers, see Blackstone, *Commentaries*, 2:337; and Reeve, *Baron and Feme*, 52–53.

20. On releases of dower, see chap. 2.

21. Kirk v. Dean, 2 Binney 347, 355 (Pa., 1810). For other comments by American jurists on the favored position of tenants in dower, see for example Kennedy v. Nedrow and Wife et al., 3 Sergeant and Rawle 94 (Pa., 1789); John Calder and Wife v. Caleb Bull, 2 Root 50 (Conn., 1793); and Mary Loocock v. William Clarkson et al., 1 Desaussure 471 (S.C., 1796).

22. Chew v. Gleaves' Heirs (1793–97), Chancery Records, 40:230, and Chancery Papers No. 893, MHR. In this case the woman never did release her dower right as

requested, and therefore the purchaser lost part of his property to her for the period of her widowhood. He won a suit for damages against the family.

23. Michael Lowe and Wife v. Robert Loper et al. (1779–88), Chancery Records, 16:84, MHR.

24. In Colvin v. Morris (1799), the court observed that when a man bought property he did so "at his own risk," and should be aware of the dangers dower rights entailed (2 Yeates 522).

25. On the rules respecting jointures, see Blackstone, *Commentaries*, 2:137–39; *The Laws Respecting Women*, 209–12; and Reeve, *Baron and Feme*, 41–46.

26. Blackstone, *Commentaries*, 2:182.

27. Haskins, *Law and Authority in Early Massachusetts*, 180–82; Spufford, *Contrasting Communities*, 85–90, 104–18, 159–64; Goody, Thirsk, and Thompson, *Family and Inheritance*.

28. Blackstone, *Commentaries* 2:492–93; *The Laws Respecting Women*, 221–24. I use the term "dower" because that was the word employed by contemporaries. Characteristics of dower in personalty were not the same as those for realty, however, a distinction that may cause confusion for the modern reader. Most important, husbands could deny their wives dower in personalty by disposing of it before they died. That step was not permissible for realty. Similarly, personalty became liable immediately for a man's debts, although widows received dower in realty before lands could be attached by creditors.

29. Regarding the right of widows to dower in personal property, Blackstone wrote, "In the reign of king Edward the third this right of the wife and children was still held to be the universal or common law; though frequently pleaded as the local custom of Berks, Devon, and other counties: and sir Henry Finch lays it down expressly, in the reign of Charles the first, to be the general law of the land" (*Commentaries*, 2:494).

30. Ibid., 492–93.

31. Ibid., 133–34, 493; Holdsworth, *A History of English Law*, 3:195; *The Laws Respecting Women*, 195; Griffith v. Griffith's Executors, 4 Harris and McHenry 106–7 (Md., 1798).

32. Blackstone, *Commentaries*, 2:493.

33. Cushing, *Earliest Laws of Connecticut*, 29.

34. Ibid., 95.

35. Cooper, *South Carolina Statutes*, 2:468–69; Beckman, *Pennsylvania Statutes*, 151; Lincoln, *Colonial Laws of New York*, 1:114; Cushing, *Massachusetts Province Laws*, 1:450.

36. William Kilty, ed., *The Laws of Maryland*, 2 vols. (Annapolis, Md., 1799), 1:206.

37. Griffith v. Griffith's Executors, 4 Harris and McHenry 101 (1798). See also the supporting decision of Coomes v. Clements, 4 Harris and Johnson 480 (Md., 1819).

38. Griffith v. Griffith's Executors, 4 Harris and McHenry 115.

39. Ibid., 119–20.

40. In Negro William v. Kelly (1820), it was determined that a slave could not be freed under the terms of his master's will because there was insufficient personal property to compensate the widow for dower without including him. The slave therefore became the property of the widow for her life (5 Harris and Johnson 59).

41. Edward Fenwick and Wife v. Vernon Hebb (1780–91), Chancery Records, 22:167, and Chancery Papers No. 1815, MHR. Lois Green Carr alerted me to this

source. In Courtenay v. Neill and McIntire (1788–90), a widow also received a half-and-half disposition from the Chancery Court (Chancery Records, 19:492, and Chancery Papers No. 1271, MHR).

42. Carr and Walsh, "The Planter's Wife."

43. Hening, *Laws of Virginia*, 2:212.

44. "An Act for establishing the dowers of widdows," in ibid., 303.

45. "An Act for the distribution of intestates estates, declaring widows rights to their deceased husbands estates; and for securing orphans estates," in ibid., 3:371, 374.

46. "An Act declaring the Negro, Mulatto, and Indian slaves within this dominion, to be real estate," in ibid., 3:333.

47. Keim, "Primogeniture and Entail in Virginia," 545–51. Keim seems to have missed the passage of the statute of 1705, however. He believed that a statute enacted in 1727 for the purpose of allowing entails of slaves served the function of making slaves real property (see pp. 546–47).

48. "*An Act to explain and amend the Act*, For declaring the Negro, Mulatto, and Indian Slaves, within this Dominion, to be Real Estate; *and part of one other Act, intituled* An Act for the distribution of Intestates Estates, declaring Widows Rights to their deceased Husbands Estates; and for securing Orphans Estates" (1727), in Hening, *Laws of Virginia*, 4:222.

49. Ibid., 223.

50. "An Act declaring slaves to be personal estate, and for other purposes therein mentioned," in ibid., 5:432.

51. Ibid., 441.

52. Ibid., 440–42.

53. "An Act for the distribution of Intestates estates" (1748), in ibid., 444.

54. Ibid., 443.

55. Keim, "Primogeniture and Entail in Virginia," 548 n. 9.

56. Hening, *Laws of Virginia*, 9:226; *A Collection of All Such Acts of the General Assembly of Virginia, of a Public and Private Nature, As Are Now in Force* (Richmond, Va., 1803), 191.

57. McCargo, Executor of James Callicott v. Susanna Callicott, 2 Munford 501 (1811).

58. Ibid., 502–4. The court admitted that before 1792 "dower" consisted of slaves as well as land. See Ball's Devisees v. Ball's Executors and Widow, 3 Munford 279 (1812).

59. Crowley, "Inheritance in South Carolina," 40.

60. Ibid., 45.

61. Ibid., 54–55.

62. Crowley discusses the use of limitations, which he refers to as conditional fees, in ibid., 48–50. He seems to be employing the term incorrectly, however, for conditional fees applied only to real property.

63. Salmon, "Women and Property in South Carolina," 665–66.

64. Lightfoot's Executors et al. v. Colgin and Wife, 5 Munford 55–56 (1813). Evidence from colonial Maryland indicates a scarcity of marriage settlements there as well (see Walsh, " 'Till Death Us Do Part,' " 137).

65. Numerous studies of the demographic history of early America have appeared

in recent years. Among the most useful on mortality and age at death are Lorena S. Walsh and Russell R. Menard, "Death in the Chesapeake: Two Life Tables for Men in Early Colonial Maryland," *Maryland Historical Magazine* 69 (1974): 211–27; Darrett B. Rutman and Anita H. Rutman, " 'Now Wives and Sons-in-Law': Parental Death in a Seventeenth-Century Virginia County," in Tate and Ammerman, *The Chesapeake in the Seventeenth Century*, 153–82; Daniel Scott Smith, "The Demographic History of Colonial New England," *Journal of Economic History* 32 (1972): 165–83; Daniel Scott Smith, "Population, Family, and Society in Hingham, Massachusetts, 1635–1880" (Ph.D. dissertation, University of California, Berkeley, 1972); Greven, *Four Generations*; and Maris Vinovskis, "Mortality Rates and Trends in Massachusetts before 1860," *Journal of Economic History* 32 (1972): 184–213.

66. Cushing, *Earliest Laws of Connecticut*, 29.

67. Ibid., 95.

68. Swift, *System of the Laws of Connecticut*, 1:255. Reeve discussed the Connecticut law on dower in *Baron and Feme*, 40.

69. Holdsworth, *A History of English Law*, 3:197.

70. The Widow Deforest's Appeal from Probate, 1 Root 50 (1772).

71. Stewart v. Stewart, 5 Connecticut Reports 317 (1824).

72. Ibid., 321.

73. Swift, *System of the Laws of Connecticut*, 1:212. See also Joel Prentiss Bishop, *Commentaries on the Law of Married Women under the Statutes of the Several States and at Common Law and in Equity*, 2 vols. (Boston, 1873–75), 1:613–14.

74. Phelps v. Jepson, 1 Root 48 (1769); Whittlesey v. Fuller et al., 11 Connecticut Reports 337 (1836).

75. "An Act for the Equal Division, and Distribution of Insolvent Estates" was enacted in 1716 and revised in 1760 to allow women this prior claim (see *The Public Statute Laws of the State of Connecticut* [Hartford, Conn., 1808], 275).

76. Reeve, *Baron and Feme*, 52–53. The decision that a widow could have dower in an equity of redemption came from the Supreme Court in Fish and Another v. Catharine Fish, 1 Connecticut Reports 559 (1816). In England a widow could not be endowed of an equity of redemption, although a tenant by the curtesy could have such an estate. Reeve criticized this rule of English law: "Some of their ablest judges and writers have, however, shown symptoms of disgust with the settled course of decisions. . . . It is remarkable that the courts refuse to place the estate by courtesy on the same footing. They allow the husband to enjoy his courtesy, in the equity of redemption, which belonged to his wife in her life time, and has descended to her heirs" (*Baron and Feme*, 53).

77. In Calder and Wife v. Bull, 2 Root 52 (Conn., 1793), the court stated that "the widow's dower is preferred to heirs or creditors." Similar sentiments were expressed in Parsons v. Hosmer, 2 Root 1 (Conn., 1793), and Fish v. Fish, 1 Connecticut Reports 559 (1816).

78. George, Nead, and McCamant, *Charter and Laws of Pennsylvania*, 141. See also the use of similar words in statutes enacted in 1693, 1697 (ibid., 231, 264), and 1700 (*Laws of Pennsylvania*, 2:31).

79. James T. Mitchell and Henry Flanders, comps., *The Statutes at Large of Pennsylvania from 1682 to 1801*, 16 vols. (Philadelphia, 1896–1911), 2 (1896): 205.

80. Ibid., 210.

81. Ibid., 349.

82. Ibid., 15:82.

83. Connecticut decisions include Dodge v. Dodge and Lathum, 1 Root 233 (1790); and Crocker v. Fox, 1 Root 227 (1790). For Maryland, see Courtenay v. Neill and McIntire (1788–90), Chancery Records, 19:492, and Chancery Papers No. 1271; Yellott v. Sterrett (1788–1810), Chancery Records, 29:154, and Chancery Papers Nos. 5893, 3986; Ogle's Creditors v. Ogle (1793–94), Chancery Records, 30:87, and Chancery Papers No. 5326; and Carroll v. Howard (1794–1820), Chancery Records, 30:430, and Chancery Papers No. 7257; all in MHR. For South Carolina, see Brown v. Cattell's Executors, 1 Desaussure 112 (1785); and Gist v. Cattell, 2 Desaussure 53 (1801). Relevant New York cases are Tabele v. Tabele et al., 1 Johnson's Chancery Reports 45 (1814); and Jackson v. O'Donaghy, 7 Johnson's Supreme Court Reports 247 (1810). For Massachusetts, see Jabez Bullard v. Deborah Briggs, 7 Pickering 533 (1829); Jeremiah Glidden v. Stevens Smith, 15 Tyng 170 (1818); and Mehitable Hastings v. William Dickinson and Elizabeth his Wife, 7 Tyng 153 (1810). For Virginia, see Dancy et al. v. Willard's Administrators (1741) in Barton, *Virginia Colonial Decisions*, 2:355; Quarles v. Lacy, 4 Munford 251 (1813); and Blanton v. Taylor, Gilmer 209 (1820).

84. *Laws of Pennsylvania*, 1:9.

85. Beckman, *Pennsylvania Statutes*, 134, 172.

86. *Laws of Pennsylvania*, 1:7–9. For a discussion of the statute, see Graff v. Smith's Administrators, 1 Dallas 481 (1789).

87. Skelton and Wife v. Basnett (1695), Docket of the Court of Quarter Sessions, Philadelphia County, Collection No. 805: Miscellaneous Court Records, HSP; Sanders v. Sanders (1703), Papers of the Court of Common Pleas, Collection No. 1364: Philadelphia Legal Papers, HSP; Margaret Thornton Petition (1755), Orphans Court Records, Bucks County, 1:105, 111–12, BCHS; Richardson v. Thornton (1756), Appearance Docket of the Court of Common Pleas, Bucks County, 1750–60, 12 June 1756, BCHS; Patterson v. Patterson (1756), Appearance Docket of the Court of Common Pleas, Bucks County, 1750–60, 16 September 1756, BCHS; Worthington v. Addis and Wife (1760), Execution Docket of the Court of Common Pleas, Bucks County, 1732–1803, March 1760, BCHS; Harvey v. Harvey (1765), Execution Docket of the Court of Common Pleas, Bucks County, 1732–1803, 11 June 1765, BCHS; Jean Wainwright Petition (1782), John Dickinson Papers, Box 10, Library Company of Philadelphia; Morris's Executors v. McConaughey, 1 Yeates 9 (1791); Hannum v. Spear, 2 Dallas 291 (1791); Morris's Lessee v. Smith, 4 Dallas 119 (1792); Thomas Nokes lessee of William Morris v. John Smith, 1 Yeates 238 (1793); John Diller v. Matthias Young, 2 Yeates 216 (1797); Deshler v. Beery, 4 Dallas 300 (1804).

88. Petition of Mary Jamison, Orphans Court Records, Bucks County, vol. B, p. 52, BCHS.

89. Petition of Elizabeth Breese (1756), Orphans Court Records, Bucks County, 1:114, BCHS; Appearance Docket of the Court of Common Pleas, Bucks County, 1732–1803, 11 March 1756, BCHS.

90. Grace Scott v. Ezra Croasdale, 1 Yeates 75 (1791). The case is also reported in 2 Dallas 127.

91. Petition of Grace Scott (1762), Sessions Docket of the Court of Common Pleas, Bucks County, 1754–82, p. 219, BCHS.

92. Scott v. Croasdale, 1 Yeates 75.

93. Morris's Lessee v. Smith, 1 Yeates 243–44 (1792).

94. Diller v. Young, 2 Yeates 261 (1797).

95. The term was used by Chief Justice Parker of the Massachusetts Supreme Court in his opinion on Elizabeth Conner v. Benjamin Shepherd, 15 Tyng 168 (1818).

96. Blackstone, *Commentaries*, 2:136.

97. "An Act for the Convenient and Speedy Assignment of Dower," in Goodell, *Acts and Resolves of Massachusetts Bay*, 1:451.

98. In Pennsylvania, widows took cash payments in lieu of dower when estates proved indivisible. See, for example, the dispositions of the Orphans Court of Bucks County in cases concerning the estates of George Logan (1766) and Edward Rice (1766), Orphans Court Records, vol. B, 1766–1801, pp. 4, 10, BCHS. For South Carolina, see James Wright v. Anna Thompson et al. (1736), in Gregorie, *Records of South Carolina*, 480. Widows in New York also released their dower rights and took annuities or cash payments when it was necessary (see Hale v. James, 6 Johnson's Chancery Reports 258 [1822]). In an early nineteenth-century New York case, Bradshaw v. Callaghan (1809), the Supreme Court determined that a widow's dower right was not subject to the statute on partitioning estates among heirs that had been enacted in 1801 (5 Johnson's Supreme Court Reports 80).

99. Private acts and resolves passed for this purpose appear in Goodell, *Acts and Resolves of Massachusetts Bay*, vols. 6–18. See, for example, "Vote Impowering Hannah Underwood [Admx] to Sell Real Estate and Making Provision as to the Proceeds" (1753), 15:77; "Order Impowering Joshua Walker, Admr, to Sell Real Estate and Making Provision in Regard to the Proceeds" (1756), 15:506; "Resolve Impowering Samuel Smead and Wife to Sell Real Estate and Making Provision in Regard to the Proceeds" (1774), 18:775; and "Order Impowering Hannah Shaw to Sell Land" (1708), 9:8.

100. See, for example, the judicial discussion in Desire Leonard v. George Leonard et al., 4 Tyng 533 (1805); and the decision on Joseph Brazer v. Jesse S. Dean and Another, 15 Tyng 183 (1818).

101. "An Act for the more easy and expeditious obtaining the admeasurement of Dower to Widows of the lands of their deceased husbands," in Cooper, *South Carolina Statutes*, 4:386.

102. Executor of Clifford v. Charles Clifford, a minor, 1 Desaussure 115 (1785).

103. The Creditors of John Scott, deceased v. Sarah Scott, Widow of the deceased, 1 Bay's South Carolina Reports 504 (1795); Petitions and Writs for Dower, Charleston District, Writ 1791, 11-A3, SCA.

104. Scott v. Scott, 1 Bay's South Carolina Reports 506.

105. Ibid., 507.

106. It became common for widows to receive cash sums in lieu of dower in postrevolutionary South Carolina. For example, of the ninety-two existing petitions for dower submitted to the Charleston County Court of Common Pleas between 1783 and 1834, eighty-two resulted in judgments giving widows one-third the value of their husbands' estates in cash. Ten women received one-third of their husbands'

real property (see Petitions and Writs for Dower, Charleston District, SCA). See also the decision of the court on Miller v. Cape et al., 1 Desaussure 109 (1784).

107. "An Act for the abolition of the Rights of Primogeniture, and for giving an equitable distribution of the Real Estate of Intestates," in Cooper, *South Carolina Statutes*, 5:162–63. Related cases include Lattimer et al. v. Robert Elgin and Wife and Lewis Gantt, 4 Desaussure 26 (1809); and Archibald Douglass et al. v. Jacob Clarke et al., 4 Desaussure 143 (1810). See also the discussions in Salmon, "'Life, Liberty, and Dower,'" 95–96; and Crowley, "Inheritance in South Carolina," 4–6. While South Carolina acted to improve the property rights of widows, North Carolina moved in the opposite direction. A statute enacted there in 1784 reduced the widow's in personalty estate to a child's share. North Carolina, *Session Laws*, April 1784, 35.

108. "An Act for the abolition of the Rights of Primogeniture," in Cooper, *South Carolina Statutes*, 5:163.

109. See, for example, the decision of the court in John Sturgineger et al. v. A. Hannah et al., 2 Nott and McCord's Law and Equity Reports 148–49 (1819).

110. The Creditors of Thomas Howe Ridgate v. Benjamin Cornish Ridgate, Heir, and Elizabeth Ridgate, Widow (1792–99), Chancery Records, 35:123, MHR.

111. Charles Wallace et al. v. Elizabeth Dowson et al. (1795–96), Chancery Records, 35:16, and Chancery Papers No. 2779, MHR.

112. Ibid., Chancery Records, 35:23. In McCormick v. Gibson (1824), the Chancery Court expressed its opinion that a cash payment was in general the most beneficial to all parties, including the widow (3 Bland 502).

113. Charlotte Heyward v. J. C. Cuthbert, Brevard's South Carolina Reports, part 2, 482 (1814).

114. Ibid., 483.

115. See, for example, the decision of Chancellor Hanson in Campbell et al. v. Digges et al., 4 Harris and McHenry 12 (1797); and Priscilla Paca et al. v. Helen Paca et al. (1798), Chancery Records, 41:575, and Chancery Papers No. 4014, MHR.

116. "A Supplement to an act, entitled, An act to direct descents" (1799), in Kilty, *Laws of Maryland*, vol. 2, chap. 49. Widows in Maryland still could receive dower as special assignments determined by the nature of the property, if its sale was not advantageous to the parties. See, for example, the decision on Hannah Chase's Case, 1 Bland 206 (1821).

117. Hanson's discussion was reported in Williams' Case, 3 Bland 270 (1827).

118. Ibid., 272.

119. Ibid., 274.

120. Ibid., 186.

121. Ibid., 281.

122. Horwitz, *The Transformation of American Law*, 3.

123. For cases in which courts ruled on charges of waste, see Beers et al. v. Strong and Wife, 1 Kirby 19 (Conn., 1786); Rose v. Hays, 1 Root 244 (Conn., 1791); Lattimer v. Elgin and Gantt, 4 Desaussure 26 (S.C., 1809); Gardiner v. Derring and Hempstead, 1 Paige's Chancery Reports 573 (N.Y., 1829); David Padelford v. Elizabeth Padelford, 7 Pickering 152 (Mass., 1828); and Erastus Sackett et al. v. Elizabeth Sackett, 8 Pickering 309 (Mass., 1829).

124. Hastings v. Crunkleton, 3 Yeates 262 (1801).

125. Goodell, *Acts and Resolves of Massachusetts Bay*, 1:451.

126. Armistead v. Swiney and Wife (1732), in Barton, *Virginia Colonial Decisions*, 1:97.

127. Ibid., 99.

128. Thomas Gantt Denwood v. William Winder et al. (1770–81), Chancery Records, 13:343, MHR. A somewhat later Maryland case demonstrates the reluctance of executors to prosecute a widow for waste committed on her dower lands by tenants (see Petition of Thomas Tongue and Joseph Cowman for sale of the real estate of Richard Cowman, deceased [1794], Chancery Records, 30:1, and Chancery Papers No. 5237, MHR).

129. Mitchell and Flanders, *Statutes of Pennsylvania*, 2:327.

130. Hastings v. Crunkleton, 3 Yeates 261 (1801).

131. Ibid. The decision on this case was supported in Lynn's Appeal (1857), in which the court wrote, "If the timber was cut in the process of clearing the land, or for other purposes required in the reasonable cultivation of it, or for keeping the premises in repair, it is not such waste as renders the tenant for life liable to the remainder-men. . . . His [the tenant for life's] privileges under the laws of Pennsylvania are much greater than those recognized by the common law of England" (31 Pa. St. 46).

132. Kent, *Commentaries*, 4:76.

133. James Paslay et al. v. William Byrd and Elizabeth his Wife (1822), Laurens District Equity Decrees, 1821–23, 125, SCA.

134. Ibid., 131.

135. Ann Mackie, Widow of James Mackie v. William Alston et al., 2 Desaussure 362 (1806).

136. Kent noted the rule on waste in Massachusetts in *Commentaries*, 4:76.

137. Crocker v. Fox and Wife, 1 Root 323 (1791).

138. Ibid.

139. Conner v. Shepherd, 15 Tyng 165 (1818).

140. Leonard v. Leonard, 4 Tyng 533 (1808).

141. Ibid.

142. Conner v. Shepherd, 15 Tyng 164 (1818).

143. Ibid., 166–68; Blackstone, *Commentaries*, 2:136.

144. Horwitz, *The Transformation of American Law*, 56–58.

145. James Kent and Jacob Radcliffe, comps., *Laws of the State of New York: In Two Volumes* (Albany, N.Y., 1802), 1:296. Virginia enacted its first statute on waste at about the same time, in 1792 (see *Acts of the General Assembly of Virginia*, 277).

146. Shaw, Widow v. White, 15 Johnson's Supreme Court Reports 179 (1816). Other liberal interpretations of the waste rule in New York include Gardiner v. Derring and Hempstead, 1 Paige's Chancery Reports 573 (1829); and Jackson ex dem. Beekman v. Sellick, 8 Johnson's Supreme Court Reports 262 (1811).

147. Webb v. Townsend, 1 Pickering 21 (1822).

148. Ibid., 21–22.

149. *Laws of the State of New York: Containing All the Acts Passed from the Revision of 1801, to the End of the 27th Session of the Legislature, 1804* (Albany, N.Y., 1804), 156; New York, *Session Laws* (March 1815), 74.

150. Mary P. Ryan, *Cradle of the Middle Class: The Family in Oneida County, New York, 1790–1865* (New York, 1981), 53, 210–18.

151. Lebsock, *Free Women of Petersburg*, 196.
152. Ibid., 214–15.

CONCLUSION

1. On the influence of the first American reports and law treatises, see Lawrence M. Friedman, *A History of American Law* (New York, 1973), 282–92. On the changing legal profession, see Murrin, "The Legal Transformation"; Nelson, *Americanization of the Common Law*; and G. Edward White, *The American Judicial Tradition* (New York, 1976).

2. Horwitz is particularly eloquent on this point: see *The Transformation of American Law*, chap. 8, "The Rise of Legal Formalism." He notes, "What does seem extremely clear . . . is that the attempt to place law under the banner of 'science' was designed to separate politics from law, subjectivity from objectivity, and laymen's reasoning from professional reasoning" (p. 257).

3. Grossberg, "Law and the Family in Nineteenth Century America," 261.

Selected Bibliography

MANUSCRIPT SOURCES

Annapolis, Maryland
  Maryland Hall of Records
    Chancery Court Records. Vols. 1–41.
    Chancery Court Papers.
Philadelphia, Pennsylvania
  Historical Society of Pennsylvania
    Gratz Collection.
    McKean Papers.
    Miscellaneous Court Records.
    Philadelphia Legal Papers.
    Francis T. Redwood Collection.
  Library Company of Philadelphia
    John Dickinson Papers.
Doylestown, Pennsylvania
  Bucks County Historical Society
    Bucks County Court of Common Pleas, Appearance Dockets. Vols. 1–14.
    ———. Continuance Dockets. Vols. 1–11.
    ———. Execution Dockets. Vols. 1–2.
    ———. Judgment Docket, 1770–92.
    ———. Sessions Docket, 1754–82.
Harrisburg, Pennsylvania
  Pennsylvania State Archives
    Records of the Pennsylvania Supreme Court. Divorce Decrees, 1800–1805.
    ———. Divorce Papers, 1786–1815.
    ———. General Motions for Divorce, 1750–1837.
Columbia, South Carolina
  South Carolina Department of History and Archives
    Camden Equity District. Journal. Vol. 1.
    Charleston District Court of Chancery. Decrees. Vols. 1–3.
    ———. Journals, 1791–1820.
    ———. Papers, 1784–1820.
    ———. Petitions, 1790–1820.
    Charleston District Court of Common Pleas. Petitions and Writs for Dower, 1783–1834.
    Laurens Equity District. Decrees, 1821–23.

Marlboro County Court of Equity. Decrees. Vol. 1.
Records of the Court of Common Pleas. Journals. Vols. 1–3.
————. Judgment Books. Vols. 1–16.
————. Judgment Dockets. Vols. 1–2.
————. Judgment Rolls, 1703–90.
Records of the Registrar of the Secretary of the Province. Vols. A–I.
Records of the Secretary of State. Marriage Settlements. Vols. 1–10.
————. Miscellaneous Records, Charleston Series. Vols. AB, BB–XX.
South Carolina Court of Chancery. Case Papers, 1721–99.
Washington Equity District. Decrees. Vol. 1.
Ithaca, New York
    Myron Taylor School of Law, Cornell University
    Samuel Church. Notebook. "Lectures on Law by Tapping Reeve," 1806.

CASE REPORTS

Addison, Alexander. *Pennsylvania Supreme Court Reports*. Vol. 1 (1791–99).
Armstrong, Edward, ed. *Record of the Court at Upland, in Pennsylvania, 1676–1681.*
    Philadelphia, 1959.
Ashmead, John W. *Reports of Cases Adjudged in the Courts of Common Pleas, Quarter
    Sessions, Oyer and Terminer, and Orphans Courts, of the First Judicial District of
    Pennsylvania, 1804–1841.* 2 vols. Philadelphia, 1831–41.
Barton, R. T., ed. *Virginia Colonial Decisions: The Reports by Sir John Randolph and by
    Edward Barradall of Decisions of the General Court of Virginia, 1728–1741.* 2 vols.
    Boston, 1909.
Bay, Elihu Hall. *South Carolina Law Reports*. Vols. 1–2 (1783–1804).
Bee, Thomas. *Reports of Cases Adjudged in the District Court of South Carolina.* . . .
    Philadelphia, 1810.
Binney, Horace. *Pennsylvania Supreme Court Reports*. Vols. 1–6 (1799–1814).
Bland, Theodorick. *Reports of Cases Decided in the High Court of Chancery of Maryland.*
    3 vols. Baltimore, Md., 1840–57.
Brevard, Joseph. *South Carolina Law Reports*. Vols. 1–3 (1793–1816).
Caines, George. *New York Common Law Reports*. Vols. 1–3 ("Caines's Reports,"
    1803–5), Vols. 1–2 ("Caines's Cases," 1801–5).
Call, Daniel. *Virginia Reports*. Vols. 1–6 (1793–1825).
Cushing, Luther. *Massachusetts Reports*. Vol. 56 (1849).
Dallas, Alexander J. *Pennsylvania Supreme Court Reports*. Vols. 1–4 (1754–1806).
Day, Thomas. *Connecticut Reports*. Vols. 1–7 (1814–29).
Desaussure, Henry William. *South Carolina Equity Reports*. Vols. 1–4 (1784–1817).
Ewell, Marshall D. *Cases on Domestic Relations*. Boston, 1891.
Faught, Albert Smith, ed. *The Registrar's Book of Governor Keith's Court of Chancery of
    the Province of Pennsylvania, 1720–1735.* Harrisburg, Pa., 1941.
Gill, Richard W., and Johnson, John. *Maryland Reports*. Vols. 1–2 (1829–30).
Gilmer, Francis W. *Virginia Reports* (1820–21).
Gregorie, Anne King, ed. *Records of the Court of Chancery of South Carolina, 1671–
    1779.* Introduction by J. Nelson Fierson. Washington, D.C., 1950.

Harris, Thomas, and Gill, Richard W. *Maryland Reports*. Vols. 1–2 (1826–29).

Harris, Thomas, and Johnson, Reverdy. *Maryland Reports*. Vols. 1–7 (1800–1826).

Harris, Thomas, and McHenry, John. *Maryland Reports*. Vols. 1–4 (1658–1799).

Hening, William H., and Munford, William. *Virginia Reports*. Vols. 1–4 (1806–10).

Hopkins, Samuel M. *New York Chancery Reports* (1823–26).

Jefferson, Thomas. *Reports of Cases Determined in the General Court of Virginia from 1730 to 1740, and from 1768 to 1772*. Charlottesville, Va., 1903.

Johnson, William. *New York Chancery Reports*. Vols. 1–7 (1814–23).

———. *New York Common Law Reports*. Vols. 1–3: *Johnson's Cases* (1799–1803).

———. *New York Common Law Reports*. Vols. 1–20: *Johnson's Reports* (1806–23).

Kirby, Ephraim. *Reports of Cases Adjudged in the Superior Court of the State of Connecticut, from the Year 1785, to May 1788: With Some Determination in the Supreme Court of Errors*. Litchfield, Conn., 1789.

———. *Reports of Cases Adjudged in the Superior Court Taken by Ephraim Kirby after the Time of His Reports*. Philadelphia, 1949.

McCord, David J. *South Carolina Equity Reports*. Vols. 1–2 (1825–27).

———. *South Carolina Law Reports*. Vols. 1–4 (1821–28).

Munford, William. *Virginia Reports*. Vols. 1–6 (1810–20).

Nott, Henry Junius, and McCord, David James. *South Carolina Law Reports*. Vols. 1–2 (1817–20).

Paige, Alonzo C. *New York Chancery Reports*. Vols. 1–11 (1828–45).

Pickering, Octavius. *Massachusetts Reports*. Vols. 1–8 (1822–29); Vols. 16–17 (1834–36).

Quincy, Josiah, Jr. *Reports of Cases Argued and Adjudged in the Supreme Court of Judicature of the Province of Massachusetts Bay between 1761 and 1772*. Boston, 1865.

Reed, Clay H., and Miller, George J., eds. *The Burlington Court Book, 1680–1709*. Burlington, N.J., 1944.

Root, Jesse. *Reports of Cases Adjudged in the Superior Court and the Supreme Court of Errors. . . .* 2 vols. Hartford, Conn., 1798–1802.

Sergeant, Thomas, and Rawle, William Jr. *Pennsylvania Supreme Court Reports*. Vols. 1–17 (1814–28).

Treadway, W. R. H. *South Carolina Law Reports*. Vols. 1–2 (1811–14, 1822).

Trumbull, J. Hammond. *The Public Records of the Colony of Connecticut, May 1678 to June 1689*. Vol. 3. Hartford, Conn., 1859. Reprint. New York, 1968.

Tyng, Dudley Atkins. *Massachusetts Reports*. Vols. 2–17 (1786–1822).

Washington, Bushrod. *Virginia Reports*. Vols. 1–2 (1790–96).

Williams, Ephraim. *Massachusetts Reports* (1804–5).

Wythe, George. *Decisions of Cases in Virginia by the High Court of Chancery: With Remarks upon Decrees by the Court of Appeals Reversing Some of Those Decisions*. Charlottesville, Va., 1903.

Yeates, Jasper. *Pennsylvania Supreme Court Reports*. Vols. 1–4 (1791–1808).

LEGAL TREATISES, ABRIDGMENTS, AND DIGESTS

Alston, Leonard, ed. *De Republica Anglorum: A Discourse on the Commonwealth of England by Sir Thomas Smith*. Cambridge, England, 1906.

Ballow, Henry. *A Treatise of Equity*. London, 1737.

Baron and Feme: A Treatise of Law and Equity, Concerning Husbands and Wives. 3d ed. London, 1738.

Blackstone, William. *Commentaries on the Laws of England*. 4 vols. Oxford, 1765–69.

Brackenridge, Henry Hugh. *Law Miscellanies*. Philadelphia, 1814.

Bridgman, Orlando. *Precedents of Conveyances*. London, 1682.

Brightly, Frederick Charles. *A Treatise on the Equitable Jurisdiction of the Courts of Pennsylvania*. Philadelphia, 1855.

Dane, Nathan. *A General Abridgment and Digest of American Law*. Vol. 1. Boston, 1823.

Doctor and Student; or, Dialogues between a Doctor of Divinity and a Student in the Laws of England. . . . 16th ed. London, 1761.

An Essay on the Nature and Operation of Fines. London, 1783.

Francis, Richard. *Maxims of Equity*. London, 1728.

Kent, James. *Commentaries on American Law*. 4 vols. New York, 1826–30.

The Law of Baron and Feme. London, 1734.

The Laws Respecting Women. Reprint ed. Foreword by Shirley Raissi Bysiewicz. London, 1777. Reprint. Dobbs Ferry, N.Y., 1974.

Powell, John Joseph. *Essay upon the Law of Contracts and Agreements: In Two Volumes*. London, 1790.

Reeve, Tapping. *The Law of Baron and Feme, of Parent and Child, of Guardian and Ward, of Master and Servant, and of the Powers of Courts of Chancery*. New Haven, Conn., 1816.

Roberts, Samuel. *A Digest of Select British Statutes in Force in Pennsylvania*. Pittsburgh, 1817.

Story, Joseph. *Commentaries on Equity Jurisprudence, As Administered in England and America*. 2 vols. 10th ed. Edited by Isaac Redfield. Boston, 1870.

Swift, Zephaniah. *A Digest of the Laws of the State of Connecticut*. 2 vols. New Haven, Conn., 1822–23.

————. *A System of the Laws of the State of Connecticut: In Six Books*. 2 vols. New Haven, Conn., 1795–96.

Swinburne, Henry. *A Treatise of Spousals, or Matrimonial Contracts*. London, 1686.

STATUTES

Acts and Laws of His Majesty's English Colony of Connecticut in New-England in America. New London, Conn., 1750.

Acts and Laws of the State of Connecticut in America. Hartford, Conn., 1805.

Acts of the General Assembly of the Commonwealth of Pennsylvania. Harrisburg, Pa., 1815.

Acts of the General Assembly of the Commonwealth of Pennsylvania. Harrisburg, Pa., 1817.

Acts of the General Assembly of Virginia. Richmond, Va., 1848.

Acts Passed at a General Assembly of the Commonwealth of Virginia. Richmond, Va., 1803.

Acts Passed at a General Assembly of the Commonwealth of Virginia. Richmond, Va., 1827.

Bacon, Thomas, ed. *Laws of Maryland at Large, with Proper Indexes: Now First Collected into One Compleat Body.* . . . Annapolis, Md., 1765.

Barnes, Thomas G., ed. *The Book of the General Lawes and Libertyes Concerning the Inhabitants of the Massachusets.* San Marino, Calif., 1975.

Beckman, Gail McKnight, ed. *The Statutes at Large of Pennsylvania in the Time of William Penn.* New York, 1976.

Bishop, Joel Prentiss. *Commentaries on the Law of Married Women under the Statutes of the Several States and at Common Law and in Equity.* 2 vols. Boston, 1873–75.

Brevard, Joseph. *Alphabetical Digest of the Public Statute Laws of South Carolina in Three Volumes.* Charleston, S.C., 1814.

Browne, William Hand. *Archives of Maryland.* Baltimore, Md., 1833–.

A Collection of All Such Acts of the General Assembly of Virginia, of a Public and Private Nature, As Are Now in Force. Richmond, Va., 1803.

Cooper, Thomas, ed. *The Statutes at Large of South Carolina.* 5 vols. Columbia, S.C., 1836–39.

Cushing, John D., ed. *The Earliest Laws of the New Haven and Connecticut Colonies, 1639–1673.* Wilmington, Del., 1977.

——. *The Earliest Printed Laws of North Carolina, 1669–1751.* 2 vols. Wilmington, Del., 1977.

——, comp. *The Laws and Liberties of Massachusetts, 1641–1691: A Facsimile Edition.* 3 vols. Wilmington, Del., 1976.

——, ed. *Massachusetts Province Laws, 1692–1699.* Wilmington, Del., 1978.

George, Staughton; Nead, Benjamin M.; and McCamant, Thomas, comps. *Charter to William Penn and Laws of the Province of Pennsylvania.* Harrisburg, Pa., 1879.

Goodell, Abner C., ed. *Acts and Resolves, Public and Private, of the Province of Massachusetts Bay.* 18 vols. Boston, 1869–1912.

Hening, William Waller, ed. *The Statutes at Large: Being a Collection of all the Laws of Virginia, from the First Session of the Legislature, in the Year 1619.* 13 vols. Richmond, Va., 1809–23. Reprint. Charlottesville, Va., 1969.

Kent, James, and Radcliffe, Jacob, comps. *Laws of the State of New York: In Two Volumes.* Albany, N.Y., 1802.

Kilty, William, ed. *The Laws of Maryland.* 2 vols. Annapolis, Md., 1799.

——. *A Report of All Such English Statutes As Existed at the Time of the First Emigration of the People of Maryland.* . . . Annapolis, Md., 1811.

Laws Made and Passed by the General Assembly of the State of Maryland. Annapolis, Md., 1842.

Laws of Maryland. Annapolis, Md., 1791.

The Laws of the Commonwealth of Massachusetts from November, 1780 . . . to February 28, 1807. 3 vols. Boston, 1807.

Laws of the Commonwealth of Pennsylvania. 10 vols. Philadelphia, 1810–44.

Laws of the State of New York: Containing All the Acts Passed from the Revision of 1801, to the End of the 27th Session of the Legislature, 1804. Albany, N.Y., 1804.

Laws of the State of New York Passed at the Sessions of the Legislature Held in the Years 1777, 1778, 1779, 1780, 1781, 1782, 1783, and 1784, Inclusive, Being the First Seven Sessions. 2 vols. Albany, N.Y., 1886.

Lincoln, Charles Z., ed. *The Colonial Laws of New York from the Year 1664 to the Revolution.* . . . 5 vols. Albany, N.Y., 1894.

McCord, David J., ed. *Statutes at Large of South Carolina.* Vols. 6–7. Columbia, S.C., 1839–40.

Maxy, Virgil, comp. *The Laws of Maryland.* 3 vols. Baltimore, Md., 1811.

Metcalf, Theron, ed. *The General Laws of Massachusetts, from the Adoption of the Constitution, to February 1822.* 2 vols. Boston, 1823.

_____, and Mann, Horace, eds. *The Revised Statutes of the Commonwealth of Massachusetts, Passed November 4, 1835.* Boston, 1836.

Mitchell, James T., and Flanders, Henry, comps. *The Statutes at Large of Pennsylvania from 1682 to 1801.* 16 vols. Philadelphia, 1896–1911.

The Perpetual Laws of the Commonwealth of Massachusetts. 3 vols. Boston, 1801.

Private Laws of the State of New-York, Passed at the Thirty-third Session of the Legislature. Albany, N.Y., 1810.

The Public Statute Laws of the State of Connecticut. Hartford, Conn., 1808.

The Public Statute Laws of the State of Connecticut. Hartford, Conn., 1835.

BOOKS AND ARTICLES

Allen, David Grayson. *In English Ways: The Movement of Societies and the Transferal of English Local Law and Custom to Massachusetts Bay in the Seventeenth Century.* New York, 1982.

Auwers, Linda. "Fathers, Sons, and Wealth in Colonial Norwich, Connecticut." *Journal of the History of the Family* 3 (1978): 136–49.

Bailyn, Bernard. "Politics and Social Structure in Virginia." In *Seventeenth-Century America: Essays in Colonial History*, edited by James Morton Smith. Chapel Hill, N.C., 1959.

Baker, J.H. "The Use upon a Use in Equity, 1558–1625." *Law Quarterly Review* 93 (1977): 33–38.

Balch, Thomas, ed. *The Examination of Joseph Galloway, Esq., by a Committee of the House of Commons.* Boston, 1972.

Ballard, James Ames. *Equity in Pennsylvania.* Philadelphia, 1895.

Barnes, Viola F. *The Dominion of New England: A Study in British Colonial Policy.* New Haven, Conn., 1923.

Basch, Norma. "Equity vs. Equality: Emerging Concepts of Women's Political Status in the Age of Jackson." *Journal of the Early Republic* 3 (1983): 297–318.

_____. *In the Eyes of the Law: Marriage and Property in Nineteenth-Century New York.* Ithaca, N.Y., 1982.

_____. "Problems and Possibilities in the Legal History of Women: From the American Revolution to the Progressive Era." Paper presented at the Sixth Berkshire Conference on the History of Women, Northampton, Mass., 1 June 1984.

Beard, Mary R. *Woman as Force in History: A Study in Traditions and Realities.* New York, 1946. Reprint, New York, 1962.

Benson, Mary Sumner. *Women in Eighteenth-Century America: A Study of Opinion and Social Usage.* New York, 1935. Reprint, Port Washington, N.Y., 1966.

Biddle, Charles. *The Autobiography of Charles Biddle*. Philadelphia, 1883.

Biemer, Linda Briggs. *Women and Property in Colonial New York: The Transition from Dutch to English Law, 1643–1727*. Ann Arbor, Mich., 1983.

Blake, Nelson Manfred. *The Road to Reno: A History of Divorce in the United States*. Westport, Conn., 1962.

Bonfield, Lloyd. "Marriage, Property and the 'Affective Family.'" *Law and History Review* 1 (1983): 297–312.

―――. "Marriage Settlements and the 'Rise of Great Estates': The Demographic Aspect." *Economic History Review*, 2d ser. 32 (1979): 483–93.

―――. *Marriage Settlements, 1601–1740: The Adoption of the Strict Settlement*. Cambridge, England, 1983.

―――. "Marriage Settlements, 1660–1740: The Adoption of the Strict Settlement in Kent and Northamptonshire." In *Marriage and Society: Studies in the Social History of Marriage*, edited by R. B. Outhwaite. London, 1981.

Bronner, Edwin B. *William Penn's "Holy Experiment": The Founding of Pennsylvania, 1681–1701*. New York, 1962.

Carlton, Charles. "Changing Jurisdictions in Sixteenth and Seventeenth-Century England: The Relationship between the Courts of Orphans and Chancery." *American Journal of Legal History* 18 (1972): 124–36.

Carr, Lois Green. "Women and Inheritance in the Colonial Chesapeake." Paper presented at the 8th annual symposium of the United States Capitol Historical Society, "Women in the Age of the American Revolution." Washington, D.C., 28 March 1985.

―――, and Walsh, Lorena S. "The Planter's Wife: The Experience of White Women in Seventeenth-Century Maryland." *William and Mary Quarterly*, 3d ser. 34 (1977): 542–71.

Chaytor, A. H. *Equity, Also, the Forms of Action at Common Law: Two Courses of Lectures by Frederic William Maitland*. Cambridge, England, 1920.

Chroust, Anton Hermann. *The Rise of the Legal Profession in America*. 2 vols. Norman, Okla., 1965.

Chused, Richard H. "Married Women's Property Law: 1800–1850." *Georgetown Law Journal* 71 (1983): 1359–1425.

Cioni, Maria L. "The Elizabethan Chancery and Women's Rights." In *Tudor Rule and Revolution: Essays for G. R. Elton from His American Friends*, edited by Delloyd J. Guth and John W. McKenna. Cambridge, England, 1982.

―――. "Women and the Law in Elizabethan England with Particular Reference to the Court of Chancery." Ph.D. dissertation, University of Cambridge, 1974.

Clay, Christopher. "Marriage, Inheritance, and the Rise of Large Estates in England, 1660–1815." *Economic History Review*, 2d ser. 21 (1968): 503–18.

Clinton, Catherine. *The Plantation Mistress: Women's World in the Old South*. New York, 1982.

Clive, John, and Bailyn, Bernard, "England's Cultural Provinces: Scotland and America." *William and Mary Quarterly*, 3d ser. 11 (1954): 200–213.

Cohn, Henry S. "Connecticut's Divorce Mechanism, 1636–1969." *American Journal of Legal History* 14 (1970): 35–55.

Cott, Nancy F. *The Bonds of Womanhood: Woman's Sphere in New England, 1780–1825*. New Haven, Conn., 1977.

————. "Divorce and the Changing Status of Women in Eighteenth-Century Massachusetts." *William and Mary Quarterly*, 3d ser. 33 (1976): 586–614.

————. "Eighteenth-Century Family and Social Life Revealed in Massachusetts Divorce Records." *Journal of Social History* 10 (1976): 20–43.

Crowley, John E. "Family Relations and Inheritance in Early South Carolina." *Histoire Sociale* 17 (1984): 35–57.

Curran, William J. "The Struggle for Equity Jurisdiction in Massachusetts." *Boston University Law Review* 31 (1951): 269–96.

Deen, James W., Jr. [Jamil Zainaldin]. "Patterns of Testation: Four Tidewater Counties in Colonial Virginia." *American Journal of Legal History* 16 (1972): 154–76.

Demos, John. *A Little Commonwealth: Family Life in Plymouth Colony.* New York, 1970.

Dexter, Elisabeth Anthony. *Career Women of America, 1776–1840.* Francestown, N.H., 1950.

————. *Colonial Women of Affairs.* 1924. Rev. ed. Boston, 1931.

Ditz, Toby L. *Ownership and Obligation: Family and Inheritance in Five Connecticut Towns, 1750–1820.* Princeton, N.J., forthcoming.

Drinker, Sophie. "Votes for Women in Eighteenth-Century New Jersey." *New Jersey Historical Society Proceedings* 80 (1962): 31–45.

————. "Women Attorneys in Colonial Times." *Maryland Historical Magazine* 56 (1961): 335–51.

Dunn, Mary Maples. *William Penn: Politics and Conscience.* Princeton, N.J., 1967.

Eastman, Frank Marshall. *Courts and Lawyers of Pennsylvania: A History, 1623–1923.* 3 vols. New York, 1922.

Ely, James W., Jr. "American Independence and the Law: A Study of Post-Revolutionary South Carolina Legislation." *Vanderbilt Law Review* 26 (1973): 939–71.

Finlason, W. F., ed. *Reeve's History of English Law.* 5 vols. Philadelphia, 1879.

Friedman, Lawrence M. *A History of American Law.* New York, 1973.

Goebel, Julius, Jr. "King's Law and Local Custom in Seventeenth-Century New England." *Columbia Law Review* 31 (1931): 416–48.

Goody, Jack; Thirsk, Joan; and Thompson, E. P., eds. *Family and Inheritance: Rural Society in Western Europe, 1200–1800.* Cambridge, England, 1976.

Gordon, Ann D., and Buhle, Mari Jo. "Sex and Class in Colonial and Nineteenth-Century America." In *Liberating Women's History*, edited by Berenice Carroll. Urbana, Ill., 1976.

Greene, Jack P. "Search for Identity: An Interpretation of the Meaning of Selected Patterns of Social Response in Eighteenth-Century America." *Journal of Social History* 3 (1969–70): 189–220.

Greven, Philip J., Jr. *Four Generations: Population, Land, and Family in Colonial Andover, Massachusetts.* Ithaca, N.Y., 1970.

Grossberg, Michael. "Law and the Family in Nineteenth Century America." Ph.D. dissertation, Brandeis University, 1979.

————. "Who Gets the Child? Custody, Guardianship, and the Rise of a Judicial Patriarchy in Nineteenth-Century America." *Feminist Studies* 9 (1983): 235–60.

Gundersen, Joan R., and Gampel, Gwen Victor. "Married Women's Legal Status in Eighteenth-Century New York and Virginia." *William and Mary Quarterly*, 3d ser. 39 (1982): 114–34.

Habakkuk, H. J. "Marriage Settlements in the Eighteenth Century." *Transactions of the Royal Historical Society*, 4th ser. 32 (1950): 15–31.

Harrison, M. Leigh. "A Study of the Earliest Reported Decisions of the South Carolina Courts of Law." *American Journal of Legal History* 16 (1972): 51–71.

Haskins, George Lee. "The Beginnings of Partible Inheritance in the American Colonies." *Yale Law Journal* 51 (1942): 1280–1315.

————. *Law and Authority in Early Massachusetts: A Study in Tradition and Design.* New York, 1960.

Hemphill, C. Dallett. "Women in Court: Sex-Role Differentiation in Salem, Massachusetts, 1630–1683." *William and Mary Quarterly*, 3d ser. 39 (1982): 164–75.

Hindus, Michael S. *Prison and Plantation: Crime, Justice, and Authority in Massachusetts and South Carolina, 1767–1878.* Chapel Hill, N.C., 1980.

————, and Withey, Lynne E. "The Law of Husband and Wife in Nineteenth-Century America: Changing Views of Divorce." In *Women and the Law: The Social Historical Perspective.* Vol. 2: *Property, Family, and the Legal Profession*, edited by D. Kelly Weisberg. Cambridge, Mass., 1982.

Holdsworth, William Searle. *A History of English Law.* 16 vols. London, 1903–66.

Horwitz, Morton J. *The Transformation of American Law, 1780–1860.* Cambridge, Mass., 1977.

Howard, George Elliott. *A History of Matrimonial Institutions, Chiefly in England and the United States.* 3 vols. Chicago, 1904.

Jones, Alice Hanson. *American Colonial Wealth: Documents and Methods.* 3 vols. 2d ed. Foreword by Stuart Bruchey. New York, 1977.

Jones, W. J. *The Elizabethan Court of Chancery.* Oxford, 1967.

Jordan, Winthrop D. *White over Black: American Attitudes toward the Negro, 1550–1812.* Chapel Hill, N.C., 1968.

Journal of the Commissioners for Trade and Plantations from April 1704. . . . 27 vols. London, 1920–.

Kammen, Michael. *Empire and Interest: The American Colonies and the Politics of Mercantilism.* Philadelphia, 1970.

Katz, Stanley N. "The Politics of Law in Colonial America: Controversies over Chancery Courts and Equity Law in the Eighteenth Century." *Perspectives in American History* 5 (1971): 257–84.

————. "Republicanism and the Law of Inheritance in the American Revolutionary Era." *Michigan Law Review* 76 (1977–78): 1–29.

Keeton, George W., and Sheridan, L. A. *Equity.* London, 1969.

Keim, C. Ray. "Primogeniture and Entail in Colonial Virginia." *William and Mary Quarterly*, 3d ser. 25 (1966): 545–86.

Kerber, Linda K. *Women of the Republic: Intellect and Ideology in Revolutionary America.* Chapel Hill, N.C., 1980.

Keyssar, Alexander. "Widowhood in Eighteenth-Century Massachusetts: A Problem in the History of the Family." *Perspectives in American History* 8 (1974): 83–119.

Koehler, Lyle. *A Search for Power: The "Weaker Sex" in Seventeenth-Century New England.* Urbana, Ill., 1980.

Konig, David Thomas. "Community Custom and the Common Law: Social Change and the Development of Land Law in Seventeenth-Century Massachusetts." *American Journal of Legal History* 18 (1974): 137–77.

————. *Law and Society in Puritan Massachusetts: Essex County, 1629–1692*. Chapel Hill, N.C., 1979.

Lebsock, Suzanne. *The Free Women of Petersburg: Status and Culture in a Southern Town, 1784–1860*. New York, 1984.

Lerner, Gerda. "The Lady and the Mill Girl: Changes in the Status of Women in the Age of Jackson, 1800–1840." *Midcontinent American Studies Journal* 10 (1969): 5–14.

"Letters of Elizabeth and Vernon Hebb." *Chronicles of St. Mary's* 11 (1963): 2–10.

Liverant, Spencer R., and Hitchler, Walter H. "A History of Equity in Pennsylvania." *Dickinson Law Review* 37 (1932–33): 156–83.

Loengard, Janet Senderowitz. "Legal History and the Medieval Englishwoman: A Fragmented View." Paper presented at the Sixth Berkshire Conference on the History of Women, Northampton, Mass., 1 June 1984.

Loyd, William H. *The Early Courts of Pennsylvania*. Boston, 1910.

McCusker, John J. *Money and Exchange in Europe and America, 1600–1775: A Handbook*. Chapel Hill, N.C., 1978.

Marcus, Gail Sussman. " 'Due Execution of the Generall Rules of Righteousness': Criminal Procedures in New Haven Town and Colony, 1638–1658." In *Saints and Revolutionaries: Essays on Early American History*, edited by David D. Hall, John M. Murrin, and Thad W. Tate. New York, 1984.

Meehan, Thomas. "Courts, Cases, and Counsellors in Revolutionary and Post-Revolutionary Pennsylvania." *Pennsylvania Magazine of History and Biography* 91 (1967): 3–34.

————. " 'Not Made Out of Levity': The Evolution of Divorce in Early Pennsylvania." *Pennsylvania Magazine of History and Biography* 92 (1968): 441–64.

Menefee, Samuel Pyeatt. *Wives for Sale: An Ethnographic Study of British Popular Divorce*. New York, 1981.

Morgan, Edmund S. *The Puritan Family: Religion and Domestic Relations in Seventeenth-Century New England*. 1944. Reprint. New York, 1966.

Morris, Richard B. *Studies in the History of American Law: With Special Reference to the Seventeenth and Eighteenth Centuries*. 1930. Reprint. New York, 1959.

Murrin, John M. "Anglicizing an American Colony: The Transformation of Provincial Massachusetts." Ph.D. dissertation, Yale University, 1966.

————. "The Legal Transformation: The Bench and Bar of Eighteenth-Century Massachusetts." In *Colonial America: Essays in Political and Social Development*, 3d ed., edited by Stanley N. Katz and John M. Murrin. New York, 1983.

Narrett, David Evan. "Patterns of Inheritance in Colonial New York City, 1664–1775: A Study in the History of the Family." Ph.D. dissertation, Cornell University, 1981.

Nelson, William E. *Americanization of the Common Law: The Impact of Legal Change on Massachusetts Society, 1760–1830*. Cambridge, Mass., 1975.

Norton, Mary Beth. "A Cherished Spirit of Independence: The Life of an Eighteenth-Century Boston Businesswoman." In *Women of America: A History*, edited by Carol R. Berkin and Mary Beth Norton. Boston, 1979.

————. "The Evolution of White Women's Experience in Early America." *American Historical Review* 89 (1984): 593–619.

_____. *Liberty's Daughters: The Revolutionary Experience of American Women, 1750–1800*. Boston, 1980.

Philbrook, Mary. "Women's Suffrage in New Jersey Prior to 1807." *New Jersey Historical Society Proceedings* 57 (1939): 87–98.

Plucknett, Theodore Frank Thomas. *A Concise History of the Common Law*. 5th ed. Boston, 1956.

Pollock, Frederick, and Maitland, Frederic William. *The History of English Law before the Time of Edward I*. 2 vols. 2d ed. Introduction by S. F. C. Milsom. Cambridge, England, 1968.

Prall, Stuart. *The Agitation for Law Reform during the Puritan Revolution*. The Hague, 1966.

_____. "Chancery Reform and the Puritan Reformation." *American Journal of Legal History* 6 (1962): 28–44.

Rabkin, Peggy A. *From Fathers to Daughters: The Legal Foundations of Female Emancipation*. Westport, Conn., 1980.

Rawle, William Henry. *Equity in Pennsylvania*. Philadelphia, 1868.

Riddell, William Renwick. "Legislative Divorce in Colonial Pennsylvania." *Pennsylvania Magazine of History and Biography* 57 (1931): 175–80.

Rogers, Kim Lacy. "Relicts of the New World: Conditions of Widowhood in Seventeenth-Century New England." In *Woman's Being, Woman's Place: Female Identity and Vocation in American History*, edited by Mary Kelley. Boston, 1979.

Rundell, Oliver S. "The Chancellor's Foot: The Nature of Equity." *University of Kansas City Law Review* 27 (1958): 71–85.

Rutman, Darrett B., and Rutman, Anita H. " 'Now Wives and Sons-in-Law': Parental Death in a Seventeenth-Century Virginia County." In *The Chesapeake in the Seventeenth Century: Essays on Anglo-American Society and Politics*, edited by Thad W. Tate and David L. Ammerman. New York, 1979.

_____. "Of Agues and Fevers: Malaria in the Early Chesapeake." *William and Mary Quarterly*, 3d ser. 33 (1976): 31–60.

Ryan, Mary P. *Cradle of the Middle Class: The Family in Oneida County, New York, 1790–1865*. New York, 1981.

_____. *Womanhood in America*. New York, 1975.

Salmon, Marylynn. "The Court Records of Philadelphia, Bucks, and Berks Counties in the Seventeenth and Eighteenth Centuries." *Pennsylvania Magazine of History and Biography* 107 (1983): 249–62.

_____. "Equality or Submersion? Feme Covert Status in Early Pennsylvania." In *Women of America: A History*, edited by Carol R. Berkin and Mary Beth Norton. Boston, 1979.

_____. "The Legal Status of Women in Early America: A Reappraisal." *Law and History Review* 1 (1983): 129–51.

_____. " 'Life, Liberty, and Dower': The Legal Status of Women after the American Revolution." In *Women, War, and Revolution*, edited by Carol R. Berkin and Clara M. Lovett. New York, 1980.

_____. "The Property Rights of Women in Early America: A Comparative Study." Ph.D. dissertation, Bryn Mawr College, 1980.

_____. "Women and Property in South Carolina: The Evidence from Marriage

Settlements, 1730–1830." *William and Mary Quarterly*, 3d ser. 39 (1982): 655–85.

Scott, Anne Firor. *The Southern Lady: From Pedestal to Politics, 1830–1930*. New York, 1970.

Senese, Donald. "Building the Pyramid: The Growth and Development of the State Court System in Antebellum South Carolina, 1800–1860." *South Carolina Law Review* 24 (1972): 357–79.

Shammas, Carole. "English-Born and Creole Elites in Turn-of-the-Century Virginia." In *The Chesapeake in the Seventeenth Century: Essays on Anglo-American Society and Politics*, edited by Thad W. Tate and David L. Ammerman. New York, 1979.

Shanley, Mary Lyndon. "Lawyers and Feminists: The Historiography of Women and the Law in Victorian England." Paper presented at the Sixth Berkshire Conference on the History of Women, Northampton, Mass., 1 June 1984.

Simpson, Alfred William Brian. *An Introduction to the History of the Land Law*. London, 1961.

Smith, Daniel Blake. *Inside the Great House: Planter Family Life in Eighteenth-Century Chesapeake Society*. Ithaca, N.Y., 1980.

Smith, Daniel Scott. "The Demographic History of Colonial New England." *Journal of Economic History* 32 (1976): 165–83.

———. "Population, Family, and Society in Hingham, Massachusetts, 1635–1800." Ph.D. dissertation, University of California, Berkeley, 1972.

Smith, Helen Evertson. *Colonial Days and Ways*. New York, 1900.

Smith, Joseph Henry. *Appeals to the Privy Council from the American Plantations*. New York, 1950. Reprint. New York, 1965.

———. "The Foundations of Law in Maryland, 1634–1715." In *Law and Authority in Colonial America*, edited by George Billias. Barre, Mass., 1965.

Somerville, James K. "The Salem Woman in the Home, 1660–1779." *Eighteenth-Century Life* 1 (1974): 11–14.

Spalletta, Matteo. "Divorce in Colonial New York." *New York Historical Society Quarterly* 39 (1955): 422–40.

Speth, Linda E. "More Than Her 'Thirds': Wives and Widows in Colonial Virginia." *Women and History*, no. 4 (1982): 5–41.

Spruill, Julia Cherry. *Women's Life and Work in the Southern Colonies*. Chapel Hill, N.C., 1938. Reprint. New York, 1972.

Spufford, Margaret. *Contrasting Communities: English Villagers in the Sixteenth and Seventeenth Centuries*. London, 1974.

———. "Peasant Inheritance Customs in the Midlands, 1280–1700." In *Family and Inheritance: Rural Society in Western Europe, 1200–1800*, edited by Jack Goody, Joan Thirsk, and E. P. Thompson. Cambridge, England, 1976.

Steele, I. K. *Politics of Colonial Policy: The Board of Trade in Colonial Administration*. Oxford, 1968.

Stone, Lawrence. *The Crisis of the Aristocracy, 1558–1641*. Oxford, 1965.

———. *The Family, Sex and Marriage in England, 1500–1800*. London, 1977.

Sumner, J. D., Jr. "The South Carolina Divorce Act of 1949." *South Carolina Law Quarterly* 3 (1951): 253–59.

Surrency, Edwin C. "The Courts in the American Colonies." *American Journal of Legal History* 11 (1967): 253–76.

_____. "The Evolution of an Urban Judicial System: The Philadelphia Story, 1683–1968." *American Journal of Legal History* 18 (1974): 95–123.

Thompson, E. P. "The Grid of Inheritance: A Comment." In *Family and Inheritance: Rural Society in Western Europe, 1200–1800,* edited by Jack Goody, Joan Thirsk, and E. P. Thompson. Cambridge, England, 1976.

Thompson, Roger. *Women in Stuart England and America: A Comparative Study.* Boston, 1974.

Thurman, Kay Ellen. "The Married Women's Property Acts." L.L.M. dissertation, University of Wisconsin Law School, 1966.

Trumbach, R. *The Rise of the Egalitarian Family: Aristocratic Kinship and Domestic Relations in Eighteenth-Century England.* London, 1978.

Ulrich, Laurel Thatcher. *Good Wives: Image and Reality in the Lives of Women in Northern New England, 1650–1750.* New York, 1982.

Van Ness, James S. "On Untieing the Knot: The Maryland Legislature and Divorce Petitions." *Maryland Historical Magazine* 67 (1972): 171–75.

Veall, Donald. *The Popular Movement for Law Reform, 1640–1660.* Oxford, 1970.

Vinovskis, Maris. "Mortality Rates and Trends in Massachusetts before 1860." *Journal of Economic History* 32 (1972): 184–213.

Walsh, Lorena S. " 'Till Death Us Do Part': Marriage and Family in Seventeenth-Century Maryland, 1658–1705." In *The Chesapeake in the Seventeenth Century: Essays on Anglo-American Society and Politics,* edited by Thad W. Tate and David L. Ammerman. New York, 1979.

_____, and Menard, Russell R. "Death in the Chesapeake: Two Life Tables for Men in Early Colonial Maryland." *Maryland Historical Magazine* 69 (1974): 211–27.

Warbasse, Elizabeth Bowles. "The Changing Legal Rights of Married Women, 1800–1861." Ph.D. dissertation, Radcliffe College, 1966.

Warren, Joseph. "Husband's Right to Wife's Services." *Harvard Law Review* 38 (1924–25): 421–46, 622–50.

Waters, John J. "Patrimony, Succession, and Social Stability: Guilford, Connecticut in the Eighteenth Century." *Perspectives in American History* 10 (1976): 131–60.

Weisberg, D. Kelly. "Under Great Temptations Here: Women and Divorce Law in Puritan Massachusetts." In *Women and the Law: The Social Historical Perspective.* Vol. 2: *Property, Family, and the Legal Profession,* edited by D. Kelly Weisberg. Cambridge, Mass., 1982.

White, G. Edward. *The American Judicial Tradition.* New York, 1976.

Wilson, Joan Hoff. "Hidden Riches: Legal Records and Women, 1750–1825." In *Woman's Being, Woman's Place: Female Identity and Vocation in American History,* edited by Mary Kelley. Boston, 1979.

_____. "The Illusion of Change: Women and the American Revolution." In *The American Revolution: Explorations in the History of American Radicalism,* edited by Alfred H. Young. Dekalb, Ill., 1976.

Woodruff, Edwin H. "Chancery in Massachusetts." *Boston University Law Review* 9 (1929): 168–92.

Wyatt-Brown, Bertram. *Southern Honor: Ethics and Behavior in the Old South.* New York, 1982.

General Index

Index to Cases